The Domestic Sources of American Foreign Policy

The Domestic Sources of American Foreign Policy

Insights and Evidence

Seventh Edition

Edited by
James M. McCormick

Iowa State University

ROWMAN & LITTLEFIELD
Lanham • Boulder • New York • London

Executive Editor: Traci Crowell
Assistant Editor: Mary Malley
Senior Marketing Manager: Kim Lyons
Cover Designer: Meredith Nelson
Cover Image: IStock/Kasia75

Credits and acknowledgments for material borrowed from other sources, and
reproduced with permission, appear on the appropriate page within the text.
Published by Rowman & Littlefield
A wholly owned subsidiary of The Rowman & Littlefield Publishing Group, Inc.
4501 Forbes Boulevard, Suite 200, Lanham, Maryland 20706
www.rowman.com

Unit A, Whitacre Mews, 26–34 Stannary Street, London SE11 4AB, United Kingdom
Copyright © 2018 by Rowman & Littlefield
Sixth edition 2012.

British Library Cataloguing in Publication Information Available

Library of Congress Cataloging-in-Publication Data

Names: McCormick, James M., editor.
Title: The domestic sources of American foreign policy : insights and evidence / edited
    by James M. McCormick.
Description: Seventh edition. | Lanham : Rowman & Littlefield, 2018. | Includes
    bibliographical references and index.
Identifiers: LCCN 2017032102 (print) | LCCN 2017032925 (ebook) |
    ISBN 9781442275379 (electronic) | ISBN 9781442275355 (cloth : alk. paper) |
    ISBN 9781442275362 (pbk. : alk. paper)
Subjects: LCSH: United States—Foreign relations—1945–1989. |
    United States—Foreign relations—1989- | United States—Foreign relations—
    Decision making. | United States—Foreign relations administration.
Classification: LCC E840 (ebook) | LCC E840 .D63 2018 (print) |
    DDC 327.73—dc23
LC record available at https://lccn.loc.gov/2017032102

♾️™ The paper used in this publication meets the minimum requirements of
American National Standard for Information Sciences—Permanence of Paper for
Printed Library Materials, ANSI/NISO Z39.48–1992.

Printed in the United States of America

To the contributors to this volume over the decades:
Their insights have taught me a great deal

Contents

Acknowledgments

"Liberal Internationalism: Why Woodrow Wilson Matters" by Tony Smith. Adapted from Tony Smith, *Why Wilson Matters: The Origins of American Liberal Internationalism and Its Crisis Today* (Princeton: Princeton University Press, 2017).

"Conservative American Realism" by Colin Dueck. Adapted and Abridged from Colin Dueck, *The Obama Doctrine* (Oxford: Oxford University Press, 2015), 197–257.

"Conservative Internationalism: An Alternative to Realism and Liberal Internationlism" by Henry R. Nau. Adapted from the preface of Henry R. Nau, *Conservative Internationalism: Armed Diplomacy under Jefferson, Polk, Truman, and Reagan* (Princeton: Princeton University Press, 2015, paperback edition).

"The Israel Lobby" by John Mearsheimer and Stephen Walt. Abridged from "The Israel Lobby," *London Review of Books*, vol. 28, no. 6 (March 23, 2006): 3–12.

"American Veterans in Government and the Use of Force" by Peter D. Feaver and Christopher Gelpi. Excerpt from "The Impact of Elite Veterans on American Decisions to Use Force," in Peter D. Feaver and Christopher Gelpi, *Choosing Your Battles: American Civil-Military Relations and the Use of Force* (Princeton, NJ: Princeton University Press, 2004), 64–94. The references were taken from pages 215, 219–20, and 222–24.

"Events, Elites, and American Public Support for Military Conflict" by Adam J. Berinsky. Abridged and edited from "Assuming the Costs of War: Events, Elites, and American Public Support for Military Conflict," *Journal of Politics*, vol. 69, no. 4 (November 2007): 975–97.

"How Media Limit Accountability in Foreign Policy-Making: Iraq and Beyond" by Robert Entman. Abridged and adapted from Robert M. Entman, Steven Livingston, and Jennie Kim, "Doomed to Repeat: Iraq News, 2002–2007," *American Behavioral Scientist*, vol. 52 (January 2009): 689–708.

"Person and Office: Presidents, the Presidency, and Foreign Policy" by Michael Nelson. An extensively revised and expanded version of "U.S. Presidency," in Joel Krieger, ed., *The Oxford Companion to the Politics of the World*, 2nd ed. (New York: Oxford University Press, 2001), 690–92.

"American Diplomacy at Risk" by the American Academy of Diplomacy. Abridged from the American Academy of Diplomacy, *American Academy at Risk* (Abridged Report) (Washington, DC: American Academy of Diplomacy, April 2015).

"The Urgent Need for Defense Reform" by Michèle Flournoy. Excerpted and slightly abridged from Testimony before the Senate Armed Services Committee, December 8, 2015, complete statement available from the Center for a New American Security at https://s3.amazonaws.com/files. cnas.org/documents/Flournoy_SASC-Written-Statement-Dec-2015.pdf

"Why Intelligence and Policymakers Clash" by Robert Jervis. Slightly abridged from "Why Intelligence and Policymakers Clash," *Political Science Quarterly*, vol. 125, no. 2 (Summer 2010): 185–204. Copyright by Cornell University Press.

"American Trade Policy-Making: A Unique Process" draws substantially on I. M. (Mac) Destler, *American Trade Politics*, 4th ed. (Washington, DC: Institute for International Economics, 2005).

"Sources of Humanitarian Intervention: Beliefs, Information, and Advocacy in U.S. Decisions on Somalia and Bosnia" by Jon Western. Adapted by the author from "Sources of Humanitarian Intervention: Beliefs, Information, and Advocacy in U.S. Decisions on Somalia and Bosnia," *International Security*, vol. 26, no. 4 (Spring 2002): 112–42.

"NATO Expansion: The Anatomy of a Decision" by James M. Goldgeier. Abridged and edited from "NATO Expansion: The Anatomy of a Decision," *Washington Quarterly*, vol. 21, no. 1 (Winter 1998): 85–102.

"Obama's Decision-Making Style" by Fred Kaplan. Slightly abridged from Fred Kaplan, "Obama's Way: The President in Practice." *Foreign Affairs*, vol. 95 (January/February 2016): 46–63.

Preface

The seventh edition of *The Domestic Sources of American Foreign Policy: Insights and Evidence* seeks to provide some of the latest analyses and most recent case studies on how American societal, institutional, and individual factors shape U.S. actions abroad. The volume is intended to serve as a comprehensive reader for undergraduate and graduate courses in U.S. foreign policy and aims to aid students and instructors in understanding and appreciating more fully the effects of domestic factors in affecting American foreign policy. Although the reader can be used as a stand-alone text for courses in foreign policy analysis, it is wholly appropriate as a complementary volume to a standard U.S. foreign policy text as well. Further, the *Domestic Sources* reader may also serve as a supplemental text in a global politics or comparative foreign policy course where American actions are analyzed.

This edition is again divided into three parts as a way to assist students in assessing different aspects of how American society influences foreign policy. Part I, consisting of eight chapters, assesses how the society at large contributes to foreign policy. Five of the chapters in this part are new to this edition, and they now include chapters on three alternative "grand strategies" that the United States may pursue in global politics and new chapters on the role of the media and public opinion. Part II, also consisting of eight chapters, examines the roles of various political institutions and bureaucracies (e.g., the presidency, Congress, Department of State, and the intelligence community) in formulating American foreign policy. Two of these chapters are new to this edition, five of them have been updated from the previous edition by the authors, and one chapter has been retained from the sixth edition. Part III, consisting of five chapters, contains case studies of foreign policymaking with a particular emphasis on the role of individual and group decisionmakers in influencing U.S. policies abroad. The cases include analyses of individual and bureaucratic factors over decision-making associated with the Vietnam War and the American intervention in Somalia near the end of the George H. W. Bush administration. The more recent cases focus on the role of President Clinton in the expansion of NATO, the role of President George W. Bush in the initiation of the Iraq War, and President Barack Obama's decision style in several foreign policy actions. The case studies for the George W. Bush and Barack Obama administrations are wholly new to this edition.

To further aid instructors and students in using this reader, the volume has an introductory chapter and chapter openers for each of the parts by the editor. The introductory chapter locates the volume in the larger study of American foreign policy and advances the argument about how these three parts fit together to create a fuller picture of the shaping of American foreign policy. The chapters that open each of the three parts focus specifically on the differing importance of societal, institutional, or individual factors in shaping foreign policy. In addition, these part openers provide a preview of each of the chapters in that section of the volume.

In the course of completing the seventh edition, I have incurred a number of debts to individuals and institutions, and I want to take the opportunity to acknowledge my thanks to them publicly. First of all, colleagues at other institutions offered their comments and suggestions for improving the book by carefully reviewing the sixth edition: Eric Blanchard, SUNY Oswego; Roshen Hendrickson, College of Staten Island (CUNY); Gyung-Ho Jeong, University of British Columbia; Dennis Jett, Pennsylvania State University; Jeremy Meyer, George Mason University; Sharon Murphy, Nazareth College of Rochester; Amy M. Skonieczny, San Francisco State University; Michael O. Slobodchikoff, Troy University; Robert Sutter, George Washington University; James P. Todhunter, Troy University; and Robert Weiner, University of Massachusetts, Boston. For their extensive reviews and very helpful suggestions, I am most grateful. Although I sought to follow some of these suggestions for various chapter inclusions, an editor's stubbornness sometimes got in the way. Nonetheless, I do appreciate their careful assessment of the various chapters in the previous edition.

Second, I want to thank Rowman & Littlefield for their support and encouragement as I was completing the seventh edition. I particularly want to thank Traci Crowell, political science editor, for her assistance and understanding as this edition was delayed somewhat by my health issues, and Mary Malley for guiding the manuscript through the production process. An author could not ask for better support than was provided by this team.

Third, I want to thank the distinguished scholars who authored the various chapters for this edition and earlier ones. I have learned a great deal about American foreign policy from their writings, and the success of the volume has been wholly dependent on their insightful and timely contributions. As such, I would like to dedicate this edition to them for their contribution in helping me prepare this reader.

Finally, I want to again acknowledge my debt to the late Eugene R. Wittkopf, who originally invited me to join this volume as a coeditor four editions ago. His confidence in me will always be a great source of personal satisfaction as well as his vision on the need for this volume for the study of American foreign policy.

Introduction

The Domestic Sources of American Foreign Policy

On November 8, 2016, Donald J. Trump won the presidency with 308 electoral votes, after carrying key battleground states (e.g., Florida, North Carolina, and Ohio) and several long-time "blue" states (Wisconsin, Michigan, and Pennsylvania). His fundamental message to the American voters and to the rest of the world was a populist and nationalist one ("Make America Great Again"). With his victory, he appeared to be fore-shadowing significant changes in America's foreign and domestic policy. Indeed, he called for a new direction in American foreign policy, one that would focus on "America First." Under his administration, the United States would seemingly emphasize a foreign policy based on what would advance American domestic interests in the world and one in which the United States would be more willing to go it alone, if necessary, to achieve them.

Although candidate Trump did not outline a comprehensive foreign policy approach during the presidential campaign, he did identify several different priorities that would be the focus of his administration and that would put him at odds with the priorities of the Obama administration.[1] On military policy, for example, candidate Trump aimed to increase military spending (and halt the sequestration policy of the previous administration), increase the size of each of the military branches, and move forward with a ballistic missile defense system. On trade policy, Trump has been particularly critical of the trade agreements negotiated by the Obama administration, stating that the "TPP [Trans-Pacific Partnership] was a disaster" and that trade with China was unfair as it was dumping its products in the United States and devaluing its currency (and thus harming American exports). As a result, he proposed imposing tariffs on imports from China and threatening American companies that moved abroad with tariffs if they

1

sought to sell their products in the United States after such a move. On the environment, Trump questioned whether globe warming was man-made and proposed withdrawing the United States from the 2015 Paris agreement on climate change. With allies, too, Trump initially raised questions about whether those American commitments would be honored. Indeed, at one juncture, he questioned whether the United States would honor its commitment to NATO and called for the European countries to spend more on their own defense. Similarly, Trump appeared to raise doubts about America's commitment to Japan and South Korea, even alluding to the possibility that these countries may need to develop their own nuclear arsenals.

Toward two major powers, Russia and China, President Trump appears to take differing attitudes. Toward Russia, Trump has praised the leadership of Vladimir Putin, and he seemed to imply a more accommodative relationship with Russia. His first national security advisor, retired General Michael Flynn, also has had friendly relations with Russia, despite that country's seizure of Crimea, continued involvement in Ukraine, and participating in the Syrian civil war in support of Bashir al-Assad. As a result, it is not clear what will be the policy direction for the United States in dealing with Russia. Toward China, however, President-Elect Trump appears ready to challenge that country not only over trade relations, but political-military issues as well. Shortly after winning the election, Trump took a congratulatory call from the president of Taiwan, raising doubts about his commitment to a one-China policy. Moreover, he has now made it clear that this call was not a spontaneous event, but, in fact, a carefully arranged one. As a result, the intent apparently was to send a signal to China about a possible new direction. Further, after the Chinese navy seized an American research drone in international waters in the South China Sea (and even outside the nine-dash line area claimed by China), Trump tweeted his strong objections to this action—again a signal of a differing approach than the Obama administration toward that state.

Trump's inaugural address reinforced many of his campaign themes and statements.[2] In this initial address, President Trump declared that "every decision on trade, on taxes, on immigration, on foreign affairs, will be made to benefit American workers and American families. We must protect our borders from the ravages of other countries making our products, stealing our companies, and destroying our jobs. Protection will lead to great prosperity and strength." In addition, he said, "We will seek friendship and goodwill with the nations of the world—but we do so with the understanding that it is the right of all nations to put their own interests first." And with his initial executive orders and pronouncements, President Trump put these beliefs in operation by withdrawing the United States from the Trans-Pacific Partnership and calling for the renegotiation of the North American Free Trade Agreement (NAFTA).

These actions and pronouncements imply that President Trump would pursue a foreign policy more narrowly driven by American interests. Further, he would seek to provide more U.S. leadership on various issues than that pursued by the Obama administration. At the same time, though, such an approach reminds us of the inevitable nexus between foreign and domestic policy.

The linkage of domestic interests with foreign policy actions for the United States (or for other countries) is hardly a new phenomenon. In recent decades, that linkage has been driven, and indeed accelerated, by the process of globalization. That is, political, economic, and social forces were drawing peoples together regardless of state boundaries or geographical distance, and these ties blurred the distinctions between foreign and domestic policies across a broad spectrum of issues. The expansion of intergovernmental organizations in the world, the rise of more and more nongovernmental organizations globally, and the growth of transnational linkages through the Information Revolution of cyberspace—all have contributed to this phenomenon.[3]

Even as these positive aspects of globalization continue, the negative sides of these globalizing processes are not very far behind. That is, the globalization process also facilitates the rapid transfer of drugs and crimes, the transmittal of diseases, and the export of terrorism on a global scale. The attacks of September 11, for example, brought home to Americans this dark side of globalization in the most dramatic way. No state was beyond reach, especially by determined nonstate actors. No borders were impenetrable for those determined to do harm. The continued threat of international terrorism—including the recent occurrences of terror attacks in Paris, Brussels, Manchester, Berlin, Boston, San Bernardino, and Orlando— reminds us of the negative aspects of globalization.

These global ties have also been an important vehicle for the spreading of the economic crises worldwide. With the problems of the mortgage industry, the failure of major banks and investment houses, and the bankruptcy of major corporations, America's Great Recession of 2008 (and beyond) in the first decade of the twenty-first century resulted in high unemployment, growing national debt, and economic uncertainty at home. Because of the centrality and the interconnectedness of the American economy to the rest of the world, other economies were not immune to these economic problems. The recovery from these economic dislocations began to occur in the second decade of this century, but the pace has been slow and uneven across and within societies. Indeed, the economic gaps have broadened between rich and poor, with the American (and world's) middle class increasingly squeezed by stagnant wages and low-paying jobs. Further, with the dislocation of large populations—owing to the conflicts in Iraq, Afghanistan, and Syria and declining economies globally—and the massive migration of peoples to other nations, discontent with the effects of globalization has risen worldwide.

The Trump presidential campaign and other nationalist movements, especially in Western Europe, have focused on these growing economic disparities and mounting migrations wrought by globalization, civil wars, and terrorism. The result has been a direct effort to halt the effects of globalization domestically and to focus on a populist and nationalist approach to guide American actions abroad. In short, American domestic well-being, for the Trump administration, would be the ultimate driver of American foreign policy.

To be sure, the responses to the challenges of globalization have taken different forms by the American administrations over the past decades. The events of September 11 and the Iraq War fueled one kind of response for the role of the United States in the world in the twenty-first century. The Bush administration argued that the United States ought to maintain a military sufficient to "assure our allies and friends; dissuade future military competition; deter threats against U.S. interests, allies, and friends; and decisively defeat any adversary if deterrence fails." The administration sought to build a "coalition of the willing" to defeat terrorists and tyrants globally, especially those with the potential to develop weapons of mass destruction. Also, it asserted that the United States reserved to itself "the option of preemptive actions to counter a sufficient threat to our national security."[4] With the initiation of wars in Afghanistan and Iraq, the Bush administration implemented these imperatives to fight international terrorism.

Another response came from the Obama administration. That administration advanced a strategy that emphasized a cooperative and comprehensive involvement by the United States with the world, whether friend and foe, and that focused on strengthening the international order to solve common economic, political, and military problems. Put differently, the Obama administration's national security strategy approach, labeled a "strategy of engagement," sought to restore American leadership worldwide and to promote a "just and sustainable international order."

And now the Trump administration has initiated yet a third response. It is perhaps best summarized by the phrase, "America First." In all actions abroad, the primary and fundamental concern would be the relative gain for the United States and its people in addressing economic dislocation and global migration. In the first days of the Trump presidency, the administration announced the United States' withdrawal from the Trans-Pacific Partnership, called for the renegotiations of the North American Trade Agreement, pronounced its approval for the Keystone XL pipeline with Canada, and initiated the building of a wall with Mexico over continuing immigration. By the end of its first week in office, the administration attempted to put in place a temporary ban on citizens from seven Muslim-majority countries entering the United States because those countries had been linked to international terrorism and also placed a permanent ban for refugees from Syria.

Much as the dark side of globalization shaped debates and responses by recent administrations over the direction of American foreign policy, it also reshaped the potency of domestic participants in the foreign policy process. Foreign policy was now viewed as a sustained domestic concern, with increased public and media attention directed toward both global issues and homeland security. In that context, the American people were willing to afford the president a greater degree of latitude in shaping America's global posture in the immediate aftermath of 9/11. Over the past decade and more, that leeway has diminished as a result of American actions in Iraq and Afghanistan, the perceived rise of China in global importance, the migrations of large populations, and the economic difficulties experienced by the American people. The public has now become more sharply divided on the merits of globalization and the threat posed by mass integration. Republicans and Trump supporters see immigration and globalization as critical threats to the United States while Democrats and independents generally are somewhat more circumspect about these phenomena. Still, majorities of both political parties "favor a continued shared leadership role for the United States internationally" and share some similar foreign policy goals. That is, the American public "remains united around combatting a similar set of top threats, including terrorism and nuclear proliferation. American of both parties share a similar view of how to deal with Russian and Chinese power, and both support the US military presence in key allied countries such as Japan and South Korea."[5]

In the immediate months after 9/11, Congress's foreign policy voice was muted and largely deferential to presidential direction. As the war in Iraq dragged on, public opposition grew, eventually resulting in the Democrats gaining control of both Houses of Congress in 2006. That institution then sought to reassert its foreign policy role and challenge the Bush administration, although with limited success. With the Obama administration Congress continued to be more assertive, whether over the closing of the U.S. prison at Guantanamo Bay, the approval of the New START Treaty, debating immigration policy, or critiquing American policy toward Syria and ISIS. With the Republicans gaining control of both Houses of Congress and the presidency in 2016, however, some uncertainty exists over whether Congress will continue to be assertive on foreign policy. Still, there are already signs that some issues such as altering sanctions toward Russia over Ukraine and Crimea, resurrecting the use of waterboarding against terrorist suspects, or changing American trade policy may prompt concerted congressional actions.

Finally, immediately after the events of 9/11, some interest groups lost the prominence that they had gained following the collapse of the Berlin

Wall and the implosion of the Soviet Union. Increasingly, though, these groups have found their voice on foreign affairs once again. Indeed, the proliferation of both the number and kind of foreign policy interest groups today is greater and more vocal than in perhaps any recent period.

DOMESTIC POLITICS AND FOREIGN POLICY

The proposition that domestic politics explains foreign policy stands in sharp contrast to the realist tradition in the study of foreign policy. Political realism, a perspective that enjoyed widespread acceptance among policy-makers and scholars during the Cold War and before, argues that foreign policy is primarily a function of what occurs outside national borders. In this tradition, states are the principal actors; power and national interests are the dominant policy considerations; and maintaining the balance of power among states is the principal policy imperative. Furthermore, all states—democratic and nondemocratic—operate on the same assumptions and respond similarly to changes in the international system. In short, from a realist perspective, domestic politics exerts little if any impact on state behavior.

While political realism provides valuable insights into the motivations and actions of states, particularly at times of heightened concern about national security, it surely underestimates the effects of the domestic environment, both historically and today. Even the Greek philosopher Thucydides, perhaps the first political realist, recognized the importance of domestic politics in shaping the external behavior of Athens and Sparta. In language with a decidedly contemporary ring, he observed that the actions leaders of Greek city-states directed toward one another often sought to affect the political climates within their own polities, not what happened between them.

Centuries later, Immanuel Kant argued in his treatise *Perpetual Peace* that democracies are inherently less warlike than autocracies, because democratic leaders are accountable to the public, which restrains them from waging war. Because ordinary citizens would have to supply the soldiers and bear the human and financial costs of imperial policies, he contended, liberal democracies are "natural" forces for peace.

History has been kind to Kant's thesis—democracies rarely fight one another. That theme highlighted the Clinton administration's foreign policy in the decade of the 1990s, which held that the spread of democratic market economies is good not only for peace but also for business and prosperity. The Bush administration embraced that theme as well. In his second inaugural address, for instance, George W. Bush declared that "it is the policy of the United States to seek and support the growth of democratic movements and institutions in every nation and culture, with the ultimate goal of ending tyranny in the world." Likewise, Barack Obama emphasized the advancement of democracy as an important foreign policy objective of the United States. In his 2009 Cairo speech, President Obama acknowledged that "no system of government can or should be imposed by one nation by any other," but he went on to say that such a stance "does not lessen my commitment . . . to governments that reflect the will of the people." The Trump administration, however, has seemingly not embraced a view of democracy promotion as a fundamental tenet of its foreign policy actions. In his inaugural address, President Trump put it this way: "We do not seek to impose our way of life on anyone, but rather to let it shine as an example for everyone to follow."[6]

The constraints of domestic politics on foreign policy actions of other nations manifested itself in several ways for the Bush and Obama administrations, and the Trump administration has already begun to face such constraints as well. For example, it is difficult to explain France's reluctance to endorse the Bush administration's approach to Iraq without taking into account its perennial skepticism of American leadership in world affairs, grounded in its own history and experience, as well as its traditional ties with Iraq itself. Saudi Arabia's hesitance to grant access to military bases important for an attack on Iraq was closely tied to its Islamic heritage and foundations. The Obama administration faced similar constraints from abroad. That is, the leadership in NATO countries generally opposed the Obama administration's call for maintaining or increasing troops in Afghanistan, with some countries deciding to withdraw their forces (e.g., Canada and the Netherlands), undoubtedly driven in part by domestic concerns. The leaders of several key G-20 nations opposed the Obama administration's call for stimulating economic growth prior to addressing budget debt issues,[7] presumably owing to their domestic constraints.

Some statements (e.g., that NATO is "obsolete" or allied states need to pay more for their defense) and actions (e.g., the building of a wall with Mexico) by the Trump administration have already sparked domestic constraints in allies and friends. The prime minister of the United Kingdom, for instance, has publicly defended the importance of NATO, since that organization is so crucial to Great Britain's defense posture. The Mexican president addressed his own people and, in accord with national pride, indicated that his country would not pay for the wall between the United States and Mexico. Similarly, the Trump administration has received an avalanche of criticism over its policy of temporarily banning refugees and immigrants from several Muslim countries. The domestic publics in these states could indeed be reluctant to support their governments' continued cooperation with the United States over such statements and actions. Put differently, domestic considerations and national interests undoubtedly governed the decisions of these states and their leaders—and the Trump administration will not be exempt from such pressures.

DOMESTIC POLITICS AND AMERICAN FOREIGN POLICY

America's post–Cold War and post-9/11 foreign policies, too, are rife with examples of how domestic politics shapes its actions abroad. In the latter years of the Clinton administration, for example, the president felt constrained in dealing with various humanitarian crises abroad by an American public reluctant to support sending U.S. ground forces to cope with them. Hence, when Clinton announced his decision to bomb Serbian positions in Kosovo in response to Serbia's mistreatment of its own Albanian minority there, he explicitly excluded the option of sending ground forces from any military action. Similarly, the administration's desire to ratify the Comprehensive Test Ban Treaty was halted by a reluctant Senate, where less than a majority approved it.

Upon taking office, George W. Bush also confronted a public and Congress not wholly supportive of his foreign policy plans. Early polls showed that barely a majority of Americans supported his initial foreign policy designs. An equally divided Congress also expressed skepticism about the unilateralism evident in many of the new administration's early pronouncements and actions. September 11 changed all of that, at least for a time. Congressional criticism became muted, and public enthusiasm for the president's agenda blossomed. By early 2003, however, the tides once again appeared to shift as war with Iraq loomed. While the initial success in Iraq brought some positive public reaction, that effect began to erode as reconstruction efforts in Iraq lagged and internal opposition and sectarian violence increased. Further, as American casualties increased, public support at home began to erode. While President Bush continued to hew to the policy line of "staying the course" in Iraq, the American public dealt a sharp rebuke to the administration's approach with the 2006 congressional elections.

The Obama administration came into office on a wave of popular sentiment, but it, too, quickly faced opposition at home to its foreign policy initiatives. President Obama's efforts to close the American prison at Guantanamo Bay, Cuba, and transfer the "enemy combatants" there to a mainland facility met with both public and congressional resistance. Similarly, when President Obama's attorney general announced that some prisoners held in Guantanamo Bay would be given civilian trials in New York, public and congressional opposition arose once more. Ultimately, the Obama administration decided to utilize military tribunals and to keep some prisoners at Guantanamo Bay.

Other national security issues also sparked public or congressional opposition at various times. The decision to employ a "surge strategy" in Afghanistan sparked critiques from liberals and conservatives, albeit for differing reasons. The New START Treaty with Russia produced extended Senate debate over the wisdom of ratification and whether it imperiled America's nuclear arsenal. Although the administration ultimately gained that body's approval in late 2010, it did so only after extended negotiations. The administration's policy toward Iran and North Korea over their nuclear programs, and the seeming lack of successful action in halting those programs, remain a source of criticism. Similarly, the administration's position on the requirements for negotiations between Israel and the Palestinians fostered sharp domestic criticism, especially by those with close ties to Israel. In all, the impact of domestic politics on foreign policy matters continues.

Given the nation's historical roots, the constraints domestic politics impose on American foreign policy should hardly be surprising. Since its founding, the United States has perceived itself as a different—indeed, as an exceptional—nation, one with a foreign policy driven more by domestic values than by the vagaries of international politics. Analysts who have examined the views of Thomas Jefferson and other founders conclude that they believed that "the objectives of foreign policy were but a means to the end of posterity and promoting the goals of domestic society."[8] That belief still permeates American society and its political processes.

Still, satisfying the requirements of domestic politics arguably became more critical for foreign policy over recent decades than at other times in the nation's history. Whether that is cause for concern may be debated, but it raises questions about the ability of a democratic society to pursue a successful foreign strategy. As the French political sociologist Alexis de Tocqueville observed over 150 years ago, "Foreign politics demand scarcely any of those qualities which a democracy possesses; they require, on the contrary, the perfect use of almost all those faculties in which it is deficient."

Although there may be broad agreement that domestic imperatives sometimes shape foreign policy, there is less agreement about the particulars and how they manifest themselves in the political process. For analytic purposes, we can begin our inquiry into the domestic sources of American foreign policy by grouping them into three broad categories: the nation's societal environment, its institutional setting, and the individual characteristics of its decisionmakers and the policymaking positions they occupy.

Figure I.1 illustrates the relationship between each of the domestic explanatory categories and American foreign policy and their interrelationships with one another. The figure posits that domestic policy influences are inputs into the decision-making process that converts policy demands into foreign policy. (We can define "foreign policy" as the goals that a nation's officials seek to realize abroad, the values that give rise to them, and the

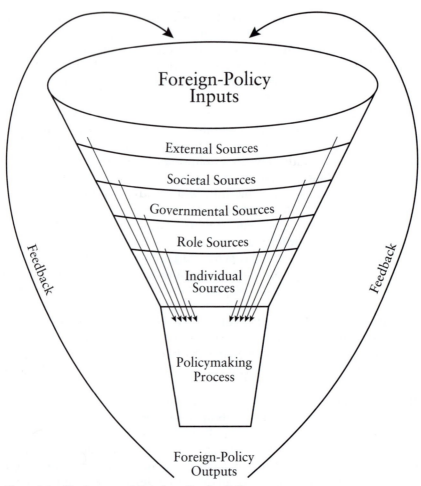

Figure I.1.   The Sources of American Foreign Policy

Source: Charles W. Kegley Jr. and Eugene Wittkopf, *American Foreign Policy: Pattern and Process*,
   5th ed. (New York: St. Martin's Press, 1996), 15.

means or instruments used to pursue them.) Conceptualized as the output
of the process that converts policy demands into goals and means, foreign
policy is typically multifaceted, ranging from discrete behaviors linked to
specific issues to recurring patterns of behavior that define the continual
efforts to cope with the environment beyond a state's borders.

   Although we can easily identify many of the discrete variables that make
up the domestic source categories, the lines between the categories themselves are not always clear-cut. To help draw these larger distinctions as well
as explicate the smaller ones, it is useful to think of the explanatory categories as layers of differing size and complexity.

THE SOCIETAL ENVIRONMENT

The broadest layer is the societal environment. The political culture of the United States—the basic needs, values, beliefs, and self-images widely shared by Americans about their political system—stands out as a primary societal source of American foreign policy. Minimally, those beliefs find expression in the kinds of values and political institutions American policymakers have sought to export to others throughout much of its history. Included is a preference for democracy, capitalism, and the values of the American liberal tradition-limited government, individual liberty, due process of law, self-determination, free enterprise, inalienable (natural) rights, the equality of citizens before the law, majority rule, minority rights, federalism, and the separation of powers.

With roots deeply implanted in the nation's history, elements of the political culture remain potent forces explaining what the United States does in its foreign policy. But as both the positive and negative aspects of globalization are more fully recognized, the domestic roots of foreign policy may increasingly be found elsewhere. While industry, labor, and environmental interests seek to place their own stamp on U.S. responses to globalization issues (like wages, labor trafficking, and World Trade Organization dispute-settlement rulings), other entities, particularly ideological, ethnic, and single-issue groups, have expressed concern about American targets abroad in its anti-terror campaign and have sought to impose their imprint on policy positions.

Since the end of the Vietnam War, American opinion toward foreign policy issues has consistently revealed domestic divisions about what is the appropriate role of the United States in world affairs. While American opinion leaders and policymakers remain overwhelmingly internationalist in orientation, fissures have continued to be evident among the public over the nature of America's internationalism—and the involvements in the Afghanistan and Iraq Wars surely exacerbated those divisions. Indeed, while majorities of those who identify themselves as Republicans or Democrats still agree on most foreign policy issues, partisan differences on some are quite deep and persistent. These include sharp gulfs between Democrats and Republicans over the benefits of globalization, the threat posed by immigration, and the dangers of Islamic fundamentalism. At the same time, majorities of the American public favor an active role for the United States in world affairs, maintaining the commitment to NATO and supporting U.S. participation in such international agreements as the Paris accord on climate change, the International Criminal Court, and lifting sanctions on Iran in exchange for limitation on its development of nuclear capability.[9] Divisions among the public on key and current foreign policy issues can and do make it difficult for policymakers to fashion and carry out a foreign policy that meets public approval. In this sense, these divisions pose a significant difficulty in producing a foreign policy consensus and a clear direction in America's actions abroad. Yet the exact shape of America's involvement is likely to be more fully contested in the ensuing presidential and congressional elections, revealing once again the close linkage between foreign and domestic politics.

Historically, American leaders have been able to define the parameters of American involvement in the world and to count on public support for their choices. Especially important was the so-called Establishment, consisting of (largely male) leaders drawn from the corporate and financial world and later supplemented by faculty members from the nation's elite universities. With roots in the early twentieth century, the Establishment was a major force defining key elements of American foreign policy prior to World War II and in the decades of Cold War conflict that followed. Its role is consistent with the elitist model of foreign policymaking, which says that public policy is little more than an expression of elites' preferences— and the interests underlying them.

A long-standing belief that public opinion will not tolerate large losses of life in situations involving American troops is consistent with another tradition known as *pluralism*. Whereas the elitist model sees the process of policymaking as one flowing from the top downward, pluralism sees the process as an upward-flowing one. Mass public opinion, which enjoys greater weight in this model, finds expression through interest groups, whose ability to shape foreign policy has been enhanced in recent years.

The media figure prominently but quite differently in these competing policymaking models. From the elitist perspective, the media are largely the mouthpieces of elites, providing the conduit through which mass public opinion is manipulated and molded to fit elite preferences. From the pluralist perspective, on the other hand, the media comprise an independent force able to scrutinize what the government is doing and provide an independent assessment of its policies. Thus, the media appear less conspiratorial in the pluralist than in the elitist model, but their role is potent nonetheless. Indeed, to some, the media are public opinion. Minimally, the media help to set the agenda for public discussion and often lay out for the American people the range of interpretations about foreign policy issues from which they might choose. Thus, the media help to aggregate the interests of more discrete groups in American society.

Political parties also aggregate interests. In the two-party system of the United States, political parties are broad coalitions of ethnic, religious, economic, educational, professional, working-class, and other sociodemographic groups. One of the most important functions these broad coalitions serve is the selection of personnel to key policymaking positions. They can also serve as referenda on past policy performance. Increasingly, the two major political parties are pursuing differing foreign policy paths, a departure from the tradition of bipartisanship in foreign affairs and another indicator of the enhanced role of domestic division on American foreign policy.

What role foreign policy beliefs and preferences play in shaping citizens' choices on these broad issues is difficult to determine. On the one hand, most citizens are motivated not by foreign policy issues but by domestic ones. Their electoral choices typically reflect those preferences, something especially evident in recent presidential elections. Still, we cannot easily dismiss the role elections play in the expression and consequences of Americans' foreign policy preferences. In the 2002 and 2006 congressional elections and in the presidential election in 2004, an abundance of evidence suggested the foreign policy issues, especially terrorism and the war in Iraq, figured prominently in the voting calculus of many Americans. In the 2008 and 2012 presidential elections, foreign policy issues for some Americans proved important in their voting decisions. In the 2016 presidential election, too, foreign policy issues such as terrorism, immigration, and global migration were prominent sources of concerns for many Americans. In this sense, foreign policy has always been an issue across presidential elections and can be crucial, especially in a closely contested election through the Electoral College system.[10] It is thus reasonable to hypothesize that the foreign policy preferences of Americans may have been pivotal in shaping the ultimate electoral outcome than we might suspect. In this sense, foreign policy issues can and do matter in presidential elections.

As these ideas suggest, the political culture, the foreign policy attitudes and beliefs of leaders and masses, and the role that the media, interest groups, and elections play in shaping Americans' political preferences and transmitting them to leaders may be potent explanations of what the United States does in the world.

THE INSTITUTIONAL SETTING

As we peel away the societal environment as a source of American foreign policy, a second category is revealed: the institutional setting, consisting of the various branches of government and the departments and agencies assigned responsibility for decision-making, management, and implementation. The category incorporates the diverse properties related to the structure of the U.S. government—notably its presidential rather than parliamentary form—that limit or enhance the foreign policy choices made by decisionmakers and affect their implementation, thus revealing the linkages between the substance of foreign policy and the process by which it is made.

Broadly speaking, the American "foreign affairs government" encompasses a cluster of variables and organizational actors that influence what the United States does—or does not do—abroad. Most striking in this regard is the division of authority and responsibility for foreign policymaking between Congress and the president. The Constitution embraces the eighteenth-century belief that the abuse of political power is controlled best not through centralization but by fragmenting it in a system of checks and balances. Hence, because authority and responsibility for American foreign policy is lodged in separate institutions sharing power, the Constitution is an "invitation to struggle."

The struggle for control over foreign policymaking between Congress and the president is most evident during periods when Congress and the presidency are controlled by different political parties (divided government). But even during periods when the government is not divided, conflict over foreign policymaking continues, often within the executive branch itself. There we find departments and agencies that grew in size and importance during nearly a half-century of Cold War competition with the Soviet Union. Each is populated by career professionals who fight both for personal gain and for what they view as the appropriate response of the United States to challenges from abroad. Not surprisingly, then, bureaucratic struggles over appropriate American policies have long been evident. They continue to leave their imprints on American foreign policy.

The growing interdependence of the United States with the world political economy reinforces these bureaucratic battles, as several executive branch departments seemingly oriented toward domestic affairs (e.g., agriculture, commerce, justice, and treasury) now are also stakeholders in the foreign policy game. This is especially evident in the fight against international terrorism. Foreign intelligence agencies (notably the CIA) and domestic law enforcement agencies (notably the FBI) are constrained by law and tradition to different policy and implementation tracks, yet today they find they must triangulate their efforts on common external threats, including not only terrorism in its physical sense but also cyberterrorism and other such challenges as trafficking in illicit drugs. While there have been numerous efforts to encourage such interdepartmental cooperation, the differing cultural traditions within these bureaucracies remain formidable, and conflicts continue.

Fragmentation of authority over policymaking within the executive branch itself is a product of the complexity and competition evident within the foreign affairs government. That characterization takes on a special meaning when we consider the often overlapping roles of the White House and National Security Council staffs, the State Department, the Defense Department, the Treasury Department, the intelligence community, and other decision-making units, including the Department of Homeland

Security established after 9/11. This last department's charge is particularly challenging, since it is directed to integrate intelligence-gathering and law-enforcement responsibilities now spread across many different departments and agencies. The 2004 legislation creating a national director of intelligence as a means to integrate the disparate elements of the intelligence community is yet another case in point of the festering problem of fragmentation within the foreign affairs government—and this effort at restructuring has not been without growing pains.

As more agencies have achieved places in the foreign affairs government, and as the domestic political support they enjoy has solidified, the management of policymaking by the president, whose role in the conduct of foreign affairs is preeminent, has become more difficult. To many, blame for the incoherence and inconsistency sometimes exhibited in American foreign policy lies here. Ironically, however, efforts to enhance presidential control of foreign policymaking by centralizing it in the White House have sometimes exacerbated rather than diminished incoherence and inconsistency, by encouraging competition and conflict between the presidency, on the one hand, and the executive branch departments and agencies constituting the permanent foreign affairs government, on the other.

In sum, understanding the institutional setting as a source of American foreign policy requires an examination of the responsibilities of numerous institutions and their relations with one another: the institutionalized presidency, Congress, the cabinet-level departments, and other agencies with foreign affairs responsibilities. These, then, will be our concerns in part II.

DECISIONMAKERS AND THEIR POLICYMAKING POSITIONS

When we peel away the institutional setting as a domestic source of American foreign policy, the people who make the policies, their policymaking positions, and the bureaucratic environments in which they work become the focus of our attention. The underlying proposition is that the personal characteristics of individuals (personality traits, perceptions, and psychological predispositions), the role responsibilities that the individual assumes within the decision process (as president, national security adviser, or secretary of the treasury), and the differing bureaucratic environments (the FBI versus the CIA, for instance) in which individuals operate affect policy choices. Still, and despite the combination of these forces, it is important to keep in mind that the individual decisionmaker is the ultimate source of influence on policy, the final mediating force in the causal chain linking the other domestic sources to the ends and means of American foreign policy.

There are several ways in which personality and perceptual factors may impinge upon foreign policymaking. Ideas about communism and the Soviet Union instilled early in life, for example, likely affect the attitudes and behaviors of many now responsible for negotiating with the leaders of the post-Soviet states, including Russia. Similarly, policymakers' orientation toward decisionmaking may profoundly affect the nation's foreign policy strategies. It has been suggested, for example, that American leaders can be characterized as either crusaders or pragmatists. The hallmark of a crusader is a "missionary zeal to make the world better. The crusader tends to make decisions based on a preconceived idea rather than on the basis of experience. Even though there are alternatives, he usually does not see them." The pragmatist, on the other hand, "is guided by the facts and his experience in a given situation, not by wishes or unexamined preconceptions . . . . Always flexible, he does not get locked into a losing policy. He can change direction and try again, without inflicting damage to his self-esteem."[11] Woodrow Wilson is the preeminent twentieth-century crusader, Harry S. Truman the personification of the pragmatist. Others, including Ronald Reagan, Bill Clinton, George W. Bush, Barack Obama, and Donald Trump, could easily be characterized in these terms as well.

Personality factors also help to explain how presidents manage the conduct of foreign affairs. A president's approach to information processing, known as his or her "cognitive style," that person's orientation toward political conflict, and his or her sense of political efficacy are all important in understanding how he or she will structure the policymaking system and deal with those around the chief executive. In this case, personal predispositions form a bridge between the institutional setting of American foreign policymaking and the process of decision-making itself.

Presidents sometimes engage in foreign policy actions not to affect the external environment but to influence domestic politics. Foreign policy can be used to mobilize popular support at home (the "rally 'round the flag" effect), to increase authority through appeals to patriotism, and to enhance prospects for reelection using macroeconomic policymaking tools or distributing private benefits through trade policy or other mechanisms, such as defense spending distributions. Again, the connection between domestic politics and foreign policy is apparent.

Although policymakers doubtless use foreign policy for domestic purposes, it is unclear whether they do so because of who they are or because of the positions they occupy. Because of the frequency with which policymakers in the United States and other countries alike allegedly engage in this type of behavior, it seems that leaders' role requirements, not their personal predilections, explain this behavior. Policymakers' positions thus appear to stimulate certain predictable patterns of behavior. Conversely, the position an individual holds may constrain the impact of personality on policymaking behavior. Institutional roles thus reduce the influence of idiosyncratic factors on policy performance.

Individuals can, of course, interpret the roles they occupy differently. That fact blurs the distinction between decisionmakers and their policy positions as competing rather than complementary explanations of American foreign policy. Clearly, however, policymaking positions, or roles, severely circumscribe the freedom and autonomy of the particular individuals who occupy them and thus diminish the range of politically feasible choices. Hence, we must understand the relationship between the person and the position and how each separately and in combination affects policy outcomes. In no way can that conclusion be illustrated more clearly than with a simple aphorism drawn from bureaucratic politics: "Where you stand depends on where you sit."

In sum, a focus on decisionmakers and their policy positions as a category of domestic influences on American foreign policy draws attention to the capacity of individuals to place their personal imprints on the nation's conduct abroad, while simultaneously alerting us to the need to examine the forces that constrain individual initiative. Principal among these are the role-induced constraints that occur within bureaucratic settings. Because the making and execution of American foreign policy is fundamentally a group or organizational enterprise, we can surmise that these constraints are considerable. The essays in part III will focus on these ideas and how they relate to American foreign policymaking.

NOTES

1. For a discussion of foreign policy positions of Candidate Trump across an array of issues, see Council on Foreign Relations, "Transition 2017: The Next Commander in Chief," at http://www.cfr.org/campaign2016/, accessed January 30, 2017. Also see Damian Paletta, "Clinton vs. Trump: Where They Stand on Foreign Policy Issues," WSJ.com, 2016 at http://graphics.wsj.com/elections/2016/donald-trump-hillary-clinton-on-foreign-policy/, accessed August 30, 2016.

2. "Inaugural Address: Trump's Full Speech" CNNPolitics.com, January 20, 2017 at http://www.cnn.com/2017/01/20/politics/trump-inaugural-address/, accessed January 20, 2017.

3. On the information revolution, or what he labels the "Third Industrial Revolution," and the various ramifications of its impact on global politics, see Joseph S. Nye Jr., *The Future of Power* (New York: Public Affairs, 2011), 113–51.

4. The quoted passages are from *The National Security Strategy of the United States* (Washington, DC: The White House, September 17, 2002).

5. Dina Smeltz, Ivo Daalder, Karl Friedhoff, and Craig Kafura, *America in the Age of Uncertainty: American Public Opinion and US Foreign Policy* (Chicago: Chicago Council on Global Affairs, 2016), 8.

6. "Inaugural Address: Trump's Full Speech."

7. James M. McCormick, "The Obama Presidency: A Foreign Policy of Change?" in Steven E. Schier, ed., *Transforming America: Barack Obama in the White House* (Lanham, MD: Rowman & Littlefield, 2011), 244–45.

8. Robert W. Tucker and David C. Hendrickson, "Thomas Jefferson and American Foreign Policy," *Foreign Affairs* 69 (Spring 1990): 139.

9. See Smeltz, Daalder, Friedhoff, and Kafura, *America in the Age of Uncertainty: American Public Opinion and US Foreign Policy* for the evidence on these partisan divisions among the public on some issues as well as the support across the public for other issues.

10. On the importance of foreign policy in elections, including some evidence for the 2008 presidential election, see Miroslav Nincic, "External Affairs and the Electoral Connection," in James M. McCormick, ed., *The Domestic Sources of American Foreign Policy: Insights and Evidence*, 6th ed. (Lanham, MD: Rowman & Littlefield, 2012), 139–55.

11. John G. Stoessinger, *Crusaders and Pragmatists: Movers of Modern American Foreign Policy* (New York: Norton, 1985), xiii–xiv.

I

THE SOCIETAL ENVIRONMENT

"Politics stops at the water's edge." That aphorism, popular during much of the Cold War, embraces the notion that domestic differences should not cloud American efforts abroad. The domestic unity implied by the phrase waned in the aftermath of the Vietnam War and, later, with the end of the Cold War as foreign policy disputes became frequent. The tragic events of September 11 seemingly resurrected this aphorism as the public rallied behind its leaders and partisan divisions were put aside to confront international terrorism. The Iraq War of 2003 and its aftermath, the Afghanistan War, the Great Recession of 2008, the tragic civil war in Syria, and the rise of the Islamic State of Syria and Iraq (ISIS) shattered this temporary unity, and the constraints of the societal environment once again were fully in evidence by the end of the first decade, and into the second decade, of the twenty-first century.

The events of September 11, 2001, did indeed have a profound effect on public and partisan unity, and politics stopped at the water's edge for a time. After that spectacular event, the public's foreign policy mood shifted perceptibly with Americans becoming more committed to an "active role" for the United States than at any time in recent decades.[1] Not surprisingly, terrorism topped the list when people were asked to name "one of the two or three biggest problems facing the country," and the American public embraced a greater willingness to endorse a series of military measures against that threat. Further, partisan and ideological divisions on foreign policy among American policymakers were altered. Within days of this attack, Congress, by overwhelming margins, passed Senate Joint Resolution 23, which authorized the president to employ force "against those nations, organizations, or persons, he determines planned, authorized, committed, or aided the terrorist attacks." A month later, Congress passed the USA Patriot Act, which granted even more discretion to the president in pursuing terrorist suspects, even to the extent of easing some civil liberty protections. And a year later, Congress passed another joint resolution authorizing the president to use force against Iraq.

The Iraq War, initiated in March 2003, however, shattered this bipartisan unity and created a broad array of domestic challenges to the Bush administration's foreign policy. Although the toppling of the Iraqi regime occurred quite quickly, and Bush announced the end of combat on an American naval vessel standing before a banner proclaiming "Mission Accomplished," the challenge of the Iraq invasion, it turns out, was just beginning. The effort at reconstruction and reconciliation proved a daunting task. As the insurgent opposition and sectarian violence grew, as weapons of mass destruction could not be found in Iraq, and as the number of Americans killed in Iraq increased, domestic opposition did as well. The foreign policy unity of several months earlier began to erode. The Democratic opposition, of course, led these attacks, but dissent within the president's own Republican ranks emerged as well. Politics no longer stopped at the water's edge.

Congress was now engaged once again in the foreign policy debate, and the 2006 congressional elections, widely viewed as a referendum on the Iraq War and the Bush administration's handling of foreign policy, resulted with Democrats gaining control of both houses of Congress. The new Congress sought to hold the president accountable for his actions in Iraq and elsewhere and attempted to put its own stamp on foreign policy, albeit with limited success. Still, the social environment for American foreign policy had seemingly changed quite perceptibly in the space of a few years and in response to a major foreign policy event.

With Barack Obama's victory in the 2008 presidential election, continuing Democratic control of Congress, and the president's call for bringing people together, the stage seemed set to move back to more domestic unity on foreign policy. Indeed, Candidate Obama had pledged to bring a new style of American leadership, restore America's reputation in the world, and reverse some of the foreign policy actions of the Bush administration. Efforts to close the Guantanamo Bay facility, however, almost immediately sparked congressional and public opposition. The public did not want these terrorist suspects housed near them and on American soil. One public opinion survey in 2010 indicated that 60 percent of the American public wanted the prisons at Guantanamo Bay to remain open. Congress ultimately passed legislation blocking funding to renovate a facility in Illinois.[2] The Obama administration's adoption of a "surge strategy" toward the deteriorating situation in Afghanistan also sparked criticism from both sides of the political aisle. Later, that administration's decision to support a "no-fly zone" over Libya in March 2011 to halt Muammar

Qaddafi's assaults on his people sparked domestic controversy as well. Some objected that no vital national interests were at stake in Libya, and the United States was yet again involving itself in an internal war of another nation.

In the Obama administration's second term, the foreign policy divide at home continued. In 2012, President Obama set out a "redline" for American action if the Bashar al-Assad regime in Syria used chemical weapons. When evidence emerged that this use had occurred in 2013, and the president failed to follow through with a U.S. response, domestic partisan divisions quickly emerged. Similarly, the limited response of the Obama administration to Russia's seizure of Crimea and its involvement in Ukraine sparked more domestic divisions on foreign policy a year later. Finally, the agreement among the P5+1 countries (the United States, France, Britain, Russia, China, and Germany) and Iran in 2015 over the potential development of nuclear weapons by the latter immediately stoked public and party divisions within the United States.

Such partisan divisions have not ceased in the early days of the Trump administration; arguably, they have increased. The issuance of a temporary ban on immigration by the administration sparked demonstrations across the country, legal challenges in the courts, and partisan (and intraparty) division on Capitol Hill. Similarly, controversial statements by President Trump about American policy toward Russia and toward traditional American allies also stimulated partisan divisions on the direction of American foreign policy.

Understanding the degree of unity and division in American foreign policy over the past two decades requires a fuller understanding of the domestic political and social environment, the topic of part I. What are the competing societal forces shaping America's responses abroad today? Which among them play pivotal roles in charting the direction of foreign policy? How have these events of the past decade or more shaped and reshaped the societal environment and its impact on American foreign policy? What is the appropriate foreign policy strategy or approach that will begin to garner more support across partisan and social divides?

We begin to explore such questions with three readings that focus on differing "grand strategies" in which the United States as a society may embrace in dealing with the world in the second decade of the twenty-first century. Each of these chapters advances an argument that the United States needs to alter the basis of its foreign policy approach from the past and rely on different values and assumptions about the world. Each chapter, too, introduces students to key foreign policy approaches—liberal internationalism, realism, and conservative internationalism—that have been utilized in the past, albeit with each one providing its own insights and revisions of the approaches.

In the first chapter, "Liberal Internationalism: Why Woodrow Wilson Matters," political scientist Tony Smith provides an authoritative account of the development and meaning of liberal internationalism, offers a critique of how it has been applied to U.S. foreign policy recently, and outlines how it should be changed for the current era.

Liberal internationalism was the grand strategy of foreign policy that the United States largely embraced since its sustained engagement in the international system over the past century and had its origins fundamentally out of the American experience in World War I. President Woodrow Wilson sought "to promote a concept of world order that would take [the U.S.] permanently out of isolationism." Liberal internationalism, or "what came to be called Wilsonianism," had four main components, as Smith points out: "cooperation among democratic governments," ties among states through "economic openness," functional and "well-structured multilateral institutions" that were operating, and American leadership of the democratic nations in the global system. These components and their synthesis "yields an effective unity greater than the mere sum of its parts" in the international system. Moreover, these interrelated parts can create a "zone of democratic peace" in the world and, as Smith argues, various periods in recent history reflected this outcome (e.g., the 1940s and the early 1990s).

This liberal international approach thus assumed a prominent and continued basis for American actions abroad, particularly with its promotion of liberal values worldwide. But, Smith argues, proponents of this approach in recent years tended to exaggerate "the appeal of liberal values, practices, and institutions as well as the ease of putting them in place." The result has been the rise of "neo-Wilsonianism" (in Smith's terminology). In this view, force could be used to impose democracy on nations (as illustrated by the Bush administration's national security strategy statement) or to bypass sovereignty (as embodied in "the responsibility to protect" doctrine to protect citizens as occurred in the Obama years). Smith contends that "never would Wilson have entertained such astonishing presumptions." Although Wilson championed "democratic life . . . he was chary of thinking that its progress abroad could be easily assumed." Instead of initiating "a crusade to democratize the world," he favored an effort "to make the world safe for democracy by protecting such elements as were at hand." Any new "burst of democracy" worldwide will need to be home-grown, not imposed. "Neo-Wilsonians," however, were not listening to Wilson's original imperatives as both the Bush and Obama administrations embraced the spread of democracy. Neoconservatives, Smith argues, bear some of the responsibility for this, but not all. Neoliberals do as well.

Hence, Smith concludes that liberal internationalism is "in crisis." To restore this approach to its original intent as the basis of American foreign policy, Smith offers three important recommendations. Democracies, including the United States, must "put their own houses in order"; they must work with authoritarian states and not lecture them "on human rights and democracy"; and they should aid countries "to promote human rights and democratization, but only where the ground seems genuinely propitious."

In the second chapter, "Conservative American Realism," Colin Dueck outlines a distinct view that American foreign policy should take, one largely at odds with liberal internationalism that Smith discusses. Instead, Dueck advances the argument for a *conservative American realism*. This approach would be conservative, by "working to preserve America's international status"; American, by "aiming to energetically promote concrete U.S. interests"; and realist, by recognizing the competitive nature of the international system that the United States confronts.

There are some key components of this approach that Dueck identifies and some key advantages that the United States possesses to achieve them. Conservative American realism would focus on achieving U.S. interests, maintaining U.S. primacy in the world, and sustaining a "forward military presence overseas" to reassure allies and friends and deter enemies and adversaries. Such actions provide for greater stability in the international system and for retaining the American role in global affairs. Despite some recent analyses of American decline, Dueck points out a host of ways in which U.S. capabilities and resources continue to be paramount to allow America to play this central role internationally. At the same time, Dueck acknowledges that challenges exist from state and nonstate actors for the United States from Russia, China, rogue states (e.g., Iran, North Korea), and jihadist terrorists. For each of these challengers, he outlines how a conservative American realist and American foreign policy should respond to them.

Dueck concludes by drawing some policy lessons from the American experience in Iraq for the past two decades from the Bush and Obama administrations and draws some general principles for the future conduct of a conservative American realism. From the latter administration, conservative realism would emphasize "credible deterrence and robust strategies of pressure against clearly identified U.S. adversaries, rather than retrenchment, accommodation, and autobiographical complacency." From the former administration, Dueck's approach would reject the notion "that a doctrine of regime change via preventive warfare lies at the heart of [U.S.] foreign policy." Instead, greater attention should be placed on "when and how to use force wisely." In all, Dueck argues, U.S. foreign policy should be less about transforming the international system and more about maintaining American dominance in world affairs.

In "Conservative Internationalism," political scientist Henry Nau offers a foreign policy approach that combines the elements of liberal internationalism, nationalism, and realism, and it stands in contrast to the first two chapters. As Nau notes, the United States has vacillated between being too aggressive and too restrained in its foreign policy over the decades (and even historically), and neither approach has served the United States very well.

Nau sees these differing cycles as rooted in competing foreign policy traditions domestically. The liberal (and liberal internationalist) tradition in foreign policy is exemplified by the presidencies of Woodrow Wilson and Franklin Delano Roosevelt. Wilson, for instance, sought to "tame international violence and spread democracy largely by multilateral diplomacy and economic interdependence." His approach eschewed military force except as a last resort. By contrast, the other prominent traditions, nationalism and realism, view the international system as competitive, not inclined toward cooperation, and thus the United States must be willing to use its national power and capabilities to defend its interests. Military force, moreover, is the key to protecting those interests. Nau identifies the presidencies of Andrew Jackson and James K. Polk as reflecting this nationalist tradition, and Theodore Roosevelt and Richard Nixon, the realist one.

As an alternative to these approaches, Nau calls for one that "combines the commitment of *liberal internationalism* to spread democracy . . . with the instruments of *realism* to back-up diplomacy with military force." This conservative internationalism, as he labels it, has already been utilized by Harry Truman and Ronald Reagan as well as earlier presidents, and it should be again because it offers key foreign policy advantages for the United States. Conservative internationalism "would insist that the United States continue efforts to improve the world by increasing the number of democratic states." In order for the United States to promote democracies and negotiate with authoritarian states that may resist, "the United States needs to arm its diplomacy." In other words, the balance of power must be operative and American defense must be strong. At the same time, Nau cautions that using force to advance diplomacy should be selective, and "the United States has to set priorities." Indeed, he argues that the United States should use force "to deter or reduce threats from any country but promote democracy only in countries that lie on the border of existing free countries."

Finally, Nau set outs how conservative internationalism has been used previously and discusses how it is applicable to the United States defending Ukraine, Turkey, and the Korean peninsula, but not to Iraq and Afghanistan. In defending freedom, however, Nau makes clear that the conservative internationalist "respects and preserves, not transcends, national sovereignty. It expects little from international institutions of civil society, especially free markets. It envisions a decentralized world of separate nations in which democracies grow from the bottom up."

If the first three chapters of part I focus on alternate "grand strategies" that the United States might apply to its foreign policy approach, the next three chapters address the impact of differing specific domestic interests that affect the direction of American foreign policy. One looks at the role of the Jewish lobby and its impact on American foreign policy toward the Middle East. The second examines how military experience impacts the attitudes and behaviors of political elites on their support for the use of American force abroad. The third assesses the effect of media on the foreign policy process with a case analysis of the "surge strategy" during the Iraq War.

The first of these three, "The Israel Lobby," by John Mearsheimer and Stephen Walt, is an abridged version of a longer piece on this topic published in the *London Review of Books* in March 2006. Their argument is that American policy toward Israel and toward the Middle East is driven less by moral and strategic concerns and more by the impact of the domestic Jewish lobby. And this lobby has been very successful, in their estimate. The United States has provided Israel with substantial foreign assistance on a year-to-year basis, ensured "consistent diplomatic support" through the use of the veto in the UN Security Council on resolutions that were critical of Israel, and made available "top-drawer weaponry."

Mearsheimer and Walt claim that this substantial support cannot be accounted for by strategic or moral considerations. To be sure, Israel did prove an asset to the United States during the Cold War, but Israel also "complicated America's relations with the Arab world." In addition, Israel complicates the efforts against terrorism since America's close ties with Israel partly serve as a source of anti-U.S. terrorism. As a moral imperative, Mearsheimer and Walt do acknowledge that "there is a strong moral case for supporting Israel's existence, but that is not in jeopardy." Instead, they claim that, "viewed objectively," Israel's "past and present conduct offers no moral basis for privileging it over the Palestinians." They also question whether there is an imperative to support Israel so strongly simply because it is a fellow democracy, because of its isolated position in the Middle East, or because of its past history.

Instead, their explanation for the continued American support "is the unmatched power of the Israel Lobby." As they note, this lobby is a "loose coalition of individuals and organizations who actively work to steer U.S. foreign policy in a pro-Israel direction." As such, they map out the nature and extent of the lobby—the organizations and individuals associated with it. Moreover, they argue that its effectiveness is particularly tied to "its influence in Congress," but they also note its impact on the media, think tanks, and the academic community. Mearsheimer and Walt conclude by discussing whether the "lobby's power can be curtailed." While they are skeptical about that prospect, they do call for more open debate on this topic. Perhaps needless to say, their analysis sparked considerable controversy and a series of exchanges among academics and the public on the issue of foreign policy lobbying.[3] By indirection, their analysis and the discussions also highlight the role that domestic groups—and especially domestic ethnic groups—play in the foreign policy process.

The next chapter, "American Veterans in Government and the Use of Force," by Peter D. Feaver and Christopher Gelpi, points to another kind of societal influence, the military, on one important aspect of American foreign policy—namely, the use of force abroad. In particular, they evaluate how military experience among policymakers affects the propensity of the United States to initiate and escalate the use of force abroad. To examine this relationship, Feaver and Gelpi first identify the number of "militarized disputes" that the United States initiated from 1816 to 1992 and the number of such disputes that were escalated. Next, they determine the degree of military experience among the executive and legislative branches since both branches may impact the use of force abroad. Feaver and Gelpi also consider the impact of the type of disputes abroad— disputes that affect the core values of the United States (what they call "realpolitik" targets) and disputes that do not ("interventionist" targets). Finally, Feaver and Gelpi also enter a number of other "control" variables into their analysis that might plausibly account for America's decision to use or escalate force.

The results "provide strong and striking support" for their argument that as the percentage of military veterans among policymakers increase, the United States is less likely to initiate the use of force abroad. They also found that, as the proportion of policymakers with military experience increases, the propensity to use force against interventionist targets is even less likely than against realpolitik targets. They also report that none of the control variables "can account for the impact of elite veterans" on their results. In addition, Feaver and Gelpi also find that, while policymakers with military experience may be reluctant to initiate force, elite veterans are more likely to support the escalation of American force once some forces have been initiated. In all, then, their results have important substantive implications for the future use of American force abroad, but they also point to the important role that a societal interest, the military, may have on American foreign policy.

In the last chapter among these three, "How Media Limit Accountability in Foreign Policymaking: Iraq and Beyond," noted media analyst, Robert Entman, illustrates how the media can limit "the influence of public opinion in U.S. foreign policy," how the executive branch can utilize the media to shape its foreign policy message, and how the difficulties that opposition forces face with the media in getting their message out. Entman uses a comprehensive study of the American "surge" during the Iraq War to demonstrate these arguments, but the general findings are likely applicable to other foreign policy events.

Entman's basic construct for demonstrating the effect of the media on the foreign policy process is what he calls the "accountability gap." This gap refers to the continuing deference by the media to White House pronouncements even as the costs to the country at large may be increasing, and this gap tends to enlarge over time on a given issue. The result is, in Entman's estimation, that public officials are not held accountable by news organizations—or the public—as a result. As noted, Entman uses the coverage of the Iraq surge that the Bush administration initiated in early 2007 to illustrate this accountability gap. Although the majority of the American public disapproved of the increase in troops to Iraq and a number of public officials dissented from this action, the media "revealed a marked preference for the White House frame" in covering the surge issue. Further, Entman shows how the Bush administration was markedly successful in preempting "an opposition frame" and in portraying the opposition position as fostering a rapid withdrawal of American troops from Iraq. In all, the administration was effective in seeking "to control and steer media and political debates on the surge."

What explains such accountability gaps? Entman points to "commercial necessity and professional custom" as part of the explanation. The ability of an American administration to make "big news" and to form "a coherent and reassuring argument" also accounts for these gaps. Opposition forces to the current policy often confront difficulty in developing and promoting an alternative news frame in the context of the dominance of the administration and the sometimes contradictory and ambiguous public opinion polls. As a result, Entman proposes that "a realistic goal for journalists in the U.S. might be to more self-consciously adjust proportionality" in reporting on foreign policy events and actions. In all, the analysis demonstrates how the media can affect and shape foreign policy.

The final two chapters in part I take a broader look at societal influences on foreign policy by examining how the public at large affects the foreign policy process. Adam J. Berinsky provides an explanation for public support or opposition to military conflict with particular emphasis on the Iraq War. His "elite cue" theory points to the importance of domestic politics, and particularly partisanship, as crucial for determining such support. Dina Smeltz and her colleagues at the Chicago Council on Global Affairs outline the current state of public and leadership opinion toward foreign policy, based upon that organization's 2016 survey results as well as the surveys over the past four decades.

In "Events, Elites, and American Public Support for Military Conflict," Adam J. Berinsky advances an explanation for when American public opinion will support or oppose a military conflict. The explanation is fundamentally rooted in domestic politics. His "elite cue" theory argues that the public's decision to support or oppose military actions turns on "listening

to trusted sources—those politicians who share their political predispositions." In turn, Berinsky presents evidence from two surveys during the Iraq
War to support his theory.

Berinsky's theory, of course, stands in contrast to other leading theories
about public support or opposition to conflicts. One traditional view is the
"casualties hypothesis" that has been used to account for the level of support or opposition to war. Put simply, as the number of American deaths
increases, public support declines. A second conventional explanation
points to the success of the mission as the crucial factor for public support.
The clearer the objectives of the conflict and their probability of success,
the greater the level of public support for American actions in a conflict.
Yet Berinsky contends that such "event-response" theories, as he calls them,
are problematic for at least three reasons. First, these theories assume more
knowledge about politics than is warranted among the public. Second,
these theories are based on aggregate analyses of public responses and
do not provide any explanation for individual calculations of support or
opposition to war. Third, these theories appear to leave out the partisan
nature and the impact of *domestic politics* in accounting for war support or
opposition.

He thus seeks to address these problems with his elite cue theory. Berinsky
begins his theory by drawing on the work of political scientist John Zaller.
Zaller argues that the balance of elite discourse on a particular policy position is important as to whether the public will support or oppose a policy.
While this focus on elite discourse is important, it is also incomplete.
Berinsky contends that the actors on both sides of "a controversy [may]
provide persuasive messages." Hence, how does the public decide whether
to support or oppose such a policy in this instance? Berinsky contends that
it becomes a political choice for the public: "citizens could use the positions of prominent elites [to] . . . decide whether to support or oppose a
policy." In this sense, Berinsky expects that day-to-day events about a conflict will have little effect on support or opposition. Instead, the "patterns of
elite discourse—the stated positions of leading Democrat and Republican
politicians—will play a large role in determining public support for war."
In this way, the public take their cues from their preferred partisans, not
from foreign events.

To test his theory, Berinsky reports on two surveys that he conducted
on support and opposition to the Iraq War. In the first survey experiment,
Berinsky's results show that the American public had considerable difficulty in estimating the number of war deaths in the Iraq War, and that the
estimates individuals made were tied to their political views. In particular, those who are "overestimators" of battle deaths in Iraq tended to be
Democrats, while "underestimators tend[ed] to be Republicans." Within
this first survey, some respondents were provided correct information about

the number of deaths for the "underestimators" and "overestimators." Yet such information did not affect their resultant attitudes to the war. In this sense, information about events was not crucial to their position on the war. In a second survey of the public a year later, Berinsky utilized six different survey question wordings, each with varying levels of information about the costs and benefits of the Iraq War. Berinsky reports that these differing questions made virtually no difference in levels of support by the public. In this case, he argues that these results imply that the respondents had already decided on the war and that they were not influenced by events or information.

In sum, Berinsky concludes that event-response theories do not explain support or opposition to the Iraq War. Instead, partisanship, as the elite cue theory would predict, was the more likely explanation of the level of support or opposition to the Iraq War. Furthermore, and by implication, this elite cue theory would operate for other conflicts as well.

In the final chapter in this section, Dina Smeltz and her colleagues outline three possible areas of gaps regarding public opinion. The populist gap focuses on the differences between the public and foreign policy leaders, the partisan gap examines the differences between Democrats and Republicans, and the perception gap assesses how the opinion leaders misread the views of the public. Using these gaps as analytic tools, Smeltz et al. then summarize the views of the public and their leaders across a wide array of issues and concerns—trade policy, immigration, climate change, terrorism, nuclear proliferation, and several others. In addition, they report on the differing views on the role of the United States in global affairs and the support for American alliances and bases worldwide.

Their systematic analyses provide important conclusions about the current state of American opinion on foreign policy and how those views might shape the direction of U.S. action abroad. There exists an "apparent consensus" among leaders and the public in support of "globalization, the Trans-Pacific Partnership, and many aspects of international trade." At the same time, there is a gap between the leaders (who provide strong support for trade and globalization) and the public (who more narrowly support these items). Immigration issues largely divide the parties and even within parties. Further, the parties are divided as to the direction of American foreign policy with Republicans (both leaders and the public) emphasizing "US military superiority and military strength as key element" of foreign policy, while Democrats "are more likely to say that strengthening the United Nations is an effective way of achieving US foreign policy." Finally, a perception gap also exists between leaders and the public on a range of foreign policy issues.

Importantly, Smeltz and her colleagues conclude by cautioning against overstating "the level of division between the parties on many core articles of foreign policy." The American public and its leaders still provide substantial support on America's global engagement, its commitment to NATO, its alliances abroad, and addressing nuclear proliferation. In this sense, some components of a foreign policy consensus remain among the public and its leaders.

Editor's Note: At the end of each chapter is a series of discussion questions for use by the students and instructor.

NOTES

1. See Chicago Council on Foreign Relations, "A World Transformed: Foreign Policy Attitudes of the U.S. Public after September 11," http://worldviews.org/key_findings/us_911_report.htm, for the immediate results after 9/11. For recent results on American attitudes and how attitudes have changed and remained the same, especially on actions against terrorism, see Chicago Council on Global Affairs, *Constrained Internationalism: Adapting to New Realities, Results of a 2010 National Survey of American Public Opinion* (Chicago: Chicago Council on Global Affairs, 2010).

2. See David Welna, "Democrats Block Funding to Close Guantanamo," May 20, 2009, www.npr.org/templates/story/story.php?storyId=104334339; and Charles Savage, "Closing Guantanamo Fades as a Priority," *New York Times*, June 25, 2010, www.nytimes.com/2010/06/26/us/politics/26gitmo.html.

3. The original article generated so much debate that the *London Review of Books* sponsored a debate on September 28, 2006, at the Great Hall of the Cooper Union (see www.lrb.co.uk/v28/n06/mear9]1_html). *Foreign Policy* magazine devoted a substantial portion of its July/August 2006 issue to this topic as well.

1

Liberal Internationalism

Why Woodrow Wilson Still Matters

Tony Smith

With the centennials starting in 2017 to commemorate America's entry into the Great War in April 1917, and continuing through 2018 and 2019 recalling the birth of the League of Nations two years later in Paris in 1919, debates over the character of American liberal internationalism, or what came to be called "Wilsonianism," will be very much of the moment. But how well will Woodrow Wilson's policies be understood as we reflect back on these years? Indeed, how is his influence felt still today as we recall his hope that the gift of his years in office (1913–1921) would be, in his most celebrated phrase, "a world made safe for democracy?"

Wilson and Wilsonianism are far from the only subjects to be debated as we consider the legacies of World War I—that is, the way this terrible conflagration between 1914 and 1918 decisively shaped the rest of the twentieth century and remains very much with us still today. Three momentous developments are commonly asserted to have arisen from the conflict. First, we can attribute to the war the success of Lenin's daring act of seizing power through the Russian Revolution of 1917 and his sponsorship of the international spread of communism to every corner of the planet in an astonishingly short period thereafter. Second, in reaction to the expansion of communism as well as to the Treaty of Versailles of June 28, 1919, with Germany (and to the treaties that followed with Austria-Hungary, Bulgaria, and the Ottoman Empire), we can attribute a major impetus to the rise of fascism, a form of political organization also international in scope, but whose most deadly consequences came with the rise of Nazism in Germany and the horrors of World War II that followed. Third, the moral and physical weakness of the European powers, glaringly evident by 1918, combined with the two factors already mentioned to give critical stimulation to the

31

growth of nationalist movements not only of colonized peoples under the direct rule of London and Paris but also of ancient civilizations in the Middle East and most of Asia (especially in China). Here was a prelude to the rise of these peoples after World War II completed the destruction of Europe's global power that World War I had initiated.

A fourth legacy of enormous importance that arose from World War I is less well understood: the logic of Woodrow Wilson's thinking between 1917 and 1919 and its impact on American foreign policy a generation later as Washington began to plan in the early 1940s the outlines of a postwar order after the defeat of Germany and Japan. As he took office as president in 1913, Wilson dealt first with a response to the Mexican Revolution and the question of how to assure a stable Western Hemisphere with the opening of the Panama Canal in 1914 and the advent of war in Europe. Far more critically, once conflict began in earnest in Europe and the United States joined the war, Wilson tried to promote a concept of world order that would take his nation permanently out of isolationism, founding its leadership position in the name of promoting democratic governments, open markets, and a mutual defense pact that came to be called collective security.

The result was an argument for American "exceptionalism" that has persisted until today. Its claim is not simply that the United States is the "indispensable nation" because its relative power position makes us a party to all major international issues. Rather, its primary reason to expect deference from other states is that we do not seek to pursue our own narrow self-interest so much as to insure an international order that at a minimum could deliver on Wilson's conviction that democratic nations could find their security through the organization of a community of like-minded peoples.

Given the role liberal internationalism played in the success of the United States in the cold war with the Soviet Union, and the part that it has continued to play with even more self-assurance over the past three decades, certainly Wilsonianism deserves the kind of attention as a legacy of World War I that communism, fascism, and the rise of nationalism in Asia, Latin America, and Africa have received. Here were three ideologies fighting for world dominion—fascism collapsing in 1945, communism losing its international appeal in 1989, and liberal internationalism still alive but increasingly living on borrowed time.

BUT WHAT IS "WILSONIANISM?"

Yet we must raise a delicate question: Is there, in fact, much of a consensus on the character of the Wilsonian tradition? It often appears that there are as many definitions of Wilson's legacy as there are scholars and policymakers invoking (often enough to debunk) his legacy. If liberal internationalism bids to be a basic part of the framework for American foreign policy, then some agreement on what Wilsonianism amounts to is necessary. Otherwise, the tradition is in danger of losing its identity—and so its direction—in the wave of efforts to give meaning to the term, a cacophony of concepts that threaten any meaningful discussion as to Wilson's legacy and an appreciation of its impact on American foreign policy over the last seventy-five years.

To promote a consensus, I propose that four separate, but interrelated, elements constitute its essence: (1) cooperation among democratic governments, (2) linked through economic openness, (3) negotiating differences and common interests through well-structured multilateral institutions that foster a robust sense of the importance of economic integration, international law, and a commitment to mutual defense, and (4) dependent on an America that willingly assumes the responsibilities of leadership of a community of liberal democratic nations pledged to peace through collective security, even if this means going to war to preserve it.

To envision the integration of the concepts that typify liberalism more graphically, imagine a four-sided diamond, each point of which represents one of the elemental features of liberal internationalism. Each facet of the diamond has its own distinctive quality, yet each relates to the other three in ways that are not only mutually reinforcing but that actually work to mix the characteristic features of each element into compounds that are equally distinctive. More, the synthesis created by the integration of the four elements yields an effective unity greater than the mere sum of its parts. *For the promise of this unity is mutual defense and the hope of a stable peace,* "a world made safe for democracy," which no aspect alone can be expected convincingly to deliver, but whose possible establishment, thanks to the synergy of these forces, is the prime tenet of liberal internationalism's secular faith.

Hence, when the admixture of these forces is achieved in practice—when theory is embodied in values, interests, institutions, and policies that endure over time—the result is what came by the 1990s to be called by "democratic peace theory" a "pacific union," a "zone of democratic peace." Today, the European Union is the leading historical example of the freedom, prosperity, and peace that liberal practices may bring—although others have looked at American–Canadian relations or at the cooperation apparent in Mercosur, founded in 1991 in the southern cone of Latin America. The brilliance given by the facets of the diamond of synergistically related forces arises from the radiance of its promise—Immanuel Kant's "perpetual peace," a conviction shared by a variety of American presidents from Woodrow Wilson's time on, including most especially Franklin D. Roosevelt, Ronald Reagan (who made the approach firmly bipartisan), George W. Bush, and Barack Obama.

If the complexity of this set of concepts is one factor that has prevented its coherent exposition, the opposition to its spirit of leading international relations theorists of the 1930s and 1940s made its recognition all the more difficult to appreciate. Writers of the eminence of Walter Lippmann, Hans Morgenthau, George Kennan, and later Henry Kissinger dismissed as "moralistic" and "idealistic" thinking the notion that this congeries of concepts could be a meaningful framework for American foreign policy.

Yet it was a meaningful framework. Indeed, the 1940s might be called the Wilsonian decade. High points are obvious: from the creation of the Bretton Woods system to open and integrate the world's capitalist markets in 1944 to the creation of the North Atlantic Treaty Organization in 1949, passing by perhaps the most critical of all initiatives—innovations introduced during the American occupations of Japan and Germany, which democratized them, opened their markets to the world on the basis of most favored nation status, and brought them into the leading multilateral institutions of the free market democratic world. In *World Order*, which appeared in 2014, Henry Kissinger said no less: "Wilson's principles were so pervasive, so deeply related to the American perception of itself, that when two decades later the issue of world order came up again, the failure of the interwar period did not obstruct their triumphal return. Amidst another world war, America turned once more to the challenge of building a new world order essentially on Wilsonian principles."

Here Washington laid the basis for its eventual triumph between 1989 and 1991 in the epic contest with the Soviet Union. With the fall of the Berlin Wall in November 1989 and the implosion of the Soviet Union at the end of 1991, democracy movements that had been gathering strength in Central Europe, Latin America, and East Asia since the 1970s redoubled their efforts to take power politically. Critical to these developments was Washington's determination to create a world order typified not only by human rights and democratic government but also by its leadership of efforts to establish the terms of an open and integrated world economy, and by the development of a complex set of multilateral institutions to coordinate the policies of mutual cooperation.

In fact, none other than Mikhail Gorbachev confirmed this interpretation of events when in May 1992 he traveled to Fulton, Missouri, to speak at the very spot where in 1946, Winston Churchill had declared that an "Iron Curtain" was falling across Europe, heralding a global struggle between communism and democracy from which the West must not flinch in its commitment to self-defense. At Fulton, Gorbachev declared the end of the cold war:

> a victory for common sense, reason, democracy. [The United Nations] should create structures . . . which are authorized to impose sanctions, to make use of other means of compulsion when rights of minority groups especially are being violated." [We must endorse] the universality of human rights . . . the acceptability of international interference wherever human rights are violated . . . Today democracy must prove that it can exist not only as the antithesis of totalitarianism. This means it must move from the national to the

international arena. On today's agenda is not just a union of democratic states, but also a democratically organized world community.

THE RISE OF NEO-WILSONIANISM

However, as I had warned as early as 1994 in my book *America's Mission: The United States and the Worldwide Struggle for Democracy* (republished by Princeton University Press in an expanded edition in 2012), by exaggerating the appeal of liberal values, practices, and institutions, as well as the ease of putting them in place, liberals could fail to anticipate the strength of the resistance that cultures as powerful as those in the Muslim world, Russia, and China would likely throw up to oppose these foreign ways. More, democracy activists might well underestimate the ability of anarchic forces, typical of societies based on weak social contracts and the absence of democratizing political traditions and institutions, to foil the efforts of outsiders to bring them new ways quite foreign to established patterns of social, economic, and political interaction.

The birth of what I call "neo-Wilsonianism" in the 1990s, with its extraordinary self-confidence and self-righteousness, which soon translated into military action in the Muslim world, confirmed my fears. Here was the origin of the thinking that led American liberal intellectuals and policymakers into believing that democracy had—as Presidents George W. Bush and Barack Obama (as well as British prime minister Tony Blair) repeatedly put it—"universal appeal," that it was "a universal value." Accordingly, in world affairs, "our interests and our values are one and the same." Hence, the West had "a responsibility to protect" populations against outrages committed locally in the name of a doctrine of sovereignty that could impose democracy abroad by the terms of a new concept of "just war," which overthrew the terms of state sovereignty as understood under the terms of the Westphalian peace agreement in vigor since 1648. A clash of civilizations had been unleashed, its terms explicit in the Bush Doctrine (generally understood as the National Security Strategy of the United States, of September 2002):

> In pursuit of our goals, our first imperative is to clarify what we stand for: the United States must defend liberty and justice because these principles are right and true for all people everywhere. No nation owns these aspirations, and no nation is exempt from them . . . America must stand firmly for the nonnegotiable demands of human dignity: the rule of law; limits on the absolute power of the state; free speech; freedom of worship; equal justice; respect for women; religious and ethnic tolerance; and respect for private property . . . the national security of the United States must start from these core beliefs and look outward for possibilities to expand liberty.

With this fervent conviction came the most decisive and dangerous break in the history of liberal internationalism. Never would Wilson have entertained such astonishing presumptions. As an academic, Woodrow Wilson had been a "comparativist," a term still used in political science departments today. Comparativists study discrete political forces as they locally gather expression and form. For Wilson, democratic government, especially as it had come to manifest itself in the United States, was his life-long preoccupation. In his commitment, he was rightly considered one of the leading intellectuals of his era. However, the insights he gained through his investigations of the course of democracy over time and worldwide convinced him that its progress abroad would not come quickly or easily or perhaps at all. Even for the United States itself, "eternal vigilance" was his watchword as he feared especially what he called the "predatory" tendencies of an unregulated capitalism to undermine democracy at home.

The result was that while Wilson was a moralist and an idealist in championing democratic life for possessing a social and political character above all others, he was chary of thinking that its progress abroad could be easily assumed. That is, he was not a utopian and so he was not an imperialist either. Thus, he left Mexico to its own devices after intervening between March 1913 and April 1914 on the margins of its great revolution. His reward was the creation by the Mexicans themselves of their Constitution of 1917, generally considered to be one of the most progressive in the world (to be studied by both the Bolsheviks in 1918 and the founders of the Weimar Republic in 1919).

For the same reason (as he pointed out himself), Wilson rejected Churchill's advice to march on Russia in 1918 (to "strangle in the cradle" infant Soviet communism) just as he ignored the counsel of Theodore Roosevelt to send troops to take Berlin that same year. Remembering the negative impact of international efforts to crush the French Revolution, and steeped as he was in decades of studying the origins and character of democratic government, the president did what he could short of outright military intervention, leaving domestic forces to determine the fate of their governments.

The tension in Wilson's approach to world affairs was thus at one and the same time his fear of autocratic governments as a threat to the peace yet his recognition of the limits on America's ability to control the flow of events everywhere around the globe. So in 1919, he found Germany to be "the perfect flower" of a malignant country. It was at once autocratic and oppressive internally, ruthlessly imperialist, economically protectionist, and deeply militaristic. In contrast, the United States was indeed, in Lincoln's phrase, "the last, best hope of earth," as it championed free societies, a minimum military establishment, anti-imperialism, and open-door international economic policies. As the president put it repeatedly, ultimately the outcome of the Great War turned on whether balance-of-power politics among states could be replaced by institutions ensuring collective security, a solution democracies were by their character best able to organize. So, he told the Congress in January 1917:

> The question upon which the whole future peace and policy of the world depends is this: Is the present war a struggle for a just and secure peace, or only for a new balance of power? If it be only a struggle for a new balance of power, who will guarantee, who can guarantee, the stable equilibrium of the new arrangement? Only a tranquil Europe can be a stable Europe. There must be, not a balance of power, but a community of power; not organized rivalries, but an organized common peace.

However, this summons to action was not an appeal for a crusade to democratize the world but rather a defensive request to make the world safe for democracy by protecting such elements as were at hand. To resolve the tension between his hopes and his realism, Wilson would do as best he might to protect democracy, but in full awareness that the undertaking was fraught with obstacles.

On the one hand, stood his resolute commitment to the solidarity of democratic peoples as the key to an enduring peace. Hence his most famous appeal, a call in his request on April 2, 1917 to the Congress for a declaration of war against Germany on specific terms to win the peace that would follow victory.

> The world must be made safe for democracy. Its peace must be planted upon the tested foundations of political liberty . . . A steadfast concert for peace can never be maintained except by a partnership of democratic nations. No autocratic government could be trusted to keep faith within it or observe its covenants. It must be a league of honor, a partnership of opinion . . . Only free peoples can hold their purpose and their honor steady to a common end and prefer the interests of mankind to any narrow interest of their own.

But on the other hand, it would be a gross overstatement to go from this declaration to allege, as many do, that Wilson had a "messiah complex" that made him a world "crusader" for the American way. Our twenty-eighth president was far too aware from his academic background of the inability of outsiders to push events abroad to count on either example or force of arms to move history in a dramatic way. As he had put it in *The State*, in a statement first published in 1889, then repeated in the edition of 1911, the year before his election as president:

> In politics nothing radically novel may safely be attempted. No result of value can ever be reached in politics except through slow and gradual development, the careful adaptations and nice modifications of growth. Nothing may be done by leaps. More than that, each people, each nation, must live upon the lines of its own experience. Nations are no more capable of borrowing experience than individuals are. The histories of other peoples may furnish us with

light, but they cannot furnish us with conditions of action. Every nation must constantly keep in touch with its past; it cannot run towards its ends around sharp corners.

Here was the essentially prudent, restrained, and indeed conservative sentiment that lay behind Wilson's hopes on the League of Nations. Just as he did not send troops to Mexico City, Moscow, or Berlin so that he would husband American strength for its self-defense and that of its legitimately democratic allies. Not for a minute did he consider the league to constitute an offensive organization.

The president's concerns were well-founded. In those parts of the world that called themselves democratic, he feared its roots did not go deep. Cooperation among democracies had greatly disappointed him at the Paris Peace Conference ending the war. More, the new states emerging from the disintegration of the Russian, Austro-Hungarian, and Ottoman empires were far too weak to encourage much optimism as to their eventual democratic character (exception made for Czechoslovakia). Neither the Soviet Union nor Germany was a member of the league nor likely to be friendly to its intentions. Most importantly of all, opposition to leadership of the league was widespread in the United States itself. Faced with these challenges, Wilson declared in 1918 that he was "playing for a hundred years hence."

Wilson's skepticism that democracy would necessarily be the wave of the future in 1919 was shared by many liberal intellectuals and policymakers during the cold war. In the struggle against international communism, the high ground was more often than not occupied by Leninist forces, such that Washington felt itself obliged to make common cause with authoritarian governments. If such calculations were exaggerated in many instances— most clearly with respect to Latin America, from Guatemala in the early 1950s to Chile in the early 1970s to Nicaragua in the early 1980s—in others, beginning with Greece in the late 1940s, they unfortunately made good sense. Only after the mid-1970s, as democracy took root in Greece and the Iberian Peninsula, might a new optimism begin to stir.

That the confidence of the 1970s was warranted as heralding a new age seemed ratified by the burst of democracy in important parts of East Asia, Central Europe, and Latin America after the end of the cold war. As political scientist Samuel Huntington persuasively argued in 1991, world events were certainly part of this process. Yet on closer inspection (and as Huntington well understood, as would Wilson), the peoples capable of making the transition from authoritarian to democratic governments had cultural, social, political, and historical characteristics that made such changes possible. These factors included strong feelings of national unity based on social contracts that could negotiate differences within the population; traditions of centralized government with responsible bureaucracies combined with elite codes of personal honor and civic duty; and levels of education and forms of economic development that created middle classes friendly to democratic ways.

In a word, what Huntington called "the third wave" of world democracy had its limits. So in 1996, he warned the United States against launching a "clash of civilizations" by trying to impose its ways on cultures sure to be hostile to the effort. But the neo-Wilsonians were not listening. Neither were the commanding leaders of the foreign policy elite. The policy that resulted came nearly two years after the fateful invasion of Iraq in the famous declaration of President George W. Bush in his second inaugural address:

> We are led by events and common sense to one conclusion: The survival of liberty in our land increasingly depends on the success of liberty in other lands. The best hope for peace in our world is the expansion of freedom in all the world . . . So it is the policy of the United States to seek and support the growth of democratic movements and institutions in every nation and culture, with the ultimate goal of ending tyranny in our world.

That such a mood was widespread in Washington is demonstrated by the extent to which in his first administration President Barack Obama picked up much the same themes. Late in 2009, he expressed his determination to return to Afghanistan to win the nation- and state-building agenda. Washington now had as a blueprint for success. In 2011, Obama declared his commitment to further the liberalizing ambitions of the Arab Spring (with especially deadly consequences in Libya).

The mistake of the neo-Wilsonians would be apparent to anyone familiar with the traditional American liberal internationalist thinking. In their exaggeration of the appeal to others of democracy lay the betrayal of their American liberal heritage as it was formulated by Woodrow Wilson (in its "classic stage") and adopted by most of America's foreign policy elite during the cold war (in its "hegemonic stage"). The result was an "imperialist stage" manifest in the March 2003 invasion of Iraq.

Those most responsible for the ensuing disaster were surely the neo-conservatives. The men and women gathered in the Project for the New American Century created by Robert Kagan and William Kristol in the mid-1990s militarized and popularized the mistaken belief that all the world was waiting for salvation at the hands of an activist, imperialist America. Figures close to Bush such as Paul Wolfowitz and Nathan Sharansky, and the legitimate claims of a number of neoconservative thinkers that their ideas made them the authors of the Bush Doctrine, put their ownership of the invasion of Iraq beyond doubt.

Yet it would be grossly simplistic to reserve for the neoconservatives all the responsibility for the intellectual mistakes of American liberals from the 1990s. There should be no forgetting the powerful assist given the neoconservatives from the neoliberal Democrats most notably assembled in that party's Progressive Policy Institute. Or consider the neoliberal imperialist sentiments that appeared in 2006 in the conclusions of the Princeton Report's study "Forging a World of Liberty Under Law" codirected by John Ikenberry and Anne-Marie Slaughter, leading liberal Democratic lights at none other than the Woodrow Wilson School. That all of this bipartisan enthusiasm for democracy promotion by force of arms combined with the series of optimistic reports on nation and state building published at the time by the apparently nonpartisan RAND corporation in a series of studies led by James Dobbins (a man with high official rank in both Republican and Democratic administrations), or again by General David Petraeus in his widely influential *Counterinsurgency Field Manual*, demonstrates the tsunami of argument that swept all before it. How else do we understand the mistaken policies of Barack Obama, first "surging" in Afghanistan, then hailing the Arab Spring? That neo-Wilsonianism had a decidedly bipartisan provenance is unquestionable.

RESUSCITATING AMERICAN LIBERAL INTERNATIONALISM

American liberal internationalism is today in crisis. Its problem is two-fold. On the one hand, its support for human rights and democracy globally is rightly seen as part and parcel of legitimizing Washington's imperialist interference in the Middle East. On the other, as Nobel Economics Prize winner Joseph Stiglitz has perhaps best persuasively argued, neoliberalism has been used to justify the deregulation and opening of markets worldwide in a fashion that has undermined working- and middle-class status in the United States and elsewhere, imperiling democracy even at home, much as Wilson had warned a full century ago now.

In these circumstances, to resuscitate liberal internationalism, three obvious recommendations are in order. First, the United States and its free-market democratic partners need to work first and foremost to put their own houses in order. The undermining of democratic politics at home by an unregulated capitalist system and an imperialist national security state must come to an end. Whether it is a matter of taxation rates, accounts sheltered internationally, or the export of jobs, technology, and capital that undergird the working and middle classes, a drastic overall is called for. At the same time, a prudent restraint needs to be introduced into the nation's defense planning. That this involves close cooperation with our democratic allies, themselves today in crisis, should be apparent.

Second, the United States needs to learn to work with what the American liberal political philosopher John Rawls called in his final book "relatively decent hierarchical states" rather than giving pious lectures to them on human rights and democracy. The danger of what Rawls called "outlaw states" may need to be addressed with military and diplomatic might. But to conceive of the world as a binary choice between democratic "us" and authoritarian "them" must come to an end. However much we should be concerned by the rise of hostile great powers, the contempt with which Russia and China are routinely treated in the liberal media carries with it a tone of superiority that is unwarranted in the light of the last fifteen years of American foreign and domestic policies.

Third, aid may be given to promote human rights and democratization, but only where the ground seems genuinely propitious. This may turn out to be the case in post-Castro Cuba as it is in countries as different as Iran and Tunisia. In the process, nongovernmental actors may be especially effective. These would include groups as varied as Human Rights Watch, Transparency International, the Argentine Anthropological Forensic Team, and the Open Society Institute. Most agree that the demand for equality for women should remain a paramount concern of these nongovernmental groups.

As obvious as these suggestions may be, the question is whether they (like environmental concerns) can in fact be implemented. Put differently, can democratic peoples solve their own internal contradictions both domestically and in a community of democratic states? Can the physician heal himself? As the great liberal theologian Reinhold Niebuhr warned in 1952 (in *The Irony of American History*) in words that we should take to heart today:

> If we should perish, the ruthlessness of the foe would be only the secondary cause of the disaster. The primary cause would be that the strength of a great nation was directed by eyes too blind to see all the hazards of the struggle, and the blindness would be induced not by some accident of nature or history but by hatred and vainglory.

DISCUSSION QUESTIONS

1. What are some legacies of World War I for international politics today?
2. What was Woodrow Wilson's aim of his world order design for U.S. foreign policy? How did this design contribute to the notion of "American exceptionalism"?
3. What are the key components of "Wilsonianism" or liberal internationalism?

4. To what extent has Wilsonianism or liberal internationalism been part of American foreign policy?
5. What is "neo-Wilsonianism," and when did it arise?
6. How does neo-Wilsonianism represent a break with traditional liberal internationalism and the principles of Woodrow Wilson?
7. Who supports this neo-Wilsonianism today?
8. What does Smith recommend for resuscitating liberal internationalism?

2

Conservative American Realism

Colin Dueck

FOREIGN POLICY REALISM

Foreign policy realists see the international system as a competitive arena. They caution against moralistic crusades disconnected from geopolitical conditions. They welcome the intelligent use of diplomacy. But realists also warn that diplomacy must be backed by force; that strategic competition between major powers is historically normal and will continue; and that military instruments are by no means outmoded as a central tool of world politics in our own time. Realist foreign policy recommendations therefore tend to look different from classically liberal ones. Rather than relying too heavily on the promotion of global governance, international law, multilateral institutions, economic interdependence, democracy, and human rights, realists focus on what Hans Morgenthau called the "workmanlike manipulation of perennial forces" to promote achievable national interests including a peaceful and favorable balance of power overseas.[1] These perennial forces and techniques of influence include concrete military and economic rewards as well as punishments—or stick and carrots, in more prosaic terms—to give diplomatic injunctions real bite.

For Americans, foreign policy realism is a corrective, rather than a starting point. Americans of all parties have long believed that the spread of classically liberal norms, free exchange, and popular forms of self-government abroad will ultimately lead to a more peaceful and friendly international system. That belief is not likely to disappear. Still, it can and should be tempered by a realist understanding of international security dilemmas as they actually exist.

A conservative American realism would draw on realist insights from international relations. But it would be *conservative*, literally, in working to preserve America's international status, security, and influence. It would furthermore be distinctly *American* in aiming to energetically promote concrete U.S. interests against some very real adversaries overseas—and in accepting that Americans by nature neither will nor should completely abandon long-term hopes for the betterment of the international system. What international strategy for the United States would follow from such a conceptual readjustment?

U.S. INTERESTS AND AMERICAN PRIMACY

Any strategy should begin with a specification of national interests. America's vital interests include the defense of U.S. territory from attack, terrorist, or otherwise; the protection of U.S. national sovereignty; the preservation of America's system of limited government at home; guarding the lives and property of U.S. citizens overseas; the promotion and defense of American trade and investment internationally; the security of oil supplies from the Persian Gulf; and the maintenance of regional balances of power within Europe, the Middle East, and East Asia. Beyond that, Americans have a vital interest in the preservation of what can only be called U.S. primacy. Indeed the protection of America's other national interests will be more likely if U.S. primacy is maintained.

American primacy refers to a set of interlocking conditions in which the United States retains more broad-based economic and military capabilities than any other major power, along with a greater ability than any rival to shape the international environment.[2] Primacy is a circumstance and an interest, not a strategy. In the case of the United States, however, primacy is also a historical reality, dating back to the end of World War II.

It ought to be self-evident, but seems to need repeating, that the preservation of American primacy is in the American interest. By definition, whatever other international and domestic interests, values, and goods Americans seek to conserve or pursue are more easily done if the United States is more powerful rather than less so. Under the conditions of U.S. primacy, this advantageous power position has gone hand in hand with a specifically American-led international order outside the spheres of major authoritarian powers, and the continued existence of that U.S.-led order has been of tremendous benefit to the United States. Economically, for example, Americans as a whole have benefitted materially and dramatically from the operation of a global trading system in which the United States is the largest economy and final guarantor, and from the existence of an international financial system in which the U.S. dollar remains—to this day—the leading reserve currency. This is not to mention the political, economic, and security benefits American primacy has brought for dozens of U.S. allies. What Samuel Huntington said over twenty years ago is no less true today:

> A world without U.S. primacy will be a world with more violence and disorder and less democracy and economic growth than a world where the United States continues to have more influence than any other country in shaping global affairs. The sustained international primacy of the United States is central to the welfare and security of Americans and to the future of freedom, democracy, open economies, and international order in the world.[3]

AMERICA'S FORWARD STRATEGIC PRESENCE

U.S. primacy including a relatively benign international order has been buttressed and maintained through America's forward military presence overseas. This forward presence includes a great network of U.S. defensive alliances, peacetime strategic commitments, force deployments, and military bases around the perimeter of the Eurasian continent. It also necessarily entails the maintenance of superior U.S. military capabilities, along with a credible readiness to use them. America's forward strategic presence in Europe and Asia has undergone many important adjustments over the years, but the underlying continuities are striking. Basically, during the 1940s, Americans rejected their traditional stance of strategic disengagement from the Eurasian continent, and they have never returned to that stance. The question today is whether such a return or at least partial return to disengagement might be tempting.

The most interesting arguments for strategic disengagement, deep retrenchment, and offshore balancing do not disparage the value of a favorable power position for the United States. Rather, they suggest that America's forward military presence on the Eurasian continent actually undermines the U.S. power position by leading it into unnecessary costs and unnecessary wars.[4] This is a serious argument, and it deserves an answer. There is no doubt that numerous U.S. military interventions under conditions of American primacy have been ill-managed, and in a few cases ill-advised. The key is to avoid confusing either the poor management or the unpopularity of specific interventions with the underlying argument for a forward strategic presence.

America's forward presence of alliances, bases, and strategic commitments serves several worthwhile purposes, when properly managed.[5] It deters and contains U.S. adversaries and competitors. It reassures U.S. allies, which in turn prevents those allies from pursuing dangerous levels of armament including nuclear weapons programs. It helps buffer and dampen destabilizing military competition between allies and adversaries, by clarifying that the United States will act as a security provider of last resort. It upholds regional balances of power, making it more difficult for authoritarian competitors to gather strength uncontested. It protects global sea lanes and maritime choke points, easing the free flow of commerce and shipping worldwide. A forward presence further allows the United States to more easily protect its economic interests overseas, including American trade, investment, and the steady flow of oil supplies issuing from the Persian Gulf. It permits the U.S. to perform humanitarian and disaster relief efforts abroad when it chooses to do so. It allows the United States, when necessary, to intervene against its enemies, including terrorists, from an advanced posture rather than an impossibly distant one. It leaves the United States better able to protect the lives of its citizens overseas. These all are distinctly U.S. interests. One need not be a hyperinterventionist to grasp that, on the whole, the basic U.S. strategic posture since World War II has done far more good than harm for Americans as well as for the rest of the world. It is in fact a crucial buttress not only of U.S. capabilities but also of a relatively democratic, prosperous, and peaceful international order. If America's forward strategic posture did not exist, we would have to invent it. Why throw it away?

U.S. CAPABILITIES AND RESOURCES

After specifying vital national interests, any serious strategy should offer a kind of net assessment of a country's available resources and capabilities, particularly as compared to those of its international competitors. There has been a great deal of talk in recent years about rising multipolarity, relative decline in U.S. power, and the coming of a "post-American" era. Certainly when it comes to the possibility of constructive U.S. influence overseas, the mood in America is far more pessimistic than it was for example in 2002–2003, and to some extent this pessimism has been hard earned. The combination of wartime sacrifices and frustrations in Iraq and Afghanistan, together with a severe recession followed by mediocre economic recovery, has encouraged a widespread feeling of strict U.S. limitation and possibly national decline. This is a subjective mood, with real political consequences, and it has some factual basis. But the mood of pessimism and decline has now overshot its basis in reality. Those familiar with U.S. history will understand this is hardly the first time such a pattern has repeated itself. As they did after Sputnik, Vietnam, and the 1980s economic challenge from Japan, Americans cyclically and periodically enter into earnest internal debate over their country's relative decline. Excessive optimism alternates with and is replaced by excessive and unrealistic gloom. If anything, Americans today tend to underestimate how powerful the United States really is.

America's multidimensional advantages on the world stage can be measured in several ways. No other country enjoys the range of capabilities and resources possessed by the United States. These advantages and capabilities include, but are not limited to, the following:

- the single largest national economy in the world;
- financial markets of unmatched depth;
- an extremely favorable geographical location, surrounded by friendly countries and separated by two oceans from any other major power;
- abundant natural resources including food, vital minerals, oil and gas on a continental scale;
- dramatic improvements in the domestic production of shale gas;
- favorable demographics compared to any other major power;
- an ability to receive and integrate large numbers of immigrants with relative success;
- one of the three largest populations on the planet;
- a high per capita income by international standards;
- most of the leading universities and research institutions in the world;
- a persistent edge in technological and scientific innovation;
- an exceptionally robust civil society;
- an ideological framework in liberal democracy of sometimes broad and subversive appeal overseas;
- a global alliance system, including most of the world's leading democracies, centered on the United States rather than any other country;
- an armed forces far stronger than that of any potential challenger;
- one of the two largest nuclear weapons arsenals in the world;
- unmatched military capabilities at sea and in the air;
- a continued lead in the ongoing revolution in military affairs, combining the use of precision strike with the latest information technology; and
- an underlying domestic political and constitutional order that is stable, peaceful, solid, and almost universally revered by U.S. citizens of either party.

No other major power holds this full-spectrum combination of resources and capabilities. The European Union is a vast conglomeration of wealthy democracies, peacefully integrated in many ways, but it does not perform as a single actor on key issues of international strategy, war, and peace. China is America's most plausible peer competitor, and of course Chinese economic weight has risen dramatically over the past quarter century. Over the past decade, furthermore, the balance of military capabilities along the East Asian littoral has shifted in favor of the Chinese and against the United States. Still, China does not possess a full range of capabilities like those listed above—and Chinese leaders know it. Other powers like Russia and India are either rising or resurgent, but again, they are not world powers akin to the United States. Nor is the U.S. share of world GDP (gross domestic product)—one obvious measure of material power and potential—actually in dramatic decline. The point of all these comparisons is not to beat American chests. Rather, the point is to locate some objective measure of comparative great power resources and to show that current talk of a post-American era under a new multipolarity is typically overstated.[6]

The United States does face a considerable range of very serious challenges, both domestic and international, to its continued primacy. Yet in strictly material terms, the United States has the resources and the capabilities to pursue a wide variety of international strategies, including some that preserve a forward U.S. presence overseas. In truth, this is as much a question of American political will and choice, as of resources. If America's underlying share of material capabilities internationally were terribly unfavorable, or in genuinely steep and inevitable decline, then of course a grand strategy of continued overarching retrenchment might be the most responsible option. But the United States still holds unmatched capabilities, and their imminent demise is hardly inevitable. If anything, under current circumstances, there is a risk that excessive or ill-managed U.S. retrenchment and accommodation feed into perceptions of American decline unnecessarily.

CHALLENGES AND THREATS

A coherent strategy should specify threats to the national interest, and distinguish between them. What are the chief international threats to American interests right now? An identification of threat best refers to specific groups of human beings—whether state or nonstate actors—pursuing policies hostile or at least dangerously competitive toward the United States. There are three such categories of actor today. The first category contains great power competitors, namely Russia and China. The second category contains rogue state adversaries, primarily Iran and North Korea, although Syria and Venezuela could certainly be included. The third category contains Islamist jihadist terrorists—starting with but not limited to ISIS and Al Qaeda—that wage transnational war against the United States and its allies. More will be said about each of these categories in a moment, along with how to address them. The point for now is that important phenomena such as globalization, disease, failed states, ethnic conflict, climate change, humanitarian disaster, and even nuclear weapons are not necessarily threats to U.S. national security, unless they interact with and are taken up by specific groups of human beings in ways hostile to the United States.

National governments and nonstate actors that pursue adversarial behavior toward the United States can be pictured along a continuum. Some, like the government of China, pursue highly competitive and assertive policies within the strategic realm, but at the same time hold multiple common interests with America—economically, for example. In such cases, there is considerable room for negotiation and mutual gain, alongside serious competition. At the other end of the continuum, there are bitter and intractable enemies like ISIS and Al Qaeda, actively at war with the United States, with whom negotiation is impossible. American strategies must be calibrated toward the nature of the adversary, not to mistake a competitor for an enemy or vice versa. At the same time, none of these should be mistaken for simple partners, allies, or friends.

GREAT POWER COMPETITORS

We can count on rising and resurgent authoritarian great powers to be a continuing challenge to American statecraft. The impact of multilateral institutions and economic interdependence has not led great power competition to altogether disappear. Russia and China are both autocracies possessed of considerable material capabilities, keen national pride, and a determination to assert their influence regionally and geopolitically. The United States can work with each of these powers in certain issue areas. But strategic competition between Washington, Beijing, and Moscow will persist, requiring steady American diplomacy, strong regional alliances, and a forward military presence on the part of the United States.

With regard to *Russia*, that country's 2014 seizure of Crimea and intervention in Ukraine represents nothing less than an attack and dismemberment on the territory and integrity of a major European nation. This is part of a long-term pattern whereby Putin attempts to rebuild a Russian sphere of influence within nearby countries. Thus far, the West's response has been inadequate. If Putin and Russia are not forced to pay a heavy price for such aggressions, then naturally they will continue, raising the risk of not only further Russian assertion but even dangerous misunderstanding and possible deterrence failure in relation to America's existing NATO allies in Central and Eastern Europe. The United States can do a great deal more against these dangers, without placing major combat units directly inside Ukraine. This would at least impose genuinely heavy costs on Putin's regime, and make him think twice before his next move. In fact, it would make dangerous misunderstandings with Moscow less likely, because it would clarify that America will not tolerate incremental aggression against existing NATO allies in Central and Eastern Europe—allies it is bound to defend in any event.[7]

Putin's Russia is in fact engaged in a competition for influence with the United States and its allies in key regions including Central Europe, with implications for the success of democracy as well as multiple American interests throughout such regions. Much greater emphasis must therefore be placed on deterring, containing, and balancing Russian power assertions in a meaningful, credible manner within the former Soviet Union and beyond. The United States should and will continue to work with Moscow in a businesslike fashion on a number of issues including Afghanistan, counterterrorism, and nuclear nonproliferation, but the United States should stop operating under the assumption that generous accommodation toward Russia in any of these or other areas will lead to broader cooperation from the Putin government, because the record shows it will not. As James Sherr, the former head of the Russia and Eurasia Program at London's Chatham House, says of Moscow's foreign policy: "Partners, competitors and opponents who are ill-prepared for hyper-competition are at risk of being outmaneuvered, irrespective of the wealth, power or technology at their disposal. Those who believe that the West faces a choice between 'partnership' and 'confrontation' with Russia will be outmaneuvered systematically."[8]

In relation to *China*, the United States faces the likely prospect of a long-term peaceful strategic competition with a well-financed and sophisticated rival—less openly aggressive than Russia, but on balance more challenging. The first task is for Americans to realize that such a competition is already underway. Despite a fascinating variety of internal debates and pragmatic tactical adjustments, China's government has been perfectly capable for many years now of promoting the expansion of Chinese economic, political, and military power relative to the United States. With the American "pivot" to Asia, President Obama rightly declared a bolstered U.S. presence in the region. Yet there are profound doubts overseas about the substance, constancy, and reliability of this presence—and the U.S. desire for cooperation and accommodation with Beijing has reaped surprisingly few concrete policy rewards. America's China policy should therefore be recalibrated.

The United States should place greater emphasis on deterring China and reassuring U.S. allies, rather than the reverse. While Beijing may not like it, this will actually lead to a reduced chance of deterrence failure arising from Chinese misperceptions of American weakness or disengagement. Rather than emphasizing legalistically that it takes no partial stance on maritime disputes between China and its neighbors, the United States should make it quite clear that it supports its own allies and will not tolerate regional aggression. Washington will continue to engage Beijing diplomatically and economically in any case, but the current need is for an adjustment in the direction of strengthened, believable, and convincing U.S. balancing and deterrence, as opposed to mixed messages or sporadic detachment.

It is time to disabuse ourselves of the notion that simply trading with, investing in, and cooperating with China will necessarily liberalize that country's political system. This has been a central premise of U.S. policy for a quarter century, and the promised political liberalization has not occurred. Meanwhile, China has only grown stronger, with its one-party dictatorship intact. The United States cannot and will not try to isolate China from the global economy, as it once did with the Soviet Union; levels of economic interdependence with China are much too high for that. Still, the United States can and should pursue a more energetic and focused strategy of pressure, power balancing, and deterrence in relation to Beijing, both in order to support U.S. allies and to bolster America's relative position within the Asia-Pacific. Nobody, including the Chinese, wants a Sino-American competition to turn violent. But the best way to prevent that, and at the same time secure a peaceful and free order within the Asia-Pacific, is to make it clear to Beijing that Washington is in earnest about maintaining its commitments in the region.

ROGUE STATE ADVERSARIES

American strategy toward *Iran* needs to start from a clear recognition of the country's current regime and its foreign policy implications. Specific Iranian leaders like President Rouhani may be skillful tactical negotiators, but they are part of an Islamist dictatorship that is basically a determined and bitter adversary toward the United States and its allies within the Middle East and beyond. In recent years, Tehran has supported terrorism in multiple countries around the globe, regularly lied about the nature of its nuclear weapon ambitions, plotted assassination attempts on American soil, and helped to kill U.S. troops in Iraq and Afghanistan. In fact, the current regime holds a violent anti-Americanism as one of its founding tenets. To be sure, some of Iran's leaders such as Rouhani have proven capable of pursuing all of these ends in operationally flexible ways. Still, this regime is not about to become a cooperative partner in U.S. designs for a benign regional security architecture, and American strategy should not be based on that false hope. Any serious U.S. strategy must comprehend the full range of Tehran's international aggression and push back against it, rather than self-limiting to the nuclear issue alone.

Tehran works actively to promote violence and instability, further Iranian interests, and counter American ones in Syria, Lebanon, Iraq, the Persian Gulf, and Palestinian territories. The United States could do considerably more to counteract this, with sophisticated, multidimensional, and competitive efforts of its own. This could, for example, include a bolstered U.S. deterrent in the region; fresh naval exercises, military coordination, and enhanced intelligence sharing with American allies; effective, strengthened theater missile defenses in Europe; and a more regular U.S. carrier task force presence in and around the Eastern Mediterranean and Persian Gulf. It could also involve foreign aid redirected to strategic ends; intensified economic sanctions, fully enforced; and increased covert action along with better intelligence gathering inside Iran itself. American diplomacy in the region should work outward from U.S. alliances, rather than frightening allies by going over their heads in an effort to accommodate Tehran. Both Iran and U.S. allies need to understand and believe that the United States is not abandoning the Middle East. The region is certainly a frustrating one for Americans. It will be even more frustrating and dangerous if the belief continues to spread that U.S. allies are not supported, and U.S. adversaries not resisted.

With regard to *North Korea*, the Obama administration settled on a default policy of "strategic patience"—essentially, containing North Korea. This policy at least had the advantage of avoiding further extracted concessions followed by predictably broken promises on North Korea's part. Yet strategic patience in this case carries its own dangers as well.

North Korea continues to work on the development of nuclear-tipped ICBMs (intercontinental ballistic missiles) capable of reaching the mainland United States.[9] Thus far, the North has been deterred from another major attack southward since the cease-fire of 1953, but it is not clear that it will be deterred forever. Kim and his surrounding circle may not understand that they do not have a reliable second-strike nuclear capability against the United States. They may believe or come to believe that they possess massive coercive leverage against the United States and its allies—and they may choose to use it. Deterrence may fail. Indeed on a certain level it already has, if we consider Pyongyang's repeated violent aggressions and nuclear and missile tests against multiple American warnings.[10]

According to Georgetown University professor Victor Cha, director for Asian affairs at the National Security Council from 2004 to 2007, what North Korea really wants is not a grand bargain whereby it denuclearizes in exchange for a range of economic and security benefits, but potentially a grand bargain whereby Pyongyang receives the following: continued possession of nuclear weapons; a wide range of economic and security benefits, including strategic assurances from the United States; equal recognition by Washington as a legitimate nuclear weapons state; and active American support in the continuation of the current regime.[11] In other words, Pyongyang wants an astonishingly one-sided and from an American perspective unappealing deal that no U.S. president can or will accept. Yet the North may press for such a deal with continual threats, triggering repeat crises that carry with them deliberately escalated risk. For this reason, strategic patience by itself is inadequate, since it simply allows Kim to become ever more bold and demanding.

The Obama administration really developed no satisfactory answer to the challenge of North Korea. Indeed there is no easy answer. There is, however, the possibility of a more carefully calibrated and tightly focused strategy designed to pressure and deter Pyongyang while avoiding the very worst dangers. Managing the North Korean security challenge is for Washington a constant tightrope walk. The United States should of course be extremely careful not to take actions that might trigger another Korean war. Yet the equal, parallel danger is that North Korea's rulers may think they can proceed unimpeded with continually greater aggressions, because of a perceived weakness in America's deterrent posture—and that seems to be the current risk.

If Washington gives more teeth to its declared Asia pivot, this will help deter North Korea as well as China. Pyongyang is best deterred by robust U.S. preparations, alliances, capabilities, and commitments that are crystal clear rather than the least bit uncertain. Beyond that, an American strategy of pressure should aim to weaken, frustrate, and erode North Korea's aggressive capabilities—not just contain them. An intensification and fuller enforcement of international financial sanctions, to which the North's shadow economy is vulnerable, is definitely in order. The U.S. government also needs to pay greater attention to how the United States, South Korea, and China would each respond were the government of North Korea to collapse. China prefers to maintain North Korea as a buffer state. But this dysfunctional regime cannot last forever, and it is imperative that Beijing and Washington avoid open conflict should such a collapse occur. The United States could privately offer, for example, not to station American forces in the north—a clear Chinese concern—in order to reassure Beijing over some possible consequences of Pyongyang's collapse. An explicit policy of rollback or regime change is not actually necessary. Still, the implicit long-term American goal here can only be the peaceful unification of the Korean peninsula under a democratic and friendly government. There is no other long-term solution.[12]

JIHADIST TERRORISTS

Al Qaeda's many affiliates and associates often aid one another in practical ways, for example with weapons, fighters, advice, and funding, and work to win over local Islamists to the cause of transnational jihadist terrorism. The spectacular rise of these regional associates and affiliates means that both the United States and Al Qaeda operate in a different environment compared to only a few years ago. If anything, jihadist terrorists took advantage of the disorder engendered by the Arab Spring to expand their operations across large tracts of North Africa and the Middle East. Ironically, the single greatest challenge to Al Qaeda today may be the Islamic State of Iraq and Syria (ISIS). With any luck these various groups might undermine one another, but this is hardly an excuse for complacency since all of them are violently hostile toward the United States and its allies. Indeed their competition for new recruits may lead jihadist terrorists to engage in ever more dramatic attacks against Western targets.

Working from this more realistic understanding of the continuing threat, the United States should develop strategies of intensified pressure against jihadist terrorists. This need not involve major American combat units or "boots on the ground" all or even most of the time, but it cannot rely so overwhelmingly on drones. According to their own words, Al Qaeda and like-minded groups seek to violently expunge Western influence from the Muslim world, topple secular governments, establish a series of ministates culminating in a transnational Islamic caliphate, retake historically Muslim lands, acquire weapons of mass destruction, and kill millions of Americans. It is a grave mistake to believe that such deadly and implacable foes can be effectively combated by simply declaring that various wars have ended, blaming previous American presidents, or instructing Muslims on the true nature of their own religion.

It has become fashionable to say that jihadist terrorism cannot be defeated, it can only be managed or contained. But suicide bombers seeking death cannot really be contained. It was precisely the insight of diplomat George Kennan—the author of containment—that communism could be contained precisely because communists were not suicidal. Groups like ISIS and Al Qaeda are a different sort of challenge, and with them there can truly be no negotiation, compromise, or even containment. If jihadist terrorists are not preempted, they will continue to pursue mass casualty attacks against innocent civilians including Americans. The nature of this particular enemy leaves no superior alternative other than an assertive and determined strategy of rollback.

THE LESSONS OF IRAQ

U.S. foreign policy under President Obama operated under the assumption of several important historical lessons learned from America's wartime experience in Iraq. We know from political psychology that foreign policy decisionmakers, past and present, tend to operate under such assumptions, analogies, or "lessons of history." We also know that such lessons and analogies tend to be overly simplistic, badly drawn, and not infrequently the source of their own distinctive mistakes.[13] For example, when the 1938 Munich conference is compared to every single negotiation internationally, this is not especially helpful. Similarly, the historical pattern is that after very frustrating wartime experiences, Americans say "never again": no more Vietnams, no more Koreas, no more great power wars in Europe, and so on. What this implies, however, is debatable, since events are never quite repeated, and historical lessons are open to competing interpretations. Today, the injunction is clear: no more Iraqs. But what exactly does this imply?

Some of Obama's lessons from Iraq were quite right. A president really should take great care before sending America's armed forces into combat. The question then is whether Obama actually did this—and whether he supplemented this sense of care with an also necessary sense of decision and determination. Unfortunately, the answer was often no. The particular way in which Obama drew lessons from Iraq encouraged a number of persistent problems in his management of American grand strategy. For example, it led him to see multiple new cases of international conflict as very much akin to Iraq 2003, when really they were not. It frequently blinded him to the many U.S. foreign policy instruments that exist between major ground interventions and doing very little, for fear of "another Iraq." It more than once allowed the term "multilateralism" to become an excuse for American inaction, since genuinely multilateral solutions to leading international problems are not always possible. It often prevented him from seeing that retrenchment and accommodation can be taken as signs of weakness rather than benevolent self-restraint. And it played havoc with several half-hearted efforts to create believable U.S. deterrent threats.

When armed force is used, or even threatened in defense of existing allies, it must be done with sufficient credibility and assertion so as to secure the desired purpose. This too is a kind of care, and anything else is positively irresponsible in relation to such deadly weapons. Successful deterrence requires a believable willingness to fight, and when force is finally employed, however reluctantly, it should be used in a robust and decisive way.

When President George W. Bush authorized the 2003 invasion of Iraq, he did so with far too little preparation toward foreseeable complications of postwar occupation, counterinsurgency, and stability operations. Indeed one of the most compelling arguments made by Bush's critics was that the United States should have sent more troops into Iraq from the very start, with better preparation for all possible contingencies. Even many Republicans now admit this mistake in initial Iraq war planning. Now there are two possible "lessons" that might be drawn from this mistake. One is that the United States should never again go to war overseas. The other is that if and when it does go to war, it should do so with much more serious and realistic forethought and preparation. The second lesson is at least as plausible as the first, but many including President Obama seemed reluctant to draw and then act upon the obvious implication: namely, that when American military intervention is finally deemed necessary, it should be undertaken with adequate determination and seriousness of purpose so as to get it right.

As noted by former secretary of defense Robert Gates, the United States has never been especially good at predicting future wars.[14] We cannot simply say, as the Obama administration's 2012 defense guidance said, that America will no longer plan for major stability operations overseas. U.S. adversaries may not be so obliging as to go along with our plans. President Obama did not plan to attack Libya when he first entered the Oval Office. Similarly, Bush did not expect to invade Iraq when he first ran for president, any more than Bill Clinton expected to forcibly liberate Kosovo from Serbian rule. Clearly, every recent U.S. president has encountered some felt necessity, once in office, to use force abroad in ways they did not originally anticipate. The real question is not whether some future U.S. presidents will engage in military intervention. The odds are, they will. The real question is whether American intervention will be undertaken with the kind of wisdom and competence appropriate to matters of life and death. That—and not an overpowering sense of indecision—would be a good lesson to draw from Iraq.

In sum, a conservative American realism would differ from both the Obama doctrine and the Bush doctrine in significant ways. It would differ from the Obama doctrine in emphasizing credible deterrence and robust strategies of pressure against clearly identified U.S. adversaries, rather than retrenchment, accommodation, and autobiographical complacency. The United States should distinguish clearly between America's friends and its enemies, supporting its friends and resisting its enemies with a full array of policy tools. Diplomatically, it should work from traditional alliances outward rather than the other way around, and back its warnings with force rather than issuing toothless declarations. There is no reason to be half-hearted in protecting the essence of American primacy, status, and influence internationally. In all of these ways, a strategy based upon conservative American realism would differ from the Obama doctrine. At the same time, a strategy based upon conservative American realism would differ in important ways from the approach pursued by President George W. Bush. Specifically, there is no need for the United States to announce that a doctrine of regime change via preventive warfare lies at the heart of its foreign policy. A president's right to preempt deadly attacks can really be taken for granted. The practical question is when and how to use force wisely. Bungled U.S. interventions only discredit American foreign policy and undermine a president's domestic agenda. In relation to most U.S. adversaries apart from ISIS and Al Qaeda, the baseline preference should be peace through strength, assertive containment, and strategies of exhaustion and attrition. Direct military intervention should only be undertaken after great care and consideration—and then, with full capability and decision. Here is where an attitude adjustment is in order since the end of the Cold War, of greater skepticism toward supposedly transformational foreign policy approaches of any kind. The great challenge today is not so much to transform a U.S.-led international order, as to defend it. Americans should expect to engage in some long-term competition with a variety of bold adversarial forces overseas. These adversaries will not be quickly transformed simply through presidential rhetoric, attempted accommodation, human rights promotion, or American disengagement. But by tapping into its underlying strengths and following tough-minded strategies under effective leadership, the United States can outlast and eventually prevail over these competitors, just as it always has before.

DISCUSSION QUESTIONS

1. What are the principal assumptions of political realists?
2. How is conservative American realism both "conservative" and "American"?
3. What are some key American interests and why is American primacy important?
4. What is meant by an American "forward strategic presence," and how does it benefit the United States?
5. What are some of the capabilities and resources that the United States enjoys in the global arena today?
6. What are the three categories of threats for the United States that Dueck identifies? What policies should be pursued toward each state or nonstate actors in those categories (at least three)?
7. What are the lessons from Iraq that Dueck discusses?
8. In Dueck's view, how does conservative American realism differ from the Obama doctrine and the Bush doctrine?

NOTES

1. Hans Morgenthau, *Politics among Nations: The Struggle for Power and Peace* (New York, NY: McGraw Hill, 2006).
2. Samuel Huntington, "Why International Primacy Matters," *International Security* 17:4 (Spring 1993), 68–83.
3. Huntington, "Why International Primacy Matters," 83.
4. See, for example, Christopher Layne, *Peace of Illusions* (Ithaca, NY: Cornell University Press, 2007).

5. On the previous paragraph, see Stephen Brooks and William Wohlforth, *America Abroad* (New York, NY: Oxford University Press, 2016); and Robert Art, *A Grand Strategy for America* (Ithaca, NY: Cornell University Press, 2003), 8–9, 42–43, 136–45, 172–222.

6. Regarding the continued and relative extent of U.S. capabilities and resources from a comparative international perspective, see Michael Beckley, "China's Century? Why America's Edge Will Endure," *International Security* 36:3 (Winter 2011/12), 41–78; Eric Edelman, *Understanding America's Contested Primacy* (Washington, DC: Center for Strategic and Budgetary Assessments, 2010); Josef Joffe, *The Myth of America's Decline* (New York, NY: Liveright, 2013); and Robert Lieber, *Power and Willpower in the American Future* (New York, NY: Cambridge University Press, 2012).

7. Edward Lucas, A. Wess Mitchell, et al., "Report No. 35: Central European Security after Crimea," *Center for European Policy Analysis*, March 25, 2014.

8. James Sherr, *Hard Diplomacy and Soft Coercion: Russia's Influence Abroad* (London: Chatham House, 2013), 113.

9. David Sanger, "U.S. Confronts Consequences of Underestimating North Korean Leader," *New York Times*, April 24, 2014.

10. Patrick Cronin, *If Deterrence Fails: Rethinking Conflict on the Korean Peninsula* (Washington, DC: Center for a New American Security, March 2014).

11. Victor Cha, *The Impossible State: North Korea, Past and Future* (New York, NY: Ecco, 2013), 297–305.

12. Sue Mi Terry, "A Korea Whole and Free," *Foreign Affairs* 93:4 (July/August 2014), 153–62.

13. Some of the classic works on this topic include Yuen Khong, *Analogies at War: Korea, Munich, Dien Bien Phu, and the Vietnam Decisions of 1965* (Princeton, NJ: Princeton University Press, 1992); Ernest May, *"Lessons" of the Past: The Use and Misuse of History in American Foreign Policy* (New York, NY: Oxford University Press, 1975); Richard Neustadt and Ernest May, *Thinking in Time: The Uses of History for Decision-Makers* (New York, NY: Free Press, 1988).

14. Robert Gates, *Duty: Memoirs of a Secretary at War* (New York, NY: dKnopf, 2014), 590.

3

Conservative Internationalism

An Alternative to Realism and Liberal Internationalism

Henry R. Nau

No one tried harder during his presidency to end old wars and avoid new ones than President Obama. Yet he failed. When his term ended, the United States was sending troops back to war in Iraq, retaining substantial forces to fight escalating violence in Afghanistan, and new wars had broken out in Syria, Ukraine, Yemen, Libya, and central Africa. Why does this happen?

One explanation is that it happens because the United States becomes too ambitious and aggressive. As critics including Obama contended, President George W. Bush pushed a worldwide freedom agenda and relied too heavily on military force to achieve it. He provoked terrorists and other rivals, and they pushed back increasing conflict. But another explanation is that war happens when the United States is not ambitious or aggressive enough, and other more aggressive nations step up and attack the interests of the United States and its allies because there is no one to stop them.

Obama dialed back America's democracy goals and abandoned the global war on terror to target specific isolated threats. He relied heavily on diplomacy to regain the trust of other countries. And he lanced military boils like U.S. forces in Iraq and prisoners at Guantanamo Bay, which, he believed, incited violence against the United States. Yet war followed that strategy too. The barbaric terrorist organization, known as the Islamic State (alternatively ISIS or ISIL), seized broad swaths of territory in northern Syria and Iraq not because Americans were there but after U.S. troops pulled out. The jihadist Taliban group in Afghanistan and Pakistan massacred school children and stepped up suicide bombings, as American forces ended their combat role and planned to leave

Afghanistan altogether by the end of 2016 (later rescinded by Obama). A nationalist-obsessed Russia annexed Crimea and destabilized eastern Ukraine even after President Obama did all he could, including giving up NATO missile defense installations in eastern Europe, to reset relations with Russia. And China belligerently pressed claims to disputed islands in the South and East China Seas even after Obama touted a G-2 partnership with Beijing to address common problems of climate change, energy, and economic recovery.

Did aggressive behavior by Obama provoke these war-like responses? Not likely. Nor is it likely that earlier U.S. policies, such as NATO expansion, caused them. NATO expansion into Eastern Europe was entirely political and economic, offering stability against internal, not external, threats and greater opportunities for economic integration with global markets. NATO did not station any military forces in Eastern Europe, let alone slip "little green men" (Russian troops without insignia that infiltrated Ukraine) across the border to seize territory in Ukraine, Belarus, or Georgia. And NATO kept that commitment until Russia invaded Crimea. Would Russia be less aggressive today if Poland and other Eastern European countries were not members of NATO?

EXCESSIVE AMBITION AND RESTRAINT

Is it possible to be too modest and restrained in foreign affairs, just as it is possible to be too ambitious and aggressive?

It is, and America has done both. The classic case of excessive ambition was President Woodrow Wilson's proposal for a League of Nations. The League committed the United States to provide for the security of every country in the world. The classic case of excessive restraint was the 1920s and 1930s. The United States rejected the League and provided for the security of no country, including in effect its own. The Japanese attacked Pearl Harbor.

But the pattern persisted. After World War II, the United States put its faith in the United Nations (UN) and withdrew most of its military forces from Europe. The Soviet Union did not. And in 1948, Moscow blockaded West Berlin, and another war, the Cold War, began.

As the Cold War ended, the United States put its faith again in the UN. For a moment, the UN worked. In the first Persian Gulf War, the entire world community isolated Iraq for invading Kuwait, imposed economic sanctions, and, as a last resort, collectively went to war to expel Iraq from Kuwait. But then ethnic conflict erupted in Yugoslavia. Wars in Bosnia and Kosovo followed. Russia blocked UN action. NATO stepped in. Elsewhere, terrorism escalated, and jihadists struck the twin towers and Pentagon. America was back at war.

Admirably, America won all of these wars, Afghanistan and Iraq included. But, after each war, it lost the peace. In 2005, George W. Bush declared "a policy . . . to seek and support the growth of democratic movements and institutions in every nation and culture, with the ultimate goal of ending tyranny in our world." That excessive ambition died painfully in the long occupations of Afghanistan and Iraq. As costs mounted, President Obama resolved not to end tyranny but to end wars. He brought America home and declared that if America minds its own business, other countries will mind theirs.

This latest episode of excessive ambition and excessive restraint is also ending badly. After America pulled out of Iraq, the Iraqi army disintegrated. Syria imploded, and President Obama announced that the Syrian government of Bashar al-Assad had to go. But then he refused to support any opposition group to replace Assad, and the militant Islamic State filled the gap. He brokered a deal with Russia to get rid of Assad's chemical weapons, inadvertently strengthening Assad. Now, the United States confronts ISIS from the air in northern Syria and Iraq with few friendly boots on the ground, while Assad barrel-bombs his own people and ISIS controls territory and trains terrorists to attack the west. Isn't this the scenario in Afghanistan that produced 9/11?

STANDARD FOREIGN POLICY TRADITIONS

Why does America cycle like this between excessive ambition and excessive restraint, always followed by a new attack, which precipitates a much bigger war than might have been necessary earlier? The reason lies deep in America's foreign policy traditions and debate. Since its origins, America has had only three principal ways of thinking about its role in the world. Thomas Jefferson introduced the *internationalist* way, the ambition that America could not only change domestic politics from monarchy to republicanism but also world politics from war to peaceable trade and diplomacy. Alexander Hamilton championed the *realist* way, advocating national power, alliances, and territorial filibusters to defend the new nation's western borders. George Washington advocated the *nationalist* (in extreme form, isolationist) way, prioritizing independence and warning against both ambition and alliances in foreign affairs.

These three approaches—nationalist, realist, and internationalist— became America's standard foreign policy traditions. Andrew Jackson and James K. Polk epitomized the nationalist approach, Teddy Roosevelt and

Richard Nixon the realist approach, and Woodrow Wilson and Franklin Roosevelt the internationalist approach.

The standard approaches push American foreign policy back and forth between excessive zeal and excessive restraint. The *internationalist* tradition, labeled *liberal internationalism* after the twentieth-century Democratic presidents Woodrow Wilson and Franklin Roosevelt who developed it, leads the United States to believe that it can tame international violence and spread democracy largely by multilateral diplomacy and economic interdependence. This tradition downplays military force, uses it only as a last resort after diplomacy fails, and eventually hopes to replace the balance of power with a world government that consolidates military force and authorizes it only by multilateral consent. President Obama came into office promising a rebirth of American diplomacy that would dispel the distrust spawned by American military interventions in Afghanistan and Iraq. If the United States practiced peaceful diplomacy, other nations would do so as well. Obama extended an open hand to Russia and China as well as the Muslim world and expected that they would reciprocate with friendly responses.

But what if other nations do not reciprocate? What if they choose not to work with other countries in international institutions but to compete for political, economic, and military advantage? What if they, like Russia and China, stall UN efforts to stop nuclear proliferation in Iran and North Korea or to defeat terrorism in Syria and Libya and initiate military interventions of their own in Ukraine and the South and East China Seas to roll back Western influence?

The other two standard traditions, *nationalism* and *realism*, expect other countries to behave this way, to compete rather than cooperate. These traditions consider it naïve to believe that America can change the world through democracy and international institutions. They empathize when other countries push back and defy Western encroachment. Why should Russia let Ukraine join NATO when Moscow has naval bases in Crimea? *Realists* and *nationalists* have always said that America must accept the world as it is, not as we might wish it to be. Other countries value their independence and form of government as much as we value ours, and often their values and our values clash. Better to minimize these domestic differences and get along with authoritarian countries as President Nixon did with China and President Obama did with Russia.

America finds no stable presence in the world. Under the influence of liberal internationalism, it overextends to transform the world at what it expects to be low military cost; and under the influence of nationalism and realism, it retreats to concentrate on territorial defenses with little hope to improve the world. Each overreach encounters pushback by other countries and eventually higher military costs, and each retreat is followed by renewed anarchy in the world and fresh attacks on the United States or its allies, more devastating than these attacks might have been if the United States had acted earlier.

AN ALTERNATIVE TRADITION

What to do about this cycling? There is no silver bullet, especially in the short term. But over the longer run, an intermediate tradition exists that might improve the American debate and from time to time anchor America's role in the world, moderating the tendency toward cycling. This tradition, called conservative internationalism, combines the commitment of *liberal internationalism* to spread democracy and make the world a better place with the instruments of *realism* to back up diplomacy with military force. But then it disciplines this combination of freedom and force by prioritizing the spread of freedom on the borders of existing free countries, primarily in Europe and Asia, not in "every nation and culture" worldwide, and by tying military actions closely to diplomatic offers to achieve incremental improvements in despotic regimes, not military victory followed by interminable nation-building. In the end, conservative internationalism aims for a world that is much closer to *nationalism* than internationalism in which nation-states remain separate, sovereign, and armed yet, as democracy spreads, live side by side in peaceful competition under the democratic peace.

The conservative internationalist tradition is not simply a theoretical construct. It has been a part of America's historical experience from the beginning. It goes back to Thomas Jefferson, James K. Polk, and, more recently, Harry Truman and Ronald Reagan. These presidents promoted the expansion of liberty in their day and did so by a combination of force and diplomacy that narrowed the options for authoritarian adversaries. (Jefferson and Polk, though slave holders, acquired the territories that enabled more white male citizens to own land and vote than in any other country at the time.) Jefferson tacked deftly toward Great Britain to pry the Louisiana territory away from France; Polk used diplomacy backed by force to secure the Oregon territory without war and then force backed by diplomacy to defeat Mexico in war but by leaving Mexico quickly and taking only the territory he initially sought to purchase; Truman and Reagan believed the Cold War could be won, not just managed, and mobilized Western strength to contain and eventually undermine the Soviet Union. Conservative internationalists recognize that tyrants do not willingly cooperate to spread freedom and will use force to achieve their objectives outside negotiations if they know the other side will use force only after negotiations fail.

The standard traditions resist a conservative version of internationalism. Nationalists and realists object because they do not support the goal of spreading freedom, and liberal internationalists object because they do not support the use of force while negotiations are going on and insist on multilateral consent even after negotiations fail. In recent years, the standard traditions have spared no effort to discredit an alternative conservative internationalist tradition.

They have been particularly bitter toward neoconservatives. Neoconservatives were defectors from the standard traditions. Some, like Senator Henry "Scoop" Jackson and Jeane Kirkpatrick, were liberal internationalists who were unhappy with the excessive focus on détente (diplomacy) and favored a more assertive military policy to negotiate with the Soviet Union. Others like Condoleezza Rice and Charles Krauthammer were realists who decided that it was not enough to use military power simply to balance power and coexist with despots forever but that it was necessary to "tilt the balance of power toward freedom." Neoconservatives joined many traditional conservatives, who like nationalists valued national defense but like internationalists considered America an exceptionalist nation.

Neoconservatism does not define conservative internationalism, however, any more than one world government defines liberal internationalism. The conservative internationalist space is varied, just like the liberal internationalist and realist space. Henry Wallace, vice president under Franklin Roosevelt, believed in one world government; Franklin Roosevelt did not. Yet they were both liberal internationalists. Teddy Roosevelt believed in imperial American power; Richard Nixon and George H. W. Bush believed only in balancing power. All three were realists, but Roosevelt was an offensive realist, Nixon and H. W. defensive realists. Similarly, Harry Truman believed more in the UN than Ronald Reagan. Yet they both stressed anticommunism, not just the balance of power, and built up military and economic strength to negotiate with Moscow. They were both conservative internationalists.

FREEDOM AND FORCE

What difference would conservative internationalism make in the world today?

First, it would insist that the United States continue efforts to improve the world by increasing the number of democratic states. A world with more democratic states is without question a safer world for America. To grasp this fact, compare Europe and Japan in 2014 with Europe and Japan in 1914. If no effort had been made to democratize Germany and Japan, the world today would look much more like it did in 1914 (or 1940); America would be surrounded by ideologically hostile states. National defense depends on how friendly or hostile the world is, not just on how much relative power a country has. In a world that is drifting toward despotism, as it was in 1914, America needs a lot of national power to defend itself. In a world moving steadily toward democracy, as the world did after 1945 and especially after 1991, it needs much less.

Since 2006, the world is drifting again toward despotism. As *Freedom in the World 2016* reports, "over the past 10 years, 105 countries have seen a net decline [in freedom], and only 61 have experienced a net improvement."[1] Make no mistake, advances by authoritarian states like Russia, China, and Iran cause neighboring states to recalibrate. Hungary becomes more friendly to Moscow, South Korea becomes more dependent on China, and Iraq becomes more subservient to Iran. As Ronald Reagan put it, "[F]reedom wither[s] through a quiet, deadening accommodation with totalitarian evil." And while Islamic fundamentalism today is not the existential threat to the United States that the Soviet Union was during the Cold War, it is a horrific ideology that, if married with weapons of mass destruction and aided indirectly by Russia and China, could roll back Western freedom. To hunker down now, to go into a defensive crouch, and give up the battle to advance freedom, is simply to wait for the world to deteriorate again and the next war to come—as it always has in the past.

If America is serious about making the world a better place by increasing the number of democratic states in the world, however, it will face blowback by undemocratic or despotic regimes. Therefore, unlike liberal internationalism, conservative internationalism does not expect authoritarian countries to cooperate in international institutions. It expects them to resist. Russia and China use the UN to restrain human rights and free governments, not to facilitate them. To have serious negotiations with these countries, the United States needs to arm its diplomacy. It needs to bring the balance of power to bear before and during negotiations, not just after negotiations fail, to ensure that these countries do not achieve their objectives by force outside or without negotiations.

Ronald Reagan exemplified this kind of armed diplomacy. He built up U.S. defenses early before he started negotiations with the Soviet Union, and he deployed strategic and covert forces—missile deployments in Europe and freedom fighters in Afghanistan and Central America—to prevent Moscow from gaining military advantage outside negotiations. He then used military and economic leverage to offer the Soviet Union a way out—reducing nuclear arms and expanding the world economy.

How does this approach play out in Iran? As long as Iran is achieving its military objectives outside negotiations, why should it compromise inside negotiations? The nuclear agreement concluded in 2015 does not end Iran's nuclear program; it simply delays it for ten years. Nevertheless, liberal internationalists argue the agreement builds trust that now makes it possible for Iran to moderate its support of terrorism throughout the Middle East—in

Iraq, Syria, Lebanon, and, most recently, Yemen. Conservative internation-alists doubt this prospect. Only a credible threat to deny Iran further gains outside the agreement could restrain its aggression. That does not mean invade Iran. Force is never a substitute for diplomacy even in the case of regime change, as the United States learned bitterly in Iraq and Afghanistan. But it does mean the deployment and manipulation of smaller amounts of force while negotiations are going on to avoid having to use much greater force later after negotiations fail. If the United States had paid more atten-tion to its defense budget instead of cutting it carelessly through seques-tration, left behind some forces in Iraq to limit Iranian influence, aided opposition groups in Syria in a more timely fashion, backed Israel solidly including veiled threats that Israel might attack Iranian nuclear facilities, and most importantly *not* "pivoted" declining overall U.S. naval forces from the Mediterranean to the Pacific, Iran might have realized sooner that it could not achieve its objectives outside negotiations and conceded more inside negotiations.

Second, conservative internationalism recognizes that using force to make negotiations with despotic countries succeed is potentially costly and therefore must be conserved. The United States has to set clear priori-ties. It should use force to deter or reduce threats from *any* country but to promote democracy *only* in countries that lie on the border of existing free countries.

The United States invaded Afghanistan to repulse the Taliban threat, and it resumed the war in Iraq to repulse the ISIS threat. Once threat is repulsed, however, America should get out of countries like Afghanistan and Iraq—within two to three years at the most. Use a light footprint or heavy foot-print, whatever it takes. But, most importantly, use a "swift footprint." Why? Because the chances of spreading democracy to these countries are minimal. They are far from the borders of existing free countries, and there are no strong nearby alliances and free markets to support liberalism.

Moreover, the United States simply cannot deploy military forces indefi-nitely in an unlimited number of places wherever terrorists may be training—Libya, Syria, Yemen, Iraq, Afghanistan, Pakistan, and so on. That would only play into a terrorist strategy of spreading out and exhausting U.S. and allied resources. The U.S. objective in these countries is to keep the terror-ists off balance through a combination of working with local governments, even though they are often oppressive, and of intervening for short terms and repeatedly from offshore if local governments fall apart or fail to stanch the terrorist threat. The United States provides military advice and assistance and seeks to improve local governments as time goes on, such as a more inclusive government in Iraq and Afghanistan or a less oppressive military government in Egypt. But when the United States stays too long in these countries and leaves behind governments that after ten years are no more democratic or stable than they were after three years, the American people lose their appetite for intervening altogether.

The objective is different, however, if the threat comes from a country on the central borders of existing free countries, essentially the fault lines today between free Europe and Russia and between free Asia and China (secondary fault lines exist around India and Israel). On these borders, much more is at stake. The United States and its allies, with powerful nearby military and economic assets (NATO, EU, Japan), should not only repulse the threat but stay on to win the struggle for freedom. In this sense, the critical battles today are in Ukraine, Turkey, and the Korean peninsula, not in Iraq and Afghanistan. Sadly, in the past decade, the United States did exactly the opposite, investing heavily in democracy promotion in Iraq and Afghanistan, while weakening the prospects of freedom in Ukraine, Turkey, and potentially South Korea.

It was a mistake, for example, to invade Iraq without the support of Turkey, a democratizing and NATO country. Since then, Turkey has drifted ominously away from democracy, Israel, and the United States. And it is a mistake today, as some argue, to regard Ukraine as a buffer state, that it "must not be either side's outpost against the other."[2] Ukraine stands at the epicenter of the geopolitical struggle for freedom in Europe. The Western allies should support it with defensive weapons and economic assistance. Like Germany in 1991, Kiev has the right to be free and to choose its own alliances. So does a future Korea. When Korea reunites, it will do so under democratic control and ideological alliances with Japan and the United States, or it will slide inexorably toward China, its more powerful authoritarian neighbor. The borderline of freedom moves forward or backward, and a permanent accommodation with despotism increases the prospects of war.

Third, while aiming high, conservative internationalism has more modest expectations about what and how change might be achieved in the world. Unlike liberal internationalism and more like nationalism, it respects and preserves, not transcends, national sovereignty. It expects little from international institutions and more from the institutions of civil society, especially freer markets. It envisions a decentralized world of separate nations in which democracies grow from the bottom up, especially on the borders of existing free countries, and despotic states become increasingly weaker.

America's goal, as the world's first large liberal republic, was never to impose democracy on any country but to show the world that democracy was possible and that it could be chosen by other countries based on their own traditions. As Harvey Mansfield, the conservative Harvard professor once wrote, "American patriotism has always said to others not 'We are inherently superior,' but 'You can have it too.' This is conservative pride and tradition mixed with liberal inclusiveness and innovation."[3] As Mansfield implies, the sprouts of freedom exist in every country; but they struggle to emerge against the overgrowth of autocracy. And in that struggle, as Ronald Reagan declared, America takes sides: "there is one boundary that can never be made legitimate, and that is the dividing line between freedom and oppression."

Conservative internationalism does not have all the answers but it adds an indispensable alternative to the American foreign policy debate. That debate, balanced and respectful, is the best answer for foreign policy crises. No one can know compellingly which tradition is appropriate in any given set of circumstances. Therefore, all traditions should be included in the debate. Then, the American public can make the best decision that takes account of existing circumstances. And if they choose wrong, they have that right in a democratic republic. But then, they also have the responsibility to learn from that experience.

DISCUSSION QUESTIONS

1. How has the United States been too ambitious and too aggressive and too restrained and modest in its foreign policy? What is the consequence of each one?
2. What are three foreign policy traditions that Nau identifies? How is each different from one another?
3. Which presidents in their foreign policies represent these traditions?
4. What is the alternative tradition that Nau proposes? How does it differ or complement the previous traditions?
5. How do freedom and force play a role in conservative internationalism?
6. Under conservative internationalism, should force be used alone? How should it be employed?
7. Is democracy promotion compatible with conservative internationalism? When and under what circumstances?

NOTES

1. *Freedom in the World 2016*, https://freedomhouse.org/report/freedom-world/freedom-world-2016
2. Henry A. Kissinger, "To settle the Ukraine crisis, start at the end," *The Washington Post*, March 5, 2014, http://www.washingtonpost.com/opinions/henry-kissinger-to-settle-the-ukraine-crisis-start-at-the-end/2014/03/05/46dad868-a496-11e3-8466-d34c451760b9_story.html
3. Harvey C. Mansfield, "You Can Have It Too," *The Atlantic*, November 2007, http://www.theatlantic.com/magazine/archive/2007/11/you-can-have-it-too/306315/

4

The Israel Lobby

John Mearsheimer and Stephen Walt

For the past several decades, and especially since the Six-Day War in 1967, the centerpiece of U.S. Middle Eastern policy has been its relationship with Israel. The combination of unwavering support for Israel and the related effort to spread "democracy" throughout the region has inflamed Arab and Islamic opinion and jeopardized not only U.S. security but also that of much of the rest of the world. This situation has no equal in American political history. Why has the United States been willing to set aside its own security and that of many of its allies in order to advance the interests of another state? One might assume that the bond between the two countries was based on shared strategic interests or compelling moral imperatives, but neither explanation can account for the remarkable level of material and diplomatic support that the United States provides.

Instead, the thrust of U.S. policy in the region derives almost entirely from domestic politics, and especially the activities of the "Israel Lobby." Other special-interest groups have managed to skew foreign policy, but no lobby has managed to divert it as far from what the national interest would suggest, while simultaneously convincing Americans that U.S. interests and those of the other country—in this case, Israel—are essentially identical.

Since the October War in 1973, Washington has provided Israel with a level of support dwarfing that given to any other state. It has been the largest annual recipient of direct economic and military assistance since 1976, and is the largest recipient in total since World War II, to the tune of well over $140 billion (in 2004 dollars). Israel receives about $3 billion in direct assistance each year, roughly one-fifth of the foreign aid budget, and worth about $500 a year for every Israeli. This largesse is especially striking since

Israel is now a wealthy industrial state with a per capita income roughly equal to that of South Korea or Spain.

Other recipients get their money in quarterly installments, but Israel receives its entire appropriation at the beginning of each fiscal year and can thus earn interest on it. Most recipients of aid given for military purposes are required to spend all of it in the United States, but Israel is allowed to use roughly 25 percent of its allocation to subsidize its own defense industry. It is the only recipient that does not have to account for how the aid is spent, which makes it virtually impossible to prevent the money from being used for purposes the United States opposes, such as building settlements on the West Bank. Moreover, the United States has provided Israel with nearly $3 billion to develop weapons systems, and given it access to such top-drawer weaponry as Blackhawk helicopters and F-16 jets. Finally, the United States gives Israel access to intelligence it denies to its NATO allies and has turned a blind eye to Israel's acquisition of nuclear weapons.

Washington also provides Israel with consistent diplomatic support. Since 1982, the United States has vetoed thirty-two UN Security Council resolutions critical of Israel, more than the total number of vetoes cast by all the other Security Council members. It blocks the efforts of Arab states to put Israel's nuclear arsenal on the International Atomic Energy Agency's agenda. The United States comes to the rescue in wartime and takes Israel's side when negotiating peace. The Nixon administration protected it from the threat of Soviet intervention and re-supplied it during the October War. Washington was deeply involved in the negotiations that ended that war, as well as in the lengthy "step-by-step" process that followed, just as it played a key role in the negotiations that preceded and followed the 1993 Oslo Accords. In each case there was occasional friction between U.S. and Israeli officials, but the United States consistently supported the Israeli position. One American participant at Camp David in 2000 later said, "Far too often, we functioned . . . as Israel's lawyer." Finally, the George W. Bush administration's ambition to transform the Middle East was at least partly aimed at improving Israel's strategic situation.

This extraordinary generosity might be understandable if Israel were a vital strategic asset or if there were a compelling moral case for U.S. backing. But neither explanation is convincing. One might argue that Israel was an asset during the Cold War. By serving as America's proxy after 1967, it helped contain Soviet expansion in the region and inflicted humiliating defeats on Soviet clients like Egypt and Syria. It occasionally helped protect other U.S. allies (like King Hussein of Jordan), and its military prowess forced Moscow to spend more on backing its own client states. It also provided useful intelligence about Soviet capabilities.

Backing Israel was not cheap, however, and it complicated America's relations with the Arab world. For example, the decision to give $2.2 billion in emergency military aid during the October War triggered an OPEC oil embargo that inflicted considerable damage on Western economies. For all that, Israel's armed forces were not in a position to protect U.S. interests in the region. The United States could not, for example, rely on Israel when the Iranian Revolution in 1979 raised concerns about the security of oil supplies, and had to create its own Rapid Deployment Force instead.

The first Gulf War revealed the extent to which Israel was becoming a strategic burden. The United States could not use Israeli bases without rupturing the anti-Iraq coalition, and had to divert resources (e.g., Patriot missile batteries) to prevent Tel Aviv doing anything that might harm the alliance against Saddam Hussein. History repeated itself in 2003: although Israel was eager for the United States to attack Iraq, President Bush could not ask it to help without triggering Arab opposition. So Israel stayed on the sidelines once again.

Beginning in the 1990s, and even more after 9/11, U.S. support has been justified by the claim that both states are threatened by terrorist groups originating in the Arab and Muslim world, and by "rogue states" that back these groups and seek weapons of mass destruction. This is taken to mean not only that Washington should give Israel a free hand in dealing with the Palestinians and not press it to make concessions until all Palestinian terrorists are imprisoned or dead, but also that the United States should go after countries like Iran and Syria. Israel is thus seen as a crucial ally in the war on terror, because its enemies are America's enemies. In fact, Israel is a liability in the war on terror and the broader effort to deal with rogue states.

"Terrorism" is not a single adversary, but a tactic employed by a wide array of political groups. The terrorist organizations that threaten Israel do not threaten the United States, except when it intervenes against them (as in Lebanon in 1982). Moreover, Palestinian terrorism is not random violence directed against Israel or "the West"; it is largely a response to Israel's prolonged campaign to colonize the West Bank and Gaza Strip.

More important, saying that Israel and the United States are united by a shared terrorist threat has the causal relationship backwards: the United States has a terrorism problem in good part because it is so closely allied with Israel, not the other way around. Support for Israel is not the only source of anti-American terrorism, but it is an important one, and it makes winning the war on terror more difficult. There is no question that many al Qaeda leaders, including Osama bin Laden, are motivated by Israel's presence in Jerusalem and the plight of the Palestinians. Unconditional support for Israel makes it easier for extremists to rally popular support and to attract recruits.

As for so-called rogue states in the Middle East, they are not a dire threat to vital U.S. interests, except inasmuch as they are a threat to Israel. Even if these states acquire nuclear weapons—which is obviously undesirable—neither America nor Israel could be blackmailed, because the blackmailer could not carry out the threat without suffering overwhelming retaliation. The danger of a nuclear handover to terrorists is equally remote, because a rogue state could not be sure the transfer would go undetected or that it would not be blamed and punished afterward. The relationship with Israel actually makes it harder for the United States to deal with these states. Israel's nuclear arsenal is one reason some of its neighbors want nuclear weapons, and threatening them with regime change merely increases that desire.

A final reason to question Israel's strategic value is that it does not behave like a loyal ally. Israeli officials frequently ignore U.S. requests and renege on promises (including pledges to stop building settlements and to refrain from "targeted assassinations" of Palestinian leaders). Israel has provided sensitive military technology to potential rivals like China, in what the State Department inspector-general called "a systematic and growing pattern of unauthorized transfers." According to the General Accounting Office, Israel also "conducts the most aggressive espionage operations against the U.S. of any ally." In addition to the case of Jonathan Pollard, who gave Israel large quantities of classified material in the early 1980s (which it reportedly passed on to the Soviet Union in return for more exit visas for Soviet Jews), a new controversy erupted in 2004 when it was revealed that a key Pentagon official, Larry Franklin, had passed classified information to an Israeli diplomat. Israel is hardly the only country that spies on the United States, but its willingness to spy on its principal patron casts further doubt on its strategic value.

Israel's strategic value isn't the only issue. Its backers also argue that it deserves unqualified support because it is weak and surrounded by enemies; it is a democracy; the Jewish people have suffered from past crimes and therefore deserve special treatment; and Israel's conduct has been morally superior to that of its adversaries. On close inspection, none of these arguments is persuasive. There is a strong moral case for supporting Israel's existence, but that is not in jeopardy. Viewed objectively, its past and present conduct offers no moral basis for privileging it over the Palestinians.

Israel is often portrayed as David confronted by Goliath, but the converse is closer to the truth. Contrary to popular belief, the Zionists had larger, better equipped, and better led forces during the 1947–1949 War of Independence, and the Israel Defense Forces won quick and easy victories against Egypt in 1956 and against Egypt, Jordan, and Syria in 1967—all of this before large-scale U.S. aid began flowing. Today, Israel is the strongest military power in the Middle East. Its conventional forces are far superior to those of its neighbors, and it is the only state in the region with nuclear weapons. Egypt and Jordan have signed peace treaties with it, and Saudi Arabia has offered to do so. Syria has lost its Soviet patron, Iraq has been devastated by three disastrous wars, and Iran is hundreds of miles away. The Palestinians barely have an effective police force, let alone an army that could pose a threat to Israel. According to a 2005 assessment by Tel Aviv University's Jaffee Centre for Strategic Studies, "The strategic balance decidedly favours Israel, which has continued to widen the qualitative gap between its own military capability and deterrence powers and those of its neighbours." If backing the underdog were a compelling motive, the United States would be supporting Israel's opponents.

That Israel is a fellow democracy surrounded by hostile dictatorships cannot account for the current level of aid: there are many democracies around the world, but none receives the same lavish support. The United States has overthrown democratic governments in the past and supported dictators when this was thought to advance its interests—it has good relations with a number of dictatorships today.

Some aspects of Israeli democracy are at odds with core American values. Unlike the United States, where people are supposed to enjoy equal rights irrespective of race, religion, or ethnicity, Israel was explicitly founded as a Jewish state, and citizenship is based on the principle of blood kinship. Given this, it is not surprising that its 1.3 million Arabs are treated as second-class citizens, or that a recent Israeli government commission found that Israel behaves in a "neglectful and discriminatory" manner toward them. Its democratic status is also undermined by its refusal to grant the Palestinians a viable state of their own or full political rights.

A third justification is the history of Jewish suffering in the Christian West, especially during the Holocaust. Because Jews were persecuted for centuries and could feel safe only in a Jewish homeland, many people now believe that Israel deserves special treatment from the United States. The country's creation was undoubtedly an appropriate response to the long record of crimes against Jews, but it also brought about fresh crimes against a largely innocent third party: the Palestinians.

This was well understood by Israel's early leaders. David Ben-Gurion told Nahum Goldmann, the president of the World Jewish Congress,

> If I were an Arab leader I would never make terms with Israel. That is natural: we have taken their country. . . . We come from Israel, but two thousand years ago, and what is that to them? There has been anti-Semitism, the Nazis, Hitler, Auschwitz, but was that their fault? They only see one thing: we have come here and stolen their country. Why should they accept that?

Since then, Israeli leaders have repeatedly sought to deny the Palestinians' national ambitions. When she was prime minister, Golda Meir famously remarked that "there is no such thing as a Palestinian." Pressure from extremist violence and Palestinian population growth has forced subsequent Israeli leaders to disengage from the Gaza Strip and consider other territorial compromises, but not even Yitzhak Rabin was willing to offer the Palestinians a viable state. Ehud Barak's purportedly generous offer at Camp David would have given them only a disarmed set of Bantustans under de facto Israeli control. The tragic history of the Jewish people does not obligate the United States to help Israel today no matter what it does.

Israel's backers also portray it as a country that has sought peace at every turn and shown great restraint even when provoked. The Arabs, by contrast, are said to have acted with great wickedness. Yet on the ground, Israel's record is not distinguishable from that of its opponents. Ben-Gurion acknowledged that the early Zionists were far from benevolent toward the Palestinian Arabs, who resisted their encroachments—which is hardly surprising, given that the Zionists were trying to create their own state on Arab land. In the same way, the creation of Israel in 1947–1948 involved acts of ethnic cleansing, including executions, massacres, and rapes by Jews, and Israel's subsequent conduct has often been brutal, belying any claim to moral superiority. Between 1949 and 1956, for example, Israeli security forces killed between 2,700 and 5,000 Arab infiltrators, the overwhelming majority of them unarmed. The Israel Defense Forces (IDF) murdered hundreds of Egyptian prisoners of war in both the 1956 and 1967 wars, while in 1967, it expelled between 100,000 and 260,000 Palestinians from the newly conquered West Bank, and drove 80,000 Syrians from the Golan Heights.

During the first intifada, the IDF distributed truncheons to its troops and encouraged them to break the bones of Palestinian protesters. The Swedish branch of Save the Children estimated that "23,600 to 29,900 children required medical treatment for their beating injuries in the first two years of the intifada." Nearly a third of them were aged ten or under. The response to the second intifada was even more violent, leading *Ha'aretz* to declare that "the IDF . . . is turning into a killing machine whose efficiency is awe-inspiring, yet shocking." The IDF fired one million bullets in the first days of the uprising. Since then, for every Israeli lost, Israel has killed 3.4 Palestinians, the majority of whom have been innocent bystanders; the ratio of Palestinian to Israeli children killed is even higher (5.7:1). It is also worth bearing in mind that the Zionists relied on terrorist bombs to drive the British from Palestine, and that Yitzhak Shamir, once a terrorist and later prime minister, declared that "neither Jewish ethics nor Jewish tradition can disqualify terrorism as a means of combat."

The Palestinian resort to terrorism is wrong but it isn't surprising. The Palestinians believe they have no other way to force Israeli concessions. As Ehud Barak once admitted, had he been born a Palestinian, he "would have joined a terrorist organization."

So if neither strategic nor moral arguments can account for America's support for Israel, how are we to explain it?

The explanation is the unmatched power of the Israel Lobby. We use "the Lobby" as shorthand for the loose coalition of individuals and organizations who actively work to steer U.S. foreign policy in a pro-Israel direction. This is not meant to suggest that the Lobby is a unified movement with a central leadership, or that individuals within it do not disagree on certain issues. Not all Jewish Americans are part of the Lobby because Israel is not a salient issue for many of them. In a 2004 survey, for example, roughly 36 percent of American Jews said they were either "not very" or "not at all" emotionally attached to Israel.

Jewish Americans also differ on specific Israeli policies. Many of the key organizations in the Lobby, such as the American-Israel Public Affairs Committee (AIPAC) and the Conference of Presidents of Major Jewish Organizations, are run by hard-liners who generally support the Likud Party's expansionist policies, including its hostility to the Oslo peace process. The bulk of U.S. Jewry, meanwhile, is more inclined to make concessions to the Palestinians, and a few groups—such as Jewish Voice for Peace—strongly advocate such steps. Despite these differences, moderates and hard-liners both favor giving steadfast support to Israel.

Not surprisingly, American Jewish leaders often consult Israeli officials, to make sure that their actions advance Israeli goals. As one activist from a major Jewish organization wrote, "It is routine for us to say: 'This is our policy on a certain issue, but we must check what the Israelis think.' We as a community do it all the time." There is a strong prejudice against criticizing Israeli policy, and putting pressure on Israel is considered out of order. Edgar Bronfman Sr., the president of the World Jewish Congress, was accused of "perfidy" when he wrote a letter to President Bush in mid-2003 urging him to persuade Israel to curb construction of its controversial "security fence." His critics said that "it would be obscene at any time for the president of the World Jewish Congress to lobby the president of the United States to resist policies being promoted by the government of Israel."

Similarly, when the president of the Israel Policy Forum, Seymour Reich, advised Condoleezza Rice in November 2005 to ask Israel to reopen a critical border crossing in the Gaza Strip, his action was denounced as "irresponsible": "There is," his critics said, "absolutely no room in the Jewish mainstream for actively canvassing against the security-related policies . . . of Israel." Recoiling from these attacks, Reich announced that "the word 'pressure' is not in my vocabulary when it comes to Israel."

Jewish Americans have set up an impressive array of organizations to influence American foreign policy, of which AIPAC is the most powerful and best known. In 1997, *Fortune* magazine asked members of Congress and their staffs to list the most powerful lobbies in Washington. AIPAC was ranked second behind the American Association of Retired People (AARP), but ahead of the AFL-CIO and the National Rifle Association. A *National*

Journal study in March 2005 reached a similar conclusion, placing AIPAC in second place (tied with AARP) in the Washington "muscle rankings."

The Lobby also includes prominent Christian evangelicals like Gary Bauer, Jerry Falwell, Ralph Reed, and Pat Robertson, as well as Dick Armey and Tom DeLay, former majority leaders in the House of Representatives, all of whom believe Israel's rebirth is the fulfillment of biblical prophecy and support its expansionist agenda; to do otherwise, they believe, would be contrary to God's will. Neo-conservative gentiles such as John Bolton; Robert Bartley, the former *Wall Street Journal* editor; William Bennett, the former secretary of education; Jeane Kirkpatrick, the former UN ambassador; and the influential columnist George Will are also steadfast supporters.

The U.S. form of government offers activists many ways of influencing the policy process. Interest groups can lobby elected representatives and members of the executive branch, make campaign contributions, vote in elections, try to mold public opinion, and so on. They enjoy a disproportionate amount of influence when they are committed to an issue to which the bulk of the population is indifferent. Policymakers will tend to accommodate those who care about the issue, even if their numbers are small, confident that the rest of the population will not penalize them for doing so.

In its basic operations, the Israel Lobby is no different from the farm lobby, steel or textile workers' unions, or other ethnic lobbies. There is nothing improper about American Jews and their Christian allies attempting to sway U.S. policy: the Lobby's activities are not a conspiracy of the sort depicted in tracts like the *Protocols of the Elders of Zion*. For the most part, the individuals and groups that compose it are only doing what other special interest groups do, but doing it very much better. By contrast, pro-Arab interest groups, in so far as they exist at all, are weak, which makes the Israel Lobby's task even easier.

The Lobby pursues two broad strategies. First, it wields its significant influence in Washington, pressuring both Congress and the executive branch. Whatever an individual lawmaker or policymaker's own views may be, the Lobby tries to make supporting Israel the "smart" choice. Second, it strives to ensure that public discourse portrays Israel in a positive light, by repeating myths about its founding and by promoting its point of view in policy debates. The goal is to prevent critical comments from getting a fair hearing in the political arena. Controlling the debate is essential to guaranteeing U.S. support because a candid discussion of U.S.-Israeli relations might lead Americans to favor a different policy.

A key pillar of the Lobby's effectiveness is its influence in Congress, where Israel is virtually immune from criticism. This in itself is remarkable because Congress rarely shies away from contentious issues. Where Israel is concerned, however, potential critics fall silent. One reason is that some key members are Christian Zionists like Dick Armey, who said in September 2002, "My No. 1 priority in foreign policy is to protect Israel." One might think that the No. 1 priority for any congressman would be to protect America. There are also Jewish senators and congressmen who work to ensure that U.S. foreign policy supports Israel's interests.

Another source of the Lobby's power is its use of pro-Israel congressional staffers. As Morris Amitay, a former head of AIPAC, once admitted, "There are a lot of guys at the working level up here [on Capitol Hill] who happen to be Jewish, who are willing . . . to look at certain issues in terms of their Jewishness. . . . These are all guys who are in a position to make the decision in these areas for those senators. . . . You can get an awful lot done just at the staff level."

AIPAC itself, however, forms the core of the Lobby's influence in Congress. Its success is due to its ability to reward legislators and congressional candidates who support its agenda, and to punish those who challenge it. Money is critical to U.S. elections (as the scandal over lobbyist Jack Abramoff's shady dealings reminded us), and AIPAC makes sure that its friends get strong financial support from the many pro-Israel political action committees. Anyone who is seen as hostile to Israel can be sure that AIPAC will direct campaign contributions to his or her political opponents. AIPAC also organizes letter-writing campaigns and encourages newspaper editors to endorse pro-Israel candidates.

There is no doubt about the efficacy of these tactics. Here is one example: In the 1984 elections, AIPAC helped defeat Senator Charles Percy from Illinois, who, according to a prominent Lobby figure, had "displayed insensitivity and even hostility to our concerns." Thomas Dine, the head of AIPAC at the time, explained what happened: "All the Jews in America, from coast to coast, gathered to oust Percy. And the American politicians—those who hold public positions now, and those who aspire—got the message."

AIPAC's influence on Capitol Hill goes even further. According to Douglas Bloomfield, a former AIPAC staff member, "It is common for members of Congress and their staffs to turn to AIPAC first when they need information, before calling the Library of Congress, the Congressional Research Service, committee staff or administration experts." More important, he notes that AIPAC is "often called on to draft speeches, work on legislation, advise on tactics, perform research, collect co-sponsors and marshal votes."

The bottom line is that AIPAC, a de facto agent for a foreign government, has a stranglehold on Congress, with the result that U.S. policy towards Israel is not debated there, even though that policy has important consequences for the entire world. In other words, one of the three main branches of the government is firmly committed to supporting Israel. As one former Democratic senator, Ernest Hollings, noted on leaving office, "You can't have an Israeli policy other than what AIPAC gives you around here." Or as Ariel Sharon once told an American audience, "When people ask me how they can help Israel, I tell them, 'Help AIPAC.'"

Thanks in part to the influence Jewish voters have on presidential elections, the Lobby also has significant leverage over the executive branch. Although they make up less than 3 percent of the population, they make large campaign donations to candidates from both parties. The *Washington Post* once estimated that Democratic presidential candidates "depend on Jewish supporters to supply as much as 60 percent of the money." And because Jewish voters have high turn-out rates and are concentrated in key states like California, Florida, Illinois, New York, and Pennsylvania, presidential candidates go to great lengths not to antagonize them.

Key organizations in the Lobby make it their business to ensure that critics of Israel do not get important foreign policy jobs. Jimmy Carter wanted to make George Ball his first secretary of state, but knew that Ball was seen as critical of Israel and that the Lobby would oppose the appointment. In this way, any aspiring policymaker is encouraged to become an overt supporter of Israel, which is why public critics of Israeli policy have become an endangered species in the foreign policy establishment.

When Howard Dean called for the United States to take a more "even-handed role" in the Arab-Israeli conflict, Senator Joseph Lieberman accused him of selling Israel down the river and said his statement was "irresponsible." Virtually all the top Democrats in the House signed a letter criticizing Dean's remarks, and the *Chicago Jewish Star* reported that "anonymous attackers . . . are clogging the email inboxes of Jewish leaders around the country, warning—without much evidence—that Dean would somehow be bad for Israel."

This worry was absurd; Dean is, in fact, quite hawkish on Israel—his campaign cochair was a former AIPAC president, and Dean said his own views on the Middle East more closely reflected those of AIPAC than those of the more moderate Americans for Peace Now. He had merely suggested that to "bring the sides together," Washington should act as an honest broker. This is hardly a radical idea, but the Lobby doesn't tolerate even-handedness.

During the Clinton administration, Middle Eastern policy was largely shaped by officials with close ties to Israel or to prominent pro-Israel organizations, among them, Martin Indyk, the former deputy director of research at AIPAC and cofounder of the pro-Israel Washington Institute for Near East Policy (WINEP); Dennis Ross, who joined WINEP after leaving government in 2001; and Aaron Miller, who has lived in Israel and often visits the country. These men were among Clinton's closest advisers at the Camp David summit in July 2000. Although all three supported the Oslo peace process and favored the creation of a Palestinian state, they did so only within the limits of what would be acceptable to Israel. The American delegation took its cues from Ehud Barak, coordinated its negotiating positions with Israel in advance, and did not offer independent proposals. Not surprisingly, Palestinian negotiators complained that they were "negotiating with two Israeli teams—one displaying an Israeli flag, and one an American flag."

The situation was even more pronounced in the George W. Bush administration, whose ranks included such fervent advocates of the Israeli cause as Elliot Abrams, John Bolton, Douglas Feith, I. Lewis ("Scooter") Libby, Richard Perle, Paul Wolfowitz, and David Wurmser. These officials consistently pushed for policies favored by Israel and backed by organizations in the Lobby.

The Lobby doesn't want an open debate, of course, because that might lead Americans to question the level of support they provide. Accordingly, pro-Israel organizations work hard to influence the institutions that do most to shape popular opinion.

The Lobby's perspective prevails in the mainstream media: the debate among Middle East pundits, the journalist Eric Alterman writes, is "dominated by people who cannot imagine criticizing Israel." He lists sixty-one "columnists and commentators who can be counted on to support Israel reflexively and without qualification." Conversely, he found just five pundits who consistently criticize Israeli actions or endorse Arab positions. Newspapers occasionally publish guest op-eds challenging Israeli policy, but the balance of opinion clearly favors the other side. It is hard to imagine any mainstream media outlet in the United States publishing a piece like this one.

"Shamir, Sharon, Bibi—whatever those guys want is pretty much fine by me," Robert Bartley once remarked. Not surprisingly, his newspaper, the *Wall Street Journal*, along with other prominent papers like the *Chicago Sun-Times* and the *Washington Times*, regularly runs editorials that strongly support Israel. Magazines like *Commentary*, the *New Republic* and the *Weekly Standard* defend Israel at every turn.

Editorial bias is also found in papers like the *New York Times*, which occasionally criticizes Israeli policies and sometimes concedes that the Palestinians have legitimate grievances, but is not even-handed. In his memoirs, the paper's former executive editor Max Frankel acknowledges the impact his own attitude had on his editorial decisions: "I was much more deeply devoted to Israel than I dared to assert. . . . Fortified by my knowledge of Israel and my friendships there, I myself wrote most of our Middle East commentaries. As more Arab than Jewish readers recognized, I wrote them from a pro-Israel perspective."

News reports are more even-handed, in part because reporters strive to be objective, but also because it is difficult to cover events in the Occupied Territories without acknowledging Israel's actions on the ground. To discourage unfavorable reporting, the Lobby organizes letter-writing campaigns, demonstrations, and boycotts of news outlets whose content it considers anti-Israel. One CNN executive has said that he sometimes gets six thousand e-mail messages in a single day complaining about a story. In May 2003, the pro-Israel Committee for Accurate Middle East Reporting in America (CAMERA) organized demonstrations outside National Public Radio stations in thirty-three cities; it also tried to persuade contributors to withhold support from NPR until its Middle East coverage became more sympathetic to Israel. Boston's NPR station, WBUR, reportedly lost more than $1 million in contributions as a result of these efforts. Further pressure on NPR has come from Israel's friends in Congress, who have asked for an internal audit of NPR's Middle East coverage as well as more oversight.

The Israeli side also dominates the think tanks which play an important role in shaping public debate as well as actual policy. The Lobby created its own think tank in 1985, when Martin Indyk helped to found WINEP. Although WINEP plays down its links to Israel, claiming instead to provide a "balanced and realistic" perspective on Middle East issues, it is funded and run by individuals deeply committed to advancing Israel's agenda.

The Lobby's influence extends well beyond WINEP, however. Over the past twenty-five years, pro-Israel forces have established a commanding presence at the American Enterprise Institute, the Brookings Institution, the Center for Security Policy, the Foreign Policy Research Institute, the Heritage Foundation, the Hudson Institute, the Institute for Foreign Policy Analysis, and the Jewish Institute for National Security Affairs (JINSA). These think tanks employ few, if any, critics of U.S. support for Israel.

Take the Brookings Institution. For many years, its senior expert on the Middle East was William Quandt, a former NSC official with a well-deserved reputation for even-handedness. Today, Brookings's coverage is conducted through the Saban Center for Middle East Studies, which is financed by Haim Saban, an Israeli American businessman and ardent Zionist. The center's director is the ubiquitous Martin Indyk. What was once a nonpartisan policy institute is now part of the pro-Israel chorus.

Where the Lobby has had the most difficulty is in stifling debate on university campuses. In the 1990s, when the Oslo peace process was underway, there was only mild criticism of Israel, but it grew stronger with Oslo's collapse and Sharon's access to power, becoming quite vociferous when the IDF reoccupied the West Bank in spring 2002 and employed massive force to subdue the second intifada.

The Lobby moved immediately to "take back the campuses." New groups sprang up, like the Caravan for Democracy, which brought Israeli speakers to U.S. colleges. Established groups like the Jewish Council for Public Affairs and Hillel joined in, and a new group, the Israel on Campus Coalition, was formed to coordinate the many bodies that now sought to present Israel's case. Finally, AIPAC more than tripled its spending on programs to monitor university activities and to train young advocates, in order to "vastly expand the number of students involved on campus . . . in the national pro-Israel effort."

The Lobby also monitors what professors write and teach. In September 2002, Martin Kramer and Daniel Pipes, two passionately pro-Israel neo-conservatives, established a website (Campus Watch) that posted dossiers on suspect academics and encouraged students to report remarks or behavior that might be considered hostile to Israel. This transparent attempt to blacklist and intimidate scholars provoked a harsh reaction and Pipes and Kramer later removed the dossiers, but the website still invites students to report "anti-Israel" activity.

Groups within the Lobby put pressure on particular academics and universities. Columbia has been a frequent target, no doubt because of the presence of the late Edward Said on its faculty. "One can be sure that any public statement in support of the Palestinian people by the preeminent literary critic Edward Said will elicit hundreds of e-mails, letters, and journalistic accounts that call on us to denounce Said and to either sanction or fire him," Jonathan Cole, its former provost, reported. When Columbia recruited the historian Rashid Khalidi from Chicago, the same thing happened. It was a problem Princeton also faced a few years later when it considered wooing Khalidi away from Columbia.

No discussion of the Lobby would be complete without an examination of one of its most powerful weapons: the charge of anti-Semitism. Anyone who criticizes Israel's actions or argues that pro-Israel groups have significant influence over U.S. Middle Eastern policy—an influence AIPAC celebrates—stands a good chance of being labeled an anti-Semite. Indeed, anyone who merely claims that there *is* an Israel Lobby runs the risk of being charged with anti-Semitism, even though the Israeli media refer to America's "Jewish Lobby." In other words, the Lobby first boasts of its influence and then attacks anyone who calls attention to it. It's a very effective tactic: anti-Semitism is something no one wants to be accused of.

Can the Lobby's power be curtailed? One would like to think so, given the Iraq debacle, the obvious need to rebuild America's image in the Arab and Islamic world, and the recent revelations about AIPAC officials passing U.S. government secrets to Israel. One might also think that Arafat's death and the election of the more moderate Mahmoud Abbas would cause Washington to press vigorously and even-handedly for a peace agreement. In short, there are ample grounds for leaders to distance themselves from the Lobby and adopt a Middle East policy more consistent with broader U.S. interests. In particular, using American power to achieve a just peace between Israel and the Palestinians would help advance the cause of democracy in the region.

But that is not going to happen—not soon, anyway. AIPAC and its allies (including Christian Zionists) have no serious opponents in the lobbying world. They know it has become more difficult to make Israel's case today, and they are responding by taking on staff and expanding their activities. Besides, American politicians remain acutely sensitive to campaign contributions and other forms of political pressure, and major media outlets are likely to remain sympathetic to Israel no matter what it does.

The Lobby's influence causes trouble on several fronts. It increases the terrorist danger that all states face—including America's European allies. It has made it impossible to end the Israeli-Palestinian conflict, a situation that gives extremists a powerful recruiting tool, increases the pool of potential terrorists and sympathizers, and contributes to Islamic radicalism in Europe and Asia.

Equally worrying, the Lobby's campaign for regime change in Iran and Syria could lead the United States to attack those countries, with potentially disastrous effects. We don't need another Iraq. At a minimum, the Lobby's hostility towards Syria and Iran makes it almost impossible for Washington to enlist them in the struggle against al Qaeda and the Iraqi insurgency, where their help is badly needed.

There is a moral dimension here as well. Thanks to the Lobby, the United States has become the de facto enabler of Israeli expansion in the Occupied Territories, making it complicit in the crimes perpetrated against the Palestinians. This situation undercuts Washington's efforts to promote democracy abroad and makes it look hypocritical when it presses other states to respect human rights. U.S. efforts to limit nuclear proliferation appear equally hypocritical given its willingness to accept Israel's nuclear arsenal, which only encourages Iran and others to seek a similar capability.

Besides, the Lobby's campaign to quash debate about Israel is unhealthy for democracy. Silencing skeptics by organizing blacklists and boycotts—or by suggesting that critics are anti-Semites—violates the principle of open debate on which democracy depends. The inability of Congress to conduct a genuine debate on these important issues paralyzes the entire process of democratic deliberation. Israel's backers should be free to make their case and to challenge those who disagree with them, but efforts to stifle debate by intimidation must be roundly condemned.

Finally, the Lobby's influence has been bad for Israel. Its ability to persuade Washington to support an expansionist agenda has discouraged Israel from seizing opportunities—including a peace treaty with Syria and a prompt and full implementation of the Oslo Accords—that would have saved Israeli lives and shrunk the ranks of Palestinian extremists. Denying the Palestinians their legitimate political rights certainly has not made Israel more secure, and the long campaign to kill or marginalize a generation of Palestinian leaders has empowered extremist groups like Hamas and reduced the number of Palestinian leaders who would be willing to accept a fair settlement and able to make it work. Israel itself would probably be better off if the Lobby were less powerful and U.S. policy more even-handed.

There is a ray of hope, however. Although the Lobby remains a powerful force, the adverse effects of its influence are increasingly difficult to hide. Powerful states can maintain flawed policies for quite some time, but reality cannot be ignored forever. What is needed is a candid discussion of the Lobby's influence and a more open debate about U.S. interests in this vital region. Israel's well-being is one of those interests, but its continued occupation of the West Bank and its broader regional agenda are not. Open debate will expose the limits of the strategic and moral case for one-sided U.S. support and could move the United States to a position more consistent with its own national interest, with the interests of the other states in the region, and with Israel's long-term interests as well.

DISCUSSION QUESTIONS

1. What are two possible explanations for the bond between the United States and Israel?
2. What do Mearsheimer and Walt argue is the actual reason that the countries are so closely tied?
3. What reasons do Mearsheimer and Walt give for questioning Israel's strategic value to the United States?
4. What are four reasons for questioning the moral basis of the United States' relationship with Israel?
5. What is the Israel Lobby? What are its two broad strategies?
6. What is AIPAC and why is it important?
7. How has the Israel lobby extended its influence outside of Congress to media, think tanks, and universities?

5

American Veterans in Government and the Use of Force

Peter D. Feaver and Christopher Gelpi

In this chapter we examine whether the prevalence of military experience among the policymaking elite affects the propensity of the United States to use military force. Because veteran opinion corresponds with military opinion, we use veteran presence in the political elite as a proxy for measuring the civil-military gap over time. Relying on a composite measure of military experience across the executive and legislative branches of government, we examine the impact of elite military experience on the U.S. propensity to initiate and to escalate militarized interstate disputes between 1816 and 1992.

The results of these analyses are striking. We find that as the percentage of veterans serving in the executive branch and the legislature increases, the probability that the United States will initiate militarized disputes declines. At the same time, however, once a dispute has been initiated, the higher the proportion of veterans, the greater the level of force the United States will use in the dispute. These results are statistically robust and are not spurious; they hold even when we control for other factors that are known to affect the propensity to use force. The civil-military gap matters, at least as far as the use of force goes.

FROM BELIEFS TO BEHAVIOR: THE CIVIL-MILITARY GAP AND INTERSTATE CONFLICT

Although civilian and military preferences regarding the use of force may differ, civilians have had the final say regarding both when and how military force will be used throughout U.S. history. The American military has never openly challenged the fundamental principle of civilian control, and we do not anticipate that it will do so. Nonetheless, even under the basic rubric of civilian control, one can imagine varying levels of military influence (Feaver 2003).

Military preferences shape U.S. foreign policy to a greater or lesser extent through at least two significant mechanisms. First, while the military may not determine American policy, its advisory role is well respected and established. Given their obvious expertise regarding the use of force, military advisors will have the opportunity to persuade civilian policymakers to adopt views that reflect the beliefs and preferences of the military. Second, even if military advisors are unable to alter the views of policymakers, their preferences may constrain them because of the leverage that the military can give to competing civilian elites (that is, elite members of a competing political party or faction). The norms of civilian control may inhibit military leaders from openly and publicly challenging civilian decisions regarding the use of force, but competing civilian elites are under no such constraint. Research indicates that one of the keys to maintaining public support for the use of force is the existence of an elite consensus in support of the issue (Larson 1996). Should civilian leaders select policies that are contrary to military advice, however, competing civilian elites will be ready and willing to attack the leadership for ignoring such expert advice if the policy is eventually judged a failure. Thus military preferences may influence the civilian elite, despite the strong American norm of civilian control, to the extent that these views can either persuade or coerce civilian policymakers to alter their choices.

The linkage between military preferences and American conflict behavior may be further complicated by the fact that individuals' preferences over when and how to use military force are likely to be related to each other. That is, an individual's preferences regarding one dimension may be contingent on the policy outcome on the other dimension (Hinich and Munger 1997). For example, it would be entirely consistent for a realpolitik policymaker to oppose intervention in response to human rights abuses abroad, but also to argue that if the United States does intervene in such conflicts it should do so with a high level of force.

First, state leaders must decide whether or not to use force. If they choose not to initiate, then no force is used and the status quo prevails. If the decision is made to initiate, however, then a second decision must be made regarding how much military force will be used. This decision tree has three end-nodes: (1) no force is used and the status quo prevails, (2) limited use of force, and (3) large-scale use of force. Our contention is that civilian and military elites have different preference rankings across these three outcomes. Moreover, preference rankings within each of these groups may vary depending upon the nature of the goal for which force is being contemplated.

The specific preferences of the relevant actors can be deduced from what is known about their views in general. Both previous case study research and our own survey research suggest that civilian elite nonveterans would most prefer a limited intervention. This preference for limited involvement appears to hold regardless of whether the goals of the military operation are realpolitik issues such as the defense of Kuwait or South Korea, or interventionist issues such as the civil war in Somalia or human rights abuses in Kosovo. However, nonveteran civilian rankings of the other two outcomes—do nothing and use large-scale force—appear to switch depending on the nature of the issue. That is, faced with realpolitik threats, nonveteran civilians seem likely to prefer large-scale force to doing nothing (for example, Kuwait and Korea). With regard to interventionist issues, however, it is arguable that nonveteran civilians would prefer doing nothing to escalating to the large-scale use of force (for example, in Kosovo and Somalia).

While nonveteran civilians' preferences are defined by their focus on limited force as the most attractive option, the military elite consistently ranks this as its least preferred outcome. This preference against limited military action is consistent across policy issues. The military's relative ranking of large-scale force and doing nothing, however, changes depending upon the nature of the issue at stake. With regard to realpolitik issues, the military's most preferred option is the large-scale use of force. It is important to note that some members of the military may have a rather restrictive conception of a realpolitik threat. Given that the military views an issue as a threat to American national security, however, its most preferred outcome is to use force on a large scale, while doing nothing ranks in between large scale and limited force. With regard to interventionist issues, however, the military's most preferred outcome is to do nothing, while large-scale force remains preferable to limited force.

Given these preference rankings, what kind of advice is the military likely to offer to civilian leaders? With regard to realpolitik issues, the military would like to counsel civilians to use force on a large scale. However, it will be wary of advising civilians to do so because of the fear that once the United States becomes involved in the conflict, civilians will place constraints on how force will be used. This subsequent choice would, of course, present the military with its least preferred outcome. The cautious and restrained nature of the military advice prior to the Gulf War may serve as an example of this pattern. Many in the military saw a threat to American security, but advised caution regarding the use of force partly out of fear that civilians would constrain the nature of the operation (Betts 1991).

With regard to interventionist issues, however, military advice is likely to be adamantly opposed to using force rather than merely cautious. In this case, the military's most preferred option is to do nothing, and it will attempt to persuade civilian elites to stay out. Military advisors should be particularly adamant in this regard because they are aware that while limited intervention is civilians' most preferred outcome, a large-scale use of force is their least favorite option. Thus a decision to use force on an interventionist issue such as Kosovo or Somalia will most likely present the military with its least preferred outcome: the limited use of force.

Not surprisingly, we expect that military preferences will have a greater influence on civilian policy choices when civilian leaders share preferences that are similar to those of the military. Moreover, our earlier findings indicate that civilians who have served in the military have preferences that are closer to those of the military than are the views of civilian nonveterans. Thus we expect that American conflict behavior will tend to reflect "military views" as the proportion of civilian policymakers with military experience increases.

Once the decision has been made to use military force, the nature of the military's advice to civilian policymakers becomes more straightforward. The military always prefers the large-scale use of force to the limited use of force. Indeed, the limited use of force is always the military's least preferred outcome. Thus once civilian policymakers have decided to use force (and the "do nothing" option disappears), military advisors will always counsel strongly for using force on a large scale. Once again, we expect this advice to be more influential when the civil-military gap is small.

Of course, the decision to use force is influenced by many factors, of which civil-military relations may not be the most important. The presence of these other factors presents a challenge for testing the influence of the civil-military opinion gap over time. Even so, it should be possible to isolate the impact of civil-military relations relative to other contributing factors that shape the use of force. The hypotheses that follow, then, are all subject to the ceteris paribus condition; controlling for all the other factors that affect the decision to use force, we expect that

Hypothesis 1: As the proportion of civilian policymakers with military experience increases, the probability that the United States will initiate militarized disputes will decrease.

Hypothesis 2: The impact of policymakers' military experience on American decisions to initiate militarized disputes will be more pronounced with regard to interventionist threats rather than realpolitik threats.

Hypothesis 3: As the proportion of civilian policymakers with military experience increases, the level of force the United States uses in disputes it initiates will increase.

MEASURING THE IMPACT OF THE CIVIL-MILITARY GAP ON AMERICAN CONFLICT BEHAVIOR

To test these hypotheses, we relate the civil-military gap to U.S. conflict behavior over the nineteenth and twentieth centuries while controlling, as far as possible, for other factors that are known to shape the use of force. We discuss the results of our analyses in the next section.

Scope

We test for the impact of the elite civil-military gap on American decisions to use force with a cross-sectional time-series dataset composed of interstate dyads of which the United States was a member between 1816 and 1992. State membership is determined by the Correlates of War dataset's definition of membership in the international system. One difficulty in using such dyadic pooled time-series data is determining which states were capable of interacting. During the latter part of the twentieth century, this issue seems less salient because of the frequent opportunities for interaction among states. As we move back in time through the nineteenth century, however, it becomes less plausible to assume that all states were capable of fighting with one another. Following a number of prominent analyses of the use of force, we address this problem by analyzing only "politically relevant" dyads (Maoz and Russett 1993; Oneal and Russett 1997), which are defined as (1) any pair of states in which at least one of the states is a major power; or (2) any pair of states that share a border or are divided by less than 250 miles of water.

Since the United States became a major power (according to the Correlates of War Capabilities dataset) in 1898, this rule implies that we analyze all interstate dyads including the United States from 1898 onward. Prior to 1898, the rule implies that we analyze American relations with all of the major powers during that period as well as American interactions with Mexico. For the entire 177 years under study, there are 8,780 dyad-years involving the United States.

Dependent Variable (1): Initiation of Force by the United States

Our argument made specific predictions about how civil-military factors might affect two different aspects of the use of force. The first aspect is the *propensity* to initiate the use of force, and thus our first dependent variable is the propensity of the United States to initiate the use of force. We code American initiations of force on the basis of the Correlates of War (COW) Militarized Interstate Disputes (MIDs) dataset, which defines the initiation of militarized disputes as explicit threats to use force, displays of force, mobilizations of force, or actual uses of force (Jones, Bremer, and Singer 1996). This variable is coded on an annual basis for each dyad, set at 1 for each year that the United States initiated a militarized dispute against the other state in the dyad, and otherwise at 0. For the entire 177 years studied, there were 111 militarized disputes initiated by the United States. Over the same period, the United States was also involved in 132 other militarized disputes that were initiated by other states. But since our theory only addresses disputes initiated by the United States, we do not include them in our analysis.

Dependent Variable (2): Level of Force Used by the United States

We also predicted a relationship between civil-military factors and the *level* of force used (that is, whether unconstrained in keeping with the classical "military" preference or constrained in keeping with the classical "civilian" preference). Once again, we rely on the COW MIDs dataset for our measure of the second dependent variable, the level of force used by the United States in the disputes that it initiated. In the MIDs dataset the highest level of force used by each side in a dispute is coded on a five-point scale as follows: 1 = no militarized response to a MID initiation by the other state; 2 = threat of force; 3 = show of force; 4 = use of force; 5 = war. For our purposes, of course, the first category of this variable is irrelevant, for we analyze the level of force only if the United States initiated a dispute. Threats of force involve verbal actions that are not supported by militarized behavior. A show of force involves the actual movement and use of troops, but stops short of extended or direct combat. The use of force involves direct military hostilities but stops short of full-scale war. Wars are defined as military engagements in which the combatants suffer at least one thousand battle deaths.

Key Explanatory Variable: The Elite Civil-Military Gap

We have no way of directly measuring the preferences of policymakers regarding the use of force across the span of American history. However, we can measure the military *experience* of American policymakers. That is, we can determine whether each of these policymakers ever served in the military. As we discussed above, this measure acts as a surrogate indicator for the presence of "military views" within the civilian policymaking elite.

Focusing on military experience as a measure of the gap fits nicely within the causal chain with which we link the civil-military gap to the use of force. We view the impact of the gap as a two-stage process. First, military experience shapes individuals' attitudes and preferences regarding the use of force. Second, these differing preferences, in turn, alter American conflict behavior. That is, although our aggregate analysis of American conflict behavior draws a direct linkage between military experience and dispute behavior, we view attitudes as an intervening variable between military experience and American foreign policy.

Our approach requires us to assume that the link between opinions about the use of force and military/veteran status has been more or less constant over the time. We are not arguing that all elite civilians have always thought exactly the same way or that all elite military have always thought exactly the same way. Rather, we are assuming that the general structure of opinion has been relatively constant over time, and we believe that this assumption is both modest and plausible.

Our analyses in this chapter also treat all forms of military experience as the same. This assumption is perhaps more problematic, because intuitively there would seem to be a difference in perspective between a draftee who served his minimum tour and a career officer who rose to the highest military ranks before pursuing a political career. Likewise, it is plausible that there is a difference in perspective between serving during combat versus serving during peacetime, or serving in a combat unit versus serving as a cook, or serving in the reserves versus active duty.

For our present purposes, this limitation in the data biases our analysis *against* finding any effect. If variations in military experience matters in ways we are not able to capture, then it will show up as more noisy variation in the data, driving coefficients toward zero and lowering the likelihood of finding any statistically significant relationship. Put another way, our assumptions increase the likelihood that we will falsely reject a veteran's effect when there really is one, and decrease the likelihood that we will falsely accept a veteran's effect when there really is none.

The next issue is the determination of whose military experience might be relevant for predicting the use of force. The president's military experience should be an important aspect of this process, but should by no means be the only factor. The president inevitably relies on advice from members of his cabinet and his national security team, so surely their military experience will shape the views and the information they convey to him. In addition, the president must also be concerned about how other policymakers will respond to his decisions regarding whether and how to use force. Congress has often publicly debated American decisions to use force, and as we noted earlier, public support for a military operation may depend critically on the existence of an elite consensus in support of the operation (Larson 1996). Thus the president must be concerned with whether legislators will hold hearings or make public statements that question the administration's policy. Congress also retains an important budgetary and constitutional link to American uses of force, and the president may consult directly with prominent members of Congress who have expertise in foreign affairs.

Consequently, our measure of the military experience of policymakers encompasses the executive and legislative branches. We do not include the military experience of the Supreme Court or other aspects of the judiciary, because judges have not historically played a role in American decisions to use force or debated such decisions publicly. For the executive branch, we recorded the percentage of veterans serving in the cabinet for each year. Thus we include the military experience of the president, the vice president, and any other cabinet officers serving during that year. For Congress, we use the percentage of veterans serving in the House of Representatives for each year.

Secondary Explanatory Variable: Interventionist Versus Realpolitik Uses of Force

One important aspect of our argument is that civilians differ from those with military experience in terms of their willingness to use military force to address issues that are outside the realpolitik scope of American security policy—especially those that involve intervention inside other states. To test this hypothesis, we divided dyads into two categories: states whose actions could represent a threat to the core bases of American security, and states whose actions could not represent such a threat. The former category we labeled "realpolitik" targets and the latter we labeled "interventionist." We defined interventionist targets as any state that (1) faced worse than a 99:1 disadvantage against the United States in terms of relative military capabilities and (2) was not allied with a competing major power. Such small, non-aligned states clearly do not have the capability to threaten American security in a realpolitik manner. Instead, disputes with such states were likely to involve U.S. intervention inside the minor state because of domestic turmoil or because the United States was dissatisfied with the policies or behaviors of the ruling government of such states. States that enjoyed less than a 99:1 disadvantage against the United States or were allied with a rival major power were coded as realpolitik targets. This coding rule results in approximately 51 percent of the dyad-years in our dataset being coded as interventionist.

Control Variables

Because decisions to use force are multifaceted and complex, even if we did find a relationship between our measures of the civil-military gap and the propensity to use force, we would not expect it to be the only (or even the most important) factor influencing the use of force. A large body of literature on international conflict has already identified numerous factors that affect the use of force, including distance, military capabilities, and democracy, for example. To the extent that the elite military experience is correlated with any of these factors, the failure to include that factor in our analysis might bias our estimate of the impact of elite veterans. Control variables thus allow us to address many of the critiques we have encountered, most of which take the form of conceding a statistical correlation but denying a causal relationship on the grounds that some other factor is the true causal agent. As far as possible, we have controlled for every plausible alternative argument in our empirical analysis.

Including additional control variables cannot artificially inflate the estimated impact of our variable of interest. It can, however, introduce problems such as multicollinearity. Such problems would inflate the standard errors of the coefficients and could reduce the statistical significance of our results. Thus the inclusion of control variables can only provide a more stringent test of our hypotheses. Including these variables also allows us to compare the impact of elite military experience with the influence of other prominent causes of conflict. [*The control variables included are portrayed in tables 5.1 and 5.2, in addition to the principal explanatory variables.—Ed.*]

DOES THE CIVIL-MILITARY GAP INFLUENCE AMERICAN CONFLICT BEHAVIOR?

We conducted a logit analysis of every politically relevant interstate dyadic relationship in which the United States was a partner from 1816 to 1992. Table 5.1 presents our analysis of the propensity of the United States to initiate militarized disputes. Our results provide strong and striking support for hypotheses 1 and 2. As predicted, the negative coefficient for elite veterans is statistically significant, indicating that the more veterans there were in the political elite, the less likely the United States was to initiate the use of force. Also as predicted, the effect of veterans on the propensity to use force was even greater in interventionist cases. As indicated by column three of table 5.1, the coefficient for this variable for realpolitik dyads is only -0.019 (p < .10). With regard to interventionist dyads, in contrast, the coefficient is calculated by adding that value to the coefficient on the interaction between the percentage of veterans in the policy elite and an interventionist threat (-0.047, p < .01). Thus the overall effect of elite veterans for interventionist dyads is -0.066—more than three times the impact for realpolitik dyads.

Figure 5.1 displays the predicted probability that the United States would initiate a militarized dispute as the percentage of veterans in the cabinet and Congress ranged from its historical near-minimum of 10 percent to its historical near-maximum of 80 percent. When only one policymaker in ten had military experience, the probability that the United States would initiate a dispute within a given dyad was approximately 3.6 percent. At first glance, this might look like a relatively small risk. But because militarized disputes are rare events, a 3 percent probability of a dispute between a given pair of states actually indicates a relatively high risk. Moreover, the effect of a 3 percent probability is magnified by the large number of dyads in which the United States was involved each year. For large portions of our data set, the United States was engaged in over one hundred such dyads per year. Thus a 3 percent per dyad probability of a dispute yields a prediction that, holding all other factors that influence the decision to use force hypothetically constant, the United States might initiate several additional militarized disputes per year because so few policymakers had military experience.

Conversely, of course, as the percentage of policymakers with military experience increases, the probability of dispute initiation drops substantially. The impact of these changes is slightly nonlinear, with the greatest decreases in the probability of a dispute occurring as the percentage of veterans ranges between 10 percent and 67 percent. By the time the rate of military experience among policymakers reaches 67 percent, the probability that the United States would initiate a dispute within a given dyad drops from 3.6 percent to 0.7 percent—representing more than an 80 percent decrease from its previous value, which we call a reduction in relative risk. Further increases in elite military experience up to 80 percent reduce the probability of a dispute within a dyad to nearly 0.4 percent.

Also in figure 5.1, we compare the impact of elite veterans on the probability that the United States would initiate a crisis against realpolitik and interventionist threats. As one would expect from the results in table 5.1, the impact of elite veterans is much greater for interventionist cases. When few veterans are in office, the United States is less likely to initiate a dispute against realpolitik than interventionist targets. Specifically, when only 10 percent of policymakers are veterans, the probability of a U.S. initiation in a realpolitik dyad is 4.7 percent, and in an interventionist dyad it is approximately 6.0 percent. As the percentage of elite veterans increases, the probability of a dispute drops within both sets of dyads, but the decline is much steeper in the interventionist group. In fact, by the time the percentage of veterans reaches 50 percent, the United States is actually more than three times as likely to initiate force against a realpolitik threat. When the percentage of veterans nears its historical maximum, the probability of initiation against a realpolitik threat is 1 percent, while the probability of initiation against an interventionist threat is only 0.08 percent. These results are made all the more striking by the crude nature of our distinction between realpolitik and interventionist threats. More careful theorizing and empirical work on these categories would surely increase the decisiveness of this distinction.

Many of our control variables also have a significant impact on U.S. dispute initiation, but none of these effects can account for the impact of elite veterans. For example, our analysis supports the war-weariness hypothesis. The coefficient for the log of U.S. casualties in the previous war is negative and statistically significant, but it does not account for the impact of elite veterans.

Table 5.1. Elite Military Experience and American Militarized Dispute Initiation

Explanatory Variables	Elite Veterans Model	Elite and Mass Veterans Model	Realpolitik vs. Interventionist Threats
Percent Veteran in Cabinet and House	−0.032*** (0.011)	−0.031** (0.014)	−0.019* (0.011)
Elite Vets x Interventionist			−0.047*** (0.012)
Interventionist Threat			1.02** (0.46)
Ln of Previous War's Battle	−0.16*** (0.056)	−0.22** (0.092)	−0.17*** (0.056)
Percent Veteran in U.S. Public		−0.042 (0.059)	
Cold War Years	1.70*** (0.50)	2.17*** (0.76)	1.83*** (0.52)
Republican Administration	0.44 (0.28)	0.41 (0.31)	0.45 (0.28)
U.S. Involvement in Other	−0.070 (0.060)	−0.065 (0.063)	−0.061 (0.06)
Balance of Military Capabilities	−1.75*** (0.61)	−1.84*** (0.72)	−1.15 (0.74)
Alliance Similarity	−1.41** (0.65)	−1.36** (0.70)	−1.77** (0.79)
United States Is a Major Power	−0.39 (0.38)	−0.76 (0.69)	−0.61 (0.40)
Adversary Is a Major Power	−0.39 (0.69)	−0.43 (0.86)	−0.29 (0.70)
Adversary Level of Democracy	−0.045** (0.023)	−0.061** (0.026)	−0.037* (0.023)
Ln Distance between States	−0.30*** (0.029)	−0.30*** (0.031)	−0.28** (0.027)
Year since U.S. Initiation in Constant[a]	−1.29 (0.90)	−2.38 (1.80)	0.61 (1.04)
Number of Observations	8,739	8,464	8,739
Initial Log Likelihood	−594.92	−534.37	−594.92
Log-Likelihood at Convergence	−469.72	−419.82	−456.54
Chi-squared	601.74 (19d.f.)	727.95 (18d.f.)*	560.77 (19d.f.)*

* = p<.10, ** = p < .05, *** = p < .01

Note: Huber-White robust standard errors in parentheses. Standard errors allow for clustering by dyad.

[a] For reasons of space, the temporal dependence coefficients are not reported here. As expected, years since the previous U.S. initiation did have a significant and nonlinear effect on U.S. dispute initiation as predicted by Beck, Katz, and Tucker (1998).

The percentage of veterans among the U.S. public, in contrast, has no significant effect. The fact that elite military experience matters while military experience among the public does not fits precisely with the elite-level causal

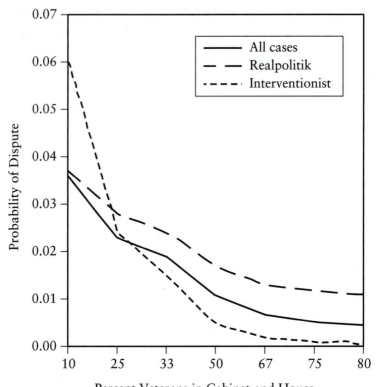

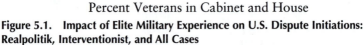

Figure 5.1.　Impact of Elite Military Experience on U.S. Dispute Initiations: Realpolitik, Interventionist, and All Cases

mechanism that we hypothesized. The coefficient for Republican administrations was consistently positive, but did not quite achieve statistical significance ($p < .11$ for model in column one). Thus any possible association between the U.S. military and the Republican Party cannot account for the relationship between elite military experience and American conflict behavior.

DOES THE CIVIL-MILITARY GAP INFLUENCE HOW AMERICA USES FORCE?

Does elite military experience also have an impact on the American escalation of disputes? The answer to this question—displayed in table 5.2—appears to be an unqualified yes. Our results indicate that higher percentages of veterans in the political elite were associated with greater levels of force by the United States—if the United States did initiate the use of force. The coefficient for the percentage of veterans in the cabinet and in Congress is positive and statistically significant, and the impact of this variable is substantial.

Table 5.2. Elite Military Experience and the Level of Military Force Used by the United States in a Dispute

Explanatory Variables	Coefficients and Standard Errors
Percent Veteran in the Cabinet and House	0.089***
	(0.024)
Republican Administration	−0.42
	(0.47)
Cold War Years	−4.31***
	(1.24)
Balance of Military Capabilities	−1.93
	(1.45)
Alliance Similarity Score	0.89
	(1.11)
U.S. Is a Major Power	1.91**
	(0.79)
Adversary Is a Major Power	−2.73***
	(1.01)
Adversary Level of Democracy	0.066
	(0.049)
U.S. Involvement in Other Disputes	−0.10
	(0.13)
Contiguous State	−0.68
	(1.016)
Distance between States	−0.0002
	(0.0002)
Adversary's Level of Force	0.61***
	(0.16)
Selection Effects Parameter	5.17*
	(3.15)
Threshold 1	−0.61
	(1.87)
Threshold 2	2.86*
	(1.90)
Threshold 3	7.08***
	(2.04)
Number of Observations	111
Initial Log-Likelihood	−112.54
Log-Likelihood at Convergence	−92.47
Chi-squared (10 d.f.)	40.13 (12 d.f.)***

Note: Huber-White robust standard errors for coefficients in parentheses.

* = p < .10, ** = p < .05, *** = p < .01.

Figure 5.2 indicates that as the percentage of veterans in the cabinet and Congress increases from 10 percent to 80 percent, the probability that the United States would engage in direct combat (use-of-force coding) increases from 2 percent to 73 percent. This same increase in the percentage of elite veterans increases the probability that the United States will escalate the

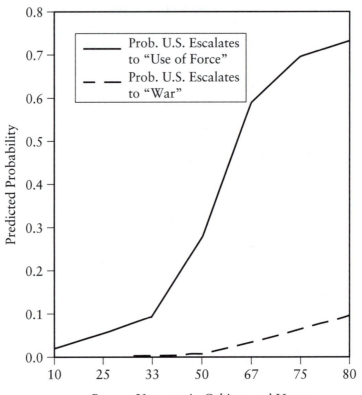

Percent Veterans in Cabinet and House

Figure 5.2. Impact of Elite Military Experience on the Level of Force Used in Dispute

dispute to the level of becoming a war from 0.06 percent to 9 percent. This latter increase is particularly substantial given the rarity of wars (0.2 percent of the dyad-years) and the gravity of escalating to such a level. Most of this impact is felt after the percentage of policymakers with military experience may well have favored something like an informal Powell Doctrine long before any such doctrine was articulated, far back in American history.

Our measure of escalation is fairly crude and developing more nuanced measures is a priority for future research. Nevertheless, it is striking that we find such statistically strong results in support of the theory's expectations, especially given the difficulties of measuring the phenomena involved. Moreover, note that the theory leads to opposite expectations from the veterans variable in these two stages of analysis: more veterans should lead to *fewer* dispute initiations but *higher* escalations. Nevertheless, the results support each apparently opposite dynamic, thus offering even stronger support for the underlying argument.

CONCLUSION

Civil-military relations at the policymaking level often seem dominated by personalities. Contrast the problems of President Clinton with those of his war-hero predecessor, President Bush; compare the rumpled tenure of Secretary Les Aspin or the academic acerbity of Secretary Madeleine Albright with the no-nonsense corporate mentality of Secretary Donald Rumsfeld; or consider the unusual charisma and political clout of General and then Secretary Colin Powell. Personalities matter and may be decisive in certain cases. Nonetheless, the findings presented here suggest that, at least when it comes to the use of force, we can identify consistent civilian and military tendencies in policymaking, irrespective of personalities.

[Earlier we have] shown that elite civilians with military experience behave like "Colin Powells" and elite civilian nonveterans are like "Madeleine Albrights"—at least where opinions on the use of force are concerned. What creates these different types? Why do civilians without military experience tend to have foreign policy views that systematically differ from the views of those who have served? We cannot definitively answer that question. We would contend, however, that service in the U.S. military is an important socialization experience that shapes individuals' attitudes. The military teaches lessons about the role of military force in American foreign policy and lessons about how military force ought to be used. These lessons do not appear to be forgotten when individuals leave the military and enter civilian life. Of course, we cannot yet specify the precise mechanisms at work in this socialization process, and our data may be consistent with other explanations as well. Nonetheless, our results suggest that the relationship among military experience, foreign policy attitudes, and conflict behavior merits further attention.

Whatever the causes of this civil-military opinion gap, we have shown that the gap had a profound effect on American military behavior from 1816 to 1992. As expected, we found that the higher the proportion of American policymakers with military experience, the lower the probability that the United States would initiate a militarized dispute. Also as expected, we found that the impact of military experience on dispute initiation became even larger when we focused on states that represented interventionist rather than realpolitik threats to the United States. Finally, also as expected, we found that the veteran's effect showed up in the level of force as well; the higher the proportion of American policymakers with military experience, the higher the level of force used by the United States, given that it had already initiated a use of force. Throughout these analyses, the impact of elite military experience was substantively large and often outweighed the impact of variables that have received considerably more attention in the study of international conflict.

It may be "normal" for military personnel and civilians to develop distinctive views regarding the use of force, but when this divergence of views begins to have an impact on American conflict behavior, one cannot simply shrug off the difference and say, "Who cares?" The difference in views between those with and without experience in the American military is a profoundly important issue that is in need of public attention and discussion. In the wake of the Cold War, the United States is faced primarily with interventionist threats such as civil wars and the violation of human rights. Undoubtedly, debates over what ought to be done in future Kosovos, Haitis, and Rwandas will be shaped by this pervasive civil-military dynamic. If veteran representation in the political elite continues to decline, we can expect American involvement in many more Kosovos, Haitis, and Rwandas to come.

DISCUSSION QUESTIONS

1. What are the underlying questions or hypotheses that Feaver and Gelpi analyze in this study?
2. What are the two ways in which military preferences affect the shaping of U.S. foreign policy?
3. How do civilians and the military likely differ in their attitudes toward the use of force?
4. What relationship do Feaver and Gelpi find between the percentage of veterans in the Cabinet and the House of Representatives and the use of force?
5. How does this relationship differ for "realpolitik" cases and "interventionist" cases?
6. What is the relationship between the percentage of veterans in the Cabinet and the House of Representatives and the probability that there will be an escalation in the use of force or in the probability of an escalation to war?
7. What are the implications of this study for understanding the relationship between military experience and the conduct of U.S. foreign policy in the future?

REFERENCES

Beck, Nathaniel, Jonathan Katz, and Richard Tucker. 1998. "Taking Times Seriously: Time-Series-Cross-Section Analysis with a Binary Dependent Variable." *American Journal of Political Science* 42, no. 4: 1260–88.

Betts, Richard K. 1991. *Soldiers, Statesmen, and Cold War Crises*. New York: Columbia University Press.

Feaver, Peter. 2003. *Armed Servants: Agency, Oversight, and Civil-Military Relations*. Cambridge, MA: Harvard University Press.

Hinich, Melvin J., and Michael C. Munger. 1997. *Analytical Politics*. New York: Cambridge University Press.

Jones, Daniel M., Stuart A. Bremer, and J. David Singer. 1996. "Militarized Interstate Disputes, 1816–1992: Rationale, Coding Rules, and Empirical Patterns." *Conflict Management and Peace Science* 15, no. 2: 163–213.

Larson, Eric V. 1996. *Casualties and Consensus: The Historical Role of Casualties in Domestic Support for U.S. Military Operations*. Santa Monica, CA: Rand.

Maoz, Zeev, and Bruce M. Russett. 1993. Normative and Structural Causes of Democratic Peace." *American Political Science Review* 87, no. 3: 624–38.

Oneal, John R., and Bruce M. Russett. 1997. "The Classical Liberals Were Right: Democracy, Independence, and Conflict, 1950–1985." *International Studies Quarterly* 41, no. 2: 267–94.

6

Events, Elites, and American Public Support for Military Conflict

Adam J. Berinsky

In recent years, a charitable view of the mass public has emerged in the public opinion and foreign policy literature. Increasingly, scholars have attributed "rationality" to public opinion concerning war. Many political scientists and policymakers argue that unmediated events—the successes and failures on the battlefield—determine whether the mass public will support military excursions. The public supports war, the story goes, if the benefits of action outweigh the costs of conflict and should therefore have a place at the policymaking table.

In this [chapter], I argue that military events may shape public opinion, but not in the straightforward manner posited by most scholars of public opinion and war. I draw upon and expand the work of scholars who contend that the balance of elite discourse influences levels of public support for war. Integrating research on heuristics and shortcuts with information-based theories of political choice, I demonstrate that patterns of conflict among partisan political actors shape mass opinion on war. It is not the direct influence of wartime events on individual citizens' decisions that determines public opinion, as "event response" theories of war support claim. Instead, consistent with the "elite cue" theory I advance in this [chapter], the nature of conflict among political elites concerning the salience and meaning of those events determines if the public will rally to war. To a significant degree citizens determine their positions on war by listening to trusted sources—those politicians who share their political predispositions.

I present evidence from the second Iraq war to come to this common conclusion. I find that significant segments of the mass public possessed

All footnotes, in-text references, and references have been deleted.

little knowledge of the most basic facts of [this conflict]. Thus, there is little evidence that citizens had the information needed to make cost/benefit calculations when deciding whether to support or oppose military action. Instead, I find that patterns of elite conflict shaped opinions during the Iraq conflict. When elites come to a common interpretation of a political reality, the public gives them great latitude to wage war. But when prominent political actors take divergent stands on the wisdom of intervention, the public divides as well. Furthermore, even in cases—such as the second Iraq war—where prominent political actors on one side of the partisan divide stay silent, the presence of a prominent partisan cue giver can lead to divergence in opinion. In sum, while members of the mass public are not lemmings—they have agency to determine their own opinion and may even, in the aggregate, reasonably react to changing events—in the realm of war, any apparent rationality arises largely through the process of elite cue taking, not through a reasoned cost/benefit analysis. The mass public is rational only to the extent that prominent political actors provide a rational lead.

THE POWER OF EVENTS?

The conventional wisdom that has emerged over the last thirty years in the public opinion and foreign policy literature holds that the course of events in a given conflict directly determines public support for war. The most prominent line of argument in this vein is what [James] Burk calls the "casualties hypothesis," the view that the American people will shrink from international involvement in the face of war deaths. This hypothesis grows out of [John] Mueller's contention that public support for war is inversely related to the log of casualties. Some modifications have been made to this basic theory over time. [Scott] Gartner and [Gary] Segura have, for instance, demonstrated the importance of local casualty rates in determining support for the war. Even so, the basic story advanced by Mueller remains a dominant view among both academics and policymakers.

Scholars have moved beyond simply investigating the impact of casualties to examine the effects of other events that affect the costs and benefits of military conflict. According to [Eric] Larson, the greater the perceived stakes, the clearer the objectives, and the higher the probability of success, the greater the level of public support for war. Building on this argument, other authors contend that the ongoing success of a mission—whether the war will come to a victorious end—determines public support for conflict. These theories differ in their particulars, yet all share the belief that "events" directly determine public support for war by altering the balance of costs and benefits related to a particular conflict. Thus, even for scholars who consider factors beyond casualties, the basic logic underlying Mueller's argument remains the dominant position: the collective mass public is rational and will support war if, and only if, the events of war ensure that the costs of military action are outweighed by the perceived benefits of a successful outcome.

Though "event-response" theories of public support for war have made important contributions, they have several potentially serious conceptual problems. First, these theories presume that members of the mass public at least implicitly incorporate knowledge of political developments into their political judgments. However, there is a long line of research that finds great heterogeneity in levels of political knowledge among the mass public. While researchers have long known that, on average, Americans know little about politics, knowledge levels are even dimmer when the focus turns to specific factual information. For instance, [Martin] Gilens found that the public's knowledge of specific policy-relevant information is low, even among those respondents who have high levels of general political knowledge.

Second, much research on the relationship between casualties and support for war has examined differences in collective public support for intervention across wars, not the differences among individuals within particular conflicts. With some important exceptions, analysis has proceeded at the aggregate level. Several existing theories, therefore, rest on untested notions of collective rationality. Larson, for instance, argues that the aggregate mass public will support war "if the aims are clear," but he does not describe the conditions under which individuals, much less the aggregate public, make such complex calculations. Thus, many existing theories of public support for military action fail to specify the mechanisms by which members of the mass public process information concerning the events of war and come to determine—both as individuals and collectives—either to support or oppose a given military operation. This aggregate-level work is certainly valuable, but it must be supplemented by individual--level analysis that accounts for individual-level variation on relevant political dimensions.

This leads to the final and most important point. Almost all the work described above ignores the partisan nature of the American political process. Treating the mass public as an undifferentiated whole—innocent of political and partisan attachments—leaves no room for the effect of domestic politics. Many researchers who study public opinion and war— even those scholars who conduct individual--level analysis—often talk about "the public" as if it were a monolithic entity. But foreign policy is often as contentious and partisan as domestic politics. Theories of war and politics must account for the effects of the domestic political process.

MEDIATED REALITY:
THE PRIMACY OF POLITICAL COMPETITION

In the early days of survey research, scholars argued that the public opinion concerning foreign policy was volatile and irrational—a fickle and changing "mood" in [Gabriel] Almond's words. However, the relative shortcoming of event-response theories does not mean that we must retreat to these dismal conclusions regarding public opinion and foreign policy. Event-response theories, after all, are not the only explanation for the dynamics of public support for war. Another possibility is to examine the influence of competition among political elites on public opinion.

The leading proponent of this theory in the context of foreign policy is [John] Zaller, who claims that elite discourse is the key to explaining war support. Zaller argues that the balance of persuasive messages carried in the political media determines the balance of opinion on a given policy controversy. Individuals who are most politically knowledgeable are most likely to receive political messages and accept those messages that accord with their personal political predispositions. The greater the volume of elite discourse favoring a particular policy position from elites of a particular political stripe, the more likely it is that the members of the mass public who share the political predispositions of those elites will adopt that position.

Zaller makes his case in the context of the Vietnam War, arguing that the decline in the support for that war was driven by a change in the balance of elite discourse across the 1960s. In the early phase of the war, when political elites were almost uniform in their support for the U.S. policy in Vietnam, Zaller found a monotonic relationship between political awareness and support for the war; those most attentive to elite discourse were most supportive of the current policy, regardless of their individual predispositions. Zaller terms this phenomenon the "mainstream pattern" of political support. On the other hand, in the later phases of the Vietnam War, when the mainstream consensus dissolved into elite disagreement, a "polarization pattern" emerged. Here, the effect of political awareness on support for the war was conditional on an individual's political values. Citizens attentive to politics followed the path of those leaders who shared their political views. For the Vietnam War, greater awareness led to higher levels of support among hawks and higher levels of opposition among doves. Zaller's story is not particular to Vietnam. [George] Belknap and [Angus] Campbell found a similar pattern of opinion during the Korean War; differences between Republican and Democratic identifiers were greatest among those respondents with high levels of political information, mirroring the corresponding differences among political elites.

The elite competition theory explicitly brings politics into the study of public opinion, allowing us to see how individuals with different political predilections react to different forms of elite discourse. At the same time, Zaller's explanation is somewhat incomplete. Zaller claims that the dynamics of opinion are driven exclusively by the net balance of partisan messages gleaned by individuals through political discourse. However, it is not clear if these messages are the only path to elite influence. Certainly, there are cases where political actors on both sides of a controversy provide persuasive messages, leading to polarized opinions among the mass public. But even in the absence of a balanced flow of discourse, individuals might have the information they need to come to a judgment regarding the fit between the policy options on the table and their political predispositions. Here the literature on cue taking and heuristics is instructive. Several studies have demonstrated that poorly informed citizens can make decisions that emulate the behavior of well-informed citizens by following the cues of politicians who share their political views. These studies suggest that even in the absence of specific policy messages, citizens can use the positions of elites to come to reasonable political decisions. We would therefore expect that citizens could use the positions of prominent elites as a reference point and decide whether to support or oppose a policy based on those positions, even in the absence of explicitly contradictory messages. In effect, citizens delegate the difficult process of arriving at an opinion on a complicated policy matter to trusted political experts. Presidents can serve as such cue givers, especially in the realm of foreign policy. For instance, if I am a Democrat, I need only know that George W. Bush supports a policy initiative to recognize that I should oppose such a course of action.

But to use this cue requires that citizens have knowledge of the positions of relevant political actors. Here is where Zaller's information-based theory can be brought into accord with cue-taking theories. As an individual's level of political information increases, their awareness of the positions of particular elites—and the distinctiveness of that position relative to other political actors—increases. Thus a pattern of opinion polarization could occur even in the absence of vocal opposition, provided a strong cue giver takes a clear position on that policy. As I will show below, this alternative mechanism of elite influence—what I call the elite cue theory—can explain the pattern of opinion in World War II, where both FDR and his Republican opponents took distinct positions. Moreover, unlike Zaller's original formulation, this theory can also explain the polarized pattern of opinion concerning the second war in Iraq, a situation where President Bush and Republican Party leaders took a strong pro-war position, but Democratic party leaders failed to express strong support or opposition.

EXPECTATIONS

Taken together, I have clear expectations regarding the relative role of events and elites in structuring opinion concerning war. Consistent with recent work on U.S. public opinion, but contrary to the expectations of scholars in the rationalist cost/benefit tradition, I expect that events will have little effect on the public's day-to-day judgments regarding the wisdom of war. This is not to say that events will never play a role in structuring opinion; certainly cataclysmic events, such as Pearl Harbor or the attacks of 9/11, can directly influence public opinion. But the events that many scholars of public opinion and war have examined—casualties and other mission indicators—play only a secondary role in determining public support for war. I therefore expect that knowledge of wartime events will not be widespread. Furthermore, correcting misperceptions of these events will have little effect on war support.

Conversely, I expect that patterns of elite discourse—the stated positions of leading Democrat and Republican politicians—will play a large role in determining public support for war. Individuals will use positions of prominent elites as a reference point, providing structure and guidance to opinions concerning war. Moreover, contrary to Zaller, I expect to find divergence without prominent elites speaking on both sides. The presence of prominent war-support cue givers can lead to a polarization of opinion as long as their political opponents do not also support war and vice versa. While citizens, in this view, do not rationally balance the costs and benefits of military action, neither do they blindly follow the messages disseminated by political elites. Rather they account for patterns of political leadership and partisan conflict to come to reasonable decisions that accord with their predispositions.

INDETERMINATE TESTS

Event-response theories, such as the casualties hypothesis (and its extensions) and the elite cue theory, which places the primary mechanism in the hands of partisan political actors, provide very different explanations for the dynamics of public support for war. These theories also carry very different normative implications: whether partisan political actors lead or follow opinion concerning war is a question with profound consequences for the practice of democracy. However, it has been difficult to assess the relative validity of the two approaches because scholars have focused on the Cold War and post–Cold War American experiences—namely, war failures and short-term military excursions. Consider, for instance, the Korea and Vietnam wars. Both the elite cue theory and the event-response theory predict that public support would decline as the conflicts unfolded. In the first view, as divisions among elites widened over time during both Korea and Vietnam, public opinion became polarized, thereby decreasing overall support for war. At the same time, since most scholars have used cumulative casualties as a measure of the war's cost, and cumulative casualties—as Gartner, Segura, and Wilkening note—are collinear with time, the casualties hypothesis predicts a secular decline in support for war over time. Thus, for both theories of public support, time is correlated with the explanatory variables of interest: real world events and how those events are discussed by elites. To distinguish the accuracy of these two theories, we need to look to new evidence.

In the rest of this [chapter], I draw upon [one case] to provide support for my elite cue theory. I present evidence from two surveys I conducted concerning the war in Iraq to reveal that citizens do not incorporate information about wartime events into their political judgments. I find instead that partisanship and attentiveness to politics can explain patterns of opinion polarization as my theory of elite cue taking implies.

THE WAR IN IRAQ

In March of 2003, the United States invaded Iraq, beginning a period of combat operations that continued through the 2006 election and beyond. Two facts about this war are particularly important for present purposes. First, dissemination of correct information about wartime events—especially the ongoing count of war dead—was prevalent in the media. We can therefore surmise that any misreporting in levels of war deaths by citizens is the result of faulty perceptions of reports of war deaths on the part of citizens, not faulty reports of the number of deaths by the media. Second, the positions of prominent cue givers regarding support for war were clear. As commander in chief, President Bush was strongly associated with support for the conflict. For much of this period, Republican Party elites followed his lead. The position of Democrats on this issue was less clear. A review of *Newsweek* articles on Iraq from February 2002 onward indicates that Democrats lacked a clear agenda for how to proceed on the Iraq question. For months after the initial invasion, there was limited dissent among Democrats. In the presidential campaign the notable dissenters on Iraq—Howard Dean and Wesley Clark—were quickly pushed aside by John Kerry, a senator who voted to authorize war in Iraq and, in line with other prominent Democrats, never took a clear position against the war. The question, then, is: Given the prominence of relevant information in media, which factor best explains variation in support for the war: casualties, as the event-response theory would suggest, or elite positions concerning the wisdom of that conflict, as the elite cue theory contends?

To answer this question, I conducted an experimental survey in the summer of 2004. My Iraq War Casualty Survey, conducted from July 23 to August 2, 2004, by Knowledge Networks, asked a random portion of a nationally representative sample of respondents the following:

> Please give your best guess to this next question, even if you are not sure of the correct answer. As you know, the United States is currently involved in a war in Iraq. Do you happen to know how many soldiers of the U.S. military have been killed in Iraq since the fighting began in March 2003?

At first glance, it appears that the public was informed about the level of troop deaths in Iraq. The mean estimate of deaths in the sample was 952 deaths, while the median response was 900 deaths. Both of these figures are extraordinarily close to the true casualty count, which rose from 901 to 915 over the span of the survey. The accuracy of the median respondent, however, disregards large variation in the casualty estimates. Respondents gave answers ranging from 0 deaths to 130,000 deaths. Even setting aside the extreme responses (casualty guesses under 10 and over 10,000), the standard deviation of the casualty estimate was 802.

A simple tabulation of the estimates illuminates the pattern of responses to the casualty question. Underestimating the casualty level of the war is a qualitatively different response than overestimating casualties. Thus, simply predicting the casualty estimate, or the absolute error of the estimate, is not informative. Instead, I created a three-category casualty estimate scale. I scored those respondents who estimated the number of war deaths to be between 801 and 1,015 (the true estimate +/- 100 deaths) as "correct." Those who gave an estimate of 800 or lower were scored as "underestimators," while those who guessed higher than 1,015 were considered "overestimators." The modal response (47 percent) was a correct answer. However, nearly as many respondents (42 percent) underestimated the number of war deaths (11 percent overestimated the number of deaths). The pattern of knowledge of casualties found in this survey extends to knowledge of the rate of American deaths in Iraq from around the same time. The Pew Research Center conducted a survey in September 2004 that asked respondents, "What's your impression about what's happened in Iraq over the past month? Has the number of American military casualties been higher, lower, or about the same as in other recent months?" Though a plurality of 46 percent gave the correct answer of "higher," a majority of respondents either gave an incorrect answer or were unable to provide an answer to the question. These knowledge levels certainly compare favorably to knowledge of other political facts, such as the percentage of budget devoted to foreign aid, but given the prominence of war deaths in the news, these studies demonstrate that even in a high salience environment, great variation existed in knowledge about events on the ground in Iraq.

More important for the purposes of this [chapter], this variation was not random; elite cues played a significant role in biasing the recall of knowledge. I examined the determinants of perceived level of casualties using measures of political engagement and partisan political leanings. I ran a multinomial logit (MNL) using the three-category casualty estimate scale (underestimator/correct/overestimator) as the dependent variable and the respondents' partisanship to account for the patterns of cue taking from partisan political actors. I also included as independent variables the amount of attention the respondent paid to news about Iraq, how much the respondent watched Fox News, and the respondent's general political information, education, and gender. The result of this analysis is presented in table 6.1. The coefficients in the second column are the effect of a given variable on the probability of underestimating the number of casualties versus correctly estimating the number of casualties. In the third column, the estimates are the effect on the probability of being an "overestimator," as compared to giving the correct answer.

Since the MNL coefficients can be difficult to interpret directly, I generated predicted probabilities of choosing the different response categories for the extreme values of the partisanship for the "typical" member of the public. These results are presented in table 6.2. As expected, compared to strong Republicans, strong Democrats are less likely to underestimate and are slightly more likely to overestimate casualty levels. By way of comparison, the effect of partisanship on the probability of underestimating casualty levels is roughly equal to the effect of moving from low information to high information. This finding is consistent with the Pew data on casualty rates described above. Among independents, 47 percent correctly stated that casualty rates were higher in the current month than in the previous month.

Table 6.1.   MNL Analysis of Determinants of Estimates of War Deaths

	Correct Answer vs. Underestimate	
Variable	*Coefficient (SE)*	*Coefficient (SE)*
Constant	1.67 (.45)*	−.08 (.70)
Information	−.94 (.31)*	−1.44 (.48)*
Education	.10 (.09)	.06 (.15)
Gender	.03 (.18)	−.02 (.29)
Follow Iraq News	−2.06 (.38)*	−1.33 (.61)*
Watch Fox News	−.14 (.53)	.42 (.85)
Party Identification (Strong Dem High)	−.51 (.26)*	.11 (.43)

N = 621.
LL = -544.58.
*=p < .05.

Table 6.2.   Predicted Probability of Causality Estimates

Information	Pr (Underestimate)	Pr (Correct Answer)	Pr (Overestimate)
Low Information	.51	.31	.18
High Information	.36	.56	.07
Difference	*–.15*	*+.25*	*–.11*
Strong Republican	.48	.44	.08
Strong Democrat	.35	.54	.12
Difference	*–.13*	*+.10*	*+.04*

Democrats were even more likely to say that casualties were higher—54 percent gave the correct answer—and Republicans were less likely to say that casualties were increasing—only 36 percent gave the correct answer. In short, perceptions of war deaths are influenced not only by information and engagement with political news, but also by the individual's political predispositions. Having demonstrated that the respondents' perceptions of events in the Iraq war were influenced by partisanship, I next move to the more important question of whether the casualty estimates had any influence on options concerning war.

Embedded in the Iraq war survey was an experiment in which one half of those respondents who were asked to estimate how many soldiers died in Iraq were then told, "Many people don't know the answer to this question, but according to the latest estimates, 901 soldiers have been killed in Iraq since the fighting began in March 2003." In other words, one-half of the respondents who were asked to estimate the number of American deaths were given a "treatment" of correct information. This experimental design allows me to compare levels of support for the war between two comparable groups: (1) the respondents in the "estimate war deaths" condition who underestimate casualties but were not told the correct number of war deaths; and (2) the respondents in the "corrected" condition who underestimate war deaths but were then told the number of U.S. soldiers who died. I can make a similar comparison for respondents who overestimate casualties. This is a powerful comparison, because the "correct information" treatment was randomly assigned. The only difference between the "estimate" group and the "corrected" group is that respondents in the "corrected" condition were subsequently told the true casualty rates. Thus, by comparing these two groups, I can assess the effect of introducing the correct information on support for war for individuals who are similarly misinformed about casualty rates.

I measured attitudes toward the Iraq war with two common measures of war support. The first question asked, "Do you think the U.S. made the right decision or the wrong decision in using military force against Iraq?" The second question asked, "All in all, considering the costs to the United States

Table 6.3.   Effect of Information Treatment on Support for War in Iraq

Among Underestimators

Did the United States Make the Right Decision in Using Military Force against Iraq?	United States Made Right Decision
Estimate War Deaths Condition	52%
Corrected Information Condition	56%
N = 252; x2(l) = .40 Pr =.53	
Has the Current War in Iraq Been Worth Fighting?	Worth Fighting
Estimate War Deaths Condition	42%
Corrected Information Condition	47%
N = 253; x2(l) = .71 Pr = .40	

Among Overestimators

Did the United States Make the Right Decision in Using Military Force against Iraq?	United States Made Right Decision
Estimate War Deaths Condition	58%
Corrected Information Condition	58%
N =57; x2(l) = .00 Pr = .95	
Has the Current War in Iraq Been Worth Fighting?	Worth Fighting
Estimate War Deaths Condition	42%
Corrected Information Condition	48%
N =57; x2(l) = .26 Pr = .61	

versus the benefits to the United States, do you think the current war with Iraq has been worth fighting, or not?" The results of these analyses are presented in table 6.3. There were no reliably significant differences between the respondents in the two conditions in either a substantive or a statistical sense. Furthermore, the direction of the treatment effect is in the incorrect direction for both the "worth fighting" and the "right decision" questions— respondents who were told that the number of war deaths was larger than they had believed were *more* supportive of the war (though the difference is small and statistically insignificant by a wide margin). Among overestimators, the effect of the treatment was in the expected direction for the "worth fighting" question only and is statistically insignificant.

THE HUMAN AND MONETARY COSTS OF WAR

One of the best-known findings from the survey research literature is that seemingly minor alterations in the wording of particular questions can lead to large changes in the answers respondents give to surveys. Recent advances in theories of the survey response have helped researchers to predict when opinion changes might occur. As Zaller argues, "Individuals do not typically possess 'true attitudes' on issues, as conventional theorizing assumes, but a series of partially independent and often inconsistent ones." Answers to survey questions are, therefore, in part determined by the balance of arguments made salient by survey questions.

Bringing additional pieces of information—to use Zaller's terminology, "considerations"—to mind alters the base of information that individuals use to come to particular decisions. From this point of view, highlighting negative information—such as the human and monetary costs of war—should cause individuals to focus on the downside of war. In the aggregate, questions that contain information about casualties and the costs of war should therefore yield lower levels of support for war than questions that omit such information.

Somewhat surprisingly, in two separate experiments, I did not find this predicted pattern of results. The design of the 2004 Iraq War Casualty Survey allowed me to directly test the effect of introducing casualty information on support for war. The Iraq War Casualty Survey was a 2 x 2 experimental design. Only one-half of the respondents were asked to estimate the number of casualties, as described above. The other half of the sample permitted a further experimental test. In the "control" condition of the survey, respondents were neither asked nor given any information concerning the casualty rates in Iraq; they were simply asked their level of support for the conflict. In the "information only" condition, respondents were not asked to provide an estimate of war deaths, but they were told the correct casualty rates. I found no statistically significant difference in the answers to the war support questions between these two conditions. Making salient a negative consideration—the scope of the human cost of war—and providing specific information about that cost did not change the aggregate shape of opinion on the war.

In the fall of 2005, I collected additional data to assess the effects of event-specific information on opinions concerning the Iraq war. Respondents to an omnibus survey were randomly assigned to one of six conditions: a "baseline" condition, a "standard survey question" condition, or one of four information conditions.

> *Form 1* (baseline): "All in all, do you think the war with Iraq was worth fighting, or not?"
> *Form 2* (standard survey question): "All in all, considering the costs to the United States versus the benefits to the United States, do you think the war with Iraq was worth fighting, or not?"
> *Form 3*: "As you may know, since the war in Iraq began in March 2003, many American soldiers have been killed. All in all, considering the costs to the United States versus the benefits to the United States, do you think the war with Iraq was worth fighting, or not?"

Form 4: "As you may know, since the war in Iraq began in March 2003, almost 2,000 American soldiers have been killed. All in all, considering the costs to the United States versus the benefits to the United States, do you think the war with Iraq was worth fighting, or not?"

Form 5: "As you may know, since the war in Iraq began in March 2003, the United States has spent a large amount of money on operations in Iraq. All in all, considering the costs to the United States versus the benefits to the United States, do you think the war with Iraq was worth fighting, or not?"

Form 6: "As you may know, since the war in Iraq began in March 2003, the United States has spent almost 200 billion dollars on operations in Iraq. All in all, considering the costs to the United States versus the benefits to the United States, do you think the war with Iraq was worth fighting, or not?"

The first (baseline) condition presented a neutral stimulus; respondents were simply asked whether or not they support the war. In the second (standard survey question) condition, respondents were explicitly asked to consider the costs and benefits of the Iraqi invasion, following the convention of poll questions asked by the *Washington Post* and Gallup. Respondents in the other four conditions were asked forms of the questions that highlighted specific information about the human and financial costs of the Iraq war, in either general (forms 3 and 5) or specific (forms 4 and 6) terms.

Given the vast amounts of research on question wording effects, we would expect to find large differences across conditions based on the types of information presented in the question. But this is not the case. In fact, as table 6.4 demonstrates, there are almost no differences in levels of support across conditions.

Why, in the face of strong negative information, did these treatments have no effect? The lack of an effect is probably not because respondents had already incorporated the information into their judgments. As the 2004

Table 6.4.   Effect of Information Treatment on Support for War in Iraq

Has the Current War in Iraq Been Worth Fighting	*United States Made Right Decision*
Baseline	40%
Standard Survey	42%
Many Soldiers Died	43%
2,000 Soldiers Died	41%
U.S. Spent a Lot of Money	40%
U.S. Spent $200 Billion	37%

N = 1,168; x2(10) = 9.48 Pr = .49.

Iraq War Survey demonstrates, many respondents did not know the correct casualty figures. Instead, I did not find substantive difference among the conditions because respondents had already made up their minds on Iraq. Citizens discounted new information in favor of more important considerations—their attachments to particular political leaders.

ELITE CUES

Though event-response theories cannot explain differences in support for war, models that account for the influence of partisan cues strongly predict patterns of war support. Recall that the elite cue theory hypothesizes that members of the mass public will look to prominent political actors as guides for their positions on the war. In the context of Iraq, the Bush administration's clear stance on the war—and the general unity of the Republican Party for much of this time—provides such a guide. Even though Democratic leaders had not taken a consistent and strong antiwar stance at the time of the survey, both Republicans and Democrats who were attentive to politics could use the strong support of the war by George Bush and Republican party leaders as a cue to influence their position on the war.

As noted above, partisanship has a larger effect on support for the war than does casualty information. More tellingly, support for the Iraq conflict followed the polarization pattern, as the elite cue theory predicts. The "polarization pattern" of political support emerges when prominent political actors take a clear position on the necessity of military action and their counterparts across the political aisle do not follow suit. Under these circumstances, citizens who are more informed will follow those political actors who share their views. If, on the other hand, elite discourse is unified in support of intervention, public opinion should be characterized by the "mainstream pattern"; more informed citizens should be more supportive of government policy, regardless of their political predispositions. To determine whether the mainstream pattern or the polarization pattern best characterizes public opinion, we need individual-level measures of three quantities: support for the war, political predispositions, and levels of political information (which, following Zaller, proxies attentiveness to elite discourse). The Iraq War Casualty Survey contains all of these quantities. Following Zaller, I ran a probit of the measures of support for war on partisanship, information, the interaction between information and partisanship, and several control variables. [*The full regression results are omitted here.—Ed.*] Figure 6.1 presents the results of an analysis of the effects of political information levels on support for the war. As the figure demonstrates, as a modal respondent's attention to political discourse increases, he adopts diametrically opposed positions on the war, depending on whether he is a Democrat or a Republican.

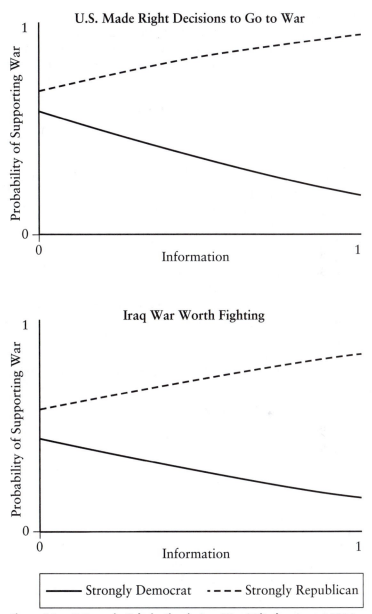

Figure 6.1.   Patterns in Polarization in Iraq War Attitudes, August 2004

Although there is a gap between Democrats and Republicans at the lowest information levels, this gap grows as information levels increase, indicating that differences in elite positions are reflected in individuals' positions on war.

All told, these results provide support for elite-centered views of war support. Perceptions of war deaths are influenced by the respondent's partisan attachments. Furthermore, perceptions of war deaths do not influence attitudes toward war, and correcting respondents' misperceptions has little effect on support for war. Whatever inconsistent effects arise from presenting correct information pale in comparison to the effects of partisanship.

DISCUSSION QUESTIONS

1. What is the usual "conventional wisdom" that is relied upon to explain the American public's support for war?
2. What is the "casualties hypothesis" in explaining war support?
3. According to the author, what are some problems with "event-response" theories of public support for war?
4. How does the competition among political elites affect public opinion and support or opposition to war?
5. What is the "elite cue" theory of public opinion?
6. What are the expectations that the author has regarding the interaction of events and elites in structuring opinion concerning support for war?
7. How does the author go about testing the impact of events, information, and partisanship with the data from the second Iraq war?
8. How does the author show that partisanship is more important than other factors in support or opposition to the second Iraq war?

7

How Media Limit Accountability in Foreign Policymaking

Iraq and Beyond

Robert M. Entman

In November 2006, the majority of U.S. voters delivered what was generally seen as a clear message of opposition to the Iraq War, as Democrats unexpectedly took control of the U.S. House and Senate. When he delivered a foreign policy address on January 7, 2007, President George W. Bush himself admitted that the tactics followed for over three and a half years after the end of "major combat operations" required major alteration (Abramowitz, Wright, and Tyson 2007). Yet, rather than reducing U.S. involvement in what had become a bitter Iraqi civil war, the Bush administration decided to escalate U.S. involvement by sending *more* troops in what was optimistically framed as a "surge." How might we explain the disconnect between apparent public opinion and the new policy? Although surely not the only factor in producing the apparent breach, the media played an important role.

We suggest the media limited the influence of public opinion on U.S. foreign policy (cf. Page with Bouton 2006; Sobel 2001) by creating an "accountability gap" that disconnected news coverage from policy outcomes. Similar gaps open up during most wars. We explore what seems to be the media's difficulty learning from past missteps, and their tendency to reenact even acknowledged mistakes from covering past wars—creating accountability gaps anew. This has the important consequence of reducing incentives for American officials to learn from and correct *their* errors by changing flawed policies.

This chapter thus serves as a case study of the relationships among media framing, foreign policy decisions, and public opinion in the United States.

Robert Entman thanks Prof. Emma Briant, Sheffield University, for her assistance in revising the present paper.

Lessons all three players (media, officials, citizens) might have learned from the early failures of U.S. Iraq policy were not applied to later Iraq policy decisions. This made it unlikely that the lessons would be generalized even further along in time, for instance when officials had to decide what, if anything, to do about the Libyan or Syrian civil wars.

THE ACCOUNTABILITY GAP

What we refer to here as the "accountability gap" is a predictable pattern of press coverage around policy developments that news organizations seem doomed repeatedly to create by deferring to the White House's framing of events no matter how often it has misled. The administration's continued capacity to dominate foreign news framing is boosted by the media's falling interest; as costs of war accumulate, they become less novel, diminishing their news value. So, as casualties and other consequences of policy in Iraq became routine, their magnitude and cultural resonance in the media declined. Figure 7.1 shows a graphical illustration.

Although the accountability gap is rooted in several news practices that seem more or less immutable whatever the specific foreign policy problem, during war itself, this novelty norm is critical. For some significant period, with occasional perturbations due to unusually costly events, we can expect that the worse the situation, and the greater the accumulated costs of the policy, the *less* well news organizations hold officials accountable for them.

We show this pattern predicted by the accountability gap in Entman, Livingston, and Kim (2009) through media treatment of casualties in Iraq, perhaps the most emotional, simple, and presumably newsworthy measure

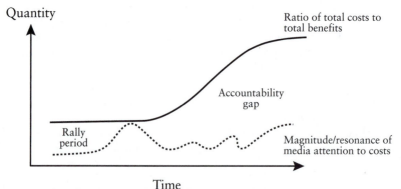

Figure 7.1. The Accountability Gap

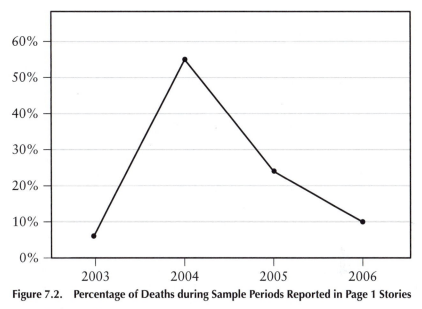

Figure 7.2.   Percentage of Deaths during Sample Periods Reported in Page 1 Stories

Source: Washington Post.

of policy cost. In this example, attention to bad news declined, while attention to apparently good news—or at least news that fits the administration's preferred frame—remained relatively high. Figure 7.2 displays the *Washington Post*'s page-one coverage of casualties peaking in 2004 and then declining sharply the following two years. The disparity in media reactions illustrates the accountability gap and news organizations' apparent tendencies to convey the administration's frames and thus its preferred problem definition and remedy, while allocating comparatively little attention to news that undermines the policy.

FRAMING THE SURGE

Our systematic content analysis of *New York Times* depictions of President Bush's surge plan between January 9 and March 15, 2007 supports this accountability gap hypothesis. It revealed a marked preference for the White House frame, even though the surge provoked criticism from policymaking elites, public intellectuals, newspaper columnists, military officials, and Iraqi political leaders. Not surprisingly, polls also indicated strong public opposition. One week following the president's address, virtually every major national opinion poll—including those by CBS News, ABC/ *Washington Post*, CNN, Pew/NPR, AP/Ipsos, and FOX News—showed that the majority of Americans disapproved of the proposed troop increase and ranked the war in Iraq as the No. 1, or "most important," problem facing the nation. These were conditions that should theoretically enable virtual parity between the White House and those promoting oppositional frames. There existed widespread and vocal elite dissent against this policy change, a newly elected Democratic majority in the Congress, bipartisan public opposition, and an attentive public. Nor was the policy decision in question— whether to send more U.S. troops—complicated or inaccessible, features that can constrain foreign policy debates (Baum 2004; Woods 1997).

The ensuing political debate over the surge made an especially compelling case for observing frame dynamics because of the White House's skill in setting the parameters of remedy endorsement. In his speech, Bush not only advanced a clear remedy—a troop increase—he also *prioritized the importance of offering a remedy* by highlighting the opposition's failure to do so, pointing out that those with different views "have a responsibility to explain how the path they propose would be more likely to succeed."

President Bush then proceeded to characterize an opposition remedy that called for any level of troop withdrawal as both counterproductive and dangerous: "To step back now would force a collapse of the Iraqi government, tear that country apart, and result in mass killings on an unimaginable scale. Such a scenario would result in our troops being forced to stay in Iraq even longer, and confront an enemy that is even more lethal." This claim achieved two powerful functions: first, it preempted an opposition frame that was clearly incompatible with White House goals; second, and more impressively, it implied that the opposition remedy *was* to quickly withdraw U.S. troops, that they were unaware of the dangers of a hasty retreat, and suggested even to Bush's critics that the new Democratic Congress could not be trusted with these dangerous realities of the current war. This instantly put the Democrats on the defensive, a very difficult position from which to advance a coherent counterframe. Furthermore, Briant (2015) emphasizes how a new sophisticated National Security Council (NSC) strategy sought to control and steer media and political debates on the surge. A so-called Fusion Cell saturated as many channels as possible (including media, think tanks, congressional staff members, and government personnel) with the administration's line or supportive third party information. Public opinion on the surge was seen as unhelpfully negative—the administration recognized that "nobody would believe anything Bush said at that time" (McCarty, quoted in Briant 2015: 168). The strategy in particular aimed to get "responsible sceptics" and "thought leaders" to change position (McCarty, quoted in Briant 2015: 168–69). NSC personnel later concluded that "armed with first hand insights" from visiting the country and the information that had been provided, "we found that the sceptics moderated, or in some cases, changed viewpoints" (McCarty and Pfeifle 2011: 8 quoted in Briant 2015: 169).

Any opposition frame would now need to advance a counterpolicy in order to be considered valid—simply rejecting the surge policy, unaccompanied by an action-oriented remedy that addressed the "unacceptable" situation in Iraq, was not enough. This presented an imbalanced challenge with respect to skill, opportunity, and the structure of American government. The White House is able to articulate policies in a unitary fashion, while the Congress must subject its policies to debate, public scrutiny, criticism, and compromise before formal passage, and debate often continues even after a bill is passed. Also, blocking the surge on its own merits—for no other reason than because it is bad policy—is as legitimate a policy option as an alternative remedy. It is poor logic to assume that "doing something" was necessarily preferable to "*not* doing something" in wartime Iraq, but the latter would not present a viable challenge to the White House frame. A leader who calls for not doing something fails to generate the emotional gratification and potential political payoff that accrues, at least in the short run, to one who whips up support for an active remedy.

For these reasons, our content analysis focused on the representation, by paragraph, of the White House (WH) frame's preferred problem definition (PD) and remedy endorsement (R)—the most influential of the four framing functions identified by Entman (2004)—compared to that of the counterframe. (The causal analysis and moral judgment aspects of framing are not unimportant, but they are less actionable than the problem definition and remedy endorsement aspects, much less likely to be subject of opinion polls, and therefore send less clear signals to policymakers.) We distinguish between *Strong* (S) and *Weak* (w) frames based upon the presence (or absence) of PD and R aspects that support one side of the debate. Strongly framed paragraphs include a problem definition and associated remedy; weakly framed paragraphs include only one or none of these two primary framing functions.

We analyzed coverage of the Iraq War surge debate from January 9, 2007, the day before its announcement, to March 15, 2007 in the *New York Times*. We included news and opinions sections, but excluded letters to the editor and arts reviews. Using Nexis, we searched for framing words—those words that have the capacity to stimulate support or opposition to the sides in a political conflict—to isolate articles and transcript segments.[1] Coding of frames was done by relevant paragraph, with a paragraph defined as containing at least fifty words. A relevant paragraph includes at least one of the following search terms: "surge," "escalate/escalation," "buildup," or "increase" *made in reference to* Bush's January 2007 decision to deploy more soldiers in Iraq.[2]

WHITE HOUSE VERSUS OPPOSITION-SUPPORTIVE
FRAMING ASPECTS

This analysis focuses on whether each paragraph contained zero, one, or two aspects of both the White House and Opposition problem definition and remedies, with those containing both for one side considered "Strong" for that side:

White House problem definition: PD_{WH} = Problem defined as: A military problem, lack of security forces, lack of U.S. troops. When defined as Iraq itself, problem can be: general situation/violence, Iraqi insurgency, terrorists, sectarian violence resulting from discrete events (e.g., 2005 Samarra mosque bombing), illegal Shi'ite militias, al-Sadr/Mahdi army, or external threats to the Iraqi government. Can also be defined as political opposition/Congress for not enacting the White House plan.

Opposition problem definition: PD_{OPP} = Problem defined as: American casualties, Iraqi casualties, troop escalation, U.S. occupation, Iraq as a political problem. When defined as Iraq itself, problem can be: Civil war or near-civil war, Iraq-as-Vietnam, naturally occurring or seemingly organic sectarian violence, Prime Minister al-Maliki, Iraqi parliament or governmental corruption.

White House Remedy: R_{WH} = Remedy: Continued and increased American troop presence, send requested troops and allow surge to take effect, demonstration of political will. Opposition Remedy: R_{OPP} = Remedy: Phased redeployment or decrease of U.S. troops, immediate and/or complete withdrawal of U.S. troops, calls for specific diplomatic initiatives in the Middle East, i.e. including Iran and/or Syria, multilateralism with regional and coalition forces.

Paragraphs containing causal and/or moral judgment aspects (the two weakest framing functions) were noted.

Table 7.1 displays the results. The disparity of frame strength between the White House and opposition sides was dramatic. Of the 519 total paragraphs, 81 percent supported at least one of the four aspects of the WH frame, and 73 percent supported at least one aspect of the OPP frame. However, when broken down into strong and weak frames, this balance disappears, with a strong administration frame (one containing its problem definition and remedy) supported in 77 percent (320) of all paragraphs, and a strong opposition frame supported in just 8 percent (30 paragraphs).

There were also far more strong WH-only framed paragraphs than strong OPP-only paragraphs, with 129, or 25 percent, of all paragraphs containing *only* a strong WH frame, and just 20, or 4 percent, featuring a strong OPP frame independently. There was a fair share of neutral or balanced weak-frame paragraphs (15 percent), but just one balanced strong-frame paragraph containing both White House and Oppositional problem definitions and remedies (rounded down to 0 percent in the data set).

Table 7.1.   Balance of White House versus Opposition Frame

	White House	Opposition	TOTAL
Any of four framing functions represented in paragraph	418 (.81)	379 (.73)	519 (1.0)
Strong framing paragraphs: include both problem definition and remedy	320 (.77)	30 (.08)	350 (.67)

Cells display number and percentage of all paragraphs (in parentheses). *Figures do not add to 1 due to paragraphs w/aspects of both WH and OPP frames.*

These cases together reveal the very opposite tendency of what many administration officials, including President Bush and Vice President Cheney, claimed, that media neglected good news and emphasized bad news.

WHY THE ACCOUNTABILITY GAP?

Why have America's major news media seemed incapable of applying the lessons of their own histories, once again opening up an accountability gap in Iraq as in the Gulf War, Vietnam, and other cases before (cf. Andersen 2007; Bennett and Paletz 1994; Entman, Aday, and Livingston 2012; Hallin 1986)? The short answer is that the construction of each novel policy problem passes through a stable configuration of forces acting on all national news organizations. Journalists respond to these predictable pressures in predictable ways. The responses are deeply rooted in commercial necessity and professional custom, and are reinforced by their very unspoken, implicit quality.

In Iraq, the president's ability to frame progress and hope swamped the unconnected sporadic news about arising negative events ranging from attacks to government reports to investigative scoops. The administration retained its ability to orchestrate dire intelligence warnings and crises, "purple finger" election rituals, other alleged milestones of progress, official visits to Iraq suffused with images of cheering Americans in uniform, and the like. These appear prominently in the media in terms that resonate with important cultural values. They made big news in part because all were new *happenings involving the most powerful American officials*, however familiar the scripts, and however dubious the officials' claims. They formed a coherent and reassuring argument that all will be well, which is much easier for everyone—journalists, governing elites, and the public—to swallow than the counterargument that all will be—as it turned out to be—rather terrible. Continued and perhaps inevitably heavy reliance on administration and military sources for wartime information permitted the government not only to keep on weaving an integrated story, but, as survey data suggest, to achieve some traction with it right up until the last part of 2006 and beyond.

Among the less informed, less attentive, and ideological Americans, media coverage interweaving assurances of progress (such as the election of Prime Minister Zarqawi) and scary warnings of threats (Iranian weapons and terrorists "following us home" if the United States withdrew from Iraq) with near-daily but disconnected reports of mounting costs, and neglect of more profoundly negative news not rooted in daily events (cf. Livingston and Bennett 2003 on event-driven news), ultimately failed to produce clear oppositional signals from public opinion as late as the autumn of 2006 if not beyond. Even by Spring 2007, survey evidence remained murky enough to discourage opponents in Congress from uniting around a failure frame built around the following elements:

1. The Iraq War could not be won by force of arms.
2. Iraq had little to do initially with the war on terrorism (though it came to because of the chaotic conditions created by the invasion itself).
3. Therefore, the invasion of Iraq undermined counterterrorism efforts and American security.
4. The best way to "support the troops" and minimize the spread of terrorism would be (as the government's own National Intelligence Estimate [2007] intimated) to end the U.S. mission expeditiously.

This counterframe was not the only one possible nor does it exhaust all potential elements of a cogent counterframe. We also do not wish to suggest that the administration's arguments for staying the course should not have been heard. Our point is merely that considering events in Iraq, elite dissent, and escalating costs, the administration obtained far more than parity with an oppositional frame, opening up the accountability gap.

A coherent, resonant frame that emphasized policy failure would have potential significance for accountability exerting independent pressure on elites *irrespective of any impacts on public opinion poll responses*. Even if ordinary citizens become less interested in bad news as time elapses, the paucity of the media images themselves may reduce pressure on officials to consider changing problematic policy. We suggest this is because elites infer current and predict future public opinion and the potential for opposition based on media reporting of the evidence of failure, not merely on what polls are saying (Entman 2004).

Continuing opposition in Congress might have reduced the administration's ability to shape news through asserting that critical coverage originated in the media's liberal bias and lack of patriotism (cf. Bennett,

Lawrence, and Livingston 2007). Yet the media environment rendered the political threats to potential elite opponents more salient and credible than they might otherwise have been. Throughout 2004–2006 and well into 2007, no matter the events on the ground, the administration skillfully deployed images and rhetorical claims to fit media needs, while the congressional opposition only fitfully raised individual voices of criticism rather than a unified critique. Journalists then used scattered rather than coherent newsworthy quotes to counterbalance the administration and the undeniably negative event news from Iraq was not organized around an alternative problem definition (the government's war policy itself) and remedy (cessation of U.S. involvement as rapidly as feasible). Such imbalance continues as long as the press relies on Congress as the main legitimate source of oppositional framing.[3] The absence of a vivid, continuing media counterframe reduced the clout and political courage of elite opponents, which in turn degraded their newsworthiness and thus the visibility and coherence of counterframing (cf. Entman and Page 1994) in the media.

These relationships help to answer the questions of why policy change took so long, and why it took the form of an escalation rather than withdrawal plan. Politicians favoring an alternative problem definition and remedy had good reason to anticipate a backlash for seeming unsupportive of the troops. The same fear apparently kept the Democratic majority in Congress from using all the tools at its disposal to force troop withdrawals throughout 2007, apparent public opinion notwithstanding.

An intriguing CNN/Gallup poll supports the latter point. Despite all the bad news from Iraq, a substantial survey majority of 57 percent felt the President Bush administration "strongly supports the troops" in May 2007, several months into a surge that a (different?) majority said they opposed. Only 31 percent said the Democrats strongly supported the troops.[4] War opponents had apparently not punched through with a convincing message that "supporting" troops meant ending the war rather than extending their tours of duty (as the Bush administration did, from twelve to fifteen months) and deploying soldiers and Marines to second and third tours of duty in Iraq (Jonsson, 2007). Moreover, only a minority (41 percent) of respondents indicated they thought the war was lost as of May 2007, with a majority still believing in the possibility of victory. Poll evidence continued to indicate limited diffusion of an oppositional frame that saw Iraq as a lost cause damaging to the fight against terrorism—despite support for that conclusion from the NIE and Iraq Study Group among other authoritative sources. Moreover, poll data offered disorganized, difficult-to-interpret information to elites that reflected the weakness and disorganization of the oppositional frame in the media even as it reinforced the disincentives for elites to invest political capital in organizing that opposing narrative.[5] This in turn bolstered the tendency for government to persist in its policy, any lessons of history notwithstanding.

CONCLUSION

As suggested by the 9:1 ratio of strong pro-administration framing in the *New York Times*'s early coverage of the surge, the administration could still supervise the *framing* of Iraq news, even if they found it impossible to stanch the flow of *negative daily event reporting* on the war. They continued to dominate the narrative even as continuing plot developments failed to fit. Media framing might well have helped to constrain the scope, depth, and coherence of opposition, maintaining sufficient freedom of maneuver for the Bush administration to mount its surge policy despite heavy political opposition and the apparent majority support for a reversal of course.

Administration influence over framing is of course inevitable, and to some degree desirable. We do not contend that in the real world it would be feasible for the dotted curve of counterframed news to precisely mirror the solid curve of rising costs in figure 7.1. Bound by objectivity rules, mainstream media cannot place many stories featuring fully elaborated, oppositional frames on page one or the lead position of newscasts. Still, when the facts on the ground suggest as much, accountability would arguably benefit from circulating an overarching narrative of policy failure and cessation to compete with the narrative of progress and possibility coming out of a White House that cannot afford to admit its mistakes (on the importance of competing frames, see Druckman and Chong 2007; Entman 2004). America's ideologically confined two-party system may also be at issue and future research could explore whether accountability gaps are larger in the United States and the conditions in multiparty systems provide more opportunities for counterframing (cf. Hallin and Mancini 2004; Sheafer and Wolfsfeld 2009). Although it has been argued that what we call the accountability gap is temporary, as citizens become more informed over several years about the costs and effects of foreign policy decisions (Baum and Groeling 2010), there is a logical problem with this sanguine conclusion. It might well be true that by, say, 2009, most citizens considered the Iraq War a policy mistake (though far from all, as nearly one-third of Americans in 2012 still believed Saddam Hussein had weapons of mass destruction; Lewis 2014). This was however far too late to sanction the administration that made the mistake, and worse, far too late to save the United States $4–6 trillion it will eventually spend on the failed Iraq and Afghanistan wars (Bilmes 2013)—or the American and foreign lives lost. That accountability gaps shrink over enough time is almost axiomatic, but usually this doesn't happen quickly enough to effect policy substantially. Worse, as we've seen, it also doesn't seem to lead media to apply lessons in future war news.

Might this case study apply only to Iraq? Although admittedly no systematic study has replicated the present one in other cases and confirmed similar accountability gaps, evidence suggests the syndrome persists. Debate over the US and NATO intervention in Libya included remarkably little sophisticated analysis of the causes and consequences of violence, or exactly what would happen after a purportedly humanitarian policy deposed that country's dictator, Muammar Qadhafi (McQuinn 2013; Nuruzzaman 2015). News coverage of America's drone attacks against terrorists slanted toward support, especially in comparison to other countries' media (Sheets, Rowling, and Jones 2015).

A realistic goal for journalism in the United States might be to more self-consciously adjust proportionality. Although many forces mentioned here and throughout the research literature (Bennett, Lawrence, and Livingston 2007; Entman 2004) militate against such an intentional calibration, some marginal improvement in the *proportions* of war coverage devoted to a failure frame seems conceivable, even if news organizations continue privileging high-visibility stories originated by the administration. To be fair, what constitutes failure and therefore success is often ambiguous—or won't become clear for a long time, often until after a president is out of office. Still, the flaws in conception, planning, and execution of U.S. Iraq policy were well documented in long-form journalism (Isikoff and Corn 2006; Packer 2005; Ricks 2006). This suggests it might be possible for journalists to make policy consequences slightly clearer in real time, and to hold government a bit more accountable in the daily news reports and editorial comment that help to shape the political environment, policymaking, and, ultimately, history itself.

DISCUSSION QUESTIONS

1. What is meant by the "accountability gap"? Who are the participants in this gap?
2. How was the accountability gap evident in Iraq casualties in 2004?
3. What period did Entman examine the accountability gap, and how did he proceed to do so?
4. In what way did the Bush administration establish "media frames" over the Iraq "surge" strategy and seek to thwart an opposition frame to this event?
5. How would you summarize the results of Entman's analysis of the *New York Times* regarding the Iraq surge?

6. What are two or three factors that might explain the media's accountability gap?
7. How would a potent counterframe assist accountability in this case?
8. What is one policy recommendation that Entman advances in his conclusion?

NOTES

1. Stories were pulled from Nexis using the following terms: [Headline, subject, or keyword: "Iraq"] AND [Full-text: "surge" OR "troop increase" OR "troop buildup" OR "escalat!" OR "withdraw!"].

2. For example, the following paragraph, from the *New York Times* article, "Yes, More Troops Would Help, a Bit" (Tom Shanker, 2006 Sept. 17, Sec. 4, Page 3) would *not* be included in the study, even if it were within the chronological scope: "Yet even with more troops, [Cordesman] said, 'the empty swaths of desert would not be worth securing,' even though insurgents are free to maneuver there. 'But more troops could help in specific cities,' Mr. Cordesman said." Although this paragraph substantively discusses a troop increase in Iraq, it does not refer to the specific troop "surge" proposal that is the concern of this study.

3. There is arguably an important partisan difference: timidity and incoherence seem more likely to characterize Democratic than Republican opposition to a president's foreign policy. Republicans' "ownership" of the defense issue—the wide perception of the GOP as "strong on defense"—enables them to strike bolder oppositional poses. When Democrats Bill Clinton and Jimmy Carter held the presidency, Republicans were able to fashion more consistent and influential oppositional frames. This point is often lost in the literature on media and U.S. foreign policy (Entman 2004).

4. CNN/Gallup Poll May 4–6, 2007 questions: 1. "Do you think President Bush strongly supports, only moderately supports, or does not support the U.S. troops currently stationed in Iraq?" 57 percent strongly; 26 percent moderately; 15 percent does not support; 2 percent unsure. 2. "Do you think the Democrats in Congress strongly support, only moderately support, or do not support the U.S. troops currently stationed in Iraq?" 31 percent strongly, 42 percent moderately, 25 percent does not support; 3 percent unsure.

5. Opinion polls suggested the surge had no appreciable impact on evaluation of Bush's handling of Iraq (67 percent disapproval in January 2007, 68 percent in November, according to the NBC News/*Wall Street Journal* survey). But there was an uptick in those responding (to a Pew Center poll) that the military effort was going very well or fairly well (from 30 percent in February 2007 to 48 percent in November 2007). (http://people-press.org/reports/display.php3?ReportID=373)

REFERENCES

Abramowitz, M., R. Wright, and A. S. Tyson. (January 7, 2007). "Critics Say 'Surge' Is More of the Same." *The Washington Post*, A01.

Baum, M. A., and T. Groeling. (2010). *War Stories: How Strategic Journalists, Citizens, and Politicians Shape the News About War*. Princeton, NJ: Princeton University Press.

Baum, M. A. (2004). "How Public Opinion Constrains the Use of Force: The Case of Operation Restore Hope." *Presidential Studies Quarterly* 34, no. 2: 187–226.

Bennett, W. Lance, Regina Lawrence, and Steven Livingston. (2007). *When the Press Fails: Political Power and the News Media from Iraq to Katrina*. Chicago: University of Chicago Press.

Bilmes, Linda J. (March 2013). "The Financial Legacy of Iraq and Afghanistan: How Wartime Spending Decisions will Constrain Future National Security Budgets." Harvard Kennedy School Faculty Research Working Paper Series RWP13-006.

Briant, Emma L. (2015). *Propaganda and Counter-Terrorism: Strategies for Global Change*. Manchester: Manchester University Press.

Druckman, J. N., and D. Chong, D. (2007). "A Theory of Framing and Opinion Formation in Competitive Elite Environments." *Journal of Communication* 57, no. 1: 99–118.

Entman, R. M. (2004). *Projections of Power: Framing News, Public Opinion and U.S. Foreign Policy*. Chicago: University of Chicago Press.

Entman, R. M., S. Aday, and S. Livingston. (2012). "News, Power, and U.S. Foreign Policy." In *Sage Handbook of Political Communication*, edited by H. Semetko and M. Scammell. London: Sage Publications.

Entman, R. M., and B. I. Page. (1994). "The News before the Storm: The Iraq War Debate and the Limits to Media Independence." In *Taken by Storm*, edited by W. L. Bennett and D. L. Paletz. Chicago: University of Chicago Press.

Hallin, D. (1986). *The Uncensored War*. New York: Oxford University Press.

Hallin, D., and P. Mancini. (2004). *Comparing Media Systems: Three Models of Media and Politics*. New York: Cambridge University Press.

Isikoff, M., and D. Corn. (2006). *Hubris: The Inside Story of Spin, Scandal, and the Selling of the Iraq war*. New York: Crown Publishers.

Jonsson, P. (January 9, 2007). "Third Round in Iraq to Test U.S. Troops. Christian Science Monitor." http://www.csmonitor.com/2007/0109/p01s01-usmi.htm

Lewis, C. (June 24, 2014). "The Lies We Believed (and Still Believe) About Iraq." http://billmoyers.com/2014/06/27/the-lies-we-believed-and-still-believe-about-iraq/

Livingston, S., and W. L. Bennett. (2003). "Gatekeeping, Indexing, and Live-Event news: Is Technology Altering the Construction of News?" *Political Communication* 20: 363–80.

McCarty, K., and M. Pfeifle. (2011). "Strategic Communication: The Iraqi Surge Strategy." Paper presented at "Strategic Communications: The Cutting Edge" Conference at King's College London, May 9–10, available through www.kcl.ac.uk/sspp/departments/warstudies/research/groups/insurgency/events.aspx

McQuinn, Brian. (October 2013). "Assessing (In)security After the Arab Spring: The Case of Libya." *PS: Political Science & Politics* 46: 716–20.

Nuruzzaman, Mohammed. (2015). "Rethinking Foreign Military Interventions to Promote Human Rights: Evidence from Libya, Bahrain and Syria." *Canadian Journal of Political Science* 48: 531–52.

National Intelligence Estimate. (2007). "Prospects for Iraq's Stability: Challenging Road Ahead." http://progressiveaustin.org/Iraq_NIE.pdf

Packer, G. (2005). *The Assassin's Gate: America in Iraq*. New York: Farrar, Straus and Giroux.

Page, B. with M. M. Bouton (2006). *Foreign Policy Disconnect: What Americans Want from Our Leaders but Don't Get.* Chicago: University of Chicago Press.

Ricks, T. (2006). *Fiasco: The American Military Adventure in Iraq.* New York: Penguin.

Sobel, R. (2001). *The Impact of Public Opinion on U.S. Foreign Policy since Vietnam: Constraining the Colossus.* New York: Oxford University Press.

Sheafer, T., and G. Wolfsfeld (2009). "Party Systems and Oppositional Voices in the News Media: A Study of the Contest over Political Waves in the United States and Israel." *International Journal of Press/Politics* 14, no. 2: 146–65.

Sheets, P., C. M. Rowling, and T. M. Jones. (2015). "The View from above (and below): A Comparison of American, British, and Arab News Coverage of US Drones." *Media, War and Conflict* 8, no. 3: 289–311.

Woods, J. L. (1997). "U.S. Government Decisionmaking Processes during Humanitarian Operations in Somalia." In *Learning from Somalia: The Lessons of Armed Humanitarian Intervention,* edited by W. Clarke and J. Herbst. Boulder, CO: Westview Press.

8

Foreign Policy Beliefs among Leaders and the Public

Dina Smeltz, Craig Kafura, Joshua W. Busby,
Jonathan Monten, and Jordan Tama

INTRODUCTION

Each year, the size and scope of partisan disputes among U.S. policymakers and the American public seem to grow louder and wider, even bleeding into the previously more neutral territory of foreign policy. Such divisions raise serious questions not only of representation but also the future of the long-standing, albeit often overstated, foreign policy consensus in the United States. Do the public and policymakers diverge on key international issues? To what extent do these divisions reflect polarization among the public and among foreign policy leaders?

The Chicago Council on Global Affairs has long been interested in measuring the differences between public and leadership opinion on foreign policy issues, tracking the extent to which policy reflects public preferences, and identifying issue areas where there are potential gaps between the views of leaders and the public. To measure these differences, the Chicago Council on Global Affairs has conducted parallel surveys of American foreign policy opinion leaders and the American public from 1978 to 2004, and revived these studies again in 2014[1] and 2016.[2]

These parallel surveys of the American public and foreign policy opinion leaders allow us to examine three areas of potential concern when it comes to differences of opinion on U.S. foreign policy issues. The first are what we call "populist" gaps: differences between the views of the American public and foreign policy opinion leaders. The second we refer to as "partisan" gaps: issue areas where Democrats and Republicans, both among the public and among opinion leaders, differ along party lines. Third are "perception" gaps: issues where opinion leaders misread the public, believing that the public opposes policies that in fact have popular support, or mistaking isolated pockets of support for policies opposed by a majority of the American public.

The 2016 Chicago Council Survey finds evidence for each of these gaps, and each produces their own unique concerns.[3]

Populist gaps between the public and opinion leaders evoke longstanding concerns of the representativeness of American policymaking institutions. If opinion leaders and the public differ on important issues for long enough, it opens the door for new, potentially more extreme political entrepreneurs to embrace those unrepresented demands. This gap of representation on trade and immigration is the gap from which Donald Trump emerged.[4] While the study of partisan conflict has mostly focused on domestic policymaking, these partisan divisions have become more apparent on foreign policy too. As dangerous as partisan rancor is when dealing with tax policy or healthcare, surely it would be better to keep it away from issues involving national security.

Lastly, perception gaps may lead opinion leaders to refrain from endorsing policies they mistakenly think are unpopular, or conversely, to endorse policies they mistakenly think have public support. As the data show, opinion leaders may be mistaking the loudest voices on issues such as immigration, international trade, and American engagement abroad for a majority of the public.[5]

In the wake of the 2016 electoral campaign, these issues of gaps between leaders and the public seem all the more relevant. The 2016 election has been widely read as a populist revolt, with average Americans rising up to reject the political elite, particularly on issues of immigration and trade. As the Council's parallel survey results show, there is an element of truth in this argument: the American public and opinion leaders are in fact divided over several key issues, including the importance of protecting American jobs, U.S. immigration policy, and the importance of protecting U.S. allies' security.

However, while there are gaps between leaders and the public on some issues, the 2016 Chicago Council Survey also reveals that elements of the foreign policy consensus remain largely intact. Americans across party lines, and among both the public and leaders, support taking an active part in world affairs and a leadership role for the United States. They share a common set of top goals and threats, and support U.S. alliances in both Europe and Asia. But in order to achieve these goals and to protect the country from these threats, there is longstanding partisan disagreement on the best way forward.

Republicans, both at the public and leadership level, emphasize U.S. military strength as a key element of U.S. foreign policy. They are also far more likely to describe Islamic fundamentalism as a critical threat and reducing illegal immigration as a very important goal.[6] Democrats, by contrast, are more supportive of multilateral approaches to achieving foreign policy goals. Both the Democratic public and Democratic opinion leaders are more likely to say that strengthening the United Nations and participating in international treaties are effective ways of achieving U.S. foreign policy.

However, this should not overstate the level of division between the parties on many core articles of foreign policy. At a time when many long-settled issues are once again being thrust back into view—such as the U.S. commitment to NATO and the importance of nuclear nonproliferation—the American public and opinion leaders across party lines still largely hold consensus views of support for the international trading system, an active U.S. role in foreign affairs, and maintaining support for U.S. alliances.

THE TRADE CONSENSUS, EXCEPT ON JOBS

Of all the issues raised in the 2016 election, international trade was one of the more unexpected issues to dominate the debate. But perhaps it should not have been so surprising: international trade and globalization are central to the functioning of the American economy, and the economy—in particular, the goal of protecting American jobs—is consistently a top priority for Americans.

American Jobs

For the American public, protecting American jobs is not only an important goal for U.S. foreign policy, it has been among the most important goals for decades. Yet opinion leaders rarely place much emphasis on protecting American jobs as a foreign policy priority.

The gap between opinion leaders and the public, of all partisan stripes, has remained remarkably consistent and stable on this issue since 1978, the year the Chicago Council on Global Affairs first conducted a parallel elite-public survey. Among the public, eight in ten Republicans, Democrats, and Independents (78 percent each) named protecting American jobs a very important goal for U.S. policy in 1978. Similar majorities said the same in 2016 (78 percent Republicans, 74 percent Democrats, 69 percent Independents).

But opinion leaders have consistently put less emphasis on this goal. In 1978, minorities of leaders (40 percent Republicans, 30 percent Democrats, 32 percent Independents) said it was a very important goal. In 2016, the results were similar (25 percent Republicans, 37 percent Democrats, 29 percent Independents) (figure 8.1).

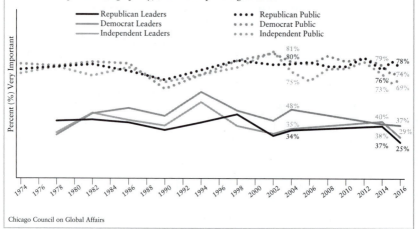

Figure 8.1

Globalization

Despite the intensity of the debate over trade in the 2016 presidential campaign, the public is by and large supportive of globalization and international trade. In the 2016 Chicago Council Survey, majorities of Republicans (59 percent), Democrats (74 percent), and Independents (61 percent) all said that globalization was mostly good for the United States. Opinion leaders agreed, by even larger margins, with roughly nine in ten saying that globalization was mostly good (90 percent Republicans, 94 percent Democrats, 85 percent Independents). Since the Council first asked this question in 1998, Democrats among the public have grown more positive on globalization, while Republicans have held steady. Opinion leaders' views over the same period have changed little, with leaders across party affiliation remaining strongly positive on globalization (figure 8.2).

Despite the public's general support for globalization, opinion leaders misread the public's views. When asked whether the American public views globalization as mostly good or mostly bad, majorities of Republican (80 percent), Democratic (69 percent), and Independent (66 percent) opinion leaders say that a majority of the American public sees globalization as mostly bad for the United States. While there is certainly a portion of the American public that holds this view, they are not a majority, nor are they a majority in one party or the other.

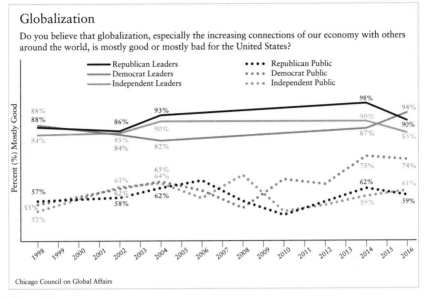

Figure 8.2

International Trade

This same positive inclination toward globalization also holds true for many of international trade's effects on the United States. A cross-partisan majority of Americans say that international trade is good for the U.S. economy, American companies, consumers like them, and their own standards of living. Opinion leaders are even more convinced that international trade is beneficial, with roughly nine in ten leaders across the political spectrum in agreement.

The public, however, is less positive on other effects of trade. Majorities of Republicans (65 percent), Democrats (52 percent), and Independents (61 percent) say that international trade is bad for creating jobs in the United States. But opinion leaders disagree, with majorities (61 percent Republican leaders, 64 percent Democratic leaders, 58 percent Independent leaders) saying international trade is *good* for U.S. job creation.

But opinion leaders do align with public views about the negative impact of international trade on U.S. workers' job security. Cross-partisan majorities among both the public and opinion leaders say that international trade is bad for the job security of American workers. Yet, this appears to be a higher concern for average Americans since leaders do not rank protecting the jobs of American workers as a top foreign policy priority.

The Trans-Pacific Partnership

While both candidates in the 2016 presidential campaign ran against the Trans-Pacific Partnership (TPP), the deal had broader support than was often appreciated. At the time the survey was fielded, majorities across party lines among the public (58 percent Republicans, 70 percent Democrats, 52 percent Independents) supported the TPP, as did even larger majorities among opinion leaders (78 percent Republican leaders, 73 percent Democratic leaders, 84 percent Independent leaders). While other surveys have found that most Americans lacked knowledge of the details of the TPP,[7] their support reflects generally positive views of international trade and trade deals that existed at least until this survey was fielded in June 2016. Since then, the TPP became more politicized over the course of the 2016 presidential election, which could have affected subsequent survey results.

THE IMMIGRATION DIVIDE

Trade is an issue included in the Chicago Council Survey that has both international and domestic impacts. Immigration, also an issue with both foreign and national implications, was another key issue for the 2016 campaign, especially the 2016 Republican primary. Unlike trade, where majorities of the public and opinion leaders largely arrive at the same conclusions about its effects, questions about immigration frequently produce both partisan, interparty splits and populist, intraparty divisions.

The Threat of Immigration

American public perceptions of the threat posed by large numbers of immigrants and refugees coming into the United States have changed dramatically over the two decades that the Chicago Council Surveys have asked Americans about the issue. In the 1990s, Americans across the political spectrum viewed immigrants and refugees coming into the country as a critical threat. But after the 2002 Chicago Council Survey, Democrats became steadily less likely to view immigration as a threat to the United States, while Republicans remained just as concerned as they had been in the 1990s. In the 2016 Chicago Council Survey, two in three Republicans (67 percent) named the issue a critical threat—a historical high point—compared to one in four Democrats (27 percent) and four in ten Independents (40 percent).

Opinion leaders, however, have never been particularly concerned about immigration. In 2016, only one in five Republican and Independent opinion leaders (19 percent each), and only five percent of Democratic opinion leaders, said they view large numbers of immigrants and refugees coming into the United States as a critical threat.

The changes in public opinion, and the stability of leaders' views, mean that while Democratic leaders and the public have come into greater accord over time, the same cannot be said for Republicans. The large majority of Republican opinion leaders do not, and have not, viewed immigration as a threat, while the Republican public has consistently named it as a critical threat. This is an example that is particularly interesting to examine because it runs counter to a commonly held assumption that the public follows the views of its trusted partisan elites.

Syrian Refugees

The issue of whether or not to accept Syrian refugees into the United States produces similar partisan and populist divisions, reflecting broader divisions on the threat of immigrants and refugees coming into the country. Among the public, a majority of Democrats (56 percent) support the United States accepting Syrian refugees, and an even stronger majority among Democratic opinion leaders agree (96 percent). While smaller majorities of Republican (54 percent) and Independent (72 percent) opinion leaders also favor accepting Syrian refugees, few Republicans (18 percent) or Independents (32 percent) among the public support doing so.

Immigration Policy

The same divisions seen in views of the threat of immigrants and refugees also apply to views on how to deal with the large population of undocumented immigrants living in the United States. Majorities among the Democratic public and among Democratic opinion leaders say that illegal immigrants living in the United States should be allowed to pursue citizenship, either immediately (43 percent Democratic leaders, 44 percent Democratic public) or after paying a penalty and waiting a period of time (49 percent Democratic leaders, 28 percent Democratic public).

Republicans, meanwhile, are internally divided, both among the Republican electorate and elites. Republican opinion leaders are divided between allowing illegal immigrants working in the United States to stay with work permits, but without a path to becoming U.S. citizens (45 percent), and allowing them to stay with a path to citizenship either immediately (11 percent) or after a fine and waiting period (34 percent). In total, nine in ten Republican opinion leaders favor some type of legal status. By contrast, relatively few Republican opinion leaders (10 percent) say that unauthorized workers should be deported.

Republicans among the public also tend to favor some type of legal status for illegal immigrants, though to a lesser degree, and they are much more inclined than opinion leaders to favor deportation. Four in ten combined support an immediate path to citizenship (20 percent) or citizenship after a fine and waiting period (23 percent). An additional 13 percent support the work permits approach. Four in ten among the Republican public (42 percent) favor deportation.

Immigration reform is another instance on which leaders misread the public. Republican leaders, in particular, overestimate public support for deportation: 60 percent of Republican leaders think the public wants illegal immigrants to be made to leave the country, despite this being a minority position, even among Republicans. Independent leaders are less likely to see the public as deportation-friendly (43 percent), and even fewer Democratic leaders do (27 percent). On immigration, leaders may be responding to their own party positions rather than the public overall.

CLIMATE CHANGE AND ENERGY

Just as Republicans are far more concerned about immigration than Democrats, Democrats are far more concerned about climate change than are Republicans. However, there is less internal division among Democrats on climate issues.

At both the public and leader levels, Democrats are far more likely to prioritize combating climate change and improving the world's environment than are Republicans or Independents (figure 8.3). Majorities among the Democratic public name climate change a critical threat (57 percent) and limiting climate change a very important goal (59 percent). Democratic opinion leaders are even more concerned: 86 percent say climate change is a critical threat, and 82 percent see limiting it as a very important goal. In fact, Democratic leaders named climate change a critical threat and a very important goal more often than any other issue, including traditional security threats such as international terrorism and nuclear proliferation. Democrats are also concerned broadly about improving the world's environment (63 percent Democratic public, 75 percent Democratic opinion leaders).

Republicans, by contrast, are much less concerned about climate change. Two in ten among the Republican public (18 percent) and opinion leaders (20 percent) name it a critical threat, and neither group sees limiting climate change as a very important goal (29 percent Republican leaders, 20 percent Republican public). A similar portion of Republican leaders (28 percent) and the public (29 percent) say that improving the world's environment is a very important goal.

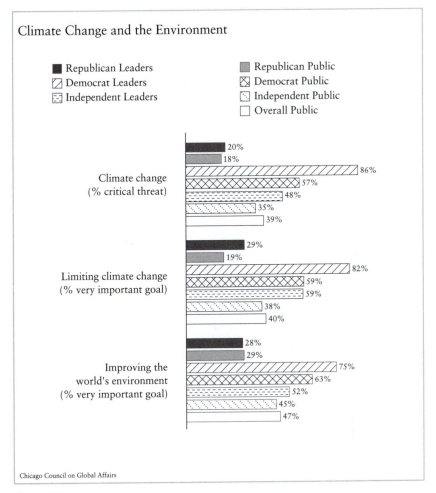

Figure 8.3

One of the key concerns around the issue of climate change is the source of Americans' energy supplies, and maintaining adequate energy reserves as well as energy independence are relatively high priorities for Americans. In 2014, majorities of opinion leaders (72 percent Republicans, 52 percent Democrats, 61 percent Independents) named securing adequate supplies of energy as a very important goal for U.S. foreign policy, a goal shared by majorities among the public (59 percent Republicans, 71 percent Democrats, 74 percent Independents).

Additionally, across party lines, the American public (63 percent Republicans, 66 percent Democrats, 64 percent Independents) is significantly more likely than opinion leaders to say that attaining energy independence is a very important goal. While politicians of all political stripes enjoy promoting energy independence in their campaigns, opinion leaders do not place nearly as high a priority on energy independence, with between two and three in ten naming it a very important goal (20 percent Republicans, 30 percent Democrats, 26 percent Independents). Elites could place less emphasis than the public on energy independence because they are more aware of growing U.S. energy self-reliance due to the rise of unconventional oil and natural gas production from fracking. Opinion leaders may also be more comfortable with the ability to meet U.S. energy needs through trade imports.

A BROADER AMERICAN CONSENSUS

Despite the elite-public or partisan gaps on trade's potential for creating jobs, immigration, and climate change, the 2016 Chicago Council Survey also reveals that a foreign policy consensus on some core issues remains largely intact.

America's Role in the World

Since the first Chicago Council Survey in 1974, the American public has consistently preferred taking an active part in world affairs over staying out of world affairs (figure 8.4). This bipartisan consensus on international engagement holds true in the 2016 Chicago Council Survey as well: among the public, majorities of Democrats (70 percent), Republicans (64 percent), and Independents (57 percent) all say that it is best for the future of the country if we take an active part in world affairs. That consensus is even stronger among opinion leaders: more than nine in ten Republican (93 percent), Democratic (99 percent), and Independent (92 percent) leaders support taking an active part in world affairs.

In the debate over America's role in the world, opinion leaders may not be aware that the public is largely on their side. When asked what percentage of the public they thought supported an active role in the world, leaders missed the mark. Republican (51 percent), Democrat (45 percent), and Independent (46 percent) opinion leaders underestimated public support by thirteen to nineteen percentage points, respectively.

There is also a similarly broad consensus that the United States should play a leadership role in the world. Few among the public, and even fewer opinion leaders, think the United States should play no leadership role at all. But there is not quite a unified consensus on the exact nature of that role. Among the public, majorities of all partisan groups (53 percent Republicans, 70 percent Democrats, 63 percent Independents) favor a shared leadership role. And both Democratic (74 percent) and Independent (59 percent) opinion leaders favor shared leadership as well. But a majority of Republican opinion leaders (64 percent) say the United States should be the dominant world leader, in line with sizeable minorities among both the Republican public and Independent opinion leaders (41 percent each).

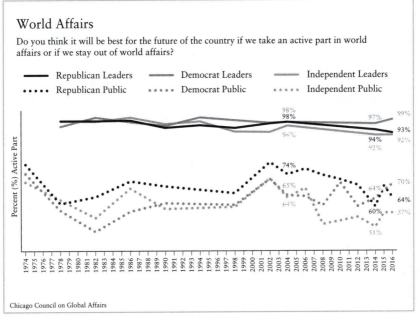

World Affairs

Do you think it will be best for the future of the country if we take an active part in world affairs or if we stay out of world affairs?

Figure 8.4

Differing Approaches to U.S. Foreign Policy

While the public and elites affirm the importance of U.S. leadership in the world, they emphasize different ways of exercising U.S. influence and achieving U.S. foreign policy goals. For example, majorities of Republicans, both among the public (60 percent) and among opinion leaders (72 percent), say that maintaining U.S. military superiority is a very effective approach to U.S. foreign policy. While a significant portion of the Democratic public agrees (43 percent), Democratic opinion leaders are less convinced, with only one in three (34 percent) naming it a very effective approach.

Rather than military superiority, Democrats are more likely to emphasize a multilateral, institutional approach such as strengthening the United Nations. Seven in ten Democratic leaders (71 percent) and eight in ten among the Democratic public (84 percent) see strengthening the United Nations as a very or somewhat effective approach, compared to only two in ten Republican leaders (22 percent) and half of the Republican public (54 percent). In the same vein, Democrats are more likely than Republicans to point to maintaining existing alliances (45 percent Democratic public, 57 percent Democratic leaders) and building new alliances (49 percent Democratic leaders, 37 percent Democratic public) as a very effective means of achieving U.S. goals.

These differing approaches to achieving the goals of U.S. foreign policy seem related to many of the differences between Republicans and Democrats when it comes to specific policy issues. Data from the 2014 Chicago Council Survey on various approaches available to the United States in dealing with the Iran nuclear program provide an excellent example. Republicans, among both the leaders and the broader public, were significantly more likely to support the use of military force to prevent Iran from acquiring a nuclear weapon, while Democrats preferred a negotiated diplomatic approach. Similarly, Democrats were more likely than Republicans to favor U.S. participation in international treaties to address climate change and the International Criminal Court.

COMMON CONCERNS, COMMON GOALS

Just as there is a general consensus on American international involvement and leadership, Americans across party lines and among both leaders and the public agree on the top threats facing the United States: terrorism and the spread of nuclear weapons. Both issues have been consistent priorities for the public and leaders alike since at least 1998. Yet this general consensus is coupled with some elite-public or partisan differences on aspects of these threats.

Terrorism

In the 2016 Chicago Council Survey, majorities of Republicans (83 percent), Democrats (74 percent), and Independents (70 percent) all named international terrorism a critical threat to the United States (figure 8.5). In fact, terrorism was the top-ranked threat among the public across party lines. Opinion leaders shared Americans' concerns: majorities of Republican (58 percent), Democratic (56 percent), and Independent leaders (63 percent) view international terrorism as a critical threat.

In turn, the public and opinion leaders also prioritize combating terrorism as a very important goal. Cross-partisan majorities among the public (81 percent Republicans, 70 percent Democrats, 66 percent Independents) and among opinion leaders (75 percent Republicans, 64 percent Democrats, 65 percent Independents) all name combating international terrorism a very important goal for U.S. foreign policy.[8]

Previous Chicago Council Surveys have shown that Americans tend to view Islamic extremism as a major factor contributing to the rise of terrorism in the Middle East.[9] In fact, American perceptions of a threat from both international terrorism and Islamic fundamentalism have increased with the emergence of the Islamic State (or ISIS) and several high-profile attacks in the United States. While partisans share concern about terrorism and ways to combat terrorism, there are some sharp differences in views concerning Islamic fundamentalism.

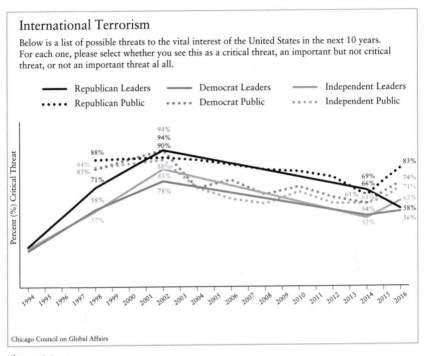

International Terrorism

Below is a list of possible threats to the vital interest of the United States in the next 10 years. For each one, please select whether you see this as a critical threat, an important but not critical threat, or not an important threat al all.

Republican Leaders — Democrat Leaders — Independent Leaders
• • • • • Republican Public • • • • • Democrat Public • • • • • Independent Public

Chicago Council on Global Affairs

Figure 8.5

Majorities of both Republican opinion leaders (66 percent) and the Republican public (75 percent) consider Islamic fundamentalism a critical threat to the United States. Democrats, by contrast, are less concerned about it: four in ten Democratic leaders (40 percent) and just under half of the Democratic public (49 percent) say Islamic fundamentalism is a critical threat.

For Republicans, the increased public fears of Islamic fundamentalism have quickly narrowed a gap in concern found in the 2014 Chicago Council Survey. Then, while seven in ten Republican leaders (72 percent) saw it as a critical threat, less than half of the Republican public (48 percent) agreed. Now Republicans are largely aligned when it comes to Islamic fundamentalism. Democrats remain relatively less concerned, though their fears about Islamic fundamentalism have also increased among Democrats since 2014.

Nuclear Proliferation

Another item of shared concern for the public and opinion leaders, and across party lines, is nuclear proliferation: both the threat of unfriendly countries becoming nuclear powers and the goal of preventing the spread of nuclear weapons.

The threat of nuclear proliferation has long been a top concern for both Republicans and Democrats, and for both opinion leaders and the public. Though concern has declined among all groups from its peak in 2002, majorities of nearly all groups see the possibility of nuclear weapons spreading to unfriendly countries as a critical threat. The exception is among Democratic leaders, with only a plurality of 49 percent naming it a critical threat, though it is one of the top five threats identified by Democratic leaders.

Given that both leaders and the public, across party lines, view nuclear proliferation as a top threat to U.S. vital interests, it should come as no surprise that they also view the prevention of the spread of nuclear weapons as a very important goal for U.S. foreign policy. And as with the threat of the spread of nuclear weapons, nonproliferation has long been a shared goal for both the public and opinion leaders, with few differences between the two or between partisan groups.

While there is shared concern over nuclear proliferation in general, Republican opinion leaders are a bit out of step with other groups in their assessment of a threat from North Korea's nuclear program. Majorities of Americans across party lines view North Korea's nuclear program as a critical threat (63 percent Republicans, 64 percent Democrats, 52 percent Independents), as do six in ten Democratic leaders (62 percent) and half of Independent leaders (50 percent). But only one in three Republican opinion leaders (35 percent) views a nuclear threat from North Korea similarly.

U.S. Alliances in Europe and Asia

Another key area of general consensus across party lines, and between the public and opinion leaders, is support for U.S. alliances in both Europe and Asia. The U.S. network of alliances around the world has been—and remains—a unifying pillar of U.S. foreign policy. And after an election in which American support for allies abroad unexpectedly became an issue, the defense of American allies is sure to be a prominent theme for years to come.

While the relevance of NATO was called into question in the 2016 Trump election campaign, majorities across party lines and among both the public and opinion leaders say that the United States should maintain its commitment to NATO. There is additional support among two in ten Republican, Democratic, and Independent leaders, as well as the Democratic public, for increasing the U.S. commitment to NATO. Very few support decreasing the U.S. commitment, and even fewer support withdrawing from NATO (figure 8.6).

Americans also value alliance partners in Asia. Majorities among all groups say that in Asia, the United States should place a higher priority on building up our strong relations with traditional allies like South Korea and Japan, even if this might diminish our relations with China.

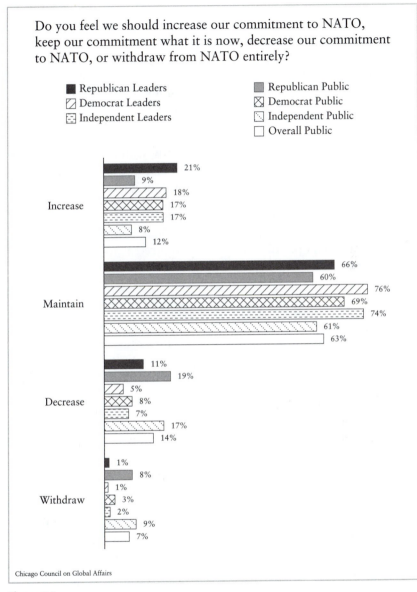

Do you feel we should increase our commitment to NATO, keep our commitment what it is now, decrease our commitment to NATO, or withdraw from NATO entirely?

■ Republican Leaders ▨ Democrat Leaders ⊟ Independent Leaders ▦ Republican Public ☒ Democrat Public ⬚ Independent Public ☐ Overall Public

Increase
21%
9%
18%
17%
17%
8%
12%

Maintain
66%
60%
76%
69%
74%
61%
63%

Decrease
11%
19%
5%
8%
7%
17%
14%

Withdraw
1%
8%
1%
3%
2%
9%
7%

Chicago Council on Global Affairs

Figure 8.6

A key aspect of the U.S. alliance structure is the network of U.S. military bases around the world. In line with their support for maintaining alliances as a means of achieving U.S. foreign policy goals, both leaders and the public support having long-term U.S. military bases in key allied nations such as Japan, South Korea, and Germany. While cross-partisan majorities of opinion leaders support maintaining bases in Australia as well, only Republicans among the public favor maintaining such bases (54 percent), along with sizable minorities of Democrats (43 percent) and Independents (44 percent).

However, defending our allies' security is a goal prioritized highly only by opinion leaders, with just minorities among the public regardless of partisan affiliation identifying it as a very important goal. This was not always the case: in the Council's cold war surveys, Americans tended to describe defending our allies' security as a very important goal. But the public became less likely to do so in the 1990s, with a boost in 2002 following the September 11 attacks. But by the 2010s, only a minority once again rated defending allies as a very important goal. Majorities among foreign policy opinion leaders, however, have consistently rated the defense of allies a very important goal for U.S. foreign policy. The decline in public support since the end of the Cold War, combined with consistent emphasis from opinion leaders, has produced a growing gap between leaders and the public.

CONCLUSION

This synthesis of parallel data offered by the 2016 Chicago Council Surveys of the American public and American opinion leaders provides some understanding of the populist energies channeled into the 2016 presidential campaign.

At a surface level, both the American public and opinion leaders express support for globalization and many aspects of international trade. Given the intensity of the political debate over trade issues on display in the 2016 campaign, this is no small thing. However, there are large differences in the degree to which publics and elites support free trade, and support among the public appears soft especially when the issue of jobs is brought into the calculus. Public opinion surveys help to measure attitudes, but it is sometimes harder to gauge whether an issue has immediate impact or strong resonance for the public. While broader public attitudes are supportive of globalization and immigration, these issues are much more salient to a vocal and politically active minority that holds opposing views. The influence of this louder minority can give candidates for elected office an incentive to adopt those minority views.

While both opinion leaders and the public consider international trade to be detrimental to American workers' job security, a leading priority for the public—but not elites—is protecting Americans jobs. Opinion leaders rate other issues, such as terrorism and nuclear proliferation, as much higher priorities for U.S. foreign policy. This priority disconnect exacerbates the gap between an elite consensus on trade and a public that, while supportive of trade, is perhaps more acutely aware of the potential downsides.

There is a similarly large and persistent gap on the issue of immigration, an issue of deep importance to the Republican public but not for most Republican opinion leaders. While Republicans among the public see immigration as a critical threat, Republican opinion leaders do not. This difference translates into significant differences of opinion on more specific policy questions, including the admission of Syrian refugees into the United States.

In light of these findings, it appears that Donald Trump, having assumed the presidency, has views that are more consistent with the positions on trade and immigration espoused by a vocal minority of the public. At the same time, his views seem to be in line with and indeed shaping the views of the Republican Party base that has become more skeptical of globalization and trade, and is far more likely than others to perceive a threat from immigration. Given Trump's stated objectives on the campaign trail, a number of the foundations of U.S. foreign policy—such as commitment to traditional alliances and a liberal trading order—appear to be in question and under strain. Future surveys will show whether Republican publics, or even Republican elites, will gravitate to his position in the coming years.

The surveys also reveal sharp partisan differences that hold true among both the public and opinion leaders. Republicans, both at the public and leadership level, are more likely than Democrats to emphasize U.S. military superiority and military strength as key elements of U.S. foreign policy. They are also far more likely to see Islamic fundamentalism as a critical threat, and reducing illegal immigration as a very important goal.

Democrats, by contrast, are more supportive than Republicans of multilateral approaches to foreign policy. Both the Democratic public and Democratic opinion leaders are more likely to say that strengthening the United Nations is an effective way of achieving U.S. foreign policy. Democrats are also far more likely to name climate change as a critical threat and see combating it as a very important goal.

In addition to gaps between the parties, and gaps between leaders and the public, there is a third gap to consider: the gap between leaders' perception of the public and their actual attitudes. The 2016 Chicago Council Survey finds that leaders consistently misperceive the public's attitudes on key issues such as trade, immigration, and international engagement. Leaders underestimate the public's support for active U.S. international engagement, and to an even greater degree, underestimate the public's support for globalization. And on immigration, opinion leaders seem to mistake the views of their own co-partisans among the public for the views of the overall American public. One possible reason for this disconnect on issues like immigration and trade is that leaders respond to the loudest and most passionate voices and mistake them for the majority view.

In sum, the 2016 Chicago Council survey reveals some of the deeper foundations of divisions in contemporary debates over U.S. foreign policy, reflecting the views of both the public and the leaders on both sides of the aisle. But one should not overstate the level of division between these key groups on many key components of foreign policy. On core questions about the U.S. role in the world, the value of alliances, and the importance of countering major security threats, consensus still largely persists. President Trump's influence and power to shape public and leader opinion will prove to be an important test of the durability of this consensus going forward.

DISCUSSION QUESTIONS

1. What are the three "gaps" that shape the analysis by Smeltz et al.? What are the differences among them?
2. To what extent is there a foreign policy consensus among the American public and its leaders?
3. To what extent do members of the public agree or disagree on trade, globalization, and the Trans-Pacific Partnership?
4. On the issues of immigration, Syrian refuges, and Islamic fundamentalism, are there partisan differences?
5. Which party is more likely to be concerned about climate change? Is the American public interested in energy independence?
6. What are two or three issues on which the public and its leaders share similar views?
7. In what ways do the two major political parties differ on how best to achieve foreign policy goals?
8. Do the American public and its leaders support American alliances in Europe and Asia? Does the public or its leaders provide stronger support for these alliances?

NOTES

1. Dina Smeltz, with Joshua Busby, Gregory Holyk, Craig Kafura, Jonathan Monten, and Jordan Tama, "United in Goals, Divided on Means: Opinion Leaders Survey Results and Partisan Breakdowns from the 2014 Chicago Council Survey

of American Opinion on US Foreign Policy," Chicago Council on Global Affairs (2015), available at https://www.thechicagocouncil.org/publication/united-goals-divided-means-opinion-leaders-chicago-council-survey-results-2014

2. The opinion leaders include persons working in Congress and executive branch agencies; fellows at top foreign policy think tanks; academics in the top universities for international relations; leaders of internationally focused interest groups and NGOs; leaders of labor unions, religious organizations, and multinational corporations; and members of the media writing on international issues. Throughout this report, the terms "foreign policy leaders," "opinion leaders," and, in some cases, just "leaders," are used interchangeably.

3. For a full description of the methodology and the questions used in the 2016 surveys, as well as the questions and methodology used in the earlier surveys, referenced here, see the website of the Chicago Council on Global Affairs at www.thechicagocouncil.org.

4. For an elaboration of this argument, see "A Party out of Step," *The Science of Trump*, July 15, 2016. First articulated in "On Immigration and Trade, It's Republican Elites, Not Donald Trump, Who Are Out of Step With Party's Voters," *The Washington Post: Monkey Cage*, April 25, 2016.

5. Joshua Busby, Craig Kafura, Jonathan Monten, Dina Smeltz, and Jordan Tama, "How the Elite Misjudge the U.S. Electorate on International Engagement," *Real Clear World* (November 7, 2016), available at http://www.realclearworld.com/articles/2016/11/07/how_the_elite_misjudge_the_us_electorate_on_international_engagement_112112.html.

6. The authors recognize that some people find the terms "Islamic fundamentalism" and "illegal immigration" objectionable. Our use of these terms is based on their use in previous historical Chicago Council survey questions, which aimed to mirror the language of contemporary public discourse in the United States at the time they were crafted. Changing the exact question wording could affect responses, so we have opted to maintain the trend wording.

7. Doug Palmer, "POLITICO-Harvard Poll: Americans Say TPP Who?" September 23, 2016, POLITICO, available at http://www.politico.com/story/2016/09/americans-say-tpp-who-228598

8. Dina Smeltz and Karl Friedhoff, "As Acts of Terrorism Proliferate, Americans See No End in Sight," The Chicago Council on Global Affairs (August 2016), available at https://www.thechicagocouncil.org/sites/default/files/survey_terror-acts-and-americans_20160822-2.pdf

9. Dina Smeltz, "ISIS Successful in Raising Public Fears about Terrorism," Chicago Council on Global Affairs, September 2015, https://www.thechicagocouncil.org/sites/default/files/ISIS%20Brief%2009%2001.pdf

II

THE INSTITUTIONAL SETTING

Foreign policy is a product of the actions officials take on behalf of the nation. Because of this, the way the government is structured for policy-making also arguably affects the conduct and content of foreign affairs. Thus, we can hypothesize that a relationship exists between the substance of policy and the institutional setting from which it derives. The proposition is particularly compelling if attention is directed not to the foreign policy goals the nation's leaders select but to the means they choose to satisfy particular objectives.

A salient feature of the American institutional setting is that the president and the institutionalized presidency—the latter consisting of the president's personal staff and the Executive Office of the President—are preeminent in the foreign policymaking process. This derives in part from the authority granted to the president in the Constitution and in part from the combination of judicial interpretation, legislative acquiescence, personal assertiveness, and custom and tradition that have transformed the presidency into the most powerful office in the world. The crisis-ridden atmosphere that characterized the Cold War era also contributed to the enhancement of presidential authority by encouraging the president to act energetically and decisively when dealing with global challenges. The widely shared consensus among American leaders and the American public that the international environment demanded an active world role also contributed to the felt need for strong presidential leadership. Although this viewpoint was sometimes vigorously debated in the years following American involvement in Vietnam, the perceived need for strong presidential leadership was generally accepted throughout the Cold War.

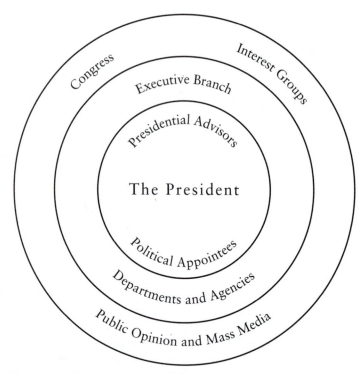

Figure II.1.   The Concentric Circles of Policymaking

Source: Adapted from Roger Hilsman, *To Move a Nation* (New York: Doubleday, 1967), 541–44.

Because of the president's key role in foreign policymaking, it is useful to consider the institutional arrangements that govern the process as a series of concentric circles that effectively alter the standard government organization chart so as to draw attention to the core, or most immediate source of the action (figure II.1).

Thus, the innermost circle in the policymaking process consists of the president, his immediate personal advisers, and such important political appointees as the secretaries of state and defense, the director of central intelligence, and various under, deputy, and assistant secretaries who bear responsibility for carrying out policy decisions. Here, in principle, is where the most important decisions involving the fate of the nation are made.

The second concentric circle comprises the various departments and agencies of the executive branch. If we exclude from that circle the politically appointed heads of agencies and their immediate subordinates, who are more properly placed in the innermost circle, we can think of the individuals within the second circle as career professionals who provide continuity in the implementation of policy from one administration to the next. Their primary tasks—in theory—are to provide top-level policymakers with the information necessary for sound decision-making and to carry out the decisions policymakers reach. The involvement of the United States in a complex web of interdependent ties with other nations in the world has led to the involvement in foreign affairs of many organizations, the primary tasks of which are seemingly oriented toward the domestic environment. The Treasury Department and the U.S. Trade Representative have become especially visible in recent years as the globalization of the world political economy has increased the salience of economic issues as foreign policy issues. The Departments of Agriculture, Commerce, and Justice (including the FBI) have also figured prominently as globalization and international terrorism have blurred the distinction between foreign and domestic politics and policy. The creation of the Department of Homeland Security in 2002 epitomizes the linking of the domestic and international arenas within one organization. While the department, as its name implies, has the explicit duty of protecting citizens at home, it also has the responsibility to gather and analyze intelligence information about foreign threats and to deter and protect against such attacks as occurred on September 11, 2001.

The departments of state and defense and the intelligence community continue to command center stage among the dozens of executive branch departments and agencies now involved in foreign affairs. The State Department's role derives from being the only department charged (in theory, at least) with responsibility for the whole range of America's relations with other nations. The Defense Department and the intelligence community, especially the CIA, on the other hand, in the Cold War years derived their importance from the threatening and crisis-ridden atmosphere; they often had ready alternatives from which top-level policymakers could choose when diplomacy and negotiation seemed destined to fail. While both bureaucracies played a diminished role in the post–Cold War world, both appear to have especially important parts to play in the post-9/11 world. Indeed, the intelligence community immediately received congressional and executive branch scrutiny over the analytic failures surrounding 9/11 and Iraq and its alleged weapons of mass destruction (WMD) during the Bush years. During the Obama administration, the intelligence community also received additional scrutiny over its handling of the attempted bombings in Detroit and New York; various terrorist attacks in Boston, San Bernardino, and Orlando; and its efforts to maintain cybersecurity for governmental agencies and the public at large against "hacking" by foreign entities. Further, the Trump administration has already clashed with the intelligence community over its effectiveness in gathering and analyzing information. To be sure, the intelligence community, composed of agencies from sixteen departments, has been restructured, and a director of national intelligence and a National Counterterrorism Center have been created to provide unity to the organization, although the effectiveness of these changes has remained a subject of debate.

Moving beyond the departments and agencies of the executive branch, the third concentric circle consists of Congress. Although technically a single institutional entity, Congress often appears to embrace many different centers of power and authority—ranging from the House and Senate leadership to the various coalitions operative in the legislative branch and from the various committees and subcommittees in which Congress does its real work to the individual senators and representatives who often vie with one another for publicity as well as power. Of all the institutions involved in foreign policymaking, Congress is least engaged in the day-to-day conduct of the nation's foreign relations, as reflected in its placement in the outermost circle.

Does this stylized description of the relative influence of various institutions and actors involved in foreign policymaking continue to hold in the wake of September 11, the turbulence of the Iraq and Afghanistan wars, the rise of the terrorism wrought by ISIS, and the devastation of Syria? Roger Hilsman, who first suggested this institutional conceptualization some five decades ago in his *To Move a Nation*, even then cautioned against a too facile reliance on this description. Although the institutional setting may affect the form and flow of policy, the politicking inherent in the process by no means conforms to the neatly compartmentalized, institutionalized paths implied by Hilsman's framework. What the nation chooses to do abroad is more often the product of an intense political struggle among the prominent players in the policymaking process, the policymaking positions or roles occupied by the key decisionmakers, and the characteristics of those individuals. The changed and changing nature of the international system is also pertinent to the contemporary institutional setting. As the constraints and opportunities in the twenty-first century unfold, the character and responsiveness of institutions largely formed during the decades of Cold War can be expected to change. It is a viewpoint we examine in the chapters in part II.

Beginning with the innermost concentric circle, a case can be made that the post-9/11 changes in the global environment have strengthened the presidency and increased its centrality in the governmental setting. Indeed, the *Economist* proclaimed shortly after September 11 that "the United States is witnessing the most dramatic expansion in presidential power for a generation."[1] In effect, we seemed to be witnessing a return of the "imperial presidency" of the Vietnam era. As the Iraq War has dragged on, as public opinion increasingly opposed presidential actions, and as Congress came under the control of the opposition party in 2006, presidential power came under more and more scrutiny and constraint. Barack Obama sought to restore the authority to the presidential office with his sweeping presidential victories, his seeming charismatic style, and his extensive use of executive orders as a governing tool. Yet he also faced the opposition party gaining control of the House of Representatives in the 2010 congressional elections and the U.S. Senate in 2014, and with his deliberative leadership style and personal characteristics came under scrutiny.[2]

As Michael Nelson argues in the first chapter in part II, "Person and Office: Presidents, the Presidency, and Foreign Policy," it is really a combination of the characteristics of the presidency and characteristics of the individual occupying the presidency that provides the fullest understanding of that institution. The presidency, as Nelson notes, possesses several important constitutional powers, although their exact operation was never made clear by the framers. Indeed, "it took well over a century for parchment to become practice" and "for all the constitutionally enumerated powers of the presidency to come to life." The activation of these powers actually came sooner in foreign policy than in domestic policy with Washington's proclamation of neutrality in the war between France and England and the declaration of the Monroe Doctrine. These (and other early unilateral actions by presidents) were defended by citing the nature of the presidency, with its unity of office and its election by the entire country. In the modern era, these arguments for presidential leadership were strengthened with the emergence of the Cold War and with the reluctance of Congress to challenge executive prerogatives in foreign affairs. Despite congressional passage of the War Powers Resolution in the aftermath of the Vietnam War, for example, succeeding presidents have not "complied with the letter, much less the spirit," of that law. Throughout much of the history of the Republic, the Supreme Court has routinely backed the executive's prerogatives in foreign affairs.

Another dimension of the office that aids presidential dominance is the president's dual role as chief of state and chief of government. The former role allows the president to represent the nation externally; the latter allows the president to lead the nation internally. Importantly, both roles afford the president the opportunity to lead the public, thus enhancing his ability to use his popularity to promote his policy.

The experiences, the personality, and the skills that an individual brings to the office are also important for understanding presidents' conduct of foreign policy. Some presidents served as secretary of state prior to assuming office, but recent ones more often come with backgrounds as state governors. As a result, recent presidents have had less experience in foreign affairs than as chief executives. The degree of self-confidence and the degree of consistency in their actions, Nelson points out, may also be helpful in understanding presidents' behavior. Finally, the leadership skills of a president—his management of authority within his own staff, his tactical political skills in dealing with Congress, and his presentation of self to the public—appear to be crucial in making the presidency function effectively as an institution.

In "Presidential Wars: Understanding Their Causes and Costs," Louis Fisher is pessimistic about the prospects of altering the balance of executive–legislative influence in foreign policy, even on issues involving the use of American force abroad. In this critical policy arena, presidents continue to act unilaterally. "Instead of coming to Congress for authority," as the Constitution calls for, presidents "justify military actions either on the commander in chief clause . . . or on decisions reached by the UN Security Council and the North Atlantic Treaty Organization (NATO)."

President Truman encouraged this process early in the Cold War by first promising to obtain congressional approval for any use of U.S. troops as part of a UN operation but then ignoring Congress when he sent American troops to Korea in June 1950. President Lyndon Johnson did get congressional approval for actions in the Vietnam War with the passage of the Gulf of Tonkin Resolution after the reporting of two attacks upon American vessels, but it turns out that one of the attacks never actually occurred.

In sending American forces to Haiti and Bosnia and using American air power in Kosovo, Clinton followed a similar strategy. To deal with Haiti, he sought and obtained a Security Council resolution authorizing an invasion and explicitly denied that he needed congressional support: "I have not agreed that I was constitutionally mandated to obtain the support of Congress." In Bosnia, he invoked authority under Article 2 of the Constitution and the NATO Treaty to deploy American forces as part of the Dayton Accords of November 1995, and he again denied that he needed congressional approval for his actions. Before the Kosovo campaign, Clinton again looked to NATO to authorize action, and he made that decision unilaterally ("I decided that the United States would vote to give NATO the authority to carry out military strikes against Serbia").

In early 2002 when George W. Bush first began discussing war against Iraq, there was little mention of going to Congress to request its support— or even going to an international forum, as his father and Clinton had done to justify earlier interventions. By the fall of that year, the administration had changed its mind and asked Congress to pass a resolution on Iraq prior to the 2002 congressional elections. In this highly partisan atmosphere and because of the popularity of the president, Bush easily succeeded in obtaining a resolution to use force against Iraq at his discretion. While a U.S. victory over Iraqi forces occurred quickly, the reconstruction of Iraq proved extraordinarily difficult, and sectarian violence was difficult to control.

In the case of Libya in 2011, President Obama followed the same practice as past presidents. As Fisher writes, "he decided to embark on a new war in Libya without seeking or obtaining authority from Congress." Instead, President Obama relied upon the passage of a United Nations Security Council Resolution (1973) to justify this action. He did notify Congress of his actions, but he did not seek their approval. His actions did result in several efforts by the members of Congress, including the passage of a resolution offered by Speaker of the House John Boehner (R-OH) admonishing the president for failing "to provide Congress with a compelling rationale" for the actions in Libya and seeking a detailed report within fourteen days. The president did send such a report, and he invoked his powers as commander in chief and as chief executive to take such actions. Fisher categorises a series of other efforts over the next several months by Congress, but those efforts did not produce any real changes in executive behavior.

More recently, President Obama did seek congressional authority to engage in an attack on Syria after that country crossed the "redline" regarding the use of chemical weapons. Congress did not act, but the president claimed authority from the commander-in-chief clause if he wanted to act unilaterally. However, a proposal from Russia with regard to turning over Syrian chemical weapons to an international body eliminated the necessity for presidential action. Finally, with actions toward the Islamic State in Iraq and Syria (ISIS), President Obama did ask Congress for authorization, but that body failed to act. "The result," as Fisher argues, "is another presidential war that lacks any statutory or constitutional authority."

In all these cases, Congress acquiesced in presidential encroachment on its powers. Indeed, Fisher argues that "Congress . . . fails to fight back but even volunteers fundamental legislative powers, including the war power and the power of the purse." While partisan politics partially explains Congress's acquiescence, members of both political parties often support presidential prerogatives. In the end, Fisher worries that the process "undermines public control, the system of checks and balances, and constitutional government."

Another important institutional mechanism within the first concentric circle of foreign policymaking is the National Security Council (NSC) system. It consists of the formal NSC, the complex of interagency committees that carry on its work, and the NSC staff, which serves the president, his advisers, and the committees making up the NSC system. The NSC staff is headed by the president's assistant for national security affairs, who has assumed a position of prominence in recent decades. Similarly, the NSC system and staff have become crucial mechanisms within the institutionalized presidency used by the White House to ensure its control of policymaking and to enhance prospects for policy coherence and consistency with presidential wishes.

Often the visibility and power of the national security assistant has been cause for conflict with other key participants in the process, notably the secretary of state. That was especially apparent during the Nixon and Carter presidencies. During the Reagan presidency, the role of the NSC staff became more contentious—indeed, infamous—as the staff engaged in the abuse of power: Lieutenant Colonel Oliver L. North undertook covert operational activities designed to divert profits from the sale of arms to Iran to the Contras fighting the Sandinista regime in Nicaragua, in apparent contravention of congressional prohibitions.

Steps were later taken to ensure that the NSC staff would no longer engage in operational activities, and both the first Bush and the Clinton presidencies were marked by the absence of public squabbles between their respective secretaries of state (James A. Baker for Bush, Warren Christopher and later Madeleine Albright for Clinton) and national security advisers (Brent Scowcroft for Bush, Anthony Lake and then Samuel Berger for Clinton). Still, Scowcroft, Lake, and Berger were powerful players in the policy process, exercising decisive influence in supporting Bush's determination to evict Iraqi forces from Kuwait and pressing Clinton to intervene in Haiti and to support the expansion of NATO.

Under President George W. Bush, the pattern of a strong and influential national security adviser continued. Condoleezza Rice, according to one assessment, played "a critical, if largely hidden, role in the overall direction of the president's foreign policy." Her successor as national security adviser in the Bush administration's second term was Stephen Hadley, her deputy from 2001 to 2004. He exercised perhaps a less public role than Rice, but he continued to be an important shaper of foreign policy. President Obama's first national security adviser, James Jones, a retired general, did not directly fit this mode in terms of dominating policymaking. After he resigned in November 2010, he was replaced by his deputy, Tom Donilon, a long-time political and foreign policy operative, who appears to be a more effective shaper of foreign policy. His replacement, Susan Rice, moved over from the American ambassadorship at the United Nations to assume this position in President Obama's second term and played a key role in shaping policy. President Trump's initial national security adviser was former three-star general and head of the Defense Intelligence Agency, Michael Flynn. After he was found not to be truthful about his discussions with a Russian official, he was replaced within one month's time by Lieutenant General H. R. McMaster. Given Trump's limited foreign policy experience, McMaster is likely to play the dominant foreign policy role that recent national security advisers have assumed.

In the next chapter, Ivo H. Daalder and I. M. (Mac) Destler provide a closer look at the role of the national security adviser in the foreign policy process. In their "How National Security Advisers See Their Role," they draw directly on the results of two roundtables with individuals who served in this position over the past four decades or so and their long experience as observers of this position. Daalder and Destler begin their analysis by identifying the reasons the role of the national security adviser has expanded since its inception. The primary reason is what they call "the presidents' need for close-in foreign policy support," but other factors have aided this expansion as well. As the NSC staff increased and became institutionalized, it assumed new functions in the policy process (e.g., crisis management). As the foreign policy agenda expanded, the NSC adviser and staff also took on more intermestic issues. As "U.S. politics no longer ends at the water's edge," the NSC, acting as the White House's surrogate, assumed responsibility to monitor the political aspects of foreign policy actions.

Within the context of these expanded responsibilities, Daalder and Destler identify three principal roles that the national security adviser undertakes: managing the foreign policy decision-making process, undertaking operational matters, and assuming public responsibilities. The most important of these is the first one, managing the decision process. In this role, the adviser needs "to ensure both that those with strong stakes are involved and that all realistic policy options are fully considered." He or she must also make certain that choices are made in a "timely manner" and must oversee "the implementation of the decisions made by the president and his or her advisers."

The operational and public roles of the national security advisers have less importance than the managerial one, but they have become increasingly used in recent years. As we have seen, in the aftermath of the Iran-Contra scandal in the mid-1980s, the NSC and its staff formally rejected an operational role. In practice, as Daalder and Destler point out, the national security adviser and the NSC staff continue to play an operational role. This role occurs for several reasons: other governments have counterparts to the adviser and require this kind of direct interaction, the traditional foreign policy bureaucracies have not been responsive to the president's directives, or the president wants to signal a fundamental shift in foreign policy through the adviser's action. The public role of the national security adviser has emerged largely with the increased politicization of foreign policy over the past three or four decades and with the expansion of media outlets, which have required that an administration have "all the bases" covered in addressing foreign affairs. With this public role, demands for more accountability of the advisers have increased, including requiring Senate confirmation of these appointments, which is not currently done.

If the institutions in the innermost (presidential) concentric circle have seemingly become more powerful since the events of September 11, that is clearly not the case with Congress during the past several years. First, it reverted to a foreign policy role reminiscent of the early years of the Cold War, with substantial deference to the president. As the war in Iraq soured, Congress then sought to be more assertive on foreign policy, and that posture has continued during the Obama administration. In "The Shifting Pendulum of Power: Executive–Legislative Relations on American Foreign Policy," James M. Lindsay surveys the changes in congressional attitudes toward the foreign policy process, especially during the past two decades or so. In 2002, Lindsay notes, the concern was that "Congress looked to have surrendered its constitutional role in foreign policymaking to the White House." By 2007, however, "Congress recovered its voice on foreign policy," and this "resurgent interest" in foreign policy has continued during the Obama administration. His explanation for this congressional volte-face lies not within "the realm of law" but within "the realm of politics." The crucial political questions for Congress are whether the country is threatened internationally and whether the president's policies are working ("Presidents who succeed find themselves surrounded by admirers; presidents who don't find themselves with fewer friends").

While the Constitution provides the framework for both Congress and president to exercise influence in the conduct of foreign policy, the political arena has often been the determinant of whether Congress actually exercises its authority. Lindsay argues that the ebbs and flows of congressional actions in foreign affairs turn largely on the perceived threat from abroad. Congressional deference was particularly evident in the immediate post–World War II years, for example, but it came "to a crashing halt" with the Vietnam War. Later, "the end of the Cold War accelerated the trend toward congressional activism." Indeed, the Clinton administration faced a series of congressional foreign policy challenges, and, more often than not, Congress prevailed.

September 11 changed that again, as "the pendulum of power swung sharply back toward the White House." Not only did members of Congress promptly provide the president with sweeping authority to retaliate against terrorism, but they also reversed policy stances that they had previously adopted. They quickly agreed to pay overdue UN dues to facilitate coalition building through that body, they lifted sanctions against Pakistan that had been imposed since the military coup in that country in 1999, and they were prepared to increase defense spending sharply. Congressional criticism of the war on terrorism was muted, and criticism that did arise was quickly challenged on patriotic grounds. By 2006, however, both Democrats and Republicans in Congress questioned the failing Iraq policy, and the stunning congressional defeats in the House and the Senate for the president's party embolden this foreign policy opposition. By early 2007, congressional criticism of foreign policy was in full throat—and across party lines—and for the balance of the Bush administration.

Congressional opposition on foreign policy continued with the Obama administration—whether over seeking to close the U.S. prison at Guantanamo Bay, Cuba, trying to pass cap-and-trade legislation, or ratifying the New START Treaty negotiated by the administration. Similarly, President Obama's action toward Libya in 2011 produced a chorus of congressional criticism, prompted by the belief that the president was usurping Congress's war powers. Proposed actions over Syria by the United States in 2013 and completion of the Iran nuclear agreement of 2015 (without the use of a treaty) produced congressional opposition as well. Despite Republican majorities in Congress, the Trump administration is unlikely to escape some congressional opposition to its foreign policy initiatives. Although Congress may not always be successful in these efforts to overturn presidential actions, that may not ultimately be necessary. As Lindsay points out, "Congress influences foreign policy not just by what it does, but what it can persuade the White House not to do."

What, Lindsay asks, is the "proper balance between activism and deference" by Congress? His judgment is that both have costs and benefits. Congressional activism forces the president and his advisers to think through their policy options, and it affords Congress the opportunity to debate and legitimate the chosen course with the American public. Yet such activism has its downside. It makes the process more cumbersome and time-consuming, and it may also lead to an incoherent policy if the two branches differ on the direction of policy. While congressional deference may avoid such problems, it may contribute to presidential "overreach" on policy. Because "presidents and their advisers are not infallible," congressional checks and balances can aid in their choices of the best policies for the nation.

According to the Constitution, the president and Congress are coequal partners in foreign policymaking. Both are elected by the American people. In practice, however, the bureaucratic organizations of the permanent foreign affairs government depicted in the second concentric circle in figure II.1 provide continuity from one administration to the next and through the continuing presidential and congressional electoral cycles. Not surprisingly, then, the organizations constituting the foreign affairs government are often described as "the fourth branch of government."

People who work in the "fourth branch" often spend their entire careers managing the routine affairs that constitute America's relations with other countries. Indeed, these career professionals and the organizations they work for are expected to be the government's "eyes and ears," searching for incipient global changes and assessing American needs and interests abroad. Thus, these key institutions can be expected to change as global challenges and opportunities change. As the last four chapters in part II suggest, organizations central to American diplomatic, military, intelligence, and economic policymaking are, in fact, responding to the changing global environment. How well they have adapted is, however, a matter of sometimes contentious political debate, and each faces an increasing set of new challenges.

In the first of these chapters, "American Diplomacy at Risk," the American Academy of Diplomacy outlines a series of challenges that the Department of State faces in advancing U.S. foreign policy and makes several important recommendations for improving the operation of this crucial bureaucracy. The chapter focuses on two major concerns that confront the Department of State at present: addressing the increased politicization of the policy and appointment process and improving the conditions and relationships between Civil and Foreign Service members within this important foreign policy bureaucracy.

Although the authors of this report acknowledge the crucial and central role that diplomacy plays in affecting the "security, safety and well-being" of Americans and that diplomacy has played an important role in America's past policy, "the sad reality is that . . . America's ability to lead globally through diplomacy is declining." This decline is related to a number of factors. First, diplomacy is increasingly politicized through the appointment of private citizens as ambassadors and key policymakers at the expense of career professionals from the U.S. Foreign Service. Indeed, with the increase in the role of money in politics, some ambassadorships are given to the important donors to an administration. Second, the demarcation between the role of Foreign Service and Civil Service members of the department has broken down, with the latter increasing performing some of the responsibilities of the former. Third, the State Department is not sufficiently educating its members "to the professional level of our competitor nations." Fourth, the opportunities for career advancements for Civil Service personnel are not sufficiently developed to ensure sustained quality performance. Finally, the department needs "broad review" to enhance and "optimize its organization, management and workforce development."

The rest of the chapter evaluates these five factors more fully and makes several recommendations of changes needed within the Department of State to address these concerns. To reduce the politicization of the department and to take advantage of the capabilities of Foreign Service officers, the authors make a number of recommendations including that Foreign Service officers occupy some of the top positions in the department and that a majority of appointments as ambassadors being those officers as well. The divisions in responsibilities between Civil Service and Foreign Service personnel, as required by the Foreign Service Act of 1980, should be recognized, rather than some actions taken lately to break down the barriers between the two sets of personnel. To maintain and enhance the professional level of the Foreign Service, the department needs to continue to maintain standards and foster the needed and important skills required for a professional diplomatic service. At the same time, the Civil Service section needs to be strengthened with career development and training opportunities. Importantly, too, there must be a path for "upward mobility" with the system as well. Finally, while the department has made considerable strides in upgrading its facilities, technology, and education and training, the final recommendation calls for addressing "the development and management of its human resources" and for "sustaining and strengthening professional identities" of the members of the Department of State.

The American military as a foreign and national security policy institution has hardly been immune from the impact of dramatic events of the past two decades, and it has not been immune from calls for significant change. Just after George W. Bush took office, for example, the U.S. Commission on National Security/Twenty-First Century (the Hart-Rudman Commission) argued that the Pentagon "needs to be overhauled" and that "strategy should once again drive the design and implementation of U.S. national security policies." More recently, and especially with the increasing budgetary difficulties of the American government and with the wars in Iraq and Afghanistan winding down during the Obama administration, the Department of Defense (DOD), and the defense budget in particular, has become a primary target for possible change in missions and funding. The Trump administration has continued this call for reform and for strengthening the military and its foreign policy posture.

In the next chapter, therefore, a former official in the DOD during the Clinton and Obama administrations, Michèle A. Flournoy, outlines what she perceives are the reforms needed in that important bureaucracy for ensuring more effective foreign and defense policy in the future. The occasion for her outlining these reforms is testimony before the Senate Armed Services Committee in its reexamination of the Goldwater-Nichols legislation (Defense Reorganization Act of 1986). That legislation increased the powers of the chairman of the Joint Chiefs of Staff as the principal military advisor to the president, created a system of commandant commanders (COCOM) for global regions who were responsible for joint or unified operations of the differing services in their region, and provided the secretary of defense with greater command authority.

In assessing whether that legislation should be changed in any way, Flournoy raises a series of reforms that should be undertaken to improve the quality of policymaking and the efficiency of the DOD. She begins her analysis by pointing to important policy process issues. There is, she contends, "the tyranny of consensus" that dominates the policymaking process within the Pentagon. Consensus "has become an end in itself in too many areas," and this has hampered the development of "compelling options or alternatives to present to senior leaders for decisions." Moreover, she also points out the "lack of clarity on the roles and responsibilities" of the various participants in the process—the Office of the Secretary of Defense, the Joint Staff of the military chiefs, and the staff of the combatant commanders. Further, as she also notes, the sheer size (and growth) of the Pentagon personnel involved in this process further complicates the policy process—and these should be reexamined.

Flournoy next turns to what she sees as the broken "strategy development process" at the DOD. She is particularly critical of the utility of the Quadrennial Defense Review (QDR) for producing good strategy for the department. That report too often becomes a document "written primarily for outside audiences" and fails to serve the needs of the department and the policy process. Instead, she recommends that the congressional requirement of the QDR be repealed and the DOD instead develop a classified defense strategy statement in the first year of each new presidential term. Further, much as the strategy process is flawed, Flournoy also views the translation of strategy into an adequate force structure that way as well. The emphasis on consensus among the various participants in developing the force leads to "lowest common denominator" decisions. Here, she recommends a more competitive process among the differing stakeholders and that the secretary of defense and the deputy secretary in charge of this process facilitate this competition. Finally, she recommends that Congress can assist in this change by supporting the secretary of defense's role, allowing some industry participation to ensure acquisitions and tolerating the possibility of some initial failure as this particular reform begins to take place.

The next set of recommendations that Flournoy set out considers the "bloated" size of the defense bureaucracy, even as the number of active duty military declines. The secretary of defense needs to undertake a comprehensive review to "delayer" the bureaucracy and eliminate redundancies. Congress also should provide the secretary the authority to "reshape the civilian workforce for the 21st century" within the DOD. Flournoy also would like to see Congress provide the secretary of defense with the ability to commission a study by an outside group to assess how greater efficiency might be achieved. Finally, in terms of organizational structure within the DOD, Congress should have the secretary of defense review and possibly streamline the combatant commands and perhaps reduce the size of their staffs.

A last set of recommendations focuses on the need for Congress to give the secretary of defense more authority to manage the department. She also would encourage Congress to alter the requirements for DOD political appointees to allow the appointment of individuals with business and management expertise. Finally, Flournoy also calls for the department to be given the authority to engage in another round of base closings as a way to use funds more efficiently.

The final section of her analysis focuses on the implications of her comments for revising the Goldwater-Nichols legislation. Although she largely supports the legislation, she reiterates the importance of allowing the secretary of defense as the "ultimate decider" in the crucial area of determining capabilities for the military and in directing the combatant commands and military services (rather than giving the chairman of the Joint Chiefs of Staff [JCS] such authority). Finally, she notes that any reform should consider the "second and third order effects," that organizational change in itself is not a panacea, and that more consistent and predictable military funding by Congress will be needed in the future.

The intelligence community is the third major foreign policy institution in the second concentric circle of policymaking. It, too, has been buffeted by recent changes in world politics. While the intelligence community has long come under criticism for its failures in intelligence estimates, the impact of September 11 produced a firestorm of criticism within Congress, as did the failures over assessing whether Saddam Hussein possessed weapons of mass destruction prior to the war with Iraq. Calls were heard for investigations of the presumed failures that had allowed the events to happen, and the 9/11 Commission offered a series of recommendations of how the intelligence community should be restructured and how changes in its operation should occur.[3] Further, Congress passed and the president signed the National Intelligence Security Reform Act of 2004, creating a new director of national intelligence to oversee and provide unity to the far-flung intelligence community.

Despite these changes, the new structure of the intelligence community has continued to have its difficulties. The attempted bombing of an airline by the "underwear bomber" on Christmas Day in 2009, the failed terrorist attack on Times Square in 2010, the Boston Marathon bombing of 2013, the San Bernardino attack of 2015, and the Orlando attack in 2016 raised questions anew about the effectiveness of intelligence in protecting the American public. To be sure, the intelligence community's (and the military's) success in killing Osama bin Laden in Pakistan in May 2011 and Anwar al-Awlaki in Yemen in September 2011 muted some criticism. Nonetheless, problems continue to exist between policymakers and the intelligence community over the quality and timeliness of information for effective action, and the Trump administration from its earliest days has renewed these concerns.

In "Why Intelligence and Policymakers Clash," political scientist Robert Jervis outlines some of these issues. In particular, he shows how the differing needs and views between policymaking and intelligence officials "guarantee conflict between them." Jervis notes that policymakers, for "both political and psychological reasons," tend "to oversell their policies" and, in doing so, they seemingly pressure the intelligence community to reinforce their policy views. Such pressure clashes with the fundamental role of intelligence—to produce information "to support better policy" and not to support a particular position of a policymaker. In all, the preferred position of policymakers for reinforcing intelligence clashes with the intelligence community's objective to produce accurate assessments. The rest of the chapter skillfully analyzes the conflicting positions of these organizations in more detail.

The run-up to the Iraq War in 2003 illustrates these competing pressures between these two important actors. The Bush administration had one view of Saddam Hussein, Iraq's nuclear weapons program, and the costs of a war with that nation. For psychological and political reasons, the Bush administration tended to link all these views together into a coherent policymaking package. Although the community believed that Iraq had a WMD program, the intelligence community's view on Saddam Hussein and the linkage with Al Qaeda and on the costs of a war with Iraq was much more differentiated. In particular, the intelligence community was more skeptical of any link between Iraq and Al Qaeda than Bush administration policymakers, and it doubted the ease of postwar reconstruction in that country. In essence, intelligence "did not feel the psychological need to bolster the case for war, [and] it did not have to pull other perceptions into line."

Beyond this fundamental tension, a series of factors may exacerbate the conflict between policymakers and the intelligence community. Jervis systematically goes through each of them and uses a series of historical examples to illustrate each one. First, policymakers are reluctant to consider an alternative option (Plan B) when a preferred option (Plan A) is not working. Yet the intelligence community, without the same stake in Plan A as policymakers, can more quickly "detect signs that the policies are failing." Jervis points to "perseverance" and "confidence" on the part of policymakers as important explanations for policymakers sticking with Plan A, even when intelligence might suggest an alternate option. That is, policymakers believe that if they stay with a policy long enough, it will succeed. Alternately, because policymakers have "confidence" in their policy choice, they are reluctant to abandon it for psychological and political reasons. Second, "cognitive predisposition" on the part of both policymakers and the intelligence community makes it difficult for the two communities to work together. Each group, Jervis argues, often comes to a policy situation with differing worldviews. As such, they may have difficulty in reconciling the information that they are receiving and processing. Third, timing is crucial with intelligence assessments and policymakers, and the intelligence community often has difficulty making the two agree. That is, intelligence "must arrive at the right time." Intelligence that arrives "too early" will be ignored by policymakers, while intelligence arriving "too late" may be put aside. Hence, to resolve this dilemma, Jervis suggests that intelligence should operate "on questions that are important, but not immediately pressing" for the policymakers. In this way, intelligence has the best prospect of making a difference. Suffice it to say, timing remains a real challenge for both participants.

Finally, Jervis tackles the issue of attempted politicization of intelligence by policymakers and discusses how that can also produce added friction between the two parties. Politicization may be attempted by policymakers in a variety of ways—from telling the intelligence community the desired conclusions in an assessment requested to demoting an official for a wrong answer to not seeking evaluations on some topics over fear of the answer. Jervis readily acknowledges that many of these efforts at politicization are ambiguous and difficult to untangle, and that fact complicates the relationship even more. Indeed, both sides have important reasons for taking differing actions that may be viewed as advancing politicization or resisting information requests. That is, policymakers want to probe for more thorough intelligence assessments (and thus they could be accused of politicizing an issue), while intelligence does not want to be pushed in a direction that they do not want to go (and they could be accused of being unresponsive to policymakers). As such, these issues "are rarely easy to settle," and tensions between the two continue.

In all, Jervis concludes where he began by arguing that "the two groups are doomed to work together and to come into conflict." And the reason is a fundamental one: "The needs and missions of leaders and intelligence officials are very different."

Recent American administrations have made trade policy a central focus of their foreign policy agendas. During the Clinton administration, for example, numerous bilateral and multilateral trade agreements (e.g., the North American Free Trade Agreement and the World Trade Organization [WTO]) were negotiated and entered into force. The Bush administration continued this process with the negotiation of several bilateral free-trade agreements (FTAs) around the world. The Obama administration has continued this process with its own ambitious trade policy agenda. The administration has declared that its "trade policy will support more American jobs and better jobs as we open world markets for Made in America products."[4] Trade policy, however, can be controversial, at home and abroad as the Clinton, Bush, and Obama administrations learned. Clinton faced substantial opposition at home in 1993 in seeking congressional approval for NAFTA and massive demonstrations by environmental, labor, and anti-globalization groups protesting against international trade regulations at the 1999 WTO meeting in Seattle. Bush had to deal with similar protests in Quebec City, Canada, over the Free Trade Area of the Americas in April 2001 and with opposition in Congress over several FTAs. Obama similarly confronted sustained congressional opposition over previously signed FTAs with Panama, Colombia, and South Korea (although ultimately prevailing in October 2011). In all, foreign economic issues remain divisive in domestic and foreign policy, and the trade process and trade politics remain crucial issues in American foreign policy.

In the last chapter in part II, "American Trade Policymaking: A Unique Process," trade analyst I. M. (Mac) Destler tackles these issues by providing a careful assessment of the trade policymaking process over the history of the Republic and by analyzing the current domestic politics of trade policy. He begins his analysis by noting that historically trade policymaking was centered in Congress and the principal issue was the tariff on importation. Indeed, the tariff issue dominated the trade agenda until the early twentieth century, reaching its apex with the passage of the Smoot-Hawley Act of 1930 that raised the average tariff to 60 percent. Such a punitive tariff, and similar ones across the world, deepened the Depression and "contributed to a fundamental change in U.S. trade policy, substantively and institutionally." Substantively, the policy turn was to lower tariffs, and institutionally, the process turn was a greater role for the executive branch in initiating trade policy.

The principal vehicle for the shift in policymaking and policy results was the Reciprocal Trade Agreements Act of 1934. Under this act, as Destler explains, the executive branch would negotiate trade tariffs under authority granted by Congress, and, in this way, the executive tends to lower rather than raise tariffs. By the end of World War II, moreover, this pattern continued beyond bilateral negotiations to include multilateral agreements as well.

Still, Congress was not entirely pleased with this arrangement, especially since the Department of State primarily carried out these negotiations and some members of Congress believed that State did not wholly understand the requirements of business. Hence, when President Kennedy sought greater negotiating authority, Congress provided it to him in the Trade Expansion Act of 1962, but it did so by creating the office of the "President's Special Representative for Trade Negotiations (STR)" within the White House. In doing so, the president (or his representative) gained even more authority over trade policymaking.

By the Trade Act of 1974, Congress transformed the STR into a statutory office and, five years later, the position was changed yet again, "renaming the STR the Office of the *United States* Trade Representative (USTR) and broadening its authority." In 1988, the Omnibus Trade and Competitiveness Act increased the power of the USTR yet again to where it is presently. As a result, the USTR "typically leads and manages on major trade issues" and "heads a statutory interagency coordinating committee structure that operates at cabinet and sub-cabinet levels."

Yet the USTR is not the sole agency involved in the formulation and implementation of U.S. trade policy. In conjunction with the United States International Trade Commission, the Department of Commerce determines whether U.S. industries have suffered "injury" by the trade actions of foreign countries. If it so determines, Commerce has the responsibility to impose countervailing duties and enforce antidumping laws for the United States on behalf of these firms. Importantly, Commerce also operates the U.S. and Foreign Commercial Service, the principal agency for promoting U.S. businesses around the world. Finally, as Destler points out, the Department of Agriculture also has trade policymaking responsibilities when issues related to agricultural trade liberalization arise.

The executive branch thus has important responsibilities in the formulation of trade policy, but the approval of Congress is still needed to implement actions. An important and recent innovation in improving interbranch coordination over formulation and implementation has been the "fast-track procedures" (later called "trade promotion authority"). Under this arrangement, the president (or more accurately, the USTR) negotiates a trade agreement with another country, and Congress agrees to vote on the negotiated agreement, without amendment, within ninety days of its submittal to Congress. At the same time, and as part of this process, the USTR is required to consult with Congress and private-sector advisory groups during the course of its negotiations. Moreover, as Destler points out, this procedure has been very important in the completion of trade agreements by the United States. Yet it also allows Congress to maintain ultimate control over the trade policy process.

Much as the process for formulating trade policy has changed over the past century, the domestic politics of trade has as well. In particular, Destler discusses two important changes in the trade policy environment that affects the effort to move toward a more open trading system. First, American business and industries have largely moved from a protectionist to a free-trade stance, hence supporting more openness, while organized labor has moved in the opposite direction, from espousing free trade to a more protectionist posture, hence seeking to slow down market openness. Second, an "anti-globalization" movement emerged in the 1990s— composed of labor unions, environmentalists, and some nongovernmental organizations—that also is skeptical of free trade and its impact at home, on developing countries, and the environment. This movement has complicated the passage of FTAs negotiated by the Bush administration, and it has further exacerbated partisan divisions over trade policy. Although a congressional compromise was negotiated in 2007 (the "May 10 agreement") to bridge the gaps between the two parties of these free-trade pacts, the agreement worked imperfectly. Instead, and as we noted earlier, it took several years to get previously negotiated agreements (e.g., Colombia, Panama, Korea) approved by Congress in late 2011. The latest trade dispute is over the Trans-Pacific Partnership that Destler discusses at the end of his analysis. In one of his first actions upon entering office, however, President Donald Trump signed an executive order withdrawing the United States from this FTA that was negotiated by the Obama administration because it did not advantage the United States. Moreover, in his inaugural address, President Trump had harsh words for trade generally and its effect domestically. Although Destler challenges such an assessment on trade, he concludes that "the gains from trade are very much at risk" and that we are entering "a new and uncertain era." In this sense, America's trade policy remains constrained by the requirements of domestic politics.

Editor's Note: At the end of each chapter is a series of discussion questions for use by the students and instructor.

NOTES

1. "The Imperial Presidency," *Economist*, November 3, 2001, 39.

2. For an example of President Obama's deliberative decision-making, especially over decision-making on Afghanistan, see Bob Woodward, *Obama's Wars* (New York: Simon and Schuster, 2010), and for an analysis of President Obama's personality and personal identity, see Stanley A. Renshon, *Barack Obama and the Politics of Redemption* (New York: Routledge, 2012). Also see Colin Dueck, *The Obama Doctrine* (Oxford: Oxford University Press, 2015) on Obama's decision style and foreign policy aims.

3. *The 9/11 Commission Report* (New York: Norton, 2004).

4. Ambassador Ron Kirk (Office of the United States Trade Representative), "President's 2011 Trade Policy Agenda Focuses on American Jobs," March 1, 2011, www.ustr.gov/about-us/press-office/press-releases/2011/presidents-2011-trade-policy-agenda-focuses-american-jobs.

9

Person and Office

Presidents, the Presidency, and Foreign Policy

Michael Nelson

Henry Jones Ford, in his classic work *The Rise and Growth of American Government*, quoted Alexander Hamilton's prediction to a friend that the time would "assuredly come when every vital question of the state will be merged in the question, 'Who shall be the next president?' " Ford cited this remark to support his argument that in creating the presidency, the Constitutional Convention of 1787 had "revived the oldest political institution of the race, the elective kingship."

Although there is much truth in Ford's evaluation of the presidency, it also displays a certain measure of ambivalence on a fundamental issue. Is the presidency best understood as a person ("Who shall be the next president?") or an office (an elective monarchy)?

Political scientists in the twentieth and twenty-first centuries have continued to grapple with Ford's conundrum. Most of them probably would agree that the best answer to the person-or-office question is some combination of both: person and office, president and presidency. The office has become important mostly because its constitutional design suited it well for national leadership in the changing circumstances of history. But because the Constitution invested so much responsibility in the person who is the president, that person's background, personality, and leadership skills are consequential as well.

Modern political scientists also tend to agree on a second matter—namely, that the presidency and the presidents who occupy the office are never more important than in the making of foreign policy. George W. Bush, a president who was more narrowly elected (2000) and reelected (2004) than any of his predecessors, showed that this is especially true of issues and challenges that concern the national security. Bush launched wars in Afghanistan and Iraq and, despite the latter's severe unpopularity by 2006, was able to increase the American military commitment even after suffering a major defeat in the midterm congressional elections. Bush's successor, Barack Obama, won a more convincing victory in 2008 and immediately faced what turned out to be the nearly insurmountable challenges of trying to bring the wars that Bush began to a reasonably successful conclusion. Obama faced many obstacles in doing so, but none of these originated in Congress or domestic politics. The same was true after Obama's reelection in 2012, when he was faced with trying to navigate between two equally unattractive opposing forces in Syria and Iraq, the brutally dictatorial regime of Syrian president Basshar al-Assad and its terrorist opponent, the Islamic State of Iraq and the Levant (ISIL).

OFFICE

The Constitutional Convention created a government marked less by separation of powers than, in political scientist Richard Neustadt's apt phrase, by "separated institutions sharing powers." Institutional separation meant that in stark contrast to parliamentary governments, which typically draw their executive leaders from the legislature, the president was forbidden by article 1, section 6, of the Constitution to appoint any sitting member of Congress to the cabinet or White House staff. These severely separated branches were, however, constitutionally enjoined to share in the exercise of virtually all the powers of the national government. Congress is empowered to "make all laws," but the president may veto them. The Senate may (or may choose not to) give "Advice and Consent" concerning presidential appointments to the executive branch and the judiciary. In matters of war, the president is "Commander in Chief of the Army and Navy," but Congress has the power to "declare war," to "raise and support Armies," and to "provide and maintain a Navy." In matters of peace, no treaty proposed by a president can take effect unless two-thirds of the Senate votes to ratify it.

Powers alone do not define power. Through history, the presidency has become much more powerful than at its inception, even though the formal powers of the office have remained the same. A second cluster of constitutional decisions, those concerning the number and selection of the executive, provides much of the explanation for the presidency's expanding influence. The framers of the Constitution, after much debate, created the presidency as a unitary, not a plural or committee-style, office and provided that the president would be elected by the entire nation, independently of Congress and the state governments. In doing so, they made the president the only national officer who can plausibly claim both a political mandate to speak for the people and their government and an institutional capacity to lead with what the Pennsylvania delegate James Wilson described as "energy, unity, and responsibility."

Lead, that is, when and in such areas of public policy as national leadership is sought—which, during the nineteenth century, it usually was not in the domestic realm. Historically, it took well over a century for parchment to become practice—that is, for all of the constitutionally enumerated powers of the presidency to come to life. Congress seized the lion's share of the government's shared powers in domestic policy nearly from the beginning, dominating even the executive appointment process. When it came to legislation, members of Congress treated with scorn most early presidential efforts to recommend or influence their consideration of bills and resolutions. Nor, until Andrew Jackson in the 1830s, were presidents able to exercise the veto power without provoking a politically disabling storm of opposition on Capitol Hill.

Although presidential disempowerment was long lived, it was not eternal. The weakness of the presidency in domestic matters was a function of the weak national government that generally prevailed during the nineteenth century. The country, then a congeries of local economies and cultures, was not seeking what the presidency was constitutionally designed to provide, namely, energetic leadership on behalf of national initiatives. But the conditions that sustained weak government began to change around the turn of the century. The widespread dissemination of railroads and telegraph lines made all but inevitable the development of a national economy, and with this transformation came demands that the national government take measures to facilitate the spread (while taming the excesses) of the new and massive corporations. Early-twentieth-century presidents Theodore Roosevelt and Woodrow Wilson roused a popular mandate for the president to make full use of the office's constitutional powers to lead Congress and the executive branch. Franklin D. Roosevelt, during the Great Depression of the 1930s, and more recent presidents, such as Lyndon B. Johnson, Ronald Reagan, and Barack Obama, also played the role of chief legislator on a grand scale.

In contrast to the slow awakening of the presidency's constitutional powers concerning domestic policy, on matters of foreign policy the powers of the office were activated early. In 1793, George Washington issued the Proclamation of Neutrality on his own authority, declaring that the United States would not take sides in the war between England and France. Critics declared that he lacked that authority. Because a declaration of war must be approved by Congress, they argued, so must a declaration not to go to war. Secretary of the Treasury Alexander Hamilton, writing as "Pacificus," replied in a series of pseudonymous newspaper articles that the president's constitutional powers were sufficient. Unlike the vesting clause of article 1, which states that "All legislative Powers herein granted shall be vested in a Congress of the United States," the vesting clause for the president lacks the words "herein granted," stating instead, "The executive Power shall be vested in a President of the United States of America." The omission of these two words, Hamilton claimed, meant that the president had constitutional powers beyond those specified by name, especially in foreign policy. Washington's proclamation stood.

Although presidents had to struggle to invigorate the domestic powers of their office during the nineteenth and early twentieth centuries, they usually were able to get their way when deciding how the United States should deal with other countries. In 1823, an otherwise weak president, James Monroe, issued the Monroe Doctrine on his own authority. The doctrine declared that the Americas were off-limits to any attempts at European colonization. James K. Polk secretly negotiated for the annexation of Texas during the mid-1840s and, by sending troops into disputed territory, provoked war with Mexico. Without congressional consultation, Presidents William McKinley, William Howard Taft, Woodrow Wilson, and Calvin Coolidge dispatched American forces into foreign countries.

Similarly, beginning with the Washington administration, presidential decisions about which foreign governments to recognize have gone uncontested as a proper exercise of the president's constitutional authority to "receive Ambassadors." Treaties gradually gave way to executive agreements as the main form of contract between the United States and other countries.

When criticized for their assertiveness in foreign policy, presidents invariably invoked the institutional nature of their office, especially its unitary character and election by the entire country. In his book *The Decline and Resurgence of Congress*, James Sundquist summarized the standard (and politically persuasive) response of presidents to their critics: "Quick decision was imperative; . . . the move had to be made, or negotiations conducted, in secret, and only the executive could maintain confidentiality; . . . only the president has the essential information; . . . effective intercourse with other nations requires the United States to speak with a single voice, which can only be the president's."

Arguments such as these became especially compelling in the post–World War II era. As in previous wars, vast temporary powers had been granted to the president during World War II. What made this war different was its aftermath. Instead of lapsing into relative isolation from world political affairs, the United States entered into a Cold War with the Soviet Union. New technologies of warfare, especially nuclear weapons and intercontinental delivery systems, raised the specter of instant and global destruction.

These developments made the president's number- and selection-based constitutional strengths appear even more significant than during past wars. Increased reliance not only on executive agreements but also on secrecy in all diplomacy made the conduct of postwar foreign policy a shared power with Congress in only the most nominal sense. The Republican Eightieth Congress (1947–1949) was angrily partisan on domestic issues, but it readily assented to Democratic president Harry S. Truman's far-reaching foreign policy initiatives, including the Marshall Plan and the North Atlantic Treaty Organization (NATO). Congress supported the American intervention in the Korean War, which it was never asked to declare, with annual military appropriations. It provided similar support for the war in Vietnam during the 1960s and early 1970s. In the years between these two wars, Congress wrote virtual blank checks in advance support of whatever actions the administrations of Dwight D. Eisenhower and John F. Kennedy might decide to take in the Middle East, Berlin, Cuba, and elsewhere.

Much was made in the post-Vietnam era of Congress's newfound assertiveness in foreign policy. In 1973, for example, Congress enacted the War Powers Resolution over President Richard Nixon's veto. The resolution requires the president to consult with Congress "in every possible instance" before sending American forces into hostile or dangerous situations. After committing the armed forces, the president is then charged to remove them within sixty (or, by special presidential request, ninety) days unless Congress votes to authorize their continued involvement.

Every president since the War Powers Resolution was enacted has questioned its constitutionality. A number of military operations have been undertaken—by Presidents Gerald Ford (the *Mayaguez* rescue), Jimmy Carter (the attempted Iranian hostage rescue), Ronald Reagan (the Grenada invasion), George H. W. Bush (the Panama invasion and the Persian Gulf War), Bill Clinton (the stationing of peacekeeping troops in Somalia, Haiti, and Bosnia), George W. Bush (the wars in Afghanistan and Iraq), and Barack Obama (the toppling of the Qaddafi regime in Libya). In few instances have these presidents complied with the letter, much less the spirit, of the War Powers Resolution. Yet Congress has seldom voted to start the sixty-day clock—and never when it mattered. The main lesson of more than four decades of experience under the resolution is that law cannot substitute for political will if Congress is to curb the president's role in war making.

Congress's weakness in foreign policymaking can be partially explained by its institutional character: large, diverse, unwieldy, and slow. As Sundquist observed, Congress can "disrupt the policy that the president pursues, but it cannot act affirmatively to carry out a comprehensive substitute policy of its own." Congress also is constrained by the public's expectations of its members. Voters want their representatives and senators to concern themselves more with local than national interests, which leaves out most foreign policies. Not surprisingly, Congress is most assertive on those few global issues that have a clear domestic policy coloration, such as trade policy and support for nations, especially Israel, that have large and well-organized domestic lobbies.

As for the Supreme Court, although it occasionally rebukes a president for exceeding the constitutional authority of the office, on the whole it has defended presidents' expansive interpretations of their powers. In *Hamdan v. Rumsfeld* (2006), the court slapped down George W. Bush's claim that the president could establish military tribunals to try suspected foreign terrorists. But no Supreme Court decision has challenged the court's most important ruling concerning presidential power in foreign affairs. In *United States v. Curtiss-Wright Export Corp.* (1936), the Court echoed Pacificus in declaring that "the President is the sole organ of the federal government in the field of international relations." The president, the court continued, "not Congress, has the better opportunity of knowing the conditions which prevail in foreign countries, and especially is this true in time of war." The court's strong defense of presidential power in foreign affairs was all the more remarkable because at the time of the decision, the justices were reining in the president's powers in domestic policy.

One other aspect of the presidential office merits special attention. In making the presidency a unitary office elected by its own national constituency, the framers of the Constitution unwittingly combined the normally separate executive leadership roles of chief of government and chief of state into one office. As chief of government, the president is called on to act as a partisan political leader in the manner of, for example, the British prime minister. As chief of state, the president is the equivalent of the British monarch—the ceremonial leader of the nation and the living symbol of national unity.

The significance of the chief of state role has little to do with the insignificant formal powers that accompany it or the activities it requires. Rather, it lies in the emotions the role arouses in citizens. Long before they have any knowledge of what the president does, young children already have positive feelings about the president's seemingly boundless power and benevolence. The death of a president causes adults to react in an equally emotional way. Surveys taken shortly after the Kennedy assassination found Americans displaying symptoms of grief that otherwise appear only at the death of a close friend or family member. Similar outpourings seem to have accompanied the deaths in office, whether by assassination or natural causes, of all presidents, whether they were young or old, popular or unpopular. In Great Britain, it is royal deaths, such as King George V's in 1936 and Princess Diana's in 1997, that occasion such deep emotions. It is the monarch whom children think of as powerful and good, not the prime minister.

The public's attachment to the president as chief of state sometimes has strong implications for the president's powers as chief of government, especially in foreign policy. In particular, the often-observed "rally 'round the flag effect" is a way in which the president benefits politically from being the nation's living symbol of unity. A rally effect is the sudden and substantial increase in public approval of the president that occurs in response to dramatic international events involving the United States. These include sudden military interventions, major diplomatic actions, and attacks on the United States. Richard Nixon's public approval rating rose twelve percentage points after his October 1969 "Vietnamization" speech. Gerald Ford's jumped eleven points after he dispatched troops to rescue the *Mayaguez*. Carter added twelve points to his approval rating as a result of the Camp David summit that achieved peace between Israel and Egypt. Reagan's approval rating leaped eight points when he invaded Grenada. George H. W. Bush's rating soared higher than any previous president's after the American victory against Iraq in the Gulf War. His record was broken by his son, George W. Bush, after he launched the war on terrorism in September 2001. The younger Bush's approval rating rose from 51 to 90 percent and remained above 75 percent for nearly a year, strengthening his hand as he directed the course of American policy toward Afghanistan and Iraq. Obama's rating improved in 2011 when he authorized a secret Special Forces mission to kill Osama bin Laden, the leader of the terrorist Al Qaeda network that conducted the 9/11 attacks on the World Trade Center and Pentagon.

PERSON

Because the presidency is important, so is the person who is president. What kinds of experience do presidents typically bring with them into office? What manner of personality? What skills of leadership?

Concerning experience, until career businessman Donald Trump's election in 2016, presidents always were drawn from the ranks of high government officials: vice presidents, members of Congress, governors, cabinet members, or generals. In most recent elections, the roster of presidential candidates was confined largely to governors, vice presidents, and senators.

The disappearance of cabinet members, generals, and members of Congress from the presidential talent pool has reduced the likelihood that the president will be experienced in foreign policy before taking office. Early in the nation's history, service as secretary of state was the main stepping-stone to the presidency. Four of the first six presidents—Thomas Jefferson, James Madison, James Monroe, and John Quincy Adams—had previously served as secretary of state. Generals in successful wars, such as Andrew Jackson (War of 1812), Zachary Taylor (Mexican-American War), Ulysses S. Grant (Civil War), and Dwight D. Eisenhower (World War II) sometimes have been elected president, but not in the modern era of warfare. In the four elections from 1960 to 1972, every major party nominee was a senator or a former senator. But in the anti-Washington political climate that has dominated presidential elections since the Vietnam War and the Watergate scandal, not a single senator has been elected president.

Instead of secretaries of state, generals, and senators, state governors have dominated the ranks of the presidency in recent decades. Trump's election was in some ways an extension of the "outsider" appeal from outside Washington to outside government altogether. Of the seven presidents chosen from 1976 to 2012, four were governors: Jimmy Carter of Georgia in 1976, Ronald Reagan of California in 1980 and 1984, Bill Clinton of Arkansas in 1992 and 1996, and George W. Bush of Texas in 2000 and 2004. (The others were, in addition to Trump, Vice President George H. W. Bush in 1988 and Senator Barack Obama in 2008, whose freshman status in the Senate meant that he, like the governors and Trump, was inexperienced in foreign policy.) Although international concerns came to dominate the administrations of all of these presidents, nearly everything they knew about foreign policy, the elder Bush excepted, came from election-year cramming and on-the-job experience.

The personality, or psychological character, that a president brings to the White House is, considering the power of the office and the pressures that weigh on its occupant, of obvious importance. In 1972, James David Barber drew scholarly attention to this concern. In his book *The Presidential Character*, Barber offered a theory that places each president into one of four character types. The most dangerous of these is the "active negative," the president who is attracted to politics by a lack of self-esteem that can be compensated for psychologically only by dominating others through the wielding of official power. When active-negative presidents feel that their hold on power is threatened, they react in rigidly defensive ways, persisting in ineffective and destructive courses of action and treating critics as enemies. In Barber's view, Wilson's failure to compromise with Senate critics on the League of Nations treaty and Johnson's unwillingness to change course in Vietnam were the products of active-negative psychological characters.

Critics have taken Barber to task for a number of fundamental weaknesses in his theory. At root, the psychological study of personality is still too murky a field to explain, much less to predict, the presidential character. But public concern remains high. For example, in 2000, doubts about character went a long way toward explaining the outcome of the presidential election. Democratic candidate Al Gore carried a reputation into the campaign as an aggressive, experienced, and skillful debater, a reputation that his Republican opponent, George W. Bush, lacked. Yet Bush ended up benefiting considerably more from their three nationally televised debates than Gore did. In the first debate, Gore treated his opponent with disdain, often speaking condescendingly when it was his turn and sighing and grimacing while Bush spoke. Chastened by the adverse public response, Gore was deferential, almost obsequious, during the second debate. He hit his stride in the third debate, but the inconsistency of his behavior from one debate to the next fed voters' doubts about who Gore really was. Bush was not strongly impressive in any of the debates, but voters saw the same person in all three of them. Gore, who had entered the debate season leading Bush by around five percentage points in the polls, left it trailing by five points.

The skills of leadership that a president requires may be more confidently described than the presidential character. In relations with the rest of the executive branch, the president is called on to be an adroit *manager of authority*, both of lieutenants on the White House staff (whose chronic sycophancy toward the president and hostility toward the president's critics perennially threaten to overwhelm the good effects of their loyalty, talent, and hard work) and of the massive departments and agencies of the bureaucracy, whose activities lie at the heart of the president's role as chief executive. For example, as a new president, George W. Bush went a long way toward reassuring foreign policy experts who doubted his understanding of international issues by appointing veteran Washington hands to important executive positions, especially Richard Cheney as vice president, Colin Powell as secretary of state, and Donald Rumsfeld as secretary of defense. Experience proved no sure guide in office, however. Cheney's and Rumsfeld's failure to anticipate the difficulties of occupying Iraq was the source of innumerable difficulties after American-led forces toppled Iraqi dictator Saddam Hussein in 2003. Nevertheless, Obama emulated Bush in appointing experienced leaders to major foreign policy positions: Joseph Biden as vice president, Hillary Clinton as first-term secretary of state and John F. Kerry as her second-term replacement, and Robert Gates (Rumsfeld's replacement during Bush's final two years) and later Chuck Hagel and Ashton Carter as secretary of defense.

Presidential leadership of Congress requires different, more *tactical political skills*. Senators and representatives, no less than the president, are politically independent and self-interested. No one has described the challenge of leading them more pithily and precisely than Neustadt in his book *Presidential Power*. To lead, Neustadt argued, is to persuade; to persuade is to bargain; and to bargain is to convince members of Congress that their interests and the president's are (or can be made to be) the same.

Ultimately, a president's standing with Congress and the bureaucracy rests on the bedrock of public opinion, which makes the *presentation of self* (a phrase invented by the sociologist Erving Goffman) to the American people an important category of leadership skills. Presentation of self involves not just speech making, press conferences, and other forms of rhetoric but dramaturgy as well. During Richard Nixon's first term, for example, he reinforced a televised speech appealing for the support of the "silent majority" of blue-collar workers and their families by dramatically donning a hard hat before a cheering crowd (and a battery of cameras) at a New York City construction site. Bill Clinton, concerned that neither the military nor the American people regarded him as a confident commander in chief, learned from studying videotapes of Ronald Reagan how to transform limp, off-hand salutes on ceremonial occasions into shoulders-back posture and crisp salutes. George W. Bush used rhetoric and dramaturgy to reassure a worried nation two days after the September 11 attacks. Standing in the midst of New York's Ground Zero with his arm around a rescue worker, Bush answered listeners who said they could not hear him by declaring "I can hear you. The rest of the world hears you. And the people who knocked these buildings down will hear all of us soon." In December 2009, Obama chose West Point as the setting in which to launch his new, two-pronged approach to the war in Afghanistan: an immediate infusion of new troops in 2010 followed by troop withdrawals starting in 2011.

Perhaps a president's most important leadership skill involves a *strategic sense* of the historical possibilities of the time. These possibilities are defined both by objective conditions (the international situation, the budget, the health of the economy, and so on) and by the public mood. Above all, the president must have a highly developed aptitude for what Woodrow Wilson called "interpretation"—that is, the ability to understand and articulate the varying, vaguely expressed desires of the American people for change or quiescence, material prosperity or moral challenge, isolation from or intervention in the problems of the world, and so on.

In the end, the background, personality, and leadership skills of the president are important because of the ways in which the Constitution and changing historical circumstances have made the presidency important. Person and office, although defined and often discussed separately, are in essence one.

DISCUSSION QUESTIONS

1. What are the constitutional powers of the presidency?
2. What does Nelson mean when he says "powers alone do not define power"?
3. How have the actions of past presidents affected the powers of the office?
4. How have presidential powers changed over time?
5. What are the key personal characteristics of a president that may affect his approach to the presidency and foreign policy?
6. What are some of the drawbacks to using a president's personality to determine his foreign policy approach?

10

Presidential Wars

Understanding Their Causes and Costs

Louis Fisher

From 1789 to 1950, all major military initiatives by the United States against foreign powers were decided by Congress, either by a formal declaration of war or by a statute authorizing the president to use military force. There were some notable exceptions, such as the actions by President James Polk, that led to hostilities between the United States and Mexico. Even on this occasion, Polk knew that the Constitution required him to come to Congress to seek authority. Presidents also used military force for various "life and property" actions, but they were typically limited, short-term engagements. By and large, the first century and a half followed the framers' expectation that matters of war and peace would be vested in the government's representative branch—Congress.

The record since 1950 has been dramatically different. Presidents for more than six decades have repeatedly acted unilaterally when using military force against other countries. Instead of coming to Congress for authority, they justify military actions either on the commander-in-chief clause in the Constitution or on decisions reached by the UN Security Council and the North Atlantic Treaty Organization (NATO). The current war against the Islamic State, which has lasted more than two years and is expected to continue for at least a decade, has never been specifically authorized by Congress.

CONSTITUTIONAL PRINCIPLES

When the American Constitution was drafted in 1787, the framers were aware that existing models of government placed the war power and foreign affairs solely in the hands of the king. Thus, matters of treaties, appointment of ambassadors, the raising and regulation of fleets and armies, and the initiation of military actions against other countries had been vested in the king. Accordingly, John Locke and William Blackstone, whose writings the framers read with care, assigned war powers and foreign affairs exclusively to the executive branch.

This monarchical model was expressly rejected at the Philadelphia convention. As revealed in the debates at the Constitutional Convention,[1] Charles Pinckney said he was for "a vigorous Executive but was afraid the Executive powers of [the existing] Congress might extend to peace & war &c which would render the Executive a Monarchy, of the worst kind, to wit an elective one." Although John Rutledge wanted the executive power placed in a single person, "he was not for giving him the power of war and peace." James Wilson supported a single executive but "did not consider the Prerogative of the British Monarch as a proper guide in defining the Executive powers. Some of these prerogatives were of a Legislative nature. Among others that of war & peace &c." Edmund Randolph worried about executive power, calling it "the foetus of monarchy."

The framers recognized that the president would need unilateral power in one area: defensive actions to repel sudden attacks, especially when Congress was not in session to legislate. An early draft of the Constitution empowered Congress to "make war." Charles Pinckney objected that legislative proceedings "were too slow" for the safety of the country in an emergency since he expected Congress to meet but once a year. James Madison and Elbridge Gerry moved to insert "declare" for "make," leaving to the president "the power to repel sudden attacks."

Debate on the Madison-Gerry amendment underscored the limited grant of authority to the president. Pierce Butler wanted to give the president the power to make war, arguing that he "will have all the requisite qualities, and will not make war but when the Nation will support it." Roger Sherman objected: "The Executive shd. be able to repel and not to commence war." Gerry said he "never expected to hear in a republic a motion to empower the Executive alone to declare war." George Mason spoke "agst giving the power of war to the Executive, because not [safely] to be trusted with it; . . . He was for clogging rather than facilitating war."

Similar statements were made at the state ratifying conventions. In Pennsylvania, James Wilson expressed the prevailing sentiment that the system of checks and balances "will not hurry us into war; it is calculated to guard against it. It will not be in the power of a single man, or a single body of men, to involve us in such distress; for the important power of declaring war is vested in the legislature at large."[2] The framers also took great pains to separate the purse and the sword. They were familiar with the efforts of English kings to rely on extra-parliamentary sources of revenue for military expeditions. After a series of monarchical transgressions, England lurched into a bloody civil war. The origin and vigor of democratic government is directly related to legislative control over the purse.

The U.S. Constitution states: "No Money shall be drawn from the Treasury, but in Consequence of Appropriations made by Law." In Federalist No. 48, Madison explained that "the legislative department alone has access to the pockets of the people." The Constitution empowers Congress to lay and collect taxes, duties, imposts, and excises; to borrow money on the credit of the United States; and to coin money and regulate its value. The power of the purse, Madison said in Federalist No. 58, represents the "most compleat and effectual weapon with which any constitution can arm the immediate representatives of the people, for obtaining a redress of every grievance, and for carrying into effect every just and salutary measure."

In making the president the commander in chief, the Constitution retained for Congress the important check over spending. Madison set forth this tenet: "Those who are to *conduct a war* cannot in the nature of things, be proper or safe judges, whether *a war ought* to be *commenced, continued,* or *concluded.* They are barred from the latter functions by a great principle in free government, analogous to that which separates the sword from the purse, or the power of executing from the power of enacting laws." At the Philadelphia convention, George Mason counseled that the "purse & the sword ought never to get into the same hands (whether Legislative or Executive)."

Distrust of executive wars was underscored by John Jay in his essay, *Federalist* No. 4. He noted:

> It is too true, however disgraceful it may be to human nature, that nations in general will make war whenever they have a prospect of getting any thing by it; nay, absolute monarchs will often make war when their nations are to get nothing by it, but for purposes and objects merely personal, such as a thirst for military glory, revenge for personal affronts, ambition, or private compacts to aggrandize or support their particular families or partisans.

Under those motivations, a single executive may "engage in wars not sanctified by justice or the voice and interests of his people."

Throughout the next century and a half, major military actions were either declared by Congress (the War of 1812, the Mexican War of 1846, the Spanish-American War of 1898, World War I, and World War II) or authorized by Congress (the Quasi-War against France from 1798 to 1800 and the Barbary Wars during the administrations of Thomas Jefferson and James Madison). In either case, presidents regularly came to Congress to seek authority to initiate offensive actions against another country.

That pattern changed radically in 1950 when President Harry Truman ordered American troops to Korea without ever coming to Congress for authority, either before or after. He based his actions in part on resolutions adopted by the UN Security Council, but nothing in the history of the UN Charter implies that Congress ever contemplated placing in the hands of the president the unilateral power to wage war.

THE UNITED NATIONS AND NATO

In 1945, during Senate debate on the UN Charter, President Harry Truman sent a cable from Potsdam stating that all agreements involving U.S. troop commitments to the United Nations would first have to be approved by both Houses of Congress. He pledged without equivocation: "When any such agreement or agreements are negotiated it will be my purpose to ask the Congress for appropriate legislation to approve them."[3] By "agreements," he meant the procedures that would permit UN military force in dealing with threats to peace, breaches of the peace, and acts of aggression. All UN members would make available to the Security Council, "on its call and in accordance with a special agreement or agreements," armed forces and other assistance for the purpose of maintaining international peace and security.

The UN Charter provided that these agreements, concluded between the Security Council and member states, "shall be subject to ratification by the signatory states in accordance with their respective constitutional processes." Each nation would have to adopt its own procedures for meeting their international obligations.

After the Senate approved the UN Charter, Congress had to decide the meaning of "constitutional processes." What procedure was necessary, under the U.S. Constitution, to bring into effect the special agreements needed to contribute American troops to UN military actions? That issue was decided by the UN Participation Act of 1945, which stated without the slightest ambiguity that the agreements "shall be subject to the approval of the Congress by appropriate Act or joint resolution."[4] The agreements between the United States and the Security Council would not result from unilateral executive action, nor would they be brought into force only by the Senate acting through the treaty process. Action by both Houses of Congress would be required.

At every step in the legislative history of the UN Participation Act— hearings, committee reports, and floor debate—these elementary points were underscored and reinforced. Executive officials repeatedly assured members of Congress that the president could not commit troops to UN military actions unless Congress first approved. Truman signed the UN Participation Act without expressing any policy or constitutional objections.

During this time, the Senate also approved the NATO treaty of 1949, which provides that an armed attack against one or more of the parties in Europe or

North America "shall be considered an attack against them all." In the event of an attack, member states could exercise the right of individual or collective self-defense recognized by Article 51 of the UN Charter and assist the country or countries attacked by taking "such action as it deems necessary, including the use of armed force." However, Article 11 of the treaty states that it shall be ratified "and its provisions carried out by the Parties in accordance with their respective constitutional processes." The Southeast Asia Treaty of 1954 also stated that the treaty "shall be ratified and its provisions carried out by the Parties in accordance with their respective constitutional processes."

These treaties do not grant the president unilateral power to use military force against other nations. First, it is well recognized that the concept in mutual security treaties of an attack on one nation being an attack on all does not require from any nation an immediate response. Each country maintains the sovereign right to decide such matters by itself. As noted in the Rio Treaty of 1947, "no State shall be required to use armed force without its consent." In the U.S. system, who decides to use armed forces?

During hearings in 1949 on NATO, Secretary of State Dean Acheson told the Senate Foreign Relations Committee that it "does not mean that the United States would automatically be at war if one of the other signatory nations were the victim of an armed attack. Under our Constitution, the Congress alone has the power to declare war." Of course, he was merely saying what is expressly provided for in the Constitution. However, nothing in the legislative history of NATO gives the president any type of unilateral authority in the event of an attack. That the president lacks unilateral powers under the UN Charter or NATO should be obvious from the fact that both are international treaties entered into by way of a presidential proposal and Senate advice and consent. The president and the Senate cannot use the treaty process to strip the House of Representatives and future Senates of their prerogatives over the use of military force.

In the words of one scholar, the provisions in the NATO treaty that it be carried out according to constitutional processes were "intended to ensure that the Executive Branch of the Government should come back to the Congress when decisions were required in which the Congress has a constitutional responsibility." The NATO treaty "does not transfer to the President the Congressional power to make war."[5] Those predictions would be eroded by practices that began during the Clinton administration and carried forward to the Obama presidency.

TRUMAN IN KOREA

With these treaty and statutory safeguards in place to protect legislative prerogatives and constitutional government, President Truman sent U.S. troops to Korea in 1950 without ever seeking or obtaining congressional authority. How could that happen? How could so many express executive assurances to Congress and explicit statutory procedures be ignored and circumvented?

On June 26, Truman announced that the UN Security Council had ordered North Korea to withdraw its invading forces to positions north of the thirty-eighth parallel and that "in accordance with the resolution of the Security Council, the United States will vigorously support the effort of the Council to terminate this serious breach of the peace." The next day he ordered U.S. air and sea forces to provide military support to South Korea. It was not until the evening of June 27 that the Security Council actually called for military action.

Truman violated the statutory language and legislative history of the UN Participation Act, including his own assurance in 1945 that he would first obtain the approval of Congress before sending U.S. forces to a UN action. He ignored the special agreements that were the guarantee of congressional control. Truman exploited the UN machinery in part because of a fluke: the Soviet Union had absented itself from the Security Council during two crucial votes taken during the early days of the crisis. It is difficult to argue that the president's constitutional powers vary with the presence or absence of Soviet (or other) delegates to the Security Council. As Robert Bork noted in 1971, "The approval of the United Nations was obtained only because the Soviet Union happened to be boycotting the Security Council at the time, and the president's Constitutional powers can hardly be said to ebb and flow with the veto of the Soviet Union in the Security Council."[6]

In an effort to justify his actions in Korea, Truman called the military initiative a UN "police action" rather than an American war. That argument was suspect from the start and deteriorated as U.S. casualties mounted. The United Nations exercised no real authority over the conduct of the war. Other than token support from a few nations, it remained an American war—measured by troops, money, casualties, and deaths—from start to finish. The euphemism "police action" was never persuasive. As a federal court concluded in 1953: "We doubt very much if there is any question in the minds of the majority of the people of this country that the conflict now raging in Korea can be anything but war."[7]

JOHNSON'S VIETNAM WAR

In August 1964, President Lyndon Johnson reported two attacks against U.S. vessels in the Gulf of Tonkin. Although there was doubt at the time about the second attack, it was later demonstrated that the second attack never occurred. In 2005, the National Security Agency (NSA) released a study that concluded what had long been suspected: there was no second attack. The NSA explained that what had been reported as a second attack consisted of late signals coming from the first.[8] This would be one of many times that the United States went to war on the basis of false information provided by presidents and executive officials.[9]

President Johnson, aware of the hazards of getting involved in Vietnam, also worried that Republicans would exploit any sign of weakness on his part in fighting communism and jeopardize his reelections chances in the November 1964 elections. That political concern surfaced during House debate on August 4, 1964, when Rep. Dante Fascell (D-Fla.) spoke about "our confidence in President Johnson's leadership in time of grave crisis." Johnson's prompt military response, he said, "should put to rest any erroneous idea that the Communists or others may have that the United States has a 'no win policy'; or that the United States is a 'paper tiger.'" President Johnson's use of force would correct any communist idea that this administration or this country "is soft on communism."[10]

On May 27, 1964, in a conversation with foreign policy adviser McGeorge Bundy, Johnson confided that "it looks to me like we're getting into another Korea. It just worries the hell out of me. . . . I don't think it's worth fighting for and I don't think we can get out. It's just the biggest damned mess that I ever saw."[11] The next month, on June 2, Johnson told Robert Anderson, former secretary of the treasury in the Eisenhower administration: "I don't want to get tied down in an Asiatic war."[12]

Johnson would use the incidents in the Tonkin Gulf and the authority he received when Congress passed the Tonkin Gulf Resolution to widen the war. However, a few weeks before the election he told an audience in Ohio that "we are not about to send American boys 9 or 10,000 miles away from home to do what Asian boys ought to be doing for themselves."[13] In that speech, he estimated there were about 18,000 American soldiers in Vietnam. Through Johnson's initiatives, starting with large bombing runs in February 1965, troop strength eventually increased until it exceeded 500,000 American troops. Heavy casualties on both sides produced a bloody stalemate, spawned a powerful antiwar movement at home, and led to Johnson's announcement in 1968 that he would not run for reelection.

CLINTON'S MILITARY INITIATIVES

During the 1992 presidential campaign, Bill Clinton projected himself as a strong leader in foreign affairs and indicated a willingness to resort to military action. He said he was prepared to use military force—in concert with other nations—to bring humanitarian aid to the citizens of Bosnia and Herzegovina. While saying that he did not relish the prospect of sending Americans into combat, "neither do I flinch from it."[14]

Once in office, Clinton's position on what to do about the military regime in Haiti fluctuated from month to month, depending on shifting political pressures. Jean-Bertrand Aristide, the island's first democratically elected president, had been overthrown in a military coup on September 30, 1991. Political repression by the military rulers produced a flood of refugees trying to reach the United States. In October 1993, Clinton sent a contingent of six hundred U.S. soldiers to Haiti to work on roads, bridges, and water supplies. A group of armed civilians, opposed to U.S. intervention, prevented them from landing. Lightly armed, the U.S. troops were instructed by their commanders not to use force but to leave the area.

Clinton soon began threatening the use of military force. On July 31, 1994, the UN Security Council adopted a resolution "inviting" all states, particularly those in the region of Haiti, to use "all necessary means" to remove the military leadership in that island. At a news conference on August 3, Clinton denied that he needed authority from Congress to invade Haiti: "Like my predecessors of both parties, I have not agreed that I was constitutionally mandated to obtain the support of Congress." In a nationwide television address on September 15, Clinton told the American people that he was prepared to use military force to invade Haiti, referring to the Security Council resolution and expressing his willingness to lead a multilateral force "to carry out the will of the United Nations." There was no mention at all of the will of Congress.

An invasion of Haiti proved unnecessary. Clinton sent former president Jimmy Carter to negotiate with the military leaders in Haiti. They agreed to step down to permit the return of Aristide. Initially, nearly twenty thousand U.S. troops were dispatched to occupy Haiti and provide stability. Both Houses passed legislation stating that "the President should have sought and welcomed Congressional approval before deploying United States Forces to Haiti."

In concert with the United Nations and NATO, the Bush I and Clinton administrations participated in humanitarian airlifts in Sarajevo and helped enforce a "no-fly zone" (a ban on unauthorized flights over Bosnia-Herzegovina). In 1993, Clinton indicated that he would have to seek support and authorization from Congress before ordering air strikes. On May 7, he stated: "If I decide to ask the American people and the United States Congress to support an approach that would include the use of air power, I would have a very specific, clearly defined strategy." He anticipated asking "for the authority to use air power from the Congress and the American people."

Later in the year, he began to object to legislative efforts to restrict his military options. Instead of seeking authority from Congress, Clinton now said he would seek from Congress advice and support. He was "fundamentally opposed" to any statutory provisions that "improperly limit my ability to perform my constitutional duties as Commander-in-Chief." Instead, he would operate through NATO, even though NATO had never used military force during its almost half century of existence.

In 1994, Clinton announced that decisions to use air power would be taken in response to UN Security Council resolutions, operating through NATO's military command. There was no talk about seeking authority from Congress. By operating through NATO, Clinton would seek the agreement of England, France, Italy, and other NATO allies but not Congress. NATO air strikes began in February 1994 and were followed by additional strikes throughout the year and into the next. The authorizing body was a multinational organization, not Congress. The next escalation of U.S. military action was Clinton's decision to introduce ground troops into Bosnia. When reporters asked him on October 19, 1995, if he would send the troops even if Congress did not approve, he replied: "I am not going to lay down any of my constitutional prerogatives here today."

In October 1998, the Clinton administration was again threatening the Serbs with air strikes, this time because of Serb attacks on the ethnic Albanian majority in Kosovo. At a news conference on October 8, Clinton stated: "Yesterday I decided that the United States would vote to give NATO the authority to carry out military strikes against Serbia if President Milosevic continues to defy the international community." An interesting sentence—"*I* decided that the United States." Whatever Clinton personally decided would be America's policy.

Clinton's chief foreign policy advisers went to Capitol Hill to consult with lawmakers but not to obtain their approval. Although Congress was to be given no formal role in the use of force against Serbs, legislatures in other NATO countries took votes to specifically authorize military action in Yugoslavia. The Italian Parliament had to vote approval for the NATO strikes, and the German Supreme Court ruled that the Bundestag, which had been dissolved with the election that ousted Chancellor Kohl, had to be recalled to approve deployment of German aircraft and troops to Kosovo.

With air strikes imminent in March 1999, the Senate voted 58–41 to support military air operations and missile strikes against Serbia. On April 28, after the first month of bombing, the House took a series of votes on war in Yugoslavia. A vote to authorize the air operations and missiles strikes lost on a tie vote, 213–213. Several resolutions were offered in the Senate to either authorize or restrict the war, but they were tabled. The Senate chose procedural remedies rather than voting on the merits.

During the bombing of Serbia and Kosovo, Rep. Tom Campbell (R-CA) went to court with twenty-five other House colleagues to seek a declaration that President Clinton had violated the Constitution and the War Powers Resolution by conducting the air offensive without congressional authorization. A district judge held that Campbell did not have standing to raise his claims. Although each House had taken a number of votes, Congress had never as an entire institution ordered Clinton to cease military operations. In that sense, there was no "constitutional impasse" or "actual confrontation" for the court to resolve.[15]

THE IRAQ WAR IN 2003

When the administration of George W. Bush first began talking about war against Iraq in 2002, the White House cautioned that a number of options were being studied. On August 21, stating that "we will look at all options," Bush said the country was too preoccupied with military action against Iraq. Yet five days later, Vice President Dick Cheney delivered a forceful speech that identified only one option: going to war. He warned that Saddam Hussein would "fairly soon" have nuclear weapons and that it would be useless to seek a Security Council resolution requiring Iraq to submit to weapons inspectors. What happened to the options carefully being weighed by Bush?

When Bush addressed the United Nations on September 12, he laid down five conditions (including inspections) that could lead to a peaceful settlement. If Hussein complied with those demands, he could stay in power. Four days after the September 12 speech, Iraq agreed to unconditional inspections. Initially, the White House concluded that Bush did not need authority from Congress. For one reason or another, Bush decided in early September to seek legislative authorization. Lawmakers were pressured to complete action on the authorizing resolution before they adjourned for the elections, inviting partisan exploitation of the war issue. Several Republican nominees in congressional contests made a political weapon out of Iraq, comparing their "strong stand" on Iraq to "weak" positions by Democratic campaigners.

The administration released various accounts to demonstrate why Iraq was an imminent threat. On September 7, Bush cited a report by the International Atomic Energy Agency that the Iraqis were "six months away from developing a weapon. I don't know what more evidence we need." However, the report did not exist. The administration promoted a story about Mohamed Atta, the 9/11 leader, meeting with an Iraqi intelligence officer in Prague in April 2001. Yet Czech president Vaclav Havel was convinced there was no evidence that the meeting ever took place.

The administration tried to make a link between Iraq and Al Qaeda, but the reports could never be substantiated. Similar unproven claims were made about Iraq seeking uranium ore from a country in Africa, using aluminum tubes to advance its nuclear weapons program, deploying mobile labs capable of generating biological weapons, and having a stock of unmanned planes (drones) able to disperse chemical and biological agents. Those claims were unproven before the vote on the Iraq Resolution in October 2002 and thoroughly repudiated after the war began the following March.

The House passed the Iraq resolution, 296–133. That evening, the Senate voted 77–23 for the resolution. It would have been better for Congress as an institution, and for the country as a whole, to have Bush request the Security Council to authorize inspections in Iraq. Bush would then come to Congress after the elections (as was done in 1990–1991 with the Persian Gulf War). Congress would have been in the position at that point to make an informed choice. It chose, instead, to vote under partisan pressures, with inadequate information, and thereby abdicated its constitutional duties to the president.[16]

On March 19, 2003, President Bush announced the deployment of combat forces to Iraq. American forces prevailed over Iraqi troops in less than a month, but the quick victory proved to be illusory. Instead of confronting the vastly superior U.S. army, the opposition decided to melt away and prepare for a long guerrilla war. American commanders soon recognized that insurgents had ready access to weapons and were determined to make the United States pay a heavy price for the occupation. There were never sufficient U.S. troops to provide political stability in Iraq. As a result, government buildings were looted, violence spread across the country, and reconstruction projects were either delayed or abandoned. Iraq, which had provided a secular check on Islamic fundamentalism in the Middle East, deteriorated into a civil war between Shia and Sunni and also factional contests within those two groups. The Bush administration had planned to install a model democratic government in Iraq, capable of spreading those ideals to neighboring states. Instead, the chief victor in the Middle East was the growing power and influence of Iran.

OBAMA'S WAR IN LIBYA

Barack Obama entered the White House with the intention to wind down the war in Iraq and add U.S. troops to the war in Afghanistan. By the spring of 2011, he decided to embark on a new war in Libya without seeking or obtaining authority from Congress. On March 17, 2011, the Security Council passed Resolution 1973 to establish a ban on "all flights in the airspace of the Libyan Arab Jamahiriya in order to help protect civilians." Of course, the ban did not apply to "all" flights. It covered only those by the Libyan government. Military flights by coalition forces would be necessary to enforce the ban. Passage of Resolution 1973 came only after the Arab League had agreed to support a no-fly zone over Libya. Russia and China were prepared to veto the resolution but abstained, as did Germany, India, and Brazil.

The term "no-fly zone" might sound like something so limited militarily that it should not be considered war. However, it required destroying the capacity of Libya to act against the United States and its allies. No matter how officials seek to downplay or minimize a no-fly zone, the use of military force against another country that has not threatened the United States is, as former secretary of defense Robert Gates has said, an "act of war."[17]

On March 21, President Obama notified Congress that, two days earlier, U.S. forces "at my direction," commenced military operations against Libya "to assist an international effort authorized by the United Nations (U.N.) Security Council."[18] The U.S. Constitution does not permit transferring congressional power to outside bodies, including the UN and NATO. However, acting under Resolution 1973, coalition partners began a series of strikes against Libya's air defense systems and military airfields. Obama promised that the strikes would be "limited in their nature, duration, and scope," but the military commitment deepened on March 21 when he announced at a news conference: "It is U.S. policy that Qaddafi needs to go." The initial no-fly zone policy now gave way to regime change. Also, the administration said that it would ask Congress for legislative authority to shift some of the $30 billion in Libyan frozen assets to assist the rebels.

In a March 28 address to the nation, Obama described his Libyan actions in this manner: "The United States has done what we said we would do."[19] His reference to "the United States" and "we" was misleading. There was no joint agreement between the executive and legislative branches. Obama alone made the military commitment. He identified certain supporting institutions: "We had a unique ability to stop that violence: an international mandate for action, a broad coalition prepared to join us, the support of Arab countries, and a plea for help from the Libyan people themselves." Absent from this picture were Congress and the American people.

On April 1, the Office of Legal Counsel (OLC) in the Justice Department released a fourteen-page legal defense titled "Authority to Use Military Force in Libya." It spoke about "widespread popular demonstrations" throughout the Middle East beginning in mid-February, seeking government reform.[20] President Obama thus had time to inform Congress of the developing program and seek legislative authorization. Instead, he devoted time and energy in attracting support from allies, Arab nations, and the Security Council, not from the legislative branch. OLC looked to the Security Council resolution for authorization, but UN actions are not constitutional substitutes for congressional support. OLC cited a number of earlier actions by presidents taken without legislative authorization, but the precedents (missions of goodwill, rescue, or protecting American lives and property) had no connection to the military action against Libya.

Obama's failure to respect the constitutional role of Congress in the exercise of the war power led to strong challenges in the House of Representatives. Both Democrats and Republicans regarded his conduct as offensive. On June 3, 2011, the House debated and voted on two resolutions that criticized Obama for not seeking legislative authorization for the war in Libya. One resolution, introduced by Rep. Dennis Kucinich (D-OH) with Republican cosponsors, directed the removal of U.S. forces from Libya within fifteen days of the resolution's adoption. It failed 148–265. Introduced as a concurrent resolution, it would not have been legally binding. At most, it would have expressed the sentiments of the two chambers.

The second resolution was introduced by Speaker John Boehner (R-OH) and adopted 268–145. It noted that Obama had "failed to provide Congress with a compelling rationale" for military activities in Libya and directed Obama within fourteen days to describe "in detail" U.S. security interests and objectives in Libya and explain why he did not seek "authorization by Congress for the use of military force in Libya." Obama submitted his report to Boehner on June 15. By that time, the military action in Libya had exceeded the sixty-day clock of the War Powers Resolution of 1973 and neared the final ninety-day deadline—the first time a president would exceed the ninety-day limit.

How did the administration respond? Would it recognize that the ninety-day limit was binding on the president, requiring Obama to obtain statutory authorization? Would it announce that the War Powers Resolution was unconstitutional and its clock had no application? It chose to do neither. Instead, on page 25 of the June 15 report, it continued to insist that President Obama "had constitutional authority, as Commander in Chief and Chief Executive and pursuant to his foreign affairs powers, to direct such limited military operations abroad." Moreover, it held that the clock started only with the existence of "hostilities," and that no hostilities existed in Libya for this reason: "U.S. operations do not involve sustained fighting or active exchanges of fire with hostile forces, nor do they involve the presence of U.S. ground troops, U.S. casualties or a serious threat thereof, or any significance chance of escalation into a conflict characterized by those factors." In other words, if the United States conducted military operations by dropping bombs at thirty thousand feet, launching Tomahawk missiles from ships in the Mediterranean, and using unmanned armed drones, there would be no "hostilities" in Libya under the terms of the War Powers Resolution, provided U.S. casualties were minimal or nonexistent. According to this legal analysis, a nation could pulverize a weaker country with heavy bombing and there would be neither war nor hostilities.[21]

On June 24, the House responded to this report by debating two other measures that rebuked Obama. The chamber voted down a resolution that would have authorized U.S. military action in Libya. The vote: 123–295.

Seventy Democrats joined Republicans in voting against the resolution. A separate measure, to provide limited funding for the war, was also rejected, 180–238. Only thirty-six Democrats favored this bill. Critics of the House action called the two votes a "mixed message." Yet the legislative communication was quite clear on the fundamental point of whether to authorize and fund the war. On both counts: No.

On July 7, the House again passed restrictive language on military activities in Libya. It adopted, 225–201, an amendment to bar funding for training, equipping, or advising the rebel forces fighting against Colonel Qaddafi. An amendment to bar the use of any funds for military force in Libya fell on a vote of 199–229. A total of 132 Republicans and 67 Democrats voted for this restriction. A shift of thirteen votes would have meant, in the House, a total bar to funding the war.

The Senate, throughout this period, was nearly silent on the war. On March 1, it passed S. Res. 85, which urged the Security Council "to take such further action as may be necessary to protect civilians in Libya from attack, including the possible imposition of a no-fly zone over Libyan territory." The resolution was introduced that day and passed late in the afternoon with no debate and only thirty-five seconds for Senate action. The no-fly provision was added late in the afternoon with inadequate notice to senators. As a Senate resolution, it had no legal meaning.[22]

On May 23, the Senate introduced S. Res. 194, another nonbinding resolution. It expressed no concern about the lack of congressional authorization for the war in Libya. It merely requested President Obama "to consult regularly with Congress regarding United States efforts in Libya." The war power of Congress is diminished—or extinguished—when a president need only "consult" with a few members. The Constitution requires a declaration or authorization by Congress when the country goes from a state of peace to a state of war. The Senate took no action on S. Res. 194.

After the Senate Foreign Relations Committee on June 28 held hearings on "Libya and War Powers," in the afternoon it marked up a bill, S. J. Res. 20, to authorize the war. As a joint resolution, it would be legally binding. The committee planned to bring the resolution to the floor for Senate action on July 5, but it was withdrawn in favor of debate on the debt-limit crisis. No further action was taken. Because of its constitutional role with treaties and appointment of ambassadors, the Senate supposedly has a more prominent role in foreign affairs than the House. But the House acted first on Libya and its legislative actions were significantly stronger in terms of defending institutional interests.[23]

With military operations in Libya exceeding ninety days, President Obama asked OLC to prepare a legal memo that "hostilities" did not exist pursuant to the War Powers Resolution. OLC declined to prepare that memo. Jeh Johnson, general counsel in the Defense Department, also refused Obama's request. Eventually, White House Counsel Robert Bauer and State Department Legal Adviser Harold Koh agreed to state that no hostilities existed in Libya.[24] If Obama did not anticipate hostilities in Libya, he had no obligation to report to Congress within the forty-eight-hour deadline of the War Powers Resolution. But he did. Through that public action, he acknowledged the existence of hostilities or imminent hostilities.[25]

In an interview with Thomas Friedman on August 8, 2014, President Obama reflected on his use of military force in Libya: "I'll give you an example of a lesson I had to learn that still has ramifications to this day," referring to the overthrow of Qaddafi. Although he "absolutely believed that it was the right thing to do," he and his European partners "underestimated the need to come in full force if you're going to do this." There has to be "a much more aggressive effort to rebuild societies that didn't have any civil traditions. . . . So that's a lesson that I now apply every time I ask the question, 'Should we intervene, militarily? Do we have an answer [for] the day after?' "[26] In other words, the administration took Step One without planning for Step Two.

When President Obama justified military action in Libya, he said in a speech on March 28, 2011, that some nations "may be able to turn a blind eye to atrocities in other countries. The United States of America is different." After considering what Qaddafi might do against opponents in Benghazi and other regions, he felt compelled to act. Inaction "would have been a betrayal of who we are."[27] Several years later, aware of even greater humanitarian concerns in Syria, he decided not to invoke moral principles to topple a leader, Syria's President Bashar Assad.

SYRIA AND THE ISLAMIC STATE

In August 2013, President Obama was prepared to use military force against Syria but decided to seek congressional authority. He had publicly warned Syria that if it used chemical weapons against its people it would cross a "red line" and invite a retaliatory response by other countries, including the United States. On August 21, Syria used nerve gas to kill over a thousand people: men, women, and children. As with Libya, Obama claimed constitutional authority to act unilaterally for "limited" military actions without seeking authority from Congress.

Unable to gain the support of the UN Security Council, as with Libya, and facing strong opposition from voters around the country, Obama decided to seek authorization from Congress. In an address on September 10, he stated that as commander in chief he possessed independent constitutional authority to act militarily against Syria, but added: "I'm also the President of the world's oldest constitutional democracy. So even though I possess the authority to order military strikes, I believed it was right, in the absence of a direct or imminent threat to our security, to take this debate to Congress. I believe our democracy is stronger when the President acts with the support of Congress. And I believe that America acts more effectively abroad when we stand together." In his judgment, he did not think "we should remove another dictator with force—we learned from Iraq that doing so makes us responsible for all that comes next."[28] He did not mention what happened after removing Qaddafi in Libya.

Congress did not pass legislation authorizing military force against Syria. Nor did Obama attempt to act unilaterally. Instead, the administration worked jointly with Russia and the world community to compel Syria to surrender its supply of chemical weapons. By 2014, a new terrorist group called the Islamic State of Iraq and Syria (ISIS) threatened the northern part of Iraq and various parts of Syria. No one questioned the authority of President Obama to use military force to protect American diplomats and military advisers as part of a defensive operation. Nor were objections raised in using military force to protect thousands of Yazidis, a minority religious sect in northern Iraq, from possible massacre by ISIS. Those actions began in August 2014. The constitutional question concerned Obama's authority to act offensively against ISIS in Iraq and Syria in a war the administration estimated would last several years and possibly a decade or more, without receiving express congressional authority.

In February 2015, the administration asked Congress to pass legislation specifically authorizing military force against ISIS. It submitted a draft bill for congressional action. No legislative action was taken in 2015, nor was there expected to be any action throughout 2016. Fault certainly lies with Congress for failing to exercise its institutional powers, but the result is another presidential war that lacks any statutory or constitutional authority.

That matter is now in the courts. On May 4, 2016, Captain Nathan Michael Smith sued President Obama over the legality of the war against the Islamic State. In doing so, he challenged the claims by the administration that new authority was not required from Congress. An intelligence officer stationed in Kuwait, Smith supported military action against the Islamic State but wanted a legal judgment that the orders he was asked to carry out were legally binding. At issue is the basic question of distinguishing between lawful and unlawful military orders.

On July 11, the Justice Department filed a brief asking the district court to dismiss Smith's lawsuit because it raised a nonjusticiable political question and he lacked standing to assert his claims. A main argument by the Justice Department concerns "an unbroken stream of appropriations" passed by Congress supporting military actions against the Islamic State. On August 18, Smith's attorneys filed a response to the government's motion to dismiss. Among its arguments is referring to Section 8(a)(1) of the War

Powers Resolution, which stipulates that appropriations bills do not represent authorization for military actions unless they say so expressly, which Congress has not done.[29]

A FAILURE OF CHECKS AND BALANCES

The framers of the Constitution assumed that each branch of the government would protect its own prerogatives. Efforts by one branch to encroach on another would be beaten back. As Madison explained in *Federalist* No. 51: "The great security against a gradual concentration of the several powers in the same department, consists in giving to those who administer each department the necessary constitutional means and personal motives to resist encroachments of the others. . . . Ambition must be made to counter ambition." To some extent, this theory has worked well. The president and the judiciary invoke a multitude of powers to protect their institutions.

Congress, on the other hand, often fails to fight back and even volunteers to surrender fundamental legislative powers, including the war power and the power of the purse. Members of Congress seem uncertain about the scope of their constitutional powers. Some claim that Congress can limit funds for presidential actions that were taken in the past but never for future actions. There is no constitutional support for that position. The decision to use military force against other nations is reserved to Congress, other than for defensive actions. Members may restrict a president's actions prospectively as well as retrospectively.

At times, legislators will suggest that a cutoff of funds will leave American soldiers stranded and without food or ammunition. Those arguments were made during House debate in 1995 on prohibiting funds from being used for the deployment of ground forces to Bosnia and Herzegovina.[30] Cutting off funds would not have that effect. A funding prohibition would force the withdrawal of whatever troops were in place and prevent the deployment of any other troops to that region. Rather than place U.S. soldiers at risk, they are redeployed to more secure locations.

Theories of presidential war power that would have been shocking more than sixty years ago are now offered as though they are obvious and free of controversy. Instead of the two branches working in concert to create a program that has broad public support and understanding, presidents act unilaterally to engage the country in military operations abroad. Typically, they not only justify their actions on broad interpretations of the Constitution but also cite "authority" granted by multinational institutions in which the United States is but one of many state actors. This pattern does not merely weaken Congress and the power of the purse. It also undermines public control, the system of checks and balances, and constitutional government.

DISCUSSION QUESTIONS

1. On what "legal" grounds do U.S. presidents justify their unilateral decisions to use U.S. forces against other countries?
2. Why did the framers empower Congress to "declare war" but not to "make war"?
3. Why are the UN Participation Act of 1945 and Article 11 of the NATO Treaty important to U.S. participation in international military operations?
4. How did President Truman manage to circumvent congressional approval for sending troops to Korea in 1950?
5. President Johnson received statutory authority to act militarily in Vietnam. Why did his problems mount thereafter?
6. What was the situation in Haiti in the early and mid-1990s, and why did President Clinton contemplate use of military force without express congressional authorization?
7. On what basis did President Clinton claim he had independent authority to send troops to Bosnia in 1995?
8. What strategies did George W. Bush employ to demonstrate that Iraq was an imminent threat?
9. Why does Fisher say that by voting for the Iraq Resolution under partisan pressure, Congress abdicated its constitutional duties to the president?
10. On what legal and constitutional basis did President Obama direct action to be taken in Libya in March 2011? Did Congress restrict presidential action in any way?
11. How did congressional opposition block Obama's intended use of military action against Syria? What are the basic constitutional issues regarding the ongoing war against the Islamic State?
12. In the end, why does Congress largely defer to executive decisions regarding the use of U.S. forces abroad?

NOTES

1. See Max Farrand, ed., *The Records of the Federal Convention of 1787* (New Haven, CT: Yale University Press, 1937), especially 1:64–66, and 2:318–19.

2. Jonathan Elliot, ed., *The Debates in the Several State Conventions, on the Adoption of the Federal Constitution* (Washington, DC: 1836–1845), 2:528.

3. 91 *Cong. Rec.* 8185 (1945).

4. 59 Stat. 521, sec. 6 (1945).

5. Richard H. Heindel et al., "The North Atlantic Treaty in the United States Senate," *American Journal of International Law* 43 (1949): 649–50.

6. Robert H. Bork, "Comments on the Articles on the Legality of the United States Action in Cambodia," *American Journal of International Law* 65 (1971): 81.

7. *Weissman v. Metropolitan Life Ins. Co.*, 112 F. Supp. 420, 425 (S.D. Cal. 1953).

8. Robert J. Hanyok, "Skunks, Bogies, Silent Hounds, and the Flying Fish: The Gulf of Tonkin Mystery, 2–4 August 1964," *Cryptologic Quarterly*, declassified by the National Security Agency on Nov. 3, 2005, available at http://www.nsa.gov/public_info/_files/gulf_of_tonkin/articles/rel1_skunks_bogies.pdf.

9. Louis Fisher, "When Wars Begin: Misleading Statements by Presidents," *Presidential Studies Quarterly* 40 (2010): 171.

10. 110 *Cong. Rec.* 18549 (1964).

11. Michael R. Beschloss, ed., *Taking Charge: The Johnson White House Tapes, 1963–1964* (New York: Touchstone, 1998), 370.

12. Ibid., 380.

13. *Public Papers of the Presidents*, 1963–64, II, 1391.

14. *New York Times*, June 28, 1992, 16; *New York Times*, August 14, 1992, A15.

15. *Campbell v. Clinton*, 52 F. Supp. 2d 34 (D.D.C. 1999), aff'd, *Campbell v. Clinton*, 203 F. 3d 19 (D.C. 2000).

16. Louis Fisher, "Deciding on War against Iraq: Institutional Failures," *Political Science Quarterly* 118 (2003): 389.

17. Robert M. Gates, *Duty: Memoirs of a Secretary at War* (New York: Vintage Books, 2015), 513.

18. www.whitehouse.gov/the-press-office/2011/03/21/letter-president-regarding-commencement-operations-libya.

19. www.whitehouse.gov/the-press-office/2011/03/28/remarks-president-address-nation-libya.

20. www.justice.gov/olc/2011/authority-military-use-in-libya.pdf.

21. Louis Fisher, "Parsing the War Power," *National Law Journal* (July 4, 2011): 51–52.

22. See pages 6–7 of testimony by Louis Fisher before the Senate Foreign Relations committee on June 28, 2011, available at http://foreign.senate.gov/imo/media/doc/Fisher_Testimony.pdf.

23. Louis Fisher, "Senate Should Protect War Powers on Libya," *Roll Call* (July 29, 2011): 17.

24. Charlie Savage, "2 Top Lawyers Lose Argument on War Powers," *New York Times*, June 18, 2011, A1. The article refers to Caroline Krass in the OLC and Jeh Johnson in the Pentagon losing the argument to Robert Bauer and Harold Koh.

25. For further analysis of Obama's actions in Libya, see Louis Fisher, "Military Operations in Libya: No War? No Hostilities?," *Presidential Studies Quarterly* 42 (2012): 176.

26. Thomas L. Friedman, "Obama on the World," *New York Times*, August 9, 2014, A19.

27. *Public Papers of the Presidents*, 2011, I, 309.

28. For debate within the administration on whether Obama should ask Congress to authorize military action in Syria, see Charlie Savage, *Power Wars: Inside Obama's Post-9/11 Presidency* (New York: Little, Brown and Co., 2015), 627–31, 650–54.

29. Louis Fisher, "A Challenge to Presidential Wars: *Smith v. Obama*," *Congress & the Presidency* 44 (2017): 259–282.

30. See remarks by Congressmen Porter Goss and George Gekas, 141 *Cong. Rec.* 36327, 36329 (1995).

11

How National Security Advisers See Their Role

Ivo H. Daalder and I. M. (Mac) Destler

Over the seventy years since the creation of the National Security Council (NSC) in 1947, the assistant to the president for national security affairs (as the national security adviser is formally known) has emerged as the most important foreign policy aide to the president. Whether the job is performed largely outside of public view (as by Brent Scowcroft—1975–77, 1989–93; Stephen Hadley—2005–2009; and Susan Rice—2013–17), or in a highly prominent manner (as was true for Henry Kissinger—1969–75, Zbigniew Brzezinski—1977–81, and Condoleezza Rice—2001–05), almost every national security adviser since McGeorge Bundy (1961–66) has emerged as a principal player in the foreign policy arena. And those who did not so emerge—Richard Allen (1981), James Jones (2009–10)—have typically found themselves replaced by persons better able to connect to their presidents.

Yet, despite the enormous power they have wielded, there has been insufficient attention to the role these advisers play in the formulation and implementation of foreign policy. Unlike the jobs of their Cabinet counterparts, their position is neither rooted in law nor accountable to Congress. As the White House point person on foreign policy, the national security adviser serves at the pleasure of the president. Moreover, while the adviser heads an important staff, his or her managerial duties are modest compared to the huge departmental responsibilities of the secretaries of state, defense, treasury, and other principal foreign policymakers. And though some advisers have not shunned the limelight, their public responsibilities are far more limited than those of, say, the secretary of state, who is the president's principal foreign policy spokesperson at home and abroad.

Nonetheless, the national security adviser and the NSC staff have become central foreign policy players. Indeed, over the years, the NSC staff has expanded from a small group of less than fifteen policy people in the early 1960s to what is today a fully ensconced, agency-like organization whose staff has over four hundred people, including over two hundred substantive professionals. This organization has its own perspective on the myriad of national security issues confronting the government. It has become less like a staff and more like an operating agency. With its own press, legislative, communication, and speechmaking offices, the NSC conducts ongoing relations with the media, Congress, the American public, and foreign governments.

The reasons for this expansion are many. The foundation, of course, has been presidents' need for close-in foreign policy support and advisers' success in meeting this need. Beyond this, three developments stand out. First, as can be expected of any organization that has operated for decades, the NSC has become institutionalized and even bureaucratized. The White House Situation Room, established under Kennedy, has become the focal point for crisis management. The NSC communications system, also inaugurated under Kennedy, has grown in sophistication with the advance of technology. It allows staff to monitor the overseas messages sent to and from the State Department, to have access to major intelligence material, and to communicate directly and secretly with foreign governments. Over time, these capacities, together with continuing presidential need, have built the NSC into a strong, entrenched, and legitimate presidential institution.

Second, the kinds of foreign policy issues that need to be addressed have both expanded in number and become more complex in nature. As a result of rapid globalization, national security issues now involve more dimensions, each linked to proponents somewhere in the executive branch. The traditional and long-recognized dividing lines—between foreign and domestic policy, and between the "high-politics" issues of war and peace and the "low-politics" issues of social and economic advancement—have blurred. As a result, the number and type of players concerned with each issue have grown as well—placing a premium on effective organization and integration of different interests. Of all the players in the executive branch, only the White House has the recognized power necessary to manage these disparate interests effectively. And within the White House, only the NSC has the demonstrated capacity to do so. (The National Economic Council [NEC], established by President Clinton, plays this role to some extent on issues linking domestic and international economics.)

Third, U.S. politics no longer ends at the water's edge—it continues right on into the mainstream of foreign affairs. Aside from extraordinary events like the war against Al Qaeda in response to September 11, few issues are easily separated from domestic political turmoil—not military intervention, not diplomatic relations, and certainly not trade and economic interactions with the outside world. The necessity to provide political oversight of executive action—to ensure not only that policy is executed in the best manner possible, but that the political consequences of doing so have been considered—naturally falls to the White House, and to the NSC acting as its surrogate.

Yet, while the national security adviser and the NSC staff have grown in importance, their specific roles and significance remain unclear not only to the American public, but even to many of the most avid followers of foreign policy in Congress, the media, and academia. Two roundtables with former national security advisers help elucidate their roles.[1] In freewheeling discussions, which ranged historically from the Eisenhower administration in the 1950s to the G. W. Bush administration in the new century, the former advisers recounted their experiences, debated their responsibilities, and reflected on the proper role of the national security adviser under present circumstances. The discussions centered on three issues: the adviser's role in managing the foreign policy decision-making process, the adviser's operational role and responsibility, and the adviser's public responsibilities, especially with respect to Congress. This essay draws primarily on these conversations, with additional material on the national security advisers of the twenty-first century.

MANAGING THE DECISION-MAKING PROCESS

Aside from staffing the president in his personal foreign policy role—by making sure he gets the necessary information and is briefed prior to meetings, visits, and negotiations—the most important role of the national security adviser is to manage the decision-making process effectively. This involves three steps. First is guiding governmental deliberations on major foreign and national security issues to ensure both that those with strong stakes in the issue are involved in the process and that all realistic policy options are fully considered—including options not favored by any agency—before these issues reach the president and his senior advisers for decision. Second is driving this process to make real choices in a timely manner. Third is overseeing the implementation of the decisions made by the president and his advisers.

Managing this process effectively is demanding in a number of ways. There is, first of all, the inherent tension between the need of the national security adviser to be an effective and trustworthy honest broker among the different players in the decision-making process and the desire of the president to have the best possible policy advice, including advice from his closest foreign policy aide. The roles are inherently in conflict. Balancing them is tricky and possible only if the adviser has earned the trust of the other key players. As Sandy Berger argued, "You have to be perceived by your colleagues as an honest representative of their viewpoint, or the system breaks down." Walt Rostow agreed: "The national security advisor ought to be able to state the point of view of each member the president consults, with sympathy. He may disagree with it, but if a Cabinet member ever looks at what is in the summary paper, nothing is more gratifying to a national security adviser than to have him say, 'The State Department couldn't have done any better itself.'" And Zbigniew Brzezinski suggested that:

> One would have to be awfully stupid to misrepresent the views of one's colleagues to the president, because you know that if the issue is important, there will be a discussion. The president will go back and discuss it, in your presence or even your absence, with his principal advisers, be they secretary of state or secretary of defense. And it would very quickly be evident that you distorted their views if you did. So you have to be absolutely precise and present as persuasively as you can the arguments that they have mustered in favor of their position.

Brent Scowcroft aptly summarized the matter in the Brookings-Maryland roundtable:

> It's always more exciting to be the adviser, but if you are not the honest broker, you don't have the confidence of the NSC. If you don't have their confidence, then the system doesn't work, because they will go around you to get to the president. . . . So in order for the system to work, you first have to establish yourself in the confidence of your colleagues to convince them you are not going to pull fast ones on them. That means when you are in there with the president alone, which you are more than anybody else, that you will represent them fairly. . . . And after you have done that, then you are free to be an adviser.

Once the national security adviser has gained the trust of his colleagues, it is also important that the president receive his unvarnished advice. And while a good White House staff person would do well to follow "empirical rule number one" of the Eisenhower administration (which Goodpaster recalled as, "The president is always right!"), at least in public, it is equally important to tell the president when he is wrong. As Berger maintained, "I think the national security advisor often has to be the one that says the president's wrong. I always felt it was my particular obligation to give the president the downsides of a particular step he was about to take or to simply state to him—there may be a consensus among his decision-makers, but this consensus does not reflect another serious point of view that he should consider."

In short, the national security adviser must balance the roles of adviser and honest broker by both earning the trust of colleagues in presenting their views fully, fairly, and faithfully to the president and giving the president his or her best advice on every issue (even—indeed, especially—if it has not been asked for), in order to ensure the president is aware of all possible points of view. Such advice, however, should be given privately, in person, or by memo; in public, the national security adviser must stand with the president at all times. As Brzezinski recalls,

> While I do agree that the president's always right in public—whenever there's a group, he's right, because the national security adviser is helping him—in private, you have the obligation to tell him that he's wrong. And I did that repeatedly, and the president wanted me to. There was only one time that he finally sent me a little note saying, "Zbig, don't you know when to stop?" when I went back several times, trying to argue that this was not right.

Of course, even in providing the president with unvarnished advice—including advice he may not like to hear—the national security adviser also must make sure that the president's own perspective and preferences are brought into the decision-making process at an early stage. After all, the president is the only person in the executive branch actually elected by the people—everyone else serves at his pleasure alone. Condoleezza Rice emphasized this role in an interview with the *New York Times*, saying of President George W. Bush, "This president has a very strong anchor and compass about the direction of policy, about not just what's right and what's wrong, but what might work and what might not work."[2] Her job, she maintained, was to translate these presidential instincts into policy.

Managing the process is also important at the sub-cabinet level. Scowcroft was particularly good at empowering his deputy, Robert Gates, to perform this function. And Tom Donilon was so skilled at coordinating from the deputy position that when President Barack Obama decided to replace General Jones in 2010, Donilon was the natural successor.

A second balancing requirement concerns making demands on the president's time—his most precious commodity. There are many, many demands—meetings with aides, meetings with members of Congress, public ceremonies, issues other than foreign policy, and so on—and only twenty-four hours in a day. A key responsibility of the national security adviser is therefore to try to minimize imposition on the president's time. Of course, many issues require his involvement and attention—but not all. Deciding where and when the president should be involved is an issue that must preoccupy any national security adviser.

To minimize imposing on the president's time, the adviser will often seek to forge a consensus on policy among the different players and interests. As Berger suggests, the objective is often to "try to bring the secretary of defense, the secretary of state and others to what I used to call the highest common denominator. If there was not a consensus at a fairly high level, it was better to bring the president two starkly different points of view. But some of this is a function of trying to clear the underbrush of decisions before they get to the president." Frank Carlucci recalls a similar process, in which, when he was secretary of defense, he met with his successor at the NSC, Colin Powell, and the secretary of state, George Shultz, every morning at seven o'clock, without substitutes or agendas "to lay out the day's events and see if we could reach agreement. And invariably, we reached agreement. And the number of decisions that had to go to the president was greatly reduced by that process."

Of course, while it is important to try to preserve the president's time, it is also important not to create a policy process that presents the president with *faits accomplis* on important policy issues. A decision-making process that is geared toward consensus will often lead to the lowest, rather than highest, common denominator policies, which invariably lack boldness or even clear direction. Equally pernicious, a consensus process can result in delay in decision-making in order to allow time for disagreements to be resolved—enhancing the prospect for ad-hoc and reactive policymaking and needlessly limiting the options that could logically be considered if decisions were made at an earlier stage. Finally, a consensus process increases the likelihood that mistakes will go uncorrected, as the need for maintaining bureaucratic comity outweighs the requirement to reexamine policy.

What can complicate matters is a headstrong president, certain in his convictions about the right course to follow. Because a president's advisers serve at his pleasure and can be effective only if they retain his confidence, it is often very difficult for any of them to go against a consensus that has formed around the president's policy preference. This appears to have been the case with President Bush and Iraq. Not long after the September 11 attacks and the subsequent rapid ouster of the Taliban from Afghanistan, the president concluded that Saddam Hussein had to be ousted from power—most likely through the use of force. There never was a formal debate within his administration, or even a process by which to assess the pros and cons of such a far-reaching action. Instead, the president decided this was necessary and a consensus to that effect guided policymaking from that point onward. By the time the downsides of this decision had become clear, it was too late to shift course.

To avoid consensus leading to costly inaction, it may be necessary for the national security adviser to act more forcefully to challenge the consensus that exists, even when the president doesn't want such a challenge. At the Brookings-Maryland roundtable, Anthony Lake recalled his early "mistake the first six months when I tried too much to be just an honest broker. I remember Colin Powell coming to me and saying that I needed to give my own views more push . . . you have to drive the process, and you have to understand that only the NSC can do that." At the same time, when consensus is achieved rapidly and with little debate, the adviser needs to be skeptical of the outcome, to make sure all aspects of a policy have been thought through and, furthermore, to be ready to be the devil's advocate to ensure the consensus reflects the best course. As the tapes of the Cuban Missile Crisis meetings have revealed, McGeorge Bundy saw it as his role to challenge any emerging consensus, no matter whether hawkish or dovish, to ensure all the consequences of a particular action had been considered. By all accounts, Condoleezza Rice failed to play a similarly constructive role with respect to Iraq—not just on the decision to go to war, but on plans to bring stable governance after the invasion was completed.

One final consideration in managing the decision-making process concerns the kinds of issues that should fall within the NSC's coordination purview. The NSC exists for the purpose of integrating a government organized along large stovepipes, among which there is insufficient interaction. The national security adviser will have to decide which issues will have to be coordinated among these different stovepipes, how, and at what level. Too little coordination, confined to too high a level, will likely result in the exclusion of relevant issues. Too much coordination at too low a level will invariably involve the NSC in micromanaging the policy process in ways that will soon overwhelm the capacity of the staff. For that reason, Brzezinski suggested that "coordination has to take place at the presidential level. That is to say, when the decisions are of a presidential-level type decisions, then NSC coordination is necessary."

Berger disagreed, insisting that among the "important functions of the National Security Council staff is to coordinate decision-making, particularly at the working level, between the various agencies." Citing the case of Bosnia, Berger asserted, "There were day-to-day decisions that needed to be made, that were not at the presidential level, but were critically important, generally made at the assistant secretary level or above . . . In those issues that are high priority and fast-moving, it is often useful, although I think you can't generalize, for the NSC to be convening the Defense Department, the State Department and others because the institutional tensions between State and Defense often are such that without a third party in the chair, things fall back on bureaucratic instinct."

The difference between Brzezinski and Berger probably cannot be resolved except on a case-by-case basis. On those issues that require presidential input or decision, NSC involvement is, of course, a must. But not all others can be left solely to the departments to resolve, for they typically have neither the incentive nor the mechanisms necessary to do so. Bureaucratic stalemate or, possibly worse, pursuit of conflicting policies that reflect departmental rather than presidential preferences, can often result. Conversely, however, an NSC staff that insists on coordinating each and every issue will soon become mired in details and incapable of concentrating on the big picture.

Moreover, the temptation for the adviser or an NSC staff member will often be to seize control of an issue, even to the point of becoming responsible for policy implementation. That, as history tells us, can sometimes be highly effective—and also exceedingly dangerous.

The other major question with regard to the issues that need to be covered by the NSC and the adviser concerns the breadth of issue competence. The NSC was originally founded to concern itself with foreign policy and defense issues—whence the restriction of its membership to the secretaries of state and defense as well as the president and vice president. However, over time, and especially in the last two decades, the issues affecting foreign policy have grown in number and complexity, and so has the need for effective policy coordination. By the end of the Clinton administration, the national security adviser not only had to deal with traditional issues of defense and regional diplomacy, but also with energy, the environment, international finance, terrorism, drug trafficking, human rights and disaster relief, and even, if was felt, Gulf War illnesses. The policy coordinating task therefore included not only the traditional NSC agencies of state, defense, and the military and intelligence communities, but also treasury, justice, transportation, and even health and human services.

The Bush administration entered office in 2001 with the view that the NSC competence had been stretched too far and too thin. Rice cut the NSC staff by more than 30 percent, and she ordered her staff to cease coordinating policy with the domestic government agencies, including Justice and the FBI. The NSC would once again focus on the hard power issues of defense and diplomacy involving the great powers. The September 11 attacks underscored that in an age of transnational threat, dividing the world and policymaking neatly between foreign and domestic policy is increasingly difficult. Yet, the Bush administration tried just that—assigning the NSC the role of coordinating counterterrorism abroad while setting up a new structure (the Office of Homeland Security) to coordinate anti-terrorism policy at home. The Obama administration reversed this by consolidating homeland security staff under the NSC.

HOW OPERATIONAL SHOULD THE NSC BE?

A perennial issue for every national security adviser is the question of the NSC's operational involvement in executing policy. The consensus view, especially after the Iran-Contra affair, is that the NSC performs a coordinating and oversight and advisory function but should never become operational. That was the view expressed in 1987 by the Tower Commission, established to review the causes of that fiasco, and it has been faithfully repeated since. Yet, the national security adviser and staff have repeatedly been operationally involved in the twenty-five years since the Iran-Contra affair became public. Advisers have traveled on solo missions abroad. They have met with foreign diplomats and ministers on an almost daily basis. As Scowcroft recalled, "Somebody from the NSC always traveled with the secretary of state or the secretary of defense," and NSC staff members often serve as members of negotiating delegations abroad. So the question is not really whether the NSC should have an operational role, but, rather, what kind and to what extent.

It is important to understand why the president might wish the national security adviser to be operationally involved. On one level, it is the result of a basic degree of confidence, comfort, and trust. Presidents know their national security advisers well and have confidence in the advisers' staffs. The same is not always true for the secretary of state and certainly not for the State Department generally, which is largely staffed by career officials. Some presidents come to power with—or develop—a distinct distrust of the State Department (Kennedy, Nixon, and the younger Bush come to mind); others want to run foreign policy out of the White House to secure a central personal role for themselves (Carter and Bush Sr., as well as Kennedy and Nixon). In either case, the NSC is the bureaucratic beneficiary of the president's desires. As Brzezinski puts it,

> If you have a president who comes to office intent on making foreign policy himself, on a daily basis, you have a different role than if the president comes to office, let's say, more interested in domestic affairs and more inclined to delegate foreign policy authority to his principal advisors. In the first instance, the national security advisor is the inevitable bureaucratic beneficiary of deep presidential involvement.

In addition, as Anthony Lake noted, an operational NSC role is "necessary because of the way other governments are structured. For the same reasons it's happening here, other governments more and more are revolving around presidencies, prime ministers, etc., and the international contacts between them. As Brent knows, I inherited his phone with the direct lines to our counterparts all around the world who simply had to be engaged."

Aside from presidential intent and international governmental evolution, the normal ebb and flow of events will also tend to influence the nature and extent of the NSC's operational involvement. One major factor propelling such involvement is the lack of bureaucratic responsiveness to presidential direction. As Bud McFarlane recalled in an oblique reference to Iran-Contra, there is the "frustration a president can experience as someone who is there for four years wanting to get something done, to be able to demonstrate leadership in X or Y area, and with the frustration of not seeing that the Department of State or others in his administration moving in that direction." The temptation in these situations is for the national security adviser or even the president to force the issue by having the NSC implement the policy as the president wants it implemented. It is a temptation that

McFarlane warns the national security adviser to resist. It should not "lead the National Security Council or the adviser to go beyond the line and take on an operational role. You simply don't have the resources, and you don't have the mandate in law to do that. So that's a big mistake."

A further reason why the national security adviser may become operationally involved is to effect a fundamental shift in policy that, if left to the State Department to implement, would risk being derailed in bureaucratic entanglement. This, of course, was the cited reason for the most famous and productive operational engagement by a national security assistant: Henry Kissinger's secret diplomacy with China (over opening relations), North Vietnam (to negotiate a peace agreement), and the Soviet Union (over arms control and détente). The NSC played a similar role in secret talks leading to Obama's decision to begin normalization of relations with Cuba in 2014.

There may be other occasions when it is logical for the president to send his national security adviser on a quiet diplomatic mission—both to keep the actual mission out of public view and to underscore the president's own commitment to the issue in question. Zbig Brzezinski recalled four such missions during his time in office: to normalize relations with China, address a particular Middle East peace issue with Egypt, to reassure the Europeans over the Euromissile question, and to organize a regional response to the Soviet invasion of Afghanistan (the first of these did not prove to be very secret). Brent Scowcroft traveled twice to Beijing in the aftermath of the Tiananmen Square massacre. Tony Lake undertook two trips to Europe in connection with Bosnia, and a trip to China to help repair badly frayed relations in 1996. Sandy Berger traveled to Moscow to gauge Russia's interest in an arms control deal. Rice also went to Moscow, arriving there even before the secretary of state had visited. And Stephen Hadley traveled to Iraq as well as to India and Pakistan. In each case, however, the actual trip was coordinated within the U.S. government. Unlike in Kissinger's diplomacy, carried out largely without the knowledge of Secretary of State William P. Rogers, the secretary of state was kept fully informed of these missions and often a senior state department representative would travel along with the president's adviser.

Clearly, then, the national security adviser has a unique operational role to play under certain circumstances. What makes them unique, however, is not just the issue at hand, but the fact that such engagement is exceptional rather than routine.

THE PUBLIC ROLE OF THE NATIONAL SECURITY ADVISER

In recent years, the national security adviser has sometimes emerged as a prominent public spokesperson on foreign policy. Whereas Brent

Scowcroft once counseled that the national security adviser "should be seen occasionally and heard even less," the reverse is increasingly the case. During their tenures, Sandy Berger and Condoleezza Rice seemed to be everywhere—giving speeches of major import, being quoted in newspapers and newsmagazines as a result of frequent press briefings and even more frequent media interviews, appearing on the Sunday morning talk show circuit.

The reason for the public emergence of the national security adviser appears to be twofold. First, the increasing politicization of foreign policy has made defense of the president's policies by the person most directly associated with the president politically more important. It is not coincidental, therefore, that the five of the most recent national security advisers (Tony Lake, Sandy Berger, Condoleezza Rice, Stephen Hadley, and Susan Rice) were key advisers to their presidents during their campaigns for office. In contrast, with the exception of Zbigniew Brzezinski and Richard Allen, prior national security advisers were not politically associated with the incoming president. The second reason for the greater public exposure of the national security adviser in recent years is changes in the media—especially proliferation in the number of media outlets. The need to cover all the bases requires a larger number of spokespeople to engage, including, by extension, the national security adviser. As Berger argues, "The pace of the news cycle is now almost continuous, and the breadth of the media tends to pull the national security adviser out more as part of a team of people who goes out, but always with the secretary of state at the lead."

One of the consequences of the public emergence of the national security adviser is the demand for increased accountability, especially on Capitol Hill, where congressmen and senators get to ask questions of the department heads but are unable to demand answers from the president's closest foreign policy adviser. As former Congressman Lee Hamilton put it to the panel of former national security assistants, "I think the national security advisor occupies a very special place. He is, if not the principal advisor, among the two or three principal advisors to the president on foreign policy. You're perfectly willing to go before all of the TV networks anytime they give you a ring, if you want to go. Why should you discriminate against the Congress?" Told by a number of the former advisers that they always were willing to meet with members in their offices, Hamilton continued: "But it is not the same thing for a national security advisor to come into the private office and meet behind closed doors with members of Congress. That's not the same thing as going into a public body and answering questions, in my judgment. They're two different things."

The absence of congressional accountability sometimes leads to the suggestion that the national security adviser should be confirmed—a suggestion reviewed, and rejected, by the Tower Commission. The former advisers all rejected that possibility. They offered a variety of reasons:

- It would prove a major diversion, because with confirmation comes the requirement to testify on the Hill. Brzezinski: "If you get confirmed you also have to testify a lot, you have to go down to the Hill a lot. The schedule demands on you are so enormous already that that would be an additional burden. Moreover, it would greatly complicate the issue we talked about earlier, namely, who speaks for foreign policy in the government besides the president? The answer should be the secretary of state. If you are confirmed, that would become fuzzed and confused."
- It would compromise the ability of the national security adviser to provide confidential advice to the president. Berger: "One benefit of not having confirmation is that you can say no to a congressional committee. In fact, most presidents have taken the view that under executive privilege their national security advisor, just like their chief of staff, can't be compelled to go up on the Hill."
- It would have a negative impact on the policy formation process. Carlucci: "If you make the national security advisor subject to Senate confirmation, you're going to degrade the process significantly. The president will have a very difficult time implementing a coherent foreign policy. I think the president would simply name another staff person to do what the national security advisor does and let this confirmed official run around on the Hill."
- It is unnecessary because there is accountability in the system. Carlucci: "These are staff people to the president. And we had a case where the president was almost brought down because of the actions of National Security Council staff—Ronald Reagan. So there is an accountability system, and the president should be free to pick whomever he wants to give him advice."

BARACK OBAMA, AND THE BEGINNING
WEEKS OF DONALD TRUMP

President Obama signaled the importance he gave to the national security adviser position by selecting a senior military officer, retired General James L. Jones. The former marine commandant and NATO commander was widely admired for his integrity, and in his first prominent press interview he declared that the Obama NSC would be "dramatically different" from its predecessors in scope and impact. Within months, however, his influence was being discounted by Washington insiders, and he did not last through Obama's second year.

In retrospect, the Obama–Jones relationship was doomed from the start. To be effective, a national security adviser must be personally close to the president and in sync with his operating style. Jones was neither. The president barely knew him, and by his own admission, the general " 'wasn't very good at' being an aide."[3] As a military man accustomed to the prerogatives of rank and to formal, hierarchical decision structures, Jones acted as if issues should come to him in an orderly manner, rather than assuring that he was the one who brought issues to the president. Meanwhile, the lawyer-professor-politician who was now president worked informally with other trusted aides, fashioning his own ad hoc decision process. One of those aides was deputy national security adviser Tom Donilon, who coordinated a range of issues through a very active interagency NSC Deputies Committee.

Interestingly, however, Jones's nonsuccess highlighted the importance of the national security adviser position, for it was widely noticed, and it generated continuing pressure for corrective action. Obama took such action in October 2010, replacing Jones with Donilon. The move had the virtue of placing in the position the man who was already doing a substantial share of the NSC's task of high-level policy coordination. Donilon was much more adept than Jones as a staff aide, and much more in tune with the president's style and priorities. And the presence of Donilon as assistant to the president for national security affairs brought organizational continuity with past White Houses.

When Donilon resigned in early 2013, Obama tapped as his replacement his longtime foreign policy adviser, Susan Rice, who had previously served as his ambassador to the United Nations. Rice gave priority to the role of policy adviser and leader, in part, perhaps, because the president took on a substantial share of the process management burden himself. His engagement in detail was early evident in his protracted decision process on Afghanistan in 2009. It continued through his presidency, evidenced, among other things, in his repeated rebuffs to advisers seeking a more active U.S. role in the tragic civil war in Syria.

Perhaps to support this role, the NSC staff expanded further under Obama—to over 200 policy professionals at one point. And his NSC was regularly accused of micromanagement, pulling up to the White House issues of less than presidential import that could appropriately have been handled by departments, and creating decision bottlenecks as issues competed for the inevitably limited presidential time. To address this situation, Rice embarked on a "rightsizing" exercise for her staff. This led to a reduction, she reported, of 17 percent "for [NSC] policy and senior staff positions." It brought the number, in January 2017, down "to fewer than 180 staff members in policy positions."[4]

That month, of course, brought the transition to the presidency of Donald Trump. His initial policy process was sloppy and *ad hoc*, with his policy aides failing to consult the relevant executive departments before he issued his controversial restrictive order on immigration, and his national security adviser, Michael Flynn, evidently not in control. [*Editor's Note*: Michael Flynn resigned in February 2017 and was replaced by General H. R. McMaster.] How it would evolve was uncertain as this essay went to press. But Flynn and his successors would have their hands full bringing order to a process featuring an assertive, quick-acting president and aides who found that disorder served their purposes.

The modern national security adviser has been a staple of the American foreign policymaking process for more than half a century. Although the role will evolve with each president and with the growing complexity of the world, the fundamental tasks are unlikely to change all that much—to staff the president and manage the foreign policy formulation and implementation process. The demands and dilemmas each occupant has faced in meeting these tasks will also surely continue. It is in reflecting on how others have handled these challenges in the past that future occupants may prove able to do a job first brought to prominence by Kennedy's McGeorge Bundy, and which, by any standard, has become difficult indeed.

DISCUSSION QUESTIONS

1. What are two or three major reasons for the expansion of the role of the national security adviser in the foreign policy process?
2. What are some specific responsibilities of the national security adviser? What are the three different roles that national security advisers play today?
3. In Daalder and Destler's view, what is the most important role of the national security adviser?
4. What do the authors mean when they state that "the national security adviser must balance the roles of advisor and honest broker"?
5. In the authors' opinion, why would the president want the National Security Council not only to perform advisory and coordinating functions but also to become operational?
6. Why has the national security adviser more recently emerged as a prominent voice on U.S. foreign policy?
7. Why do former national security advisers believe that the national security adviser should not be subject to congressional confirmation?
8. How has the role of the national security adviser been affirmed during the Obama administration with the replacement of General Jones by Tom Donilon?

NOTES

1. One roundtable, convened by the Brookings-Maryland project on the National Security Council on October 25, 1999, featured Richard Allen (1981–82), Frank Carlucci (1986–87), Walt Rostow (1966–69), Anthony Lake (1993–97), and Brent Scowcroft. The other, convened by the Woodrow Wilson Center for International Scholars and the Baker Institute at Rice University on April 12, 2001, featured Samuel Berger (1997–2001), Zbigniew Brzezinski, Frank Carlucci, Robert (Bud) McFarlane (1983–85), Rostow, and Andrew Goodpaster (who was staff secretary to President Dwight Eisenhower (1954–61), and as such performed many of the tasks of day-to-day national security policy management carried out by national security advisers from the Kennedy administration onward.). The transcript of the Brookings-Maryland Roundtable is available at http://www.cissm.umd.edu/papers/files/the_role_of_the_national_security_adviser.pdf, which also includes transcripts of interviews with Samuel Berger (1997–2001), Robert McFarlane, Colin Powell (1987–89), and John Poindexter (1985–87). The transcript of the Wilson Center/Rice roundtable is available at http://www.wilsoncenter.org/sites/default/files/nsa.pdf. Unless otherwise noted, all quotations are drawn from these transcripts.

2. Quoted in Elisabeth Bumiller, "A Partner in Shaping Foreign Policy," *New York Times,* January 7, 2004.

3. Quoted in Bob Woodward, *Obama's Wars,* (New York: Simon & Schuster, 2010), 37.

4. Susan Rice, "Reflecting on the National Security Council's Greatest Asset, Its People," White House statement of January 17, 2017.

12

The Shifting Pendulum of Power

Executive–Legislative Relations on American Foreign Policy

James M. Lindsay

In 2002, Congress looked to have surrendered its constitutional role in foreign policymaking to the White House. After voting nearly unanimously a year earlier to attack Afghanistan for harboring the plotters behind the 9/11 attacks, many lawmakers privately questioned President George W. Bush's push to overthrow Saddam Hussein. But few lawmakers aired their criticisms publicly. When President Bush asked Congress to authorize an invasion of Iraq, members quibbled with some of the language of the draft resolution. Nonetheless, they passed the revised resolution overwhelmingly, handing the president what amounted to a blank check he could cash as he saw fit. When asked why congressional Democrats had not opposed a resolution so many thought unwise or premature, Senate Majority Leader Tom Daschle (D-SD) replied, "The bottom line is . . . we want to move on."[1] Congress's eagerness to delegate its war power to the president drew the ire of Senator Robert Byrd (D-WV), a veteran of five decades of service on Capitol Hill. "How have we gotten to this low point in the history of Congress? Are we too feeble to resist the demand of a president who is determined to bend the collective will of Congress to his will?"[2]

Five years later, however, Congress recovered its voice on foreign policy. In January 2007, President Bush proposed sending 21,500 additional U.S. troops to Iraq to stop escalating sectarian violence there. Rather than applauding the president, members of Congress from both parties assailed the plan and Bush's overall handling of the Iraq War. Senator Russell D. Feingold (D-WI) accused the administration of committing "quite possibly the greatest foreign policy mistake in the history of our nation."[3] Senator Chuck Hagel (R-NE), a decorated Vietnam War veteran, called the troop increase "a dangerous foreign policy blunder."[4] Lawmakers submitted bills limiting the president's ability to send troops to Iraq. Senator Olympia Snowe (R-Maine) captured the new mood on Capitol Hill: "Now is the time for the Congress to make its voice heard on a policy that has such significant implications for the nation, the Middle East, and the world."[5]

Congress's resurgent interest in foreign policy carried over into Barack Obama's presidency. Stiff congressional opposition forced him to abandon his initial plans to close down the prison at Guantánamo Bay that held foreign terrorists and to start a nationwide program to reduce the emission of greenhouse gases. In 2010, he barely succeeded in winning Senate approval of the New START Treaty, which lowered the limit on the number of strategic nuclear warheads that Russia and United States could deploy. In 2011, Congress declined to pass legislation authorizing the U.S. military intervention in Libya, with the House going so far as to pass a bill calling on Obama to withdraw the United States from the multinational effort. Two years later, Obama abandoned his plan to launch airstrikes on Syria to punish Damascus for its chemical weapons program. He instead referred the matter to a deeply skeptical Congress, which declined to take a vote. Obama's foreign policy clashes with Congress accelerated during his final two years in office. Lawmakers repeatedly challenged the nuclear deal he struck with Iran. And Congress pointedly declined to vote on the Trans-Pacific Partnership (TPP), a massive trade deal with eleven other countries that Obama had called central to his overall policy in Asia.

The change in the tone of executive–legislative relations during the fifteen years after 9/11 was dramatic. It was not, however, unprecedented. The pendulum of power on foreign policy has swung back and forth between Congress and the president many times over the course of American history. The reason does not lie in the Constitution. Its formal allocation of foreign policy powers, which gives important authorities to both Congress and the president, has not changed since it was drafted. Rather, the answer lies in politics. How aggressively Congress exercises its foreign policy powers turns on three critical questions: Does the country see itself as threatened or secure? Are the president's policies working or not? Does the president's party control Congress or not? Times of peace favor congressional activism, while times of war favor congressional deference. Successful presidents have more followers than failed ones do. And presidents get friendlier treatment when their party is in the majority on Capitol Hill.

The Bush and Obama presidencies illustrate an equally important lesson about Congress and foreign policy that is likely to be repeated in the presidency of Donald J. Trump: congressional activism does not always equal congressional influence. Even when Congress exercises its powers, it may not get its way. Bush ultimately sent more troops to Iraq, the Senate eventually approved the New Start Treaty, and Congress failed to stop both the U.S. military intervention in Libya and the nuclear deal with Iran. Presidents typically defend their policy choices against congressional criticism, and many times they succeed.

Does it matter whether Congress exercises its foreign policy powers? The answer to this question lies in the eyes of the beholder. Americans can and do disagree over what constitutes the "national interest" and which policies will best achieve them. What is certain, though, is that the balance of power between the two ends of Pennsylvania Avenue will continue to ebb and flow with the political tides.

THE CONSTITUTION AND FOREIGN POLICY

Ask most Americans who makes foreign policy in the United States and their immediate answer is the president. And to a point they are right. But even a cursory reading of the Constitution makes clear that Congress also possesses extensive powers to shape foreign policy. Article 1, section 8, assigns Congress the power to "provide for the common Defence," "To regulate Commerce with foreign Nations," "To define and punish Piracies and Felonies committed on the high Seas," "To declare War," "To raise and support Armies," "To provide and maintain a Navy," and "To make Rules for the Government and Regulation of the land and naval Forces." Article 2, section 2, specifies that the Senate must give its advice and consent to all treaties and ambassadorial appointments. And Congress's more general power to appropriate all government funds and the Senate's power to confirm cabinet officials provide additional means to influence foreign policy.

These powers can have great consequence. To begin with, they enable Congress—or, in the case of the treaty power, the Senate—to specify the substance of American foreign policy. The most popular vehicle for doing so is the appropriations power, which, while not unlimited in scope, is nonetheless quite broad. (The Supreme Court has never struck down any use of the appropriations power as an unconstitutional infringement on the president's authority to conduct foreign policy.) Dollars are policy in Washington, DC, and the president generally cannot spend money unless Congress appropriates it. Thus, by deciding to fund some ventures and not others, Congress can steer the course of U.S. defense and foreign policy. Congress can also specify the substance of foreign policy by regulating foreign commerce. Lawmakers have repeatedly passed bills over the objections of the White House imposing economic sanctions on other countries to compel them to change their behavior. The Senate's treaty power can have similar effects. When the Senate refuses to consider a treaty, as it has declined to do with the United Nations Convention on the Law of the Sea for more than three decades, or it votes down a treaty, as it did with the

Comprehensive Test Ban Treaty in 1999, it puts its stamp on U.S. foreign policy.

Congress's power to establish and direct the business of the federal bureaucracy (e.g., to provide and maintain a navy) also enables it to influence foreign policy by changing the procedures that the executive branch must follow in making decisions. The premise underlying such procedural legislation is that changing the rules governing how the executive branch makes decisions will change the decisions it makes. In trade policy, for example, U.S. law requires the White House to consult with a wide range of consumer, industry, and labor groups whenever it is negotiating an international trade agreement. The law's sponsors calculated that including these groups in decision-making would make it more likely that U.S. trade policy would reflect U.S. economic interests. Likewise, over the years, Congress has directed the State Department to set up special offices to handle issues such as democracy, counterterrorism, and trafficking in persons. In each instance, the idea was that the executive branch would be more likely to address the issue in question if someone in the bureaucracy had clear responsibility for it.

Congress's broader powers to hold hearings, conduct investigations, and debate issues also give it the ability to *indirectly* shape the course of foreign policy. What is said—and what is not said—on Capitol Hill influences public opinion. That in turn helps determine how much leeway presidents have to act. A Congress that applauds a president's proposals makes it all but certain that the public will rally behind the White House. Conversely, a Congress that condemns presidential initiatives fuels public skepticism and forces the White House to pay a higher—and possibly unacceptable—political price to get its way.

The overarching lesson here is that when it comes to foreign affairs, Congress and the president *both* can claim ample constitutional authority. The two branches are, in Richard Neustadt's oft-repeated formulation, "separated institutions *sharing* power."[6] The question of which branch should prevail as a matter of principle when their powers conflict has been disputed ever since Alexander Hamilton and James Madison squared off in 1793 in their famed Pacificus–Helvidius debate. (Hamilton argued the president was free to exercise his powers as he saw fit; Madison argued the president could not exercise his authority in ways that constrained Congress's ability to exercise its powers.) And while the president exercises some foreign affairs powers that are off-limits to Congress—with the power to negotiate on behalf of the United States being the most prominent—the fact that the Constitution grants Congress extensive authority in foreign policy means that most executive–legislative disputes do not raise constitutional issues.

To say that Congress *can* put its mark on foreign policy, however, is not the same as saying that it *will* do so. To understand why congressional activism and influence on foreign policy varies over time, it is necessary to leave the realm of law and enter the realm of politics.

POLITICS AND FOREIGN POLICY

The explanation for why Congress's say in foreign policy ebbs and flows lies first in an observation that the famed French commentator on American life Alexis de Tocqueville made more than 150 years ago. Surprised to find that the pre–Civil War Congress played a major role in foreign policy, he speculated that congressional activism stemmed from the country's isolation from external threat. "If the Union's existence were constantly menaced, and if its great interests were continually interwoven with those of other powerful nations, one would see the prestige of the executive growing, because of what was expected from it and of what it did."[7]

Why might perceptions of threat affect how Congress behaves? When Americans believe they face few external threats—or think that international engagement could itself produce a threat—they see less merit in deferring to the White House on foreign policy and more merit to congressional activism. Debate and disagreement are not likely to pose significant costs; after all, the country is secure. But when Americans believe the country faces an external threat, they quickly convert to the need for strong presidential leadership. Congressional dissent that was previously acceptable suddenly looks to be unhelpful meddling at best and unpatriotic at worst. Members of Congress are themselves likely to feel the same shifting sentiments toward the wisdom of deferring to the president as well as profoundly aware that being on the wrong side of that shift could hurt them come the next election.

A second factor shaping executive–legislative interactions on foreign policy is how well the president's policies are faring. Presidents who succeed find themselves surrounded by admirers; presidents who don't find themselves with fewer friends. The reason is easy to understand. It is difficult to argue with success. When things go well for a White House, friends on Capitol Hill applaud and critics bite their tongues. But when policies fail, critics step up their attacks and supporters worry about their own political futures. That is precisely what happened to President George W. Bush in 2006 and 2007; as the death toll of U.S. soldiers in Iraq mounted, so too did domestic criticism of his policies. President Obama experienced the same dynamic on Syria; congressional criticism of his hands-off approach to Syria grew during his final two years in office along with the death toll there. The statement that President Kennedy made when he took responsibility for the disastrous U.S. effort to foment Fidel Castro's overthrow by landing Cuban exiles at the Bay of Pigs in 1961 captures the underlying political reality: "Victory has a hundred fathers and defeat is an orphan."[8]

The third factor shaping executive–legislation relations is whether the president's political party controls one or both houses of Congress. Lawmakers in the majority party generally, but by no means always, defer more to presidents who share their political affiliation than to presidents who don't—a dynamic that has strengthened over time as political partisanship has intensified in American life. The tendency for partisanship to influence congressional behavior partly reflects the fact that the members of the same party are more likely to have similar world views. It also reflects raw politics: opposing a president of one's own party could undercut his political standing and help the opposition win the next election. So it was not surprising that President George W. Bush found it harder to get his way on Capitol Hill after Democrats won back control of Congress in the 2006 elections. President Obama experienced a similar reversal of political advantage after Republicans won control of the House in the 2010 elections and control of the Senate in the 2014 elections.

Throughout American history, power over foreign policy has flowed back and forth between the two ends of Pennsylvania Avenue according to these three basic dynamics. In the second half of the nineteenth century, the United States was as secure from foreign attack as at any time in American history. This was also a time when Congress so dominated foreign policy that it has been called the era of "congressional government," "congressional supremacy," and "government-by-Congress." When the United States entered World War I, the pendulum of power swung to the White House. Woodrow Wilson experienced few congressional challenges during his war presidency. But once the war ended, Congress—and the Senate in particular—reasserted itself. Congressional activism persisted into the 1930s and even intensified. Convinced that America would be safe only as long as it kept out of Europe's political affairs, "isolationist" lawmakers in Congress fought bitterly to prevent President Franklin Roosevelt from doing anything that might involve the United States in the war that was brewing across the Atlantic.

Japan's bombing of Pearl Harbor punctured the argument against nonintervention and greatly expanded Roosevelt's freedom to conduct foreign policy. He made virtually all his major wartime decisions without reference to or input from Capitol Hill. When World War II ended, Congress began to reassert itself. Senior members of the House Foreign Affairs Committee and the Senate Foreign Relations Committee helped draft the UN Charter, the peace treaties for the Axis satellite states, and the NATO Treaty.

But growing concerns about the Soviet Union slowed the shift of power away from the White House. As Americans became convinced in the late

1940s that hostile communist states threatened the United States and the rest of the free world, they increasingly came to agree on two basic ideas: the United States needed to resist communist expansion, and achieving this goal demanded strong presidential leadership. Most members of Congress shared these two basic beliefs (and helped promote them); those who disagreed risked punishment at the polls. The process became self-reinforcing. As more lawmakers stepped to the sidelines on defense and foreign policy over the course of the 1950s, others saw it as increasingly futile, not to mention dangerous politically, to continue to speak out. By 1960, the "imperial presidency," the flip side of a deferential Congress, was in full bloom.[9] As one senator complained in 1965, members of Congress were responding to even the most far-reaching presidential decisions on foreign affairs by "stumbling over each other to see who can say 'yea' the quickest and loudest."[10]

The era of congressional deference to an imperial president came to a crashing halt when public opinion soured on the Vietnam War. Many Americans became convinced that communist revolutions in the Third World posed no direct threat to core U.S. security interests and that the United States could coexist peacefully with the Soviet Union. With the public more willing to question administration policies, so too were members of Congress. Many lawmakers had substantive disagreements with the White House over what America's vital interests were and how best to advance them. Moreover, members of Congress had less to fear politically by the early 1970s in challenging the White House than they had only a few years earlier. Indeed, many lawmakers calculated that challenging the president's foreign policies could actually help at the ballot box by enabling them to stake out positions their constituents favored. The result was a surge in congressional activism. Presidents Carter and Reagan received far less cooperation from Capitol Hill than Presidents Eisenhower and Kennedy did.

Activist members of Congress did not always succeed, however, in putting their stamp on foreign policy in the 1970s and 1980s. Knee-jerk support of the president was gone, but elements of congressional deference persisted among senior lawmakers (who had come of age during the era of congressional deference) and moderates (who worried that defeating the president could harm the country's credibility). Presidents from Richard Nixon through the elder George Bush often prevailed on major issues because they could rally congressional support with a simple argument: the administration's policy might not be perfect, but opposing it would damage America's standing abroad, perhaps embolden Moscow to act more aggressively, and ultimately harm U.S. interests. Yet the mere fact that the post-Vietnam presidents had to make this argument showed how much had changed from the days of the imperial presidency.

THE FALL OF THE BERLIN WALL

The end of the Cold War accelerated the trend toward greater congressional activism that Vietnam triggered. With the Soviet Union relegated to the ash heap of history, most Americans looked abroad and saw no similar threats on the horizon. When asked to name the most important problem facing the United States, polls in the 1990s rarely found that more than 5 percent of Americans named a foreign policy issue. That was a steep drop from the upward of 50 percent who named a foreign policy issue during the height of the Cold War. Moreover, many Americans had trouble identifying *any* foreign policy issue that worried them. One 1998 poll asked people to name "two or three of the biggest foreign-policy problems facing the United States today." The most common response by far, at 21 percent, was "don't know."[11]

These public attitudes meant that members of Congress who challenged the White House on foreign policy ran almost no electoral risks. With the public not caring enough to punish them for any excesses, lawmakers went busily about challenging Bill Clinton's foreign policy. In April 1999, for instance, during the Kosovo War, the House refused to vote to support the bombing. Not to be outdone, the Senate voted down the Comprehensive Test Ban Treaty in October 1999 even though President Clinton and sixty-two senators had asked that it be withdrawn from consideration. These episodes were major departures from past practice. When members of Congress had squared off against the White House in the latter half of the Cold War on issues like Vietnam, they had vocal public support. On Kosovo and the test ban, however, few Americans were urging Congress to challenge Clinton. To the extent that they had opinions—and many did not—most Americans sided with the president.

Just as important, the once powerful argument that members of Congress should defer to the White House on key issues lest they harm broader American interests fell on deaf ears. In 1997, the Clinton administration sought to convince Congress to give it "fast-track" negotiating authority for international trade agreements. (With fast-track authority, or what is now called "trade-promotion authority," Congress agrees to approve or reject any trade agreement the president negotiates without amendment. This simplifies trade negotiations because other countries do not have to worry that Congress will rewrite any trade deal.) When it became clear that he lacked the votes needed to prevail, President Clinton escalated the stakes by arguing that the fast track was needed because "more than ever, our economic security is also the foundation of our national security."[12] The decision to recast a trade issue as a national security issue—a tried and true Cold War strategy—changed few minds, however. Recognizing defeat, Clinton asked congressional leaders to withdraw the bill from consideration, marking the first time in decades that a president had failed to persuade Congress to support a major trade initiative.

THE DEFERENTIAL CONGRESS RETURNS

Congress's assertiveness in the first post–Cold War decade rested on the public's belief that what happened outside America's borders mattered little for their lives. September 11 punctured that illusion and ended America's decade-long "holiday from history."[13] Foreign policy suddenly became a top priority with the public. Not surprisingly, the pendulum of power swung sharply back toward the White House.

The impact of September 11 on American public opinion was dramatic. Shortly after the attacks, Gallup found that two out of every three Americans named terrorism, national security, or war as the most important problem facing the United States. Foreign policy had reached this level of political salience only twice since the advent of scientific polling—during the early stages of both the Korean and Vietnam wars. President George W. Bush's public approval ratings soared to 90 percent—a figure seen only once before when his father waged the Gulf War. And while the elder Bush's public approval ratings quickly returned to their prewar levels, the younger Bush's remained high for months.

Members of Congress similarly rallied behind the president. Three days after the attack, all but one member of Congress voted to give the president open-ended authority to retaliate against those responsible, authorizing him "to use all necessary and appropriate force against those nations, organizations, or persons he determines planned, authorized, committed, or aided the terrorist attacks that occurred on September 11, 2001, or harbored such organizations or persons." In short, Congress effectively declared war and left it up to President Bush to decide who the enemy was.

Over the next few months, Congress reversed course on policies that administration officials said interfered with its ability to conduct the war on terrorism. For instance, lawmakers authorized the payment of dues owed to the UN, which Congress had previously refused to pay because of concerns about how the money would be spent, and lifted sanctions imposed on Pakistan in wake of coup there two years earlier, because the Bush administration insisted that both policies hindered the effort to build a multinational coalition to defeat Al Qaeda. Congress also retreated from confrontations with the White House on issues that had nothing to do with 9/11. Democrats dropped their plans to oppose the administration's decision to withdraw from the 1972 Anti-Ballistic Missile Treaty, and Congress voted to give President Bush the fast-track negotiating authority (now renamed trade-promotion authority) it had denied President Clinton. When the White House set up special military commissions to try captured Taliban and Al Qaeda officials, lawmakers did not ask whether the Constitution in fact gave the president power to set up his own judicial system. (The U.S. Supreme Court subsequently ruled in *Hamdan v. Rumsfeld* that he did not.)

The willingness of members of Congress to defer to President Bush on foreign policy after 9/11 stemmed in part from a basic, principled motive—the crisis demanded less "second guessing" of the White House. But lawmakers who might have preferred different policies quickly understood that discretion can be the greater part of valor. They worried that if they challenged a popular wartime president, they risked being accused of playing politics with national security. Party reputations reinforced this instinct. Because President Bush was a Republican, challenges to his leadership would more likely come from Democrats than Republicans. But ever since the Vietnam War, Americans had given Democrats far lower marks than Republicans on defense and foreign policy. In times of peace and prosperity, like the 1990s, these perceptions did not create insurmountable obstacles for Democrats. In a wartime context, however, they left Democrats who offered even mild criticisms of the White House open to charges of being naïve or unpatriotic.

A desire not to give the Republicans a campaign issue, perhaps more than agreement on the substance, explains why many Democrats embraced President Bush's call in the fall of 2002 for a resolution authorizing him to wage war on Iraq. Leading congressional Democrats privately believed the request was both premature and unwise.[14] President Bush had not publicly committed the United States to invade Iraq, and most of America's traditional allies opposed his calls for regime change in Iraq. But with the 2002 midterm congressional elections looming, most Democratic political strategists looked at the polling data and urged their candidates to support the White House. They calculated that rallying around the president would deny Republicans the opportunity to question Democrats' patriotism. It would also get Iraq off the front pages and shift the national debate back to domestic policy, where Democratic positions were more popular with the voters. In the end, political calculations trumped. Congress did something unprecedented in American history—it authorized a war against another country before the United States itself had been attacked and even before the president had publicly made up his mind to wage war.

CONGRESS REGAINS ITS VOICE

Four years after Congress authorized the invasion of Iraq, many Democrats and more than a few Republicans wished they could take back their votes. The speedy U.S. conquest of Baghdad had given way to a protracted and bloody occupation. By the start of 2007, more than three thousand

U.S. troops had died, and many times that had been wounded. Rather than forging a new democracy, Iraq was spiraling into a civil war. With the death toll mounting and the prospects for a stable Iraq, let alone a democratic one, receding, George W. Bush discovered what Lyndon Johnson learned more than three decades earlier on Vietnam—the fact that lawmakers applaud the takeoff of a presidential foreign policy initiative does not mean they will remain supportive if it crashes.

A major blow to the Bush White House came when Democrats retook control of both houses of Congress in the 2006 midterm elections. No one doubted that the Republicans' stunning defeat reflected the public's unhappiness with the war in Iraq. Empowered by their status as the new majority party and not beholden to a Republican president, Democrats held hearings critical of the Bush administration. Even more troubling for the White House, the once solid Republican support for Bush's policies began to crack. The defections partly reflected doubts that the president's policies would work. "I've gone along with the president on this, and I bought into his dream," remarked Senator George V. Voinovich (R-OH), "and at this stage of the game, I don't think it's going to happen."[15] But Republican dissatisfaction also reflected political calculations. Representative Ray LaHood (R-IL) put the White House's problem bluntly: "People are worried about their political skins."[16]

In seeking to regain a say in foreign policy, members of Congress quickly discovered that authority once given away is hard to reclaim. Because Congress had approved the FY 2007 defense budget in 2006, the Bush administration already had sufficient funds to finance the major new policy initiative it unveiled in January 2007: the dispatch of 21,500 additional U.S. troops to Iraq. That funding decision could be reversed only if Congress passed a new funding bill by a veto-proof majority. And that Congress failed to do. In May 2007, President Bush vetoed a bill that would have begun the withdrawal of U.S. troops from Iraq. Congressional leaders subsequently acknowledged that while they could pass symbolic, nonbinding resolutions criticizing the administration's Iraq policy, they lacked the votes needed to override the president's veto.

Barack Obama learned that Capitol Hill could be equally unwelcoming to a Democratic president. On his third day in office, he fulfilled one of his campaign promises by ordering the closure of the U.S. prison at Guantánamo Bay, Cuba, which housed foreign fighters captured in the war on terror. However, Congress declined to approve the measures needed to carry out his decision, which ultimately forced him to reverse course. Obama had also campaigned on a promise to establish a so-called cap-and-trade-system for curtailing the emission of the greenhouse gases driving climate change. The House passed the legislation needed to start the program, but the Senate refused to act on it. After a year of fruitless efforts to spur Senate action, Obama acknowledged political reality and abandoned the cap-and-trade initiative.

Another of Obama's foreign policy priorities was the New START Treaty with Russia, which was signed in April 2010. The White House anticipated rapid Senate approval. After all, a who's who of military leaders and foreign policy luminaries, including former Republican secretaries of state Henry Kissinger, James Baker, Lawrence Eagleburger, and Colin Powell, endorsed the agreement. Instead, a group of Senate Republicans, led by Senate Minority Leader Mitch McConnell (R-KY) and Senate Minority Whip Sen. Jon Kyl (R-AZ), fought to kill the treaty. The Senate approved it in the end, but only after a protracted White House lobbying. The administration's legislative push included promising something that many of the treaty's critics wanted: a commitment to spend billions of dollars modernizing the U.S. nuclear weapons arsenal.

Obama's decision in 2011 to launch Operation Odyssey Dawn, the military operation to unseat the Libyan dictator Muammar Qaddafi, also faced congressional opposition. Some lawmakers criticized Obama for acting too slowly and ineffectively to topple the Libyan dictator. However, far more lawmakers argued that Obama had usurped Congress's war power by attacking a country that had not attacked the United States or even threatened to. The White House argued that the 1973 War Powers Resolution gave the president the authority to use military force for up to ninety days without prior congressional authorization. When the military operations continued past the ninety-day mark, the House of Representatives, which was now controlled by the Republicans, voted overwhelmingly not to authorize continued airstrikes against Libya. The effort to constrain Obama died in the Democratic-controlled Senate. Although the White House continued the airstrikes, it limited U.S. air operations and refused to send U.S. ground troops to Libya in order to avoid antagonizing Congress further.

Obama confronted even greater congressional opposition in 2013 to his plans to attack Syria for using chemical weapons against rebel forces. A year earlier Obama had said that the Syrian government would be crossing a "red line" and trigger U.S. military intervention if it used chemical weapons. Many members of Congress criticized the idea of attacking Syria. Just hours before an attack was set to begin, Obama put his plan on hold and announced he had asked Congress to authorize the attack. But it quickly became clear that Congress wasn't going to give its consent. Obama avoided a major defeat on Capitol Hill only after Russia helped negotiate a deal under which the Syrian government agreed to get rid of its chemical weapons stockpile.

Obama faced similar congressional opposition to the deal that he and other world leaders struck in 2015 to limit Iran's nuclear program. Many members of Congress, including Democrats as well as Republicans, argued that the deal did not do enough to limit Iran's nuclear ambitions.

But lawmakers discovered that they had limited leverage. While senators insisted that the deal was a treaty, and thereby required the Senate's advice and consent, the White House countered that it was an executive agreement that the president could sign on his own authority. The White House prevailed because the Senate, and Congress more broadly, could not force President Obama to call the deal a treaty. The best that congressional opponents could do was to forge a compromise measure with the White House under which Congress would get to vote on a resolution disapproving the deal. That resolution of disapproval, however, would be subject to a presidential veto, meaning that the White House could sustain its position as long as it maintained the support of thirty-four senators. In the end, President Obama never had to wield his veto pen. While the House voted down the Iran deal by a wide margin, Democratic senators blocked the disapproval measure from coming to a vote on the Senate floor.

In contrast, Obama failed to persuade Congress to approve the TPP. This major trade deal, which took seven years to negotiate and involved countries that made up nearly 40 percent of the global economy, was intended to be the cornerstone of his bid to "pivot" or rebalance U.S. foreign policy toward Asia. In this case, the Constitution's well-established rules worked against Obama. Congress had to approve the trade deal before it could go into effect. Congressional leaders, however, refused to even bring the deal to a vote on the floor of the House or Senate before he left office. One of President Donald Trump's first official acts was to formally withdraw the United States from TPP.

The surge in Iraq, Operation Odyssey Dawn, and the battle over the Iran nuclear deal show that a more assertive Congress does not necessarily get its way. When presidents are intent on exercising their constitutional authorities—and willing to pay the price for doing so—they may carry the day. This is most likely to happen in situations in which presidents can act *until* Congress stops them. This was precisely the case with Bush in Iraq and Obama in Libya and Iran. Federal courts historically are reluctant to intervene in foreign policy disputes between the White House and Congress, so Congress typically can impose its will only by passing a law with enough support to withstand an inevitable presidential veto. As the Iraq, Libya, and Iran cases show, that is enormously difficult to do. Conversely, the advantage shifts to Congress when the Constitution or existing legislation bars the president from acting *unless* he gets congressional approval. In these situations, the difficulties in assembling congressional majorities work against the president, witness the failure to close down Guantánamo, create a cap-and-trade system, and pass TPP.

Although a more assertive Congress may not win a showdown with the White House, its willingness to resist presidential initiatives can still shape foreign policy. Presidents worry about how they spend their time, energy, and political capital. They may decide against pursuing policies that Congress is likely to oppose because they doubt they will win or they judge that the political costs of winning are too high. For example, the fierce resistance Senate Republicans put up against the START Treaty persuaded the Obama administration not to resurrect an even more controversial arms control agreement, the Comprehensive Test Ban Treaty. Likewise, congressional opposition to airstrikes on Syria helped persuade Obama to abandon the idea. As a result, Congress influences foreign policy not just by what it does but also by what it can persuade the White House not to do.

CONCLUSION

The framers of the Constitution created a political system that gives Congress substantial powers to shape the course of American foreign policy. Congress's willingness to exercise those powers has ebbed and flowed over time according to the vicissitudes of politics. When Americans are at peace and believe themselves secure, congressional assertiveness grows. When Americans find themselves at war or fear great peril, congressional deference to the president comes to the fore. At the same time, how much deference the president can expect from Capitol Hill depends on whether presidential policies are seen to be succeeding. Successful presidents can push Congress to the sidelines, while struggling presidents see their policies challenged on Capitol Hill. And presidents can be greatly helped, or hurt, by whether or not their party controls Congress.

Is there any reason to believe that America's foreign policy is better served by an assertive Congress or deferential one? This question is easy to ask and impossible to answer. No objective standard exists for judging the proper balance between activism and deference. The temptation is always to judge Congress in light of whether one likes what the president wants to do. As one former national security commented, "I have been a 'strong president man' when in the executive branch and a 'strong Congress man' when out of the government in political opposition."[17] That answer hardly satisfies those who have different partisan preferences.

What is clear is that activist and deferential congresses pose different mixes of costs and benefits. Although congressional activism usually looks unhelpful from the vantage point of the White House, it has several merits. For the same reason that an upcoming test encourages students to study, the possibility that Congress might step into the fray encourages administration officials to think through their policy proposals more carefully. Members of Congress also bring different views to bear on policy debates, views that can provide a useful scrub for administration proposals. When

Capitol Hill is more hawkish than the White House, congressional activism strengthens the president's hand overseas. And congressional debate helps to legitimate foreign policy with the public. This latter virtue should not be underestimated; the success of the United States abroad ultimately depends on the willingness of Americans to accept the sacrifices asked of them.

But if congressional activism can be helpful, it can also be harmful. At a minimum, it makes an already cumbersome decision-making process even more so. More people need to be consulted, and more opportunities to derail a policy are created. Such inefficiency is not inherently disastrous—after all, the maxim "he who hesitates is lost" has its counterpoint in "decide in haste, repent at leisure." It does, however, increase the burdens on the time and energy of executive branch officials, potentially keeping them from other duties, and it can strain relations with allies that don't understand why Washington is so slow in acting. At its worst, congressional activism may render U.S. foreign policy incoherent as members of Congress push issues they do not fully understand and pursue narrow interests rather than national ones.

A deferential Congress avoids these problems but can create others. Presidents unburdened by congressional second-guessing find it easier to exploit the advantages of "decision, activity, secrecy, and dispatch" that Alexander Hamilton long ago hailed as the great virtues of the presidency.[18] But presidents and their advisers are not infallible. They can choose unwisely, and the lack of domestic checks can tempt them to overreach. President George W. Bush's critics would offer up his handling of the Iraq War as a case in point, just as Barack Obama's critics would offer up the Iran nuclear deal. But they would hardly be the only American presidents to see their foreign policy plans go awry. It was the imperial presidency, after all, that gave America the Bay of Pigs and the Vietnam War.

Fifteen years after 9/11, the political winds on foreign policy blew in the direction of Capitol Hill. Congress had shown during the Obama presidency that it was ready, willing, and able to question the White House. That does not mean that Donald Trump will necessarily meet similar resistance. He took the oath of office in January 2017 promising to do less overseas than his immediate predecessors, a sentiment applauded by many on Capitol Hill. With both the House and Senate under Republican control, he had the added advantage of having a Congress with strong political incentives to support his policies. Whether he retains that support will depend on events abroad and the consequences of his policies. Only one thing is for certain: the balance of power in U.S. foreign policy between the president and Congress is not fixed. It continues to swing back and forth between the two ends of Pennsylvania Avenue.

DISCUSSION QUESTIONS

1. According to James Lindsay, who makes foreign policy? How much power does Congress possess?
2. According to Lindsay, what are the conditions under which Congress exercises its foreign policy powers?
3. What are some legal tools that Congress possesses for directing foreign policy?
4. What are some examples of the ebbs and flows in congressional–executive relations?
5. What was the impact of the end of the Cold War on Congress's involvement in foreign affairs?
6. What happened to congressional involvement in foreign affairs after 9/11? Has Congress regained its "voice" today?
7. To what extent did Congress affect the foreign policy actions of the Obama administration?

NOTES

1. Quoted in Frank Rich, "It's the War, Stupid," *New York Times*, October 12, 2002.
2. Robert C. Byrd, "Congress Must Resist the Rush to War," *New York Times*, October 10, 2002.
3. Quoted in Thom Shanker and David S. Cloud, "Bush's Plan for Iraq Runs into Opposition," *New York Times*, January 12, 2007.
4. Shanker and Cloud, "Bush's Plan for Iraq Runs into Opposition."
5. Quoted in Carl Hulse, "Measure in Senate Urges No Troop Rise in Iraq," *New York Times*, January 18, 2007.
6. Richard E. Neustadt, *Presidential Power and the Modern Presidents: The Politics of Leadership from Roosevelt to Reagan* (New York: Free Press, 1990), 29.
7. Alexis de Tocqueville, *Democracy in America* (New York: Anchor Books, 1969), 126.
8. Quoted in Arthur M. Schlesinger Jr., *A Thousand Days* (Boston: Houghton Mifflin, 1965), 289–90.
9. Arthur M. Schlesinger Jr., *The Imperial Presidency* (Boston: Houghton Mifflin, 1973).
10. Quoted in James L. Sundquist, *The Decline and Resurgence of Congress* (Washington, DC: Brookings Institution, 1981), 125.
11. John E. Reilly, "Americans and the World: A Survey at Century's End," *Foreign Policy* 114 (Spring 1999): 111.
12. Quoted in John M. Broder, "House Postpones Trade-Issue Vote," *New York Times*, November 8, 1997.
13. Charles Krauthammer, "The Hundred Days," *Time*, December 31, 2001, 156.

14. See Elizabeth Drew, "War Games in the Senate," *New York Review of Books,* December 5, 2002, 66–68.

15. Quoted in Michael Abramowitz and Jonathan Weisman, "Bush's Iraq Plan Meets Skepticism on Capitol Hill," *Washington Post,* January 12, 2007.

16. Quoted in David Rogers, "Groundwork for a War Debate," *Wall Street Journal,* January 17, 2007.

17. John Lehman, *Making War: The 200-Year-Old Battle between the President and Congress over How America Goes to War* (New York: Scribner, 1992), xii.

18. Alexander Hamilton, "Federalist No. 70," in Alexander Hamilton, James Madison, and John Jay, *The Federalist Papers,* ed. Garry Wills (New York: Bantam Books, 1982), 356.

13

American Diplomacy at Risk

The American Academy of Diplomacy

The world beyond our borders profoundly affects every American's security, safety and well-being. America's $17 trillion economy is deeply influenced by that world; globalization and the growing influence of rising powers have changed and will continue to change the global agenda and the competition we face. One in every five jobs in our nation is dependent upon international trade. More than 50 percent of our exports now go to developing countries.

Diplomacy is, as several Secretaries of State have pointed out, America's first line of defense. Our nation's diplomacy must recognize emerging threats and work to resolve them without the use of force, if possible. If the use of force becomes necessary, America's diplomats will be there to support United States forces before, during and after combat. Diplomacy is essential to resolving a host of transnational issues such as crime, weapons of mass destruction, climate change and public health.

We are safer today because of a common effort among diplomats, our military colleagues, development experts and business, non-governmental (NGO) and other private sector leaders. For example, our "smart power" activities are supported by business associations, think tanks, military leaders, educators and faith-based organizations, all of whom see the value in the strongest possible American voice and presence in the world. It is no exaggeration to say that how well we manage our diplomacy in the broadest sense is the foundation for every other element of national influence and will determine the future of American security and the fate of American ideals and values.

The historical record is impressive. In the last half of the 20th century, American diplomacy created and sustained the political dimension of containment, which led to the implosion of the Soviet Union. Diplomacy also built the international financial system that brought long term prosperity to millions after World War II. Today's global challenges multiply daily and are ever more difficult to manage. The use of force is no longer as widely acceptable or applicable as it once was. Effective American diplomacy is critical to promoting and protecting our nation's interests.

The American Academy of Diplomacy believes that diplomacy is best executed by a State Department which has as its foundation both a strong Foreign Service and a strong Civil Service. The Department is most effective when both the Foreign Service and Civil Service work together to contribute their energy, commitment, wisdom and expertise to the nation's missions. We have the utmost respect for the job our Foreign Service and Civil Service colleagues are doing. The objective of this [chapter] is to support them as they meet today's challenges and propose a path to an even more effective American diplomacy in the future. Without the most robust possible diplomacy, American strength and prosperity are jeopardized. There are urgent issues to confront. The time to address them is now.[1]

The sad reality is that, despite the efforts of the career Foreign and Civil Service, America's ability to lead globally through diplomacy is declining. Our nation's diplomacy is becoming increasingly politicized, reversing a century-long effort to create a merit-based system based on the highest professional standards set by the 1924 Rogers Act, which aimed to combat the effects of the "spoils system." Despite recent improvements, State is neither educating its staff to equal or surpass the professional level of our allies and competitors, nor systematically preparing its future "leadership bench" to assume senior roles.

Furthermore, and in contradiction to current law, there has been an effort to transform the valid concept of a common State Department mission—one mission, one team—into a blurring of critically important distinctions between the roles and functions of the Foreign and Civil Services. This is occurring in a manner that diminishes the effectiveness of both groups and further undercuts the professionalism and discipline that America's diplomacy requires.

The Department does not have a formal policy defining the respective roles of the Civil Service and Foreign Service in Washington. In an agency with two such different systems, the need for such a policy is imperative. The alternative is continued "ad hoc" staffing decision making based on expediency and personal preferences that often look like "cronyism," rather than the full support of national interest-based specific criteria. Currently, decisions about which personnel system to use reflect a wide variety of factors.[2]

This [chapter] looks in two directions. One is at the politicization of the policy and appointment process and management's effort to nullify the law—the Foreign Service Act of 1980 ("the Act")—both of which reduce the role of a professional Foreign Service. We strongly believe this weakens the nation and the State Department and must be reversed and resisted. A second focus is on key improvements for both the Civil and Foreign Service to strengthen professional education and the formation and quality of these careers.

The rise of regional powers and the relative decline of US military and economic preeminence have made diplomacy even more central to US national security. Our analysis, however, is that the most important factors in the decline are internal. They result from our own policies and procedures. They can and must be changed to reverse the decline.

There is an increasingly politicized appointment and policy process in the State Department, resulting in a steady decrease in the use of diplomacy professionals with current field experience and long-term perspective in making and implementing policy. This is reversing a century-long effort to create a merit-based system that valued high professionalism. It is both ironic and tragic that the US is now moving away from the principles of a career professional Foreign Service based on "admission through impartial and rigorous examination" (as stated in the Act), promotion on merit, and advice to the political level based on extensive experience, much of it overseas, as well as impartial judgment at a time when we need it most.

The role of money in politics has made more egregious the practice of appointing political ambassadors who lack the appropriate experience or credentials for that role. Some highly talented citizens have served brilliantly as ambassadors. The practice of calling on private citizens, however, does not justify sending overseas ambassadors so deficient in evident qualifications as to make them laughing stocks at home and abroad. The sale of office is contrary to law. That it appears to be happening, only slightly indirectly through campaign contributions, does not justify the practice and adds nothing to either the quality or prestige of American diplomacy.

The second factor presenting a serious challenge to a strong State Department that rests on complementary but separate Foreign and Civil Services, is the policy described in official State Department April 2013 press guidance[3] that there is a "requirement" to "break down all institutional, cultural and legal barriers between the Foreign Service and the Civil Service." In pursuit of this alleged "requirement," many of the State Department's personnel actions violate the letter and the spirit of the Act.

The third factor is that, despite recent important improvements, State is neither educating its staff to the professional level of our competitor nations, nor systematically preparing its future leaders to assume senior roles. The Department needs to view assignments and rotational practices more strategically as an integral part of creating a deep reservoir of top talent, available to successive presidents in the decades to come.

Fourth, as the Foreign Service struggles to maintain its excellence and professionalism, the Civil Service is dealing with challenges of its own: how to have a career progression that encourages multifunctional knowledge and retains the best-performing personnel? How to curb a senior level appointments process that adds politically connected friends of each new administration? How to manage the occasional domestic or overseas assignment for professional development of the Civil Service without overlapping and reducing similar opportunities for the Foreign Service? A recent study notes that non-career political appointments have increased to 4,000 in the Federal Government.[4] The Civil Service, like the Foreign Service, needs public support to address these issues and fully play its complementary role in the conduct of American foreign relations. We propose a new approach that would expand Civil Service mobility and opportunities for career development.

Finally, numerous *ad hoc* practices and decisions have accumulated over many years. A broad review is needed for State to optimize its organization, management and workforce development.

Our recommendations are summarized in the five headings discussed above: reversing the politicization of the policy process; ending efforts to nullify the Foreign Service Act of 1980; improving personnel development and education; meeting the challenges of the Civil Service; and optimizing workforce development.

America's security interests and international goals require top-quality diplomacy. The Academy recognizes that our recommendations will be controversial and will take time to implement. Without a clear and complete vision of what needs to change and how that change should evolve, nothing will improve and the national interest will continue to suffer. It is past time to start.

We have two recommendations, however, that are central to all the rest.

- The Secretary and the State Department should continue to press the Office of Management and Budget (OMB) and Congress for resources—positions, people and the funds needed to support them—to restore to American diplomacy the ability to play its critical role in the country's national security.
- The Department must define the respective and distinctive roles of the Foreign Service and Civil Services to clarify their complementary functions, in accordance with legislative language.

POLITICIZATION OF AMERICAN DIPLOMACY

In recent decades, the Foreign Service and the policymaking process have been under assault from two major trends: the increasing number of short-term political appointees throughout the senior ranks and well down into the working levels; and the efforts of the Department's administrative managers to nullify the particular role of the Foreign Service and Foreign Service Officers (FSOs) embodied in the Act.

In those instances in which individuals or institutions that support the Foreign Service have objected to these trends, they have been strongly criticized by senior officials, and particularly administrative managers, and accused of "feathering the Foreign Service nest," or of "elitism," or both, but have never been rebutted on the merits or legislative basis of their arguments.

As proponents of the law and practices that we believe will strengthen American diplomacy, the Academy will likely be subject to similar attacks. Our motivation is to support the highest quality formulation and execution of the nation's foreign policy and to restore the value and role of the Foreign and Civil Services to their legislatively mandated places because that is the surest way to a State Department capable of advancing America's interests.

The numbers speak plainly: from 1975 to 2013, the proportion of FSOs in senior positions, as defined by the Department itself, has declined from over 60 percent to between 25–30 percent. The figure for 2014 is at the upper limit (30 percent) as Secretary John Kerry has appointed career FSOs to most of the regional Assistant Secretary positions.

The price for the declining representation of the professional Foreign Service at senior levels in Washington is three-fold:

Loss of long-term field perspective—Knowledge essential for melding the desirable with the possible. FSOs speak foreign languages and have extensive knowledge of foreign nations and their policies, cultures, thinking, peoples and regions. They have spent years living among and working abroad with people from all walks of life and with leaders whose cooperation we need if US policies are going to be successful. No other part of the Federal government provides this knowledge.

Loss of Washington experience—Loss of the Washington positions that provide essential experience necessary for FSOs to excel in the critical interagency aspects of making and implementing foreign policy, and loss of the benefits in the interagency process of the unique blend of field and Washington experience among those who have implemented foreign policy abroad. This result leaves too many FSOs without sufficient Washington experience to match their overseas experience, which is essential to the development of officers' careers.

Loss of merit-based incentives—Failure to motivate and to maintain high morale when career advancement depends not on professional merit, but mainly on personal networking and political affiliations. Low morale inevitably develops when either Civil Service or Foreign

Service employees see short-term, non-career appointees with less institutional knowledge moving into rungs above them on the career ladder.

Section 101 of the Act states that, "The Congress finds that—(1) a career foreign service, characterized by excellence and professionalism, is essential in the national interest to assist the President and the Secretary of State in conducting the foreign affairs" and "that the members of the Foreign Service should be representative of the American people, . . . , knowledgeable of the affairs, cultures and languages of other countries, and available to serve in assignments throughout the world" and that "should be operated on the basis of merit principles."

The Act also mandates that the Department should "provide guidance for the formulation and conduct of programs and activities of the Department and other agencies which relate to the foreign relations of the United States;" and "perform functions on behalf of any agency or other Government establishment (including any establishment in the legislative or judicial branch) requiring their services."

Section 105 of the Act states that "(1) All personnel actions with respect to career members and career candidates in the Service (including applicants for career candidate appointments) shall be made in accordance with merit principles." The guiding statute mentions only the Foreign Service to perform these functions in this manner.

The dominance of political appointees in the upper ranks of the State Department (eight out of 10 in 2014)[5] is a major reason for the significant decline of the career Foreign Service's professional input into the policy process. A related factor is the recent explosion of ambassadors-at-large, special representatives and coordinators operating separate offices. Many are not integrated into specific bureaus that have responsibilities for these issues.

There are now more than 45 functions headed by individuals titled special envoy, ambassador-at-large, representative, coordinator, etc.[6] The hiring of the appointed special envoys and their staffs is commonly outside the usual processes for bringing people into the career Foreign and Civil Services. They often bring numbers of staff from outside the Department, operate in a closed loop with other non-career staff, and pursue their issues without necessarily integrating the larger and cross-cutting national interests that must inform foreign policy decisions and implementation. Many are supposed to report directly to the Secretary; an obvious near impossibility.

The president and the Secretary of State should systematically include career diplomats in the most senior of State's leadership positions because they provide a perspective gained through years of experience and diplomatic practice, thus assuring the best available advice and support.

We make a number of specific recommendations to recognize the importance and value of the contributions made by Foreign Service professionals. Of these, the most important include:

- Ensuring that a senior FSO occupies one of the two deputy secretary positions, the undersecretary for political affairs and the director of the Foreign Service Institute (FSI);
- Changing the Deputy Secretary's committee inside State that recommends ambassadorial nominations to the Secretary (the "D" committee) to include a majority of active duty or recently retired FSOs;
- Obeying the law (the Act) on ambassadorial nominations as "normally from the career Foreign Service" and "without regard to political campaign contributions," thereby limiting the number of non-career appointees to no more than 10 percent;
- Restoring the stature of the Director General (DG) of the Foreign Service and Director of Human Resources (HR), by appointing highly respected senior officers to these positions, reflecting the intent of the law and their importance in managing the personnel system of the Foreign and Civil Service;
- Limiting the number of non-career staff in bureau front offices and limiting the size of special envoy staffs while blending them into normal bureau operations, unless special circumstances dictate otherwise.

NULLIFICATION OF THE FOREIGN SERVICE ACT OF 1980

There have been repeated previous efforts to unify the Civil and Foreign Services. They have always failed after extensive examination because the responsibilities of the services are different and because blending the services without both having the same rigorous entry requirements, responsibilities for physical and career risks, rotation, service in difficult places and "up or out" promotion systems, will fundamentally reduce the professionalism of the Foreign Service.

Some Academy members and active duty personnel who are not familiar with the Department's personnel practices may find it difficult to believe that there is a real and significant effort underway to nullify *de facto* the Act and to homogenize the Foreign and Civil Services in a manner that is fundamentally detrimental to the existence of a unique professional Foreign Service and to the Department's strength as an institution. We reluctantly conclude that this is the case.[7]

"The QDDR [Quadrennial Diplomacy and Development Review] requires that we break down institutional, cultural and legal barriers between the Foreign Service and the Civil Service."[8]

This official press guidance, approved on April 12, 2013 by the offices of the Undersecretary for Management and the DG, and cleared by representatives of both Deputy Secretaries, the political and management undersecretaries, and other officials in the offices of the DG and Undersecretary for Management, and for the Department spokesperson, is how State chose to respond to the April 2013 Washington Post op-ed, by the chairman of the Academy board, the president of the Academy and the then-president of the American Foreign Service Association (AFSA).

The "legal barriers" referred to are, of course, the provisions of the Act. Senior officials sworn "to support and defend the Constitution of the United States" and who share the president's constitutional responsibility (Article II, Section 3) "to ensure that the laws be faithfully executed," should not call for, nor take actions that result in, the "breakdown" of the law of the land.

Given the Department's declaration quoted above, we believe the intention of too many in the management side of the Department is, contrary to the Act, to homogenize the Civil and Foreign Services. This is a matter of deeds, not simply of our interpretation of words, including the conversion of Foreign Service positions in the Department to Civil Service, the establishment of programs to convert GS (General Service) personnel to FSOs or Foreign Service specialists bypassing the Act's merit standards, and a bizarre effort that appears to attempt to expunge the words and phrases "Foreign Service," "Foreign Service Officer," and "FSO" from the vocabulary of the State Department.

A separate problem relates to the distribution of Civil Service and Foreign Service positions in the regional and functional bureaus. For reasons that no doubt include the scarcity of Foreign Service personnel as well as their assignment preferences, functional bureaus now rely very heavily on Civil Service and contractual employees, with the Foreign Service component often in single-to-low double-digit percentages. There is a clear need for the technical expertise, knowledge and continuity represented by Civil Service staffing in many functional bureaus. There is a corresponding need for field perspectives that FSOs should bring and for developing skill in integrating those perspectives with technical subjects. There is a further need to educate tomorrow's senior Foreign Service leaders in articulating the policy aspects of technical issues.

VALUING THE PROFESSIONAL CAREER FOREIGN SERVICE

The basic qualities needed to pursue US national interests in the diplomatic arena are those one might expect for a profession centered on advocacy, representation, reporting, program management and negotiation: intellectual curiosity; facility for communication, both oral and written; interpersonal competence that motivates colleagues and convinces interlocutors; the ability to recognize opportunity and the exercise of judgment in pursuing and capitalizing on it to solve problems. This latter quality—judgment—is a product of two factors. One derives from study—familiarity with the theory and practice of international relations, and an understanding of diplomacy's actual role in shaping outcomes to thorny issues. The second comes from experience—the skill gained by interacting over an extended period of time across a wide spectrum of people, places and situations in the global community. As the world has become more complex, and the players more numerous and more culturally diverse, practitioners must have broad and sustained experience to bring sound judgment and the best advice to decision makers. Policy makers and implementers need more support than ever to frame and manage policies in a complicated environment.

The readiness of the Foreign Service and the Department to keep pace with these challenges has been compromised over the past several decades in many ways. Budgetary issues, as documented in previous Academy studies, are only one part of the problem. Another component is decisions attempting to solve short-term staffing problems resulting in flawed intake, promotion and retention decisions. The net result of a long series of anomalies is that in 2014, 60 percent of FSOs have less than 10 years in the Service.

State's bureaus are replete with recourse to short-term measures to meet their staffing needs, measures that fall far short of diplomatic capacity that best advances our national interests. As one inspection report by the Office of the Inspector General (OIG) in 2013[9] noted, since at least 2004, more than 20 percent of one key regional bureau's staffing was non-permanent, with interns, fellows and others on temporary duty being used to perform necessary functions for which there were no permanent, direct-hire positions. A 2004 OIG report on this same bureau noted that even with such temporary staffing, the bureau "strains to meet routine activity without virtually any surge capacity." Bureau staffing patterns were not made available to this project but it is safe to assume that other bureaus are likely required to do the same to meet their operational staffing needs.[10]

It is no surprise that Department managers, long on ingenuity and problem-solving and long accustomed to the exhortation to "do more with less," have been brilliant in finding temporary "solutions" for some of the staffing shortfalls. Innovations have filled some of the most gaping holes. These measures, however, are "Band-Aids," not permanent solutions to the problems deriving from broken government-wide budgeting, personnel, management and contracting processes cited by a wide variety of commentators.

The Department needs to put a premium on rational workforce development by encompassing the variety of experience, including management and executive leadership development, needed by senior FSOs to provide informed and judicious leadership in the policy realm. The Diplomatic Readiness Initiative of Secretary Colin Powell and the Diplomacy 3.0 Initiative of Secretary Hillary Rodham Clinton moved the Department in the right direction of increasing staff. In order to maintain this process, the Foreign Service needs to develop the skills and commitment of its senior professionals to take on the responsibilities of maintaining and building the institution.

The US will continue to have worldwide responsibilities and interests. To exercise its authority and power the US must have a distinct, diverse professional diplomatic service, defined as such, and establish self-policing mechanisms such as formal accreditation and certification, as do other professional bodies and the great majority of the world's diplomatic services.

Diplomacy today is virtually unique among professional bodies in the US in its lack of: stringent entry requirements relating to its field, formal accreditation and the absolute requirement for purposeful continuing education and re-certification during the career, according to a comparison of eight other professions. The Department is correctly proud of its delivery on its commitment to a Foreign Service reflecting diversity across a wide spectrum of background and experience. The goal of "representativeness" in the Act comes with the continuing need for professional excellence. A key responsibility of a career service is to develop a senior bench and a mentoring class, which in addition to participating in policy formulation and leading policy implementation, also should develop and manage a diverse career service. There has been major improvement in the training and education delivered by the Foreign Service Institute (FSI).

On-the-job training remains a critical component of officer preparation. It is currently uneven and insufficient to ensure a robust diplomatic service. Professional education is a critical area that has too long suffered from underinvestment.

Over the past several decades, American universities and graduate schools have focused more on theories of international relations, international development or strategic communications rather than on the practice of diplomacy itself, area studies or culture.[11] The Department needs to continue and intensify recent efforts to focus on building essential officer skills, including in strategic thinking and planning. Professional education should install pride in the profession; diplomats first and specialists later. While specialization at the entry and mid-level has merit, at the senior Foreign Service level, "specialization tracks"—the so-called "cones"—should recede. Multifunctional promotions should be re-introduced at the mid-level to supplement promotions by cone and to ensure development of a Senior

Foreign Service of broad perspective and competency. Promotion within the Senior Foreign Service ranks should not be tied to cones. The Career Development Program (CDP), underway since 2005, recognizes the need to balance institutional needs and individual preferences. Career development should combine a broad range of policy, leadership and management experience to prepare senior officers to understand, address, anticipate and manage current and future challenges.

The Department should make a long-term commitment to professionalizing the career Foreign Service. This embraces two aspects: (1) setting and assuring that appropriate standards are maintained and enforced and (2) managing the Service as a professional career diplomatic service, as envisaged in successive Foreign Service Acts, in a dynamic complex world.

STRENGTHENING THE PROFESSIONAL CIVIL SERVICE

We believe there can be no truly successful Department of State unless all elements of the Department's work force—Foreign Service, Civil Service, non-career appointees and locally engaged staff—are able not only to aspire to the highest standards of professionalism in supporting our nation's foreign policy, but also have the institutional flexibility and support to allow them to reach their full potential. Although this [chapter] is primarily focused on Foreign Service professionalism, the chances of success are exponentially greater when our colleagues in the Civil Service are also freed from constraints of the outmoded GS[General Service] system and offered opportunities to better support the Department.

We are not experts in the Civil Service and many will say that the following recommendations are impossible to implement because "OPM will never accept them" or "the Department is too constrained by existing law." Both of these may be true but we believe that the time has arrived to modernize and make the career Civil Service more flexible. We suggest changing the way Civil Service employees manage their careers as recommended by numerous recent reports and commentaries.

State stands apart from other US government agencies in having a "unique mission with a unique workforce."[12] Of the Department's 24,767 American citizen employees, 13,860 constitute an excepted service (the Foreign Service). The Civil Service component numbers 10,907. The role of the Civil Service in the Department, broadly, is to enable and facilitate the Department's ability to carry out the policy, management and operational aspects of its mandate "to serve effectively the interests of the United States and to provide the highest caliber of representation in the conduct of foreign affairs" (The Act, Sec. 101, b.10). Additionally, as our foreign policy has incurred responsibility for more technical fields, the senior Civil Service has become a key repository of knowledge and skills in areas such as arms control, climate change, communications policy and many more.

The Act also seeks "increasing efficiency and economy by promoting maximum compatibility among the agencies authorized by law to utilize the Foreign Service personnel system, as well as compatibility between the Foreign Service personnel system and other personnel systems of the Government."[13] Designed primarily to foster harmonization among the Foreign Service cohorts of the then-five foreign affairs agencies (State, USAID, Agriculture, Commerce and USIA—now integrated into State), this section of the Act calls only for compatibility between the Department's two distinct systems, not homogenization. In today's complex foreign affairs environment, the distinctions have become blurred, creating confusion and tension about the complementary roles of the Foreign and Civil Services in advancing diplomatic objectives.

The career Civil Service is facing challenges: increasing politicization within its ranks; recurring budget uncertainties; the influx of contractors throughout the Department; lack of focus on and the absence of options for career development; and limited and uneven training opportunities. Not least is the frustration engendered by the lack of upward mobility inherent in the Civil Service rank-in-job system in contrast to the opportunities, and indeed the necessity, for upward mobility that is embedded in the Foreign Service's rank-in-person system.

The creation in 1978 of the Senior Executive Service (SES), although providing for rank-in-person, contained no limits on position incumbency or competitive mandatory retirement provisions. This has produced a corps of senior officers who can stay indefinitely in positions but have no career ladder. Career advancement in the mid-levels of the Civil Service differs among agencies and bureaus within agencies. Civil Service career advancement beyond the mid-levels is extremely difficult.

In recent years the Department has devised mechanisms to allow greater fluidity between the Foreign and Civil Services. Blurring their distinctions, as called for in the first QDDR in 2010, is a mistake and a disservice to both. Much of the impetus for the blur derives from the distortions of the Foreign Service workforce over the past 20 years caused by staffing shortfalls and promotion and retention issues. Now that the problems that grew out of those situations are receding, it is time to review conversion and address the issue of career development for Civil Service employees in a different manner.

The upper ranks of the Civil Service need a career ladder. They require opportunities to broaden their professional experience in return for accepting some additional career mobility and responsibilities. The Civil Service needs more access to professional education. These are the courses the Department should pursue. What it should not do is repeat the first

QDDR's formulation nor continue policies that blur rather than clarify the roles of the two Services.

IMPROVING WORK FORCE DEVELOPMENT, ORGANIZATION AND MANAGEMENT

State is modernizing and upgrading its physical facilities in Washington and overseas, embracing new technologies and communications, and is making solid strides in improving education and training. The Foreign Service Institute and its director deserve plaudits for their receptivity to change, enthusiastic embrace of new technology, and willingness to evaluate and implement new ideas in the design and delivery of education and training. The FSI needs the full support of the Congress and the Department for resources to continue and expand on these laudable efforts.

The focus of this project is on the need for State to address the development and management of its human resources. Sustaining and strengthening professional identities includes instilling members of the professional cadres with a strong sense of their respective roles in supporting State's mission. For FSOs, basic to inculcating *esprit de corps* is an appreciation for the icons of the profession[14] and for the special obligations that membership in the profession incur, including a disciplined approach to worldwide availability, as well as the benefits that flow from being an accredited, recognized diplomatic practitioner.

DISCUSSION QUESTIONS

1. How do the authors of this report assess the importance of diplomacy as part of national security policy for the United States?
2. What is the assessment of the state of American diplomacy today?
3. What are the two major foci in the reading regarding the evaluation of the Department of State?
4. What are some of the key factors that the authors of this report identify as contributing to the decline of American diplomacy today?
5. What are two central recommendations that the authors of this report make to improve the Department of State?
6. What are some recommendations (at least two) for reducing the level of politicization of American diplomacy?
7. What is the recommendation for the relationship of the Civil Service and the Foreign Service personnel in the Department of State? How should each area be strengthened?
8. What are the key needs that the authors conclude for improving human resources in the Department of State?

NOTES

1. The past two administrations have placed emphasis on a better integration of diplomacy, defense, and development. We endorse this "3D" concept and believe that more effort should be made to effect this integration through joint training exercises and closer collaboration on country teams. While this study and its recommendations focus on the State Department, we recognize that the officer corps of the U.S. Agency for International Development (USAID) is an integral part of the Foreign Service. The development mission is closely related to the diplomatic mission, though the program management and technical skills required are uniquely related to the development profession. USAID is a statutory agency whose administrator reports to the secretary of state. Development professionals, humanitarian relief specialists, and those engaged in transitional activities work closely with State counterparts, consistent with U.S. foreign policy goals. USAID officials also may be engaged in diplomatic activities at post related to development cooperation, and Foreign Service officers (FSOs) are increasingly engaged in diplomacy related to global development objectives. Thus, many of the recommendations contained in this report that pertain to enhancing effectiveness apply equally to State and USAID Foreign Service and Civil Service officers. In many respects, they may apply also to the Foreign Services of the U.S. Commerce and Agriculture Departments.

2. See section IV B (in the Full Report—Ed.). These comments also reflect a survey of former director generals, covering a span of twenty-six years, and done for this study in July 2014.

3. The department issued this press guidance in reaction to the op-ed "Presidents are Breaking the U.S. Foreign Service," by Academy Chair Thomas R. Pickering, Academy President Ronald E. Neumann, and then AFSA President Susan R. Johnson, *The Washington Post*, April 11, 2013.

4. The Partnership for Public Service and Booz Allen Hamilton, "Building the Enterprise: A New Civil Service Framework," April 1, 2014, http://www.ourpublic-service.org/publications.

5. The positions are secretary, two deputy secretaries, six undersecretaries, and the counselor of the department.

6. State's current organizational chart shows many of the special envoys, etc., reporting directly to the secretary (see State's website, http://www.state.gov; also, see American Diplomacy at Risk, Full Report, appendix C, 55–56 at http://www.academyofdiplomacy.org/wp-content/uploads/2016/01/ADAR_Full_Report_4.1.15.pdf for the list of functions as of January 30, 2015).

7. There are currently several alternate ways to enter the FS other than via the written and oral exam process: the FS Conversion Program (also known as the Career Mobility Program), the Mustang Program, the Diplomacy Fellows Program, and Limited Non-Career Appointments (LNA).

8. STATE/M/DG/HR Press Guidance, April 12, 2013. QDDR is the Quadrennial Diplomacy and Development Review.

9. Office of the Inspector General (OIG), "Inspection of the Bureau of East Asian and Pacific Affairs," ISP-I-13–39, September 2013.

10. Ibid.

11. Donna Oglesby, "A Fine Kettle of Fish: How Diplomats and Academics Teach Diplomacy," paper presented to the British International Studies Association Conference, Dublin, Ireland, June 2014.

12. Russell Rumbaugh and John Cappel, "Exploration of the Civil Service," paper for the American Academy of Diplomacy, April 2014.

13. Foreign Service Act of 1980, Sec. 101, b .9.

14. Don M. Snider, "Modern Professions within the US Government: Are there Lessons from the US Army?" US Military Academy, paper presented at AFSA, May 29, 2014.

14

The Urgent Need for Defense Reform

Michèle A. Flournoy

I applaud the [Senate Armed Services] committee's efforts to reexamine the landmark Goldwater-Nichols legislation nearly 30 years after its passage in 1986 and to consider a broad range of possible defense reforms to ensure that the United States maintains a military that is fully capable of underwriting our indispensible leadership role in a complex and tumultuous world. I am honored to have the opportunity to share my views with you today.

The perspectives I offer you are informed by my experience serving as Undersecretary of Defense for Policy [USDP] for Secretaries Gates and Panetta in the Obama administration, as Principal Deputy Assistant Secretary for Strategy and Threat Reduction in the Clinton Administration, and as a keen observer of the Defense Department from my perch at the Center for a New American Security (CNAS). My views are also informed by my experience as a Senior Advisor with the Boston Consulting Group over the past several years, which has afforded me the opportunity to better understand best practices used in the private sector to improve organizational effectiveness and efficiency. Based on this experience, I will confess a certain bias when it comes to defense reform: While I believe that reform is imperative and urgent, I am somewhat leery of abstract solutions in search of a problem. So I would encourage this committee to start with a fact-based diagnosis of the most critical problems and areas of poor performance in the Department of Defense [DOD] today and then tailor your reform strategies to address them.

[D]efense reform is a "target rich" environment. It would be impossible for any one of us to cover the full range of issues that I hope this committee will ultimately address in the course of its important work. So I will confine myself to identifying a handful of the most serious and consequential problems I hope you will grapple with, and offer some possible recommendations for you to consider.

TYRANNY OF CONSENSUS AND DUPLICATION OF EFFORT ACROSS STAFFS

Recently, there has been a chorus of complaints about the growth of the National Security Council staff and the tendency of a larger NSC to micromanage aspects of policy development and execution that historically have been left to the departments and agencies, particularly the Defense Department. Such complaints have been heard episodically since the Kennedy administration, and they do have some merit today. Equally important though less discussed, however, are the problems that plague the policy process *within* the Department of Defense.

Perhaps the most pernicious of these is what I like to call "the tyranny of consensus" that has come to dominate the Pentagon, particularly in how the Joint Staff (and sometimes the Office of the Secretary of Defense (OSD)) integrates diverse views from the Combatant Commands and the Services in bringing issues forward to the Chairman, the Secretary of Defense, and the NSC process. Reaching consensus—"focusing on what we can all agree on"—has become an end in itself in too many areas, from strategy development to contingency planning for operations to defining acquisition requirements. Getting the concurrence of a broad range of stakeholders on a given course of action too often takes precedence over framing and assessing a set of compelling options or alternatives to present to senior leaders for decision. This consensus-driven process also takes more time, undermining the Department's agility and ability to respond to fast-moving events, let alone get ahead of them. While Goldwater-Nichols' emphasis on fostering jointness in military operations has been absolutely critical to the success of the U.S. military over the last three decades, the emphasis on jointness in policy development is misplaced. In a bureaucratic culture in which consensus is king, the result is too often "lowest common denominator" solutions. The Chairman [of the Joint Chiefs of Staff] and the Secretary [of Defense]—and ultimately the President— would be far better served if the Joint Staff were to play more of an honest broker role, ensuring that a range of views and options, including dissenting views from the Services and COCOMs [Combatant Commands], are brought forward. (A good example of this is the deployment orders process in which any non-concurrence or dissent by an affected Service or COCOM is highlighted to the Secretary of Defense before he makes a decision.)

Policy development within DoD is further complicated and confused by lack of clarity on roles and responsibilities within the process and significant overlap between OSD, the Joint Staff and COCOM staffs, as well as the Services. The primary responsibility for the development of defense and national security policy in the Pentagon rests with the Undersecretary for Policy and her staff. Yet the Joint Staff has a large Policy shop of its own (the J-5) as does each of the COCOMs and Services. When I was USDP, I often found that there were more desk officers working a given policy issue in the Joint Staff and the relevant COCOM than I had working the issue in the Policy shop. This duplication of effort is unnecessary and has contributed to the growth of headquarters staffs. And the proliferation of policy staffs is but one example of unnecessary duplication in a functional area.

In recent years, the Joint Staff and the Office of the Chairman have grown to nearly 4,000 people—10 times their size at the time of the DoD Reorganization Act in 1958. I believe the Chairman and the Department would be better served by a much smaller and more strategic Joint Staff that did not try to duplicate every function in OSD but rather focused on what should be its core function: enabling the Chairman to provide the best *military* advice possible to the Secretary of Defense and the President. The COCOM staffs, which now number nearly 38,000 military, civilian and contractor personnel have also burgeoned in size and function. Far beyond the lean operational warfighting headquarters originally envisioned in Goldwater-Nichols, they have become sprawling platforms for military diplomacy with nearly every country in the world and active participants in the Washington policy process. The appropriate functions and size of the COCOM staffs merit a fundamental reexamination with a view to reducing unnecessary duplication with OSD and the Joint Staff.

A BROKEN STRATEGY DEVELOPMENT PROCESS

The second problem I would highlight is that DoD's strategy development process is broken. At the heart of this process is the Quadrennial Defense Review (QDR), mandated by Congress. Although the need for a robust, rigorous and regular strategic planning process within the Department remains valid, the QDR routinely falls short of this aspiration. Over the years, the QDR has become a routinized, bottom-up staff exercise that includes hundreds of participants and consumes many thousands of man-hours, rather than a top-down leadership exercise that sets clear priorities, makes hard choices and allocates risk. In addition, the requirement to produce an unclassified QDR report tends to make the final product more of a glossy coffee table brochure written primarily for outside audiences, including the press, allies and partners, defense industry, and the Hill. What the

Department needs, however, is a classified, hard-hitting strategy document that can be used to guide concrete actions, resource allocation within the Department, and engagement with key oversight partners in the Congress.

As a veteran of multiple QDRs, I would like to see Congress repeal the existing QDR legislation and instead require the Secretary of Defense to lead a top-down strategy development process that engages key leaders across the department in the development of a *classified* defense strategy during the first year of each Presidential term. (A good model for this exercise was the process used to develop the 2012 Strategic Guidance.) This classified strategy could be accompanied by the public release every several years of a shorter Defense White Paper to explain U.S. defense strategy to outside audiences.

A FLAWED FORCE PLANNING PROCESS

Another critical but flawed process in the Department is force planning—the process used to translate the defense strategy into the forces and capabilities the U.S. military will need in the future. In principle, this process should inform both the size and nature of future force structure and the mix of capabilities in which the Department should invest.

The current process is led by OSD in partnership with the Joint Staff and with input from the Services and, to a lesser extent, the COCOMS. Typically, a set of future scenarios is developed against which alternative force structures and capability mixes can be tested. The results are then assessed to yield insights that should influence DoD's investment in future capabilities. Unfortunately, the value of the current force planning process is dramatically undercut by an overriding emphasis on consensus—that is, gaining the concurrence of every participant every step of the way, from the design of the scenarios, to the assumptions governing the analysis, to the nature of the insights drawn from the exercise -- such that parochial interests are often accommodated ahead of national security interests. Frequently, what results is yet another "lowest common denominator" consensus that does little to illuminate the tough tradeoffs and investment decisions the Department must make for the future.

In my experience, this approach is antithetical to what the Department needs to understand how best to design the force of the future: specifically, how new technologies and capabilities will change future warfare; how to develop new concepts of operation to prevail in more complex and contested operating environments; and how best to characterize and evaluate the key capability investment tradeoffs. What's needed is a process that creates a "safe space" in which alternative capability mixes, concepts and solutions to a given scenario or problem can compete openly and fairly. This process should welcome ideas and proposals from the full range of stakeholders, including the Services, Joint Staff, OSD, COCOMs, and industry. Proposals should be subjected to rigorous gaming and analysis to identify those that deserve to be developed in more detail through experimentation and pilot programs. Such competition is critical to true innovation and to illuminating the key programmatic choices the Department must make today to ensure the U.S. military will have the capabilities it needs to succeed on the far more challenging battlefields of tomorrow.

Fixing this problem does not require legislative change. It is within the purview of the Secretary of Defense to empower the Deputy Secretary to run such a process in which alternative concepts and solutions to priority problems can compete in order to inform future force planning. But Congress does have an important role to play in at least three respects: first, ensuring that any acquisition reform protects the Secretary of Defense's role as the ultimate decider in determining the major requirements for needed military capabilities; second, ensuring that the federal acquisition regulation (FAR) is not used as a means to prevent industry from being at the table to suggest solutions and inform the debate about what is technologically possible; and third, being willing to tolerate a degree of failure that will inevitably occur during the experimentation process. Without this support from Congress, the key entities within the Department are unlikely to take the risks necessary to enable a healthy competition of ideas and true innovation.

BLOATED HEADQUARTERS UNDERCUT PERFORMANCE AND AGILITY

In recent years, headquarters staffs—OSD, the Joint Staff, COCOMs, and the Services—have experienced substantial growth, even as the size of the active duty military has shrunk. Today, the Office of the Secretary of Defense has grown to more than 5,000 people, the Joint Staff to nearly 4,000, and the COCOM staffs to almost 38,000. As described in an earlier hearing, OSD, JCS, the Combatant Commands, and the Defense Agencies now account for some 240,000 people (excluding contractors) and $113 billion—nearly 20 percent of the DoD budget. Some attribute this growth to the increasing complexity of the security environment and the proliferation of tasks assigned to the Department of Defense. While that may account for some growth, I suspect that other, more worrisome factors are to blame: namely, the natural tendency of bureaucracies to expand over time, a lack of role clarity and accountability that fosters duplication of effort across staffs (as described above), and lack of leadership focus and authorities to fundamentally rebaseline and reshape headquarters staffs and DoD infrastructure.

This problem is not just a matter of inefficiency; it is also an issue of effectiveness. In the private sector, bloated headquarters staffs have been documented to slow decision-making, push too many decisions to higher levels, incentivize risk averse behaviors, undermine organizational performance and compromise agility. The same is certainly true in government. What's more, in the DoD context oversized staffs consume precious resources that could otherwise be invested in strengthening our warfighting capabilities. Consequently, this problem should be addressed as a matter of priority.

Specifically, I would urge Congress to take the following steps:

First, strongly encourage the Secretary Defense to undertake a comprehensive and systematic effort to delayer headquarters staffs and agencies across the defense enterprise. This would involve a top-down effort to reassess and redesign each layer of an organization according to an agreed set of design principles. Delayering focuses on reducing unnecessary bureaucracy and optimizing "spans of control" in order to improve the quality of decision-making, organizational performance and agility. It also tends to result in substantial savings. This effort should start with OSD and the Joint Staff, and extend to the COCOM staffs, the Service secretariats and headquarters staffs, and the defense agencies.

Second, in order to facilitate the delayering process, Congress should give the Secretary authorities he needs to reshape the civilian workforce for the 21st century and the ability to eliminate or consolidate organizations as needed. There is ample precedent for this: After the end of the Cold War, Secretary of Defense William Perry was given a broad range of authorities, including Reduction in Force authority, Base Realignment and Closure authority, and meaningful retirement and incentive pays, to reshape the DoD workforce and infrastructure amidst a substantial drawdown.

Third, Congress should direct the Secretary to commission a study by an outside firm with both deep experience in management best practices in the private sector and some familiarity with the unique requirements of the defense enterprise to assess the opportunities for integrating or streamlining overlapping functional staffs within the Department. It should also give the Secretary the flexibility to implement any worthwhile recommendations. Several questions are worth asking in this regard: Do the Service Secretariats and Service Chiefs' staffs need to be separate, or would more integrated civil-military Service headquarters perform better? Does it make sense for both OSD and the Joint Staff to have parallel organizations devoted to overseeing policy, personnel, intelligence, logistics, force analysis, budgeting, and other functions? Does it make sense to have separate transportation and logistics organizations (i.e., Transportation Command and the Defense Logistics Agency) when virtually every leading firm in the private sector has integrated these functions? No doubt there are other areas worthy of assessment as well. In each case, the key question should be whether there are proven approaches that could reduce unnecessary duplication and yield better outcomes for the Department at lower cost.

Fourth, Congress should ask the Secretary of Defense to examine alternative concepts for structuring the Combatant Commands. Specifically, the Secretary should be asked to consider: 1. Reducing the number of COCOMs through consolidation and/or elimination—at a minimum, consider recombining EUCOM [European Command] and AFRICOM [Africa Command] on one hand, and SOUTHCOM [Southern Command] and NORTHCOM [Northern Command] on the other; 2. Streamlining sub-commands and service components; and 3. Rethinking the size and composition of COCOM staffs to reduce unnecessary duplication with the Joint Staff, OSD and defense agencies.

FAILURE TO PROVIDE THE SECRETARY OF DEFENSE WITH AUTHORITIES TO MANAGE EFFECTIVELY

Last but not least, Congress has not given the Secretary of Defense the authorities necessary to manage the defense enterprise effectively and efficiently. In previous periods of drawdown, such as after World War II, the Vietnam War, and the end of the Cold War, Congress provided the Secretary of Defense with the authorities and flexibility necessary to reshape the civilian workforce, reorganize parts of the Department, and right-size DoD's infrastructure. Despite severe budget cuts and a mandate to reduce the size of the so-called "fourth estate," however, Congress has denied recent Secretaries many of the authorities that past Secretaries were granted, such as Reduction in Force authority, meaningful levels of early retirement and voluntary separation incentive pays, and Base Realignment and Closure authority. Furthermore, not providing such authorities has incentivized some negative institutional coping behaviors, such as: letting go of critical personnel one would otherwise wish to retain; hiring contractors to make up for gaps in key functions (due to lack of flexibility to shift and hire career staff as needed); long hiring freezes that prevent new blood from coming into the Department even as it approaches a massive retirement of Baby Boomers; and maintaining staff in excess infrastructure to "keep the lights on" when they might be better employed elsewhere.

In addition, this committee has imposed restrictions on incoming DoD political appointees that make it virtually impossible to recruit people with the kind of business and management expertise the Department desperately needs to improve its performance and efficiency. Whereas political appointees in many other agencies are allowed to avoid potential conflicts of interest by placing their financial assets in a blind trust and/or recusing themselves from certain types of decisions, the SASC [Senate Armed Services Committee] requires DoD nominees (and their immediate family members) to sell off any assets or equity they hold in any company that does business with the Department of Defense. While well intentioned, this rule in practice has stymied the Department's ability to recruit the talent it needs to lead a much-needed transformation of its business processes. For many in the private sector, the requirement to fully divest is akin to committing financial suicide in order to serve as a political appointee. If my understanding is correct, it is within this committee's power to revise this rule and adopt the blind trust and recusal standard that has served other agencies well. I would implore you to do so before the 2016 Presidential transition so that the next administration will be able to recruit more leaders from the private sector to help lead and transform the defense enterprise.

Furthermore, despite repeated testimony on the part of the Service Chiefs that an estimated 20% of the current defense infrastructure is excess to military need, despite numerous GAO reports assessing that previous Base Realignment and Closure (BRAC) rounds have saved billions of dollars, and despite repeated requests from the last several Secretaries of Defense, Congress has not given DoD the authority to conduct another round of BRAC. The time for studying this issue has long past; what's needed now is Congressional action. While I understand the difficult politics surrounding base closures and the potential impact on local jobs, I lament the fact that billions of dollars are being diverted from strengthening military readiness and investing in critical warfighting capabilities in order to sustain facilities and bases the military no longer needs or wants. Every dollar we spend on unwanted infrastructure is a dollar less to support the men and women who serve in harm's way.

In sum, I would strongly urge this committee to lead the charge to provide the Department with the flexibility and authorities described above.

IMPLICATIONS FOR REVISING GOLDWATER-NICHOLS

The obvious question is whether any of these problems requires a change to the core elements of the 1986 Goldwater-Nichols legislation.

While I support this committee's recent efforts to empower the Service Chiefs and hold them accountable for improving performance in the execution of certain acquisition programs, it is imperative that the Secretary of Defense remain the ultimate decider in determining what I call the "Big R" requirements—that is, what capabilities DoD ultimately buys for the joint force. Several examples serve to remind us of times when the Secretary's intervention was critical to ensure that warfighter needs rather than service parochialism drove key procurement decisions (e.g., the decision to increase investment in smart munitions after the Gulf War, or the rapid procurement of MRAPs [mine-resistant ambush protected vehicles] and UAVs [unmanned aerial vehicles] for the wars in Iraq and Afghanistan).

Nevertheless, I believe that Goldwater-Nichols got most of the fundamentals right. Most importantly, the legislation made the Secretary of Defense the ultimate decider on all matters within the purview of the Department. In my view, a fully empowered Secretary is absolutely critical to ensuring strong civilian control of the military in our vibrant constitutional democracy. In addition, I believe that Congress was right in making the Chairman of the Joint Chiefs of Staff the senior military advisor not only to the Secretary of Defense but also to the President as Commander in Chief. The ability of the Chairman to offer independent military advice to the President, unfettered by any political appointee, is critical to ensuring the President has the benefit of the full range of perspectives, including dissent, when making national security decisions. This is particularly important when young Americans are being sent into harm's way. As our own history suggests, suppressing military dissent can have dire consequences for the nation, whereas ensuring dissent can be heard by the Commander in Chief tends to improve the quality of the decisions made.

That said, I think it would be a mistake to insert the Chairman into the operational chain of command, as some have suggested. Giving the Chairman decision-making authority over COCOMs and Services would come at a high cost—essentially reducing the Secretary of Defense's role and decision-making authority commensurately. Decisions about where to deploy forces and whether and how to conduct military operations are fundamentally decisions about where, when and how the United States should use its power and put the nation's blood and treasure on the line. In a democracy, it is imperative that such decisions be made by civilian rather than military authorities.

FINAL THOUGHTS

It is hard to remember a time when the need for defense reform was more acute. The growing challenges the U.S. armed forces face in protecting American interests, values and allies in the coming years are truly daunting: the spread of the Islamic State and other violent extremist groups, the growing chaos in the Middle East, the resurgence of a more aggressive

Russia, the rise of an emboldened, more capable and more assertive China that is challenging the rules-based international order in Asia, persistent threats from states like Iran and North Korea, the continued proliferation of deadly technologies to both state and non-state actors, and the emergence of new threats in the cyber and space domains. With strong leadership on defense issues in both the Senate and the House, a sitting Secretary of Defense who is willing to pursue fundamental reforms, and a transition to a new presidential administration on the horizon, now is the time to develop and begin to implement a plan of action to ensure we get the most out of every taxpayer dollar invested in defense.

But as you assess various options and begin to develop a plan, I would urge you to heed three notes of caution. First, it is imperative that we think through the second and third order effects of any changes proposed. In the balance hangs the capabilities and performance of the finest military the world has ever known and our ability to secure our nation growing forward. Great care should be taken to hear the full range of views and consider the unintended consequences.

Second, based on my experience in both government and the private sector, I would warn against assuming that every problem can or should be solved by organizational change. Too often we jump to redrawing the lines on an organizational chart when a more powerful solution might lie in clarifying roles and responsibilities, better aligning authorities, or strengthening incentives and accountability to change behavior.

Lastly, however successful future reform efforts may be, they may or may not may yield enough cost savings to bring U.S. defense spending to the levels required to protect this nation given the nature of the security environment we face. It is my hope that, in addition to considering critical defense reforms in the coming year, Congress will also consider how to establish more predictable and robust levels of defense spending over the coming 5–10 years. This period of investment could not be more important: it will determine whether the United States can maintain its technological edge and its military superiority over increasingly capable state and non-state actors who are determined to constrain our ability to project power and maintain freedom of action in regions vital to our national security. The Department of Defense simply cannot afford to return to the type of budget uncertainty that has wreaked havoc in recent years—living within the constraints of Continuing Resolutions, under the threat of sequestration, and with the risk of government shutdowns. The costs of this uncertainty are enormous and they have challenged the Department's ability to set and sustain a strategic course. In short, reaching a comprehensive budget deal that includes all of the obvious elements—tax reform, entitlement reform, and smart investment in the drivers of U.S. economic vitality and growth—is not only an economic imperative, it has become a national security imperative.

Finally, I hope that through the dialogue that this committee is fostering, the Congress and the Executive branch will be able to partner more closely to make the hard choices and undertake the reforms that will be necessary to ensure that we keep faith with the men and women who serve in the best trained, best equipped fighting force in the world. They deserve nothing less.

DISCUSSION QUESTIONS

1. What is Flournoy's experience in the area of national defense?
2. What is meant by the "tyranny of consensus," and how is it a problem in the Department of Defense? How should it be addressed?
3. What is the nature of the problem of overlap in various roles in the Department of Defense, and how should it be reformed?
4. How is the strategy development process broken, and how should the Quadrennial Defense Review be used for this process?
5. How does Flournoy argue that the "force planning" process is flawed? What should be done?
6. What are some ways that the Congress can play a role in repairing the force planning process?
7. What are some of the recommendations that Flournoy makes regarding reforming the "bloated bureaucracy" in the Pentagon?
8. How does Flournoy argue that the secretary of defense is currently handicapped in managing the Department of Defense?
9. Does Flournoy believe that the Goldwater-Nichols legislation needs much reform?
10. What are two admonitions that Flournoy makes about enacting reforms?

15

Why Intelligence and Policymakers Clash

Robert Jervis

INTELLIGENCE AND POLICYMAKERS

Policymakers say they need and want good intelligence. They do need it, but often they do not like it, and are prone to believe that when intelligence is not out to get them, it is incompetent. Richard Nixon was the most vocal of presidents in wondering how "those clowns out at Langley" could misunderstand so much of the world and cause his administration so much trouble. Unfortunately, not only will even the best intelligence services often be wrong, but even (or especially) <u>when they are right, they are likely to bring disturbing news, and this incurs a cost</u>. As director of central intelligence (DCI) Richard Helms said shortly after he was let go in 1973, he was "the easiest man in Washington to fire. I have no political, military or industrial base." Although DCI James Woolsey's view was colored by his bad relations with President Bill Clinton, he was not far off the mark in saying that the best job description for his position was "not to be liked."

For the general public, intelligence is not popular, for the additional reasons that its two prime characteristics of secrecy and covert action clash, if not with American traditions, then with the American self-image, and even those who applaud the results are likely to be uncomfortable with the means. It is telling that discussions of interventions in others' internal politics, and especially attempts to overthrow their regimes, are couched in terms of Central Intelligence Agency (CIA) interventions despite the fact that the CIA acts under instructions from the president. Critics, even those on the left, shy away from the correct label, which is that it is a

---

All footnotes have been deleted.

U.S. government intervention. Political leaders see little reason to encourage a better understanding.

A New York clothing store has as its slogan "An educated consumer is our best customer." Intelligence can say this as well, but its wish for an educated consumer is not likely to be granted. Many presidents and cabinet officers come to the job with little knowledge or experience with intelligence and with less time to learn once they are in power. Even presidents like Nixon, who were more informed and who doubted the CIA's abilities, often held unreasonable expectations about what intelligence could produce. Henry Kissinger sometimes knew better, as revealed by what he told his staff about the congressional complaints that the United States had failed to anticipate the coup in Portugal:

> I absolutely resent—anytime there's a coup you start with the assumption that the home government missed it. . . . Why the hell should we know better than the government that's being overthrown. . . . I mean what request is it to make of our intelligence agencies to discover coups all over the world?

Although Kissinger was right, even he sometimes expected more information and better analysis than was likely to be forthcoming and displayed the familiar schizophrenic pattern of both scorning intelligence and being disappointed by it.

DECISION-MAKERS' NEEDS AND
HOW INTELLIGENCE CONFLICTS WITH THEM

The different needs and perspectives of decision-makers and intelligence officials guarantee conflict between them. For both political and psychological reasons, political leaders have to oversell their policies, especially in domestic systems in which power is decentralized, and this will produce pressures on and distortions of intelligence. It is, then, not surprising that intelligence officials, especially those at the working level, tend to see political leaders as unscrupulous and careless, if not intellectually deficient, and that leaders see their intelligence services as timid, unreliable, and—often— out to get them.

Although it may be presumptuous for the CIA to have chiseled in its lobby "And ye shall know the truth and the truth will make you free," it can at least claim this as its objective. No decision-maker could do so, as the more honest of them realize. When Secretary of State Dean Acheson said that the goal of a major National Security Council document was to be "clearer than truth," he understood this very well. Some of the resulting tensions came out when Porter Goss became DCI and told the members of the CIA that they should support policymakers. Of course, the job of intelligence is to inform policymakers and in this way to support better policy. But support can also mean providing analysis that reinforces policies and rallies others to the cause. The first kind of support fits with intelligence's preferred mission, the one that decision-makers pay lip service to. But given the political and psychological world in which they live, it is often the latter kind of support that decision-makers seek. They need confidence and political support, and honest intelligence unfortunately often diminishes rather than increases these goods by pointing to ambiguities, uncertainties, and the costs and risks of policies. In many cases, there is a conflict between what intelligence at its best can produce and what decision-makers seek and need.

Because it is axiomatic that a good policy must rest on an accurate assessment of the world, in a democracy policies must be—or at least be seen as being—grounded in intelligence. Ironically, this is true only because intelligence is seen as proficient, a perception that developed in the wake of the technologies in the 1960s, and the pressures on intelligence follow from its supposed strengths. When Secretary of State Colin Powell insisted that DCI George Tenet sit right behind him when he laid out the case against Iraq before the United Nations Security Council, he was following this imperative in a way that was especially dramatic but not different in kind from the norm. It is the very need to claim that intelligence and policy are in close harmony that produces conflict between them.

In principle, it could be different. President George W. Bush could have said something like this: "I think Saddam is a terrible menace. This is a political judgment, and I have been elected to make difficult calls. While I have listened to our intelligence services and other experts, this is my decision, not theirs." In other cases, the president could announce, "The evidence is ambiguous, but on balance I believe that we must act on the likelihood that the more alarming possibilities are true." But speeches that clearly separate themselves from intelligence will seem weak and will be politically unpersuasive, and it is not surprising that leaders want to use intelligence to bolster not only their arguments but also their political standing.

CONFLICTING PRESSURES

For reasons of both psychology and politics, decision-makers want to minimize not only actual value trade-offs but also their own perception of them. Leaders talk about how they make hard decisions all the time, but like the rest of us, they prefer easy ones and will try to convince themselves and others that a particular decision is, in fact, not so hard. Maximizing political support for a policy means arguing that it meets many goals, is supported by many considerations, and has few costs. Decision-makers, then, want to portray the world as one in which their policy is superior to the alternatives in many independent dimensions. For example, when a nuclear test ban was being debated during the Cold War, proponents argued both that atmospheric testing was a major public health hazard and that a test ban was good for American national security and could be verified. It would have undercut the case for the ban if its supporters had said, "We must stop atmospheric testing in order to save innocent lives even though there will be a significant cost in terms of national security."

Psychological as well as political dynamics are at work. To continue with the test ban example, proponents who were deeply concerned about public health did not like to think that they were advocating policies that would harm national security. Conversely, those who felt that inhibiting nuclear development would disadvantage the United States came to also believe that the testing was not a health hazard. They would have been discomfited by the idea that their preferred policy purchased American security at the cost of hundreds of thousands of innocent lives. Decision-makers have to sleep at night, after all.

The run-up to the war in Iraq is an unfortunately apt illustration of these processes. In its most general form, the Bush administration's case for the war was that Saddam Hussein was a great menace and that overthrowing him was a great opportunity for changing the Middle East. Furthermore, each of these two elements had several supporting components. Saddam was a threat because he was very hard to deter, had robust weapons of mass destruction (WMD) programs, and had ties to terrorists, whom he might provide with WMD. The opportunity was multifaceted as well: the war would be waged at low cost, the postwar reconstruction would be easy, and establishing a benign regime in Iraq would have salutary effects in the region by pushing other regimes along the road to democracy and facilitating the resolution of the Arab-Israeli dispute. Portraying the world in this way maximized support for the war. To those who accepted all components, the war seemed obviously the best course of action, which would justify supporting it with great enthusiasm; and people could accept the policy even if they endorsed only a few of the multiple reasons. Seeing the world in this way also eased the psychological burdens on decision-makers, which were surely great in ordering soldiers into combat and embarking on a bold venture. What is crucial in this context is not the validity of any of these beliefs but the convenience in holding them all simultaneously when there was no reason to expect the world to be arranged so neatly. This effect was so strong that Vice President Dick Cheney, who previously had recognized that removing Saddam could throw Iraq into chaos, was able to convince himself that it would not. There was no logic that prohibited the situation from presenting a threat but not an opportunity (or vice versa), or for there to have been threat of one kind—that is, that Saddam was on the verge of getting significant WMD capability—but not of another—for example, that he had no connection to al Qaeda. Logically, Cheney's heightened urgency about overthrowing Saddam should not have changed his view on what would follow. But it did.

The contrast with the intelligence community (IC) was sharp. While it did believe that Saddam had robust WMD programs, because it did not feel the psychological need to bolster the case for war, it did not have to pull other perceptions into line and so gave little support to the administration on points where the evidence was to the contrary. And this is where the friction arose. Intelligence denied any collaboration between Saddam and al Qaeda, and it was very skeptical about the possibility that Saddam would turn over WMD to terrorists. So it is not surprising that here the administration put great pressure on intelligence to come to a different view and that policymakers frequently made statements that were at variance with the assessments. It is also not surprising, although obviously it was not foreordained, that the intelligence here was quite accurate.

Intelligence also painted a gloomy picture of the prospects for postwar Iraq, noting the possibilities for continued resistance and, most of all, the difficulties in inducing the diverse and conflicting groups in the country to cooperate with one another. Because this skepticism did not receive public attention, these estimates were subject to less political pressure, although the fact that the administration not only ignored them but also frequently affirmed the opposite must have been frustrating to the analysts. Fortunately for them, however, on these points, the administration was content to assert its views without claiming that they were supported by intelligence, probably because the judgments were of a broad political nature and did not rely on secret information. Later, when the postwar situation deteriorated and intelligence officials revealed that they had, in fact, provided warnings, the conflict heightened as the administration felt that intelligence was being disloyal and furthering its own political agenda.

It is tempting to see the browbeating and ignoring of intelligence as a particular characteristic of the George W. Bush administration, but it was not. Although available evidence does not allow anything like a full inventory, it does reveal examples from other administrations. Because Bill Clinton and his colleagues were committed to returning Haiti's Jean-Bertrand Aristide to power after he had been ousted in a coup, they resented and resisted intelligence analysis that argued that he was unstable and his governing would not be effective or democratic. Neither the administration of Dwight D. Eisenhower nor that of John F. Kennedy, both of which favored a test-ban agreement, was happy with analyses that indicated that verification would be difficult. Although on many issues liberals are more accepting of value trade-offs than are conservatives and many liberals like to think of themselves as particularly willing to confront complexity, once they are in power, they, too, need to muster political support and live at peace with themselves.

Intelligence does not feel the same pressures. It does not carry the burden of decision but "merely" has to figure out what the world is like. If the resulting choices are difficult, so be it. It also is not the duty of intelligence to build political support for a policy, and so even intelligence officials who do not oppose a policy will—or should—feel no compulsion to portray the world in a helpful way. In many cases, good intelligence will then point out the costs and dangers implicit in a policy. It will make it harder for policy-makers to present a policy as clearly the best one and will nurture second thoughts, doubts, and unease. It is not that intelligence usually points to policies other than those the leaders prefer, but only that it is likely to give decision-makers a more complex and contradictory view than fits with their political and psychological needs. Ironically, it can do this even as it brings good news. One might think that Lyndon Johnson would have welcomed the CIA telling him that other countries would not fall to Communism even if Vietnam did, but since his policy was justified (to others and probably to himself) on the premise that the domino theory was correct, he did not.

RESISTANCE TO FALLBACK POSITIONS
AND SIGNS OF FAILURE

The same factors that lead decision-makers to underestimate trade-offs make them reluctant to develop fallback plans and inclined to resist information that their policy is failing. The latter more than the former causes conflicts with intelligence, although the two are closely linked. There are several reasons why leaders are reluctant to develop fallback plans. It is hard enough to develop one policy, and the burden of thinking through a second is often simply too great. Probably more important, if others learn of the existence of Plan B, they may give less support to Plan A. Even if they do not prefer the former, its existence will be taken as betraying the leaders' lack of faith in their policy. It may also be psychologically difficult for leaders to contemplate failure.

Examples abound. Clinton did not have a Plan B when he started bombing to induce Serbia's Slobodan Milosevic to withdraw his troops from Kosovo. Administration officials thought such a plan was not needed, because it was obvious that Milosevic would give in right away. In part, they believed this because they thought it had been the brief and minor bombing over Bosnia that had brought Milosevic to the table at Dayton, an inference that, even if it had been correct, would not have readily supported the conclusion that he would give up Kosovo without a fight. The result was that the administration had to scramble both militarily and politically and was fortunate to end the confrontation as well as it did. The most obvious and consequential recent case of a lack of Plan B is Iraq. Despite intelligence to the contrary, top administration officials believed that the political and economic reconstruction of Iraq would be easy and that they needed neither short-term plans to maintain order nor long-term preparations to put down an insurgency and create a stable polity. Thinking about a difficult postwar situation would have been psychologically and politically costly, which is why it was not done.

Having a Plan B means little unless decision-makers are willing to shift to it if they must; this implies a need to know whether the policy is working. This, even more than the development of the plan, involves intelligence, and so here the clashes will be greater. Leaders tend to stay with their first choice for as long as possible. Lord Salisbury, the famous British statesman of the end of the nineteenth century, noted that "the commonest error in politics is sticking to the carcasses of dead policies." Leaders are heavily invested in their policies. To change their basic objectives will be to incur very high costs, including, in some cases, losing their offices if not their lives. Indeed the resistance to seeing that a policy is failing is roughly proportional to the costs that are expected if it does. Iraq again provides a clear example. In early 2007, Senator John McCain explained, "It's just so hard for me to contemplate failure that I can't make the next step," and President Bush declared that American policy in Iraq would succeed "because it has to." This perseverance in what appears to be a losing cause may be rational for the leaders, if not for the country, as long as there is any chance of success and the costs of having to adopt a new policy are almost as great as those for continuing to the bitter end. An obvious example is Bush's decision to increase the number of American troops in Iraq in early 2007. The previous policy was not working and would have resulted in a major loss for the United States and for Bush, and even a failed "surge" would have cost him little more than admitting defeat and withdrawing without this renewed effort. Predictions of success or failure were not central to the decision. In most cases, however, predictions are involved, and it is hard for decision-makers to make them without bias.

Intelligence officials do not have such a stake in the established policies, and thus it is easier for them to detect signs that the policies are failing. The fact that the leaders of the Bush administration saw much more progress in Iraq than did the IC is not unusual. The civilian intelligence agencies were quick to doubt that bombing North Vietnam would either cut the supply lines or induce the leadership to give in; they issued pessimistic reports on the pacification campaign and gave higher estimates of the size of the adversary's forces than the military or Johnson wanted to hear.

Leaders are not necessarily being foolish. The world is ambiguous, and indicators of success are likely to be elusive. If it were easy to tell who would win a political or military struggle, it would soon come to an end (or would not start at all), and Vietnam is not unique in permitting a postwar debate on the virtues of alternative policies. Although it was a pernicious myth that Germany lost World War I because of a "stab in the back," Germany could have gained better peace terms if the top military leaders had not lost their nerve in the late summer of 1918. Furthermore, leaders can be correct even if their reasoning is not. The classic case is that of Winston Churchill in the spring of 1940. He prevailed over strong sentiment in his cabinet for a peace agreement with Germany in the wake of the fall of France by arguing that Britain could win because the German economy was badly overstretched and could be broken by a combination of bombing and guerrilla warfare. This was a complete fantasy; his foreign secretary had reason to write in his diary that "Winston talked the most frightful rot. It drives one to despair when he works himself up into a passion of emotion when he ought to make his brain think and reason." Fortunately, Churchill's emotion and force of character carried the day; intelligence can get no credit. But regardless of who is right, we should expect conflict between leaders and intelligence over whether Plan B is necessary.

CONFIDENCE AND PERSEVERANCE

We should perhaps not underestimate the virtues of perseverance, as pigheaded as it may appear to opponents and to later observers when it fails. Not a few apparently hopeless cases end well. This may prove to be true in Iraq, and despite widespread opinion to the contrary, the mujahedeen in Afghanistan were able to force the Soviets out of the country. Similarly, two scientists spent over twenty years working on what almost everyone else believed was a misguided quest to understand the workings of the hypothalamus, producing no results until they independently made the breakthroughs that earned them Nobel Prizes. Albert Hirschman points to the "hiding hand" in many human affairs. If we saw the obstacles in our path, we would not begin many difficult but ultimately successful endeavors. For example, how many scholars would have started a dissertation had they known how long and arduous it would be?

Confidence is necessary for perseverance and for embarking on any difficult venture. While it can be costly, it also is functional in many situations, which helps explain why people are systematically overconfident. Although it might seem that we would be better off if our confidence better matched our knowledge, it turns out that the most mentally healthy people are slightly over- optimistic, overestimating their skills and ability to control their lives. This is probably even more true for decision-makers, who carry heavy burdens. As Henry Kissinger says, "Historians rarely do justice to the psychological stress on a policymaker." A national leader who had no more confidence than an objective reading of the evidence would permit probably would do little or would be worn down by mental anguish after each decision. Dean Acheson understood this when he told the presidential scholar Richard Neustadt, "I know your theory [that presidents need to hear conflicting views]. You think Presidents should be warned. You're wrong. Presidents should be given confidence."

There is little reason to think that President Bush was being less than honest when he told Bob Woodward, "I know it is hard for you to believe, but I have not doubted what we're doing [in Iraq]." He was aware that a degree of self-manipulation, if not self-deception, was involved: "[A] president has got to be the calcium in the backbone. If I weaken, the whole team weakens. If my confidence level in our ability declines, it will send ripples throughout the whole organization. I mean, it's essential that we be confident and determined and united." During the air campaign phase of the Gulf War, when the CIA estimated that the damage being inflicted was well below what the Air Force reported and what plans said was needed to launch the ground attack, the general in charge, Norman Schwarzkopf, demanded that the CIA get out of his business. His reasoning was not that the CIA was wrong but that these estimates reduced the confidence of the men and women in uniform on which success depended.

Of course, there are occasions on which intelligence can supply confidence. The breaking of German codes in World War II not only gave allied military and civilian leaders an enormous amount of information that enabled them to carry out successful military operations but also provided a general confidence that they could prevail. At the height of the Cuban Missile Crisis in 1962, Kennedy was given confidence by the report from his leading Soviet expert that Nikita Khrushchev would be willing to remove the missiles the Soviets had installed in Cuba without an American promise of a parallel withdrawal from Turkey. In most cases, however, intelligence is likely to provide a complicated, nuanced, and ambiguous picture.

When they are not prepared to change, leaders are prone both to reject the information and to scorn the messenger, claiming that intelligence is unhelpful (which in a real sense it is), superficial (which is sometimes the case), and disloyal (which is rare). Intelligence may lose its access or, if the case is important, much of its role. Thus, in the 1930s, when a unit in the Japanese military intelligence showed that the China campaign, far from leading to control over needed raw materials, was draining the Japanese economy, the army reorganized and marginalized it. Something similar was attempted in Vietnam by the U.S. military, which responded to the pessimistic reporting from the Department of State's Bureau of Intelligence and Research (INR) by having Secretary of Defense Robert McNamara insist that INR should not be permitted to analyze what was happening on the battlefield.

It might be comforting to believe that only rigid individuals or organizations act in this way, but what is at work is less the characteristics of the organization and the personalities of the leaders than the desire to continue the policy, the need for continuing political support, and the psychological pain of confronting failure. When the research arm of the U.S. Forest Service turned up solid evidence that the best way to manage forests was to permit if not facilitate controlled fires, the unit was abolished, because the founding mission and, indeed, identity of the service was to prevent forest fires.

TOO EARLY OR TOO LATE

For intelligence to be welcomed and to have an impact, it must arrive at the right time, which is after the leaders have become seized with the problem but before they have made up their minds. This is a narrow window. One might think that early warning would be especially useful because there is time to influence events. But in many cases, decision-makers will have an established policy, one that will be costly to change, and early warnings can rarely be definitive.

Intelligence about most of the world is irrelevant to leaders because they are too busy to pay attention to any but the most pressing concerns. Intelligence on matters that are not in this category may be useful for building the knowledge of the government and informing lower-level officials but will not receive a hearing at the top. This was the case with intelligence on domestic politics in Iran before the fall of 1978, when it became clear that the troubles facing the Shah were serious. Intelligence was badly flawed here, rarely going beyond inadequate reports from the field or assessing the situation in any depth. But even better analysis would not have gained much attention, because the president and his top assistants were preoccupied with other problems and projects, most obviously the attempt to bring peace to the Middle East that culminated in President Jimmy Carter's meeting with President Anwar Sadat and Prime Minister Meacham Begin at Camp David. As one CIA official said to me, "We could not give away intelligence on Iran before the crisis." Almost as soon as the crisis hit, however, it was too late. Top officials quickly established their own preferences and views of the situation. This is not unusual. On issues that are central, decision-makers and their assistants are prone to become their own intelligence analysts.

Perhaps intelligence can have the most influence if it operates on questions that are important but not immediately pressing. In the run-up to the war in Iraq, there was nothing that intelligence could have reasonably told President Bush that would have affected the basic decisions. But things might have been different if intelligence in the mid-1990s had been able to see that Saddam had postponed if not abandoned his ambitions for WMD. Had this been the standard view when Bush came to power, he and his colleagues might have accepted it because they were not then far down the road to war.

As a policy develops momentum, information and analyses that would have mattered if received earlier now will be ignored. This can be seen quite clearly in military operations, because it is relatively easy to mark the stages of the deliberation. At the start, the focus is on whether the operation can succeed, which means paying careful attention to the status of the adversary's forces and the possibilities of gaining surprise. But as things move ahead, new information is likely to be used for tactical purposes rather than for calling the operation into question. The greater the effort required to mount it and the greater the difficulty in securing agreement to proceed, the greater the resistance will be to new information that indicates it is not likely to succeed.

A clear example is Operation Market Garden in the fall of 1944. After the leading British general, Bernard Montgomery, was rebuffed by Eisenhower in his arguments for concentrating all Allied forces behind his thrust toward Berlin, political as well as military reasons led Eisenhower to agree to a bold but more limited attack deep into German-held territory, culminating at Arnhem. The need for allied unity and for conciliating Montgomery, combined with the fact that Eisenhower had been urging him to be more aggressive, meant that "once he was committed, retreat for Ike was all but impossible." Shortly before the attack was to be launched, code breaking revealed that the Germans had more and better-trained forces in the area than the allies had anticipated. Had they known this earlier, the operation would not have been approved. But once the basic decision was made, the political and psychological costs of reversing it were so high that the intelligence was disregarded, to the great cost of the soldiers parachuted onto the final bridge. The refusal or inability of a leading British general to heed the intelligence indicating that the British move into Greece in 1941 would almost surely fail can be similarly explained, as can the fact that pessimistic CIA assessments about the planned American invasion of Cambodia in 1971 were not forwarded to the president when DCI Helms realized that Nixon and Kissinger had made up their minds and would only be infuriated by the reports, which turned out to be accurate.

IMPORTANCE OF COGNITIVE PREDISPOSITIONS

Intelligence often has its own strongly held beliefs, which can operate at multiple levels of abstraction, from general theories of politics and human nature to images of adversaries to ideas about specific situations. These need not be uniform, and the IC, like the policymaking community, often is divided and usually along the same lines. During the Cold War, some factions were much more worried about the USSR than were others, and the China analysts were deeply divided in their views about the role of Mao Zedong and about how internal Chinese politics functioned. In these cases, analysts, like policymakers, were slow to change their views and saw most new information as confirming what they expected to see. This is true on the level of tactical intelligence as well. A striking case was the accidental shooting down of an Iranian airliner by the USS *Vincennes* toward the end of the Iran-Iraq War. One of the key errors was that the radar operator mis-read his screen as indicating that the airplane was descending toward the ship. What is relevant here is that the *Vincennes*'s captain had trained his crew very aggressively, leading them to expect an attack and giving them a mindset that was conducive to reading—and misreading—evidence as indicating that one was under way. A destroyer that was in the vicinity had not been drilled in this way, and its operator read the radar track correctly.

Differing predispositions provide another reason why decision-makers so often reject intelligence. The answers to many of their most important questions are linked to their beliefs about world politics, the images of those they are dealing with, and their general ideas, if not ideologies. Bush's view of Saddam rested in large measure on his beliefs about how tyrants behave, for example. If intelligence had explained that Saddam was not a major threat, being unlikely to aid terrorists or to try to dominate the region, this probably would not have been persuasive to Bush, and not just because he was particularly closed-minded. This kind of intelligence would have been derived not only from detailed analysis of how Saddam had behaved but from broad understandings of politics and even of human nature. Here, it is both to be expected and legitimate for decision-makers to act on their views rather than those propounded by intelligence. It is often rightly said that "policymakers are entitled to their own policies, but not to their own facts." Facts do not speak for themselves, however, and crucial political judgments grow out of a stratum that lies between if not beneath policies and facts.

Although it was not appropriate for a member of the National Security Council staff to ask whether the Baghdad station chief who produced a gloomy prognosis in November 2003 was a Democrat or Republican, it would not have been illegitimate to have inquired as to the person's general political outlook, his predisposition toward optimism or pessimism, his general views about how insurgencies could be put down, and his beliefs about how difficult it would be to bring stability to a conflicted society. Not only is it comforting for decision-makers to listen to those who share their general values and outlook, but it also makes real sense for them to do so. They are right to be skeptical of the analysis produced by those who see the world quite differently, because however objective the analysts are trying to be, their interpretations will inevitably be influenced by their general beliefs and theories.

It is, then, not surprising that people are rarely convinced in arguments about central issues. The debate about the nature of Soviet intentions went on throughout the Cold War, with few people being converted and fewer being swayed by intelligence or competing analysis. Without going so far as to say that everyone is born either a little hawk or a little dove, to paraphrase Gilbert and Sullivan, on the broadest issues of the nature and intentions of other countries and the existence and characteristics of broad historical trends, people's beliefs are determined more by their general worldviews, predispositions, and ideologies than they are by the sort of specific evidence that can be pieced together by intelligence. The reason why DCI John McCone expected the Soviets to put missiles into Cuba and his analysts did not was not that they examined different evidence or that he was more careful than they were, but that he strongly believed that the details of the nuclear balance influenced world politics and that Khrushchev would therefore be strongly motivated to improve his position. Similarly, as early as February 1933, Robert Vansittart, the United Kingdom's permanent undersecretary in the Foreign Office, who was to become a leading opponent of appeasement, said that the Germans were "likely to rely for their military power . . . on the mechanical weapons of the future, such as tanks, big guns, and above all military aircraft." Eighteen months later, when criticizing the military for being slow to appreciate the rise of Nazi power, he said, "Prophecy is largely a matter of insight. I do not think the Service Departments have enough. On the other hand they might say that I have too much. The answer is that I know the Germans better." Although contemporary decision-makers might not refer to intuition, they are likely to have deeply ingrained beliefs about the way the world works and what a number of countries are like, and in this sense, they will be prone to be their own intelligence analysts.

"The discrepancy between the broad cognitive predispositions of the IC and those of political leaders explains why conflict has tended to be higher when Republicans are in power." With some reason, they see intelligence analysts as predominantly liberals. Their suspicions that intelligence has sought to thwart and embarrass the administration are usually false, but to the extent that the worldviews of most intelligence officers are different from those of the Republicans, the latter are justified in being skeptical of IC analysis on broad issues. For their part, intelligence analysts, like everyone else, underestimate the degree to which their own interpretations of specific bits of evidence are colored by their general predispositions and so consider the leaders' rejection of their views closed-minded and ideological. Although not all people are equally driven by their theories about the world, there is a degree of legitimacy to the leaders' position that members of the IC often fail to grasp. President Ronald Reagan and his colleagues, including DCI Bill Casey, probably were right to believe that the IC's assessments that the Soviet Union was not supporting terrorism and was not vulnerable to economic pressures were more a product of the IC's liberal leanings than of the evidence. They therefore felt justified in ignoring the IC when they did not put pressure on it, which in turn led to charges of politicization, a topic to which I will now turn.

POLITICIZATION

Politicization of intelligence can take many forms, from the most blatant, in which intelligence is explicitly told what conclusions it should reach," to the less obvious, including demoting people who produce the "wrong" answer, putting in place personnel whose views are consistent with those of the top leaders, reducing the resources going to units whose analyses are troubling, and the operation of unconscious bias by analysts who fear that their careers will be damaged by producing undesired reports. Even more elusive may be what one analyst has called "politicization by omission": issues that are not evaluated because the results might displease superiors. Also subtle are the interactions between pressures and degrees of certainty in estimates. I suspect that one reason for the excess certainty in the Iraq WMD assessments was the knowledge of what the decision-makers wanted. Conversely, analysts are most likely to politically conform when they are uncertain about their own judgments, as will often be the case on difficult and contentious questions.

Only rarely does one find a case like the one in which President Johnson told DCI Helms, "Dick, I need a paper on Vietnam, and I'll tell you what I want included in it." Almost as blatant was Kissinger's response when CIA experts told Congress that intelligence did not believe that the new Soviet missile with multiple warheads could menace the American retaliatory force, contrary to what policymakers had said. He ordered the reports to be revised, and when they still did not conform, told Helms to remove the offending paragraph on the grounds that it was not "hard" intelligence but merely speculation on Soviet intentions, a subject on which intelligence lacked special qualifications.

Even this case points to the ambiguities in the notion of politicization and the difficulties in drawing a line between what political leaders should and should not do when they disagree with estimates. Intelligence said that "we consider it highly unlikely [that the Soviets] will attempt within the period of this estimate to achieve a first-strike capability." This prediction was reasonable—and turned out to be correct—but it rested in part on judgments of the Soviet system and the objectives of the Soviet leaders, and these are the kinds of questions that the top political leadership is entitled to answer for itself. On the other hand, to demand that intelligence keep silent on adversary intentions would be bizarre, and indeed, when the hard-liners forced an outside estimate at the end of the Gerald Ford administration, the group of selected hawks who formed "Team B" strongly criticized the IC for concentrating on capabilities and ignoring intentions.

So it is not surprising that arguments about whether politicization occurred are rarely easy to settle. In some cases, the only people with first-hand knowledge will have major stakes in the dispute, and in others, even a videotape of the meeting might not tell us what happened. Was the office chief bemoaning the fact that an estimate would cause him grief with policymakers, or was he suggesting that it be changed? Was the DCI's assistant just doing his job when he strongly criticized a draft paper, arguing that the evidence was thin, alternatives were not considered, and the conclusion went beyond the evidence, or was he exerting pressure to get a different answer? When people in the vice president's office and the office of the secretary of defense told the IC analysts to look again—and again—at the evidence for links between Saddam and al Qaeda and repeatedly pressed them on why they were discounting sources that reported such links, were they just doing due diligence? Are analysts being oversensitive, or are leaders and managers being overassertive? Winks and nods, praise and blame, promotions and their absence are subject to multiple causes and multiple interpretations. In many of these cases, I suspect that one's judgment will depend on which side of the substantive debate one is on, because commentators, as well as the participants, will bring with them their own biases and reasons to see or reject claims of pressure.

Ironically, while many of the critics of the IC's performance on Iraqi WMD highlighted the dangers of politicization, some of the proposed reforms (ones that appear after every failure) show how hard it is to distinguish a good intelligence process from one that is driven by illegitimate political concerns. It is conventional wisdom that good analysis questions its own assumptions, looks for alternative explanations, examines low-probability interpretations as well as ones that seem more likely to be correct, scrutinizes sources with great care, and avoids excessive conformity. The problem in this context is that analysts faced with the probing questions that these prescriptions imply may believe that they are being pressured into producing a different answer. The obvious reply is that consumers and managers must apply these techniques to all important cases, not just when they object to the initial answers. There is something to this, and it would make sense to look back at previous cases in which politicization has been charged and see whether only those estimates that produced the "wrong" answers were sent back for further scrutiny.

But even this test is not infallible. If I am correct that political leaders and top intelligence managers are entitled to their own broad political views, then they are right to scrutinize especially carefully what they think are incorrect judgments. Thus, the political leaders insisted that the IC continually reassess its conclusion that there were no significant links between Saddam and al Qaeda not only because they wanted a different answer but also because their feeling for how the world worked led them to expect such a connection, and they thought that the IC's assessment to the contrary was based less on the detailed evidence than on the misguided political sensibility that was dominant in the IC. It is not entirely wrong for policymakers to require a higher level of proof from intelligence when the evidence cuts against their desired policy. This means that the greater probing of the grounds for judgments and the possible alternatives that are the objectives of good intelligence procedures may increase the likelihood both of politicization and of analysts' incorrectly levying such a charge.

CONCLUSION

Decision-makers need information and analysis, and intelligence gets its significance and mission from influencing those who will make policy. But this does not mean that relations between the two groups will be smooth. The grievances of the IC are several but less consequential because it has much less power than the intelligence consumers. Members of the IC often feel that policymakers shun complicated analysis, cannot cope with uncertainty, will not read beyond the first page, forget what they have been told, and are quick to blame intelligence when policy fails. In response, members of the IC grumble a great deal among themselves and, when sufficiently provoked, leak their versions to the media.

For their part, policymakers not only overestimate the subversive activities of intelligence, but also frequently find it less than helpful. This is true in two senses. First, they find that only on a few occasions can intelligence light a clear path. The evidence that can be gathered by other than supernatural methods is limited and ambiguous, and in many significant cases, other states may not even know what they will do until the last minute. Even when intentions are long-standing, they and the associated capabilities often can be disguised, and the knowledge that deception is possible further degrades the available information. Even without this problem, it is difficult for intelligence officials to see the world as others see it and to penetrate minds that think quite differently than they do. This is especially true when the other side has beliefs and plans that, even when they become known later, make very little sense.

Leaders find intelligence less than completely helpful in another sense as well. Leaders want to understand the world in which they are operating, but above all, need to act and sustain themselves psychologically and politically. These requirements often conflict with the sort of analysis that intelligence is likely to provide. Leaders need confidence and political support, and all too often, intelligence undermines both. In many cases, intelligence will increase rather than reduce uncertainty as it notes ambiguities and alternative possibilities. Even worse, intelligence can report that the policy to which the leader is committed is likely to entail high costs with dubious prospects for success. Occasionally intelligence can point to opportunities that the country can seize or to signs that the difficulties confronting a policy are only temporary. But more often, it will indicate that the preferred path is not smooth, and may be a dead end.

No leader can have risen to the top without having frequently taken risks that others would shun and found success where others expected failure. Experience will have taught them to place faith in their own judgments. But they will still seek sources of reassurance. Psychologically, they will not want to face the full costs and risks of their policies lest they become fearful, inconsistent, and hesitant. The political problems are even greater, as they need to rally others at home and abroad. The exposure of the gaps in the information, the ambiguities in its interpretation, and the multiple problems the policy is likely to confront will not be politically helpful.

The frictions between particular American presidents and the IC are often attributed to special circumstances or the personality quirks of the former and the intellectual failures of the latter. These all do abound, but the problem goes much deeper. The needs and missions of leaders and intelligence officials are very different, and the two groups are doomed both to work together and to come into conflict.

DISCUSSION QUESTIONS

1. What are some of the attitudes that policymakers have toward intelligence and those that produce it?
2. What are two differing kinds of support that intelligence can provide policymakers?
3. How does the Iraq War illustrate the conflicting pressures on policymakers and the intelligence community?
4. Why does intelligence give policymakers "a more complex and contradictory view" than policymakers may like?
5. Why are policymakers reluctant to develop a Plan B in various situations? Why do they stick with Plan A for so long?

6. How do confidence and perseverance explain policymakers' commitment to policy? How does intelligence help or hinder such confidence?
7. When must intelligence arrive to policymakers to have an impact on policy?
8. What are some factors that make policymakers resistant to new information?
9. What does Jervis mean by the "cognitive predispositions" of intelligence analysts and policymakers?
10. To what extent does Jervis argue that policymakers are more convinced by their general world view than by intelligence assessments that they receive?
11. What are the different ways in which politicization of intelligence can occur?
12. Ultimately, why are policymakers and the intelligence community likely to come into conflict?

16

American Trade Policymaking

A Unique Process

I. M. (Mac) Destler

In the long run-up to the 2016 presidential election, U.S. international trade policy took a beating from candidates in both political parties. Vermont senator Bernie Sanders highlighted growing economic inequality and declared trade to be a primary cause. Republican nominee Donald J. Trump called "bad trade deals" a job-killing disaster for Americans and promised to abrogate existing agreements and raise tariffs unless partner nations mended their ways. This, he promised, would bring millions of manufacturing jobs back to the United States. Hillary Clinton was more nuanced, but she came out against the Trans-Pacific Partnership free-trade agreement she had hitherto championed, which President Barack Obama was hoping to make a crowning final achievement of his administration.

Trade policy, in sum, rose to a prominence in the 2016 presidential campaign far greater than it had enjoyed in decades. Candidates' positions posed a serious challenge to the eighty-year-old U.S. policy of reducing trade barriers at home and abroad, a policy pursued by every president from Franklin D. Roosevelt onward. And the surprise Trump victory raised a serious prospect of a fundamental reversal of that policy.

Yet if public opinion surveys were to be believed, over 60 percent of Americans still believe that globalization, overall, is "a good thing for the United States."[1] How do we explain all this?

Trade policy in the United States flows from a process quite different from that for mainstream foreign policy or national security. Rooted in the constitutional grant of authority to the Congress, it has evolved with changes in American trade policy goals, in the structure of the U.S. economy, and in the character of domestic politics.

CONSTITUTIONAL FRAMEWORK

Trade policy centers on the regulation of imports of goods and services entering the United States. Should they be treated the same as those produced domestically, or should they be taxed or otherwise constrained to "protect" U.S. businesses and workers? Concern over this issue dates from the origins of the Republic. In fact, it arose among the original thirteen colonies as well. The framers of the Constitution were concerned about their restricting trade with one another, and the grant of authority over "commerce" to Congress in Article I, Section 8, includes that "among the several states" as well as "with foreign nations."

This power was conveyed, of course, within the overall structure of independent executive and legislative branches—what the late Richard Neustadt famously called "separated institutions sharing powers."[2] Their intertwining means that serious policy action in the United States almost always requires major contributions from both Congress and the president.

Through most of U.S. history, however, Congress was dominant on trade policy. The issue was "the tariff," which "more than any other single topic . . . engrossed Congressional energies for more than a hundred years."[3] Tariffs were also the primary source of federal income until early in the twentieth century, when they were supplanted by the income tax. The issue divided the political parties, with Republicans seeking more protection and Democrats less. The former usually controlled the government from the Civil War to the Great Depression. Members of Congress were generally responsive to interests within their districts, and Republicans responded particularly to producer interests. This, plus logrolling among such interests, brought tariffs higher and higher, culminating in the Smoot-Hawley Act of 1930.[4] That now-infamous law brought tariffs on dutiable imports to an average of 60 percent.

Smoot-Hawley was replicated across the advanced industrial world, and the consequence of multiple nations closing their markets was a deepening of the Great Depression. This contributed to a fundamental change in U.S. trade policy, substantively and institutionally. Policy shifted from a persistent tendency to raise import barriers to an equally steady inclination to lower them. And the process changed as well—Congress abruptly stopped enacting comprehensive tariff bills, with the initiative shifting to the executive branch.

The change was inaugurated in the administration of Franklin D. Roosevelt. Democrats had won large majorities in Congress, but rather than cut tariffs directly—as they had the power to do—they established a process that they hoped could outlast their existing partisan advantage. Specifically, the United States would negotiate reciprocal barrier-reducing agreements with nations that were our primary trading partners, and the president would use delegated authority from Congress to enact the lower rates. This was accomplished through the Reciprocal Trade Agreements Act of 1934. The Reciprocal Trade Agreements Act fundamentally altered the political dynamic. Though presidents were not immune to protectionist pressures, they generally pursued broader interests. In addition, the international negotiating process brought export interests into the trade policy game to balance those of trade-threatened domestic producers.

In the decades that followed, Congress frequently limited executive leeway in barrier reduction—exempting certain products, always imposing time limits. But the central question changed from how much Congress would raise a tariff, to how much the president's negotiators would bargain it down. After World War II, moreover, the negotiating arena shifted— from bilateral talks, with tariff reductions then generalized under the most-favored-nation (MFN) principle, to multilateral "rounds" under the General Agreement on Tariffs and Trade (GATT) negotiated in 1947.

In the prewar and postwar years, these negotiations were conducted by the Department of State. Indeed, Roosevelt's secretary—Cordell Hull—was the driving force behind the initiation of the new policymaking process. But members of Congress grew increasingly restive with a process where a department distant from U.S. economic interests was responsible for key decisions affecting them. So when, in 1962, President John F. Kennedy sought unprecedentedly broad and flexible authority to negotiate new barrier reductions with the recently formed European Economic Community, this concern surfaced with a vengeance. Wilbur Mills (D-AR) was then chair of the House Ways and Means Committee, which had jurisdiction over trade policy and hence the proposed legislation. He favored the proposed negotiations. He also respected the competence of State Department officials, but he didn't think they knew much about U.S. business. Commerce Department officials, by contrast, knew a lot about business but weren't as smart, Mills believed—moreover, they didn't know much about agriculture. Harry Byrd (D-VA), chair of the Ways and Means counterpart committee in the Senate, had similar reservations. Kennedy's response was to acquiesce, reluctantly, in placing responsibility for the new trade negotiations in the White House.

THE UNITED STATES TRADE REPRESENTATIVE: ESTABLISHMENT, EVOLUTION

The Trade Expansion Act of 1962 established the office of President's Special Representative for Trade Negotiations (STR) to conduct the multilateral trade talks that became known as the "Kennedy Round." In the course of those negotiations, the task of the representative's small office was to balance foreign and domestic economic interests, coordinate the executive branch, and bargain with both Congress and foreign governments. The arrangement proved successful, and the round produced cuts in U.S. tariffs averaging 35 percent—this on top of those achieved by earlier negotiations. Congress liked both the process and the product, and took regular steps to protect and strengthen the White House–based trade office.

When President Richard M. Nixon's administration showed interest in 1973 in subsuming STR under another White House economic office, Congress made it a statutory entity and gave its head a cabinet-level salary in the Trade Act of 1974. Five years later, when Congress insisted on a strengthening of executive branch trade policy institutions, President Jimmy Carter responded with a reorganization plan renaming STR the Office of the *United States* Trade Representative (USTR) and broadening its authority. When President Ronald Reagan proposed to replace it with a Department of Trade in 1983, the Senate resisted. When House members thought the president wasn't using his trade powers aggressively enough, they used the 1988 trade legislation to shift certain authorities from him to the USTR. When aides to President-Elect George W. Bush spoke, during the 2000–2001 transition, of rescinding the USTR's cabinet status, a chorus of congressional and business voices led them to reconsider.[5]

As these events illustrate, the USTR has acquired enduring constituencies— in Congress, and in the trade-minded business community. Central to these constituencies have been the trade committees: House Ways and Means, and the Senate Committee on Finance. They come by this authority through their broad jurisdiction over revenues (tariffs are taxes), and their writ extends to such major governmental enterprises as Social Security and Medicare. This makes them powerful within their chambers, which in turn attracts ambitious and competent legislators to their ranks. When U.S. trade policy has been effective, it has typically reflected cooperation between these committees and the office they saw as "their" agent within the executive branch. Presidents weren't always eager to buy into this arrangement, and retaining presidential support has been a recurrent problem for the USTR. But the basic system has now endured for fifty years, and there is no strong current pressure to change it.

Formally, the USTR is housed in the Executive Office of the President (EOP). It is, in the words of the Carter executive order of 1980, responsible for "international trade policy development, coordination, and negotiation." Coordination of trade policy with other concerns is the responsibility of the National Economic Council (NEC)—established by President Clinton, retained by his successors—and, intermittently, of the much more established National Security Council on which the NEC is modeled. But the USTR typically leads and manages on major trade issues. It is politically attuned—to Congress, to interested industries. But even in a highly partisan era it has retained a priority in technical competence and a preference to work across party lines. Lawyers are prominent among its staff, some of whom move back and forth to the staffs of the congressional committees. And former USTR officials are prominent in the Washington trade bar.

Within the trade policy sphere, the USTR heads a statutory interagency coordinating committee structure that operates at cabinet and subcabinet levels. Other important members of these committees—and trade policy participants—include the Departments of Commerce, Agriculture, Treasury, and State, and EOP units such as the Council of Economic Advisers.

Among these other U.S. agencies, second to the USTR in importance on trade is the U.S. Department of Commerce, which the Carter order made "the focus of nonagricultural operational trade responsibilities." Commerce assumed, in 1980, authority to administer the countervailing duty and antidumping laws, enacted and periodically strengthened by Congress to give producers recourse against "unfair" imports either subsidized by foreign governments or "dumped" at less than it costs to produce them. Commerce wields this authority with dense technical expertise in a petitioner-friendly manner that reflects congressional desires. That department also houses the U.S. and Foreign Commercial Service, which works with private business in Washington and overseas to promote U.S. exports. Overall, Commerce is the federal agency deepest in expertise in trade and the industries involved.

For most matters, the USTR-Commerce division of labor is relatively clear. One place where coordination can fail is at the top. For trade is the most prominent of Commerce's generally unexciting set of responsibilities, and it is not untypical for the secretary of commerce to have closer links to the president than the USTR who is supposed to lead him. Secretaries Maurice Stans (under Nixon) and Malcolm Baldrige (under Reagan) sought government-wide leadership on trade. Secretaries Robert Mosbacher (under George H. W. Bush) and Don Evans (who served George W. Bush) were also closer to their presidents than the USTRs of their time. It was Baldrige's power struggle with USTR Bill Brock in 1981–1984 that caused the greatest problems for trade policy. Baldrige was aided by the fact that some major steel negotiations involved antidumping and countervailing duty cases before his department. Interestingly, though the commerce secretary retained Reagan's support through the period, Brock eventually won out due to his strong backing on Capitol Hill.

Another consequential institution is the United States International Trade Commission (USITC). The USITC is a regulatory body, independent of the president, with six members appointed by him and confirmed by Congress. No more than three can be members of the same political party. The USITC determines whether firms petitioning Commerce for trade relief have suffered economic "injury," with an affirmative finding being a prerequisite for the relief. In escape clause (Section 201) cases, where neither subsidies nor dumping are alleged, the commission also recommends to the president the most appropriate form of import relief, though he need not follow the recommendation. (On subsidy and dumping cases, the relief is specified in statute.)

The United States Department of Agriculture (USDA) plays an important role within its sphere due to its responsibility for farm programs that are prominent in international negotiations. When USTRs advance agricultural trade liberalization proposals, they typically do so jointly with the USDA. (When the Doha talks broke down in July 2006, for example, USTR Susan Schwab and Agriculture Secretary Mike Johanns explained it together in a joint "press availability.") Treasury plays a strong role when the negotiating issue involves financial institutions, when exchange rates are a problem, or when its secretary (such as James Baker III under Reagan) is the effective overall economic policy leader of the government.

Societal economic interests are consulted regularly, particularly the interests of producers, because advancing them is an important function of trade negotiations, and because their support is needed for agreements reached. Formally, communication takes place through a statutory network of industry and labor advisory committees, which must report to Congress their views on pending trade agreements. In recent years, committees have been added and representatives appointed to reflect the interests of civil society groups—environmentalists in particular.

Senior officials in the USTR and the departments are, of course, appointed by the president and confirmed by Congress. It is through these appointments that the chief executive exercises his strongest impact on trade policy. A strong designee (Robert Strauss under Carter) brings effectiveness and priority to trade. A delayed appointment (typical for most first-term presidents) generates doubts for the same reasons. An appointee generally perceived as weak (Ron Kirk under Obama) makes an administration's overall trade policy less effective.

COORDINATING WITH CONGRESS: "FAST TRACK"

The executive branch process is significant, but the most important coordination for U.S. trade policy is that between the two branches. The USTR cannot be effective if Congress undercuts him, or if foreign or domestic interlocutors believe that it will. And the structure of "separated institutions" makes this highly likely in the absence of processes designed to promote cooperation and shared responsibility.

When trade negotiations were limited to tariffs, as was the case from the 1930s through the 1960s, coordination was straightforward: Congress told the president, through legislation, what his agents could and could not negotiate, specifically how far they could bargain down tariffs, generally and specifically. Operating within these constraints, the president could implement tariff reductions through his delegated authority and proclaim the new rates. But problems arose when U.S. negotiators struck deals that went beyond tariffs, for then implementation required detailed statutory language whose enactment could not be delegated to the president in advance. Congress refused, in fact, to implement two Kennedy Round deals negotiated by the Johnson administration in the 1960s—one on antidumping, the second on how certain U.S. duties were calculated. Other nations then withdrew concessions they had made to Washington and declared the United States an unreliable negotiating partner.

Thus, when the Nixon administration sought authority for the Tokyo Round negotiations (launched in 1973), where nontariff barriers would be central, it faced acute skepticism abroad as well as at home. In particular, it had to assuage foreign doubts about whether the United States could deliver on the deals its negotiators struck. The challenge was to establish executive credibility while maintaining congressional authority. The answer was a major innovation, which became known as the "fast-track procedures." When Congress authorized a trade negotiation, it would commit itself to act on the results, as submitted by the president, within a limited time period—ninety legislative days. It would make this commitment through rules binding on each of its two chambers. Unlike on a tariff agreement—when Congress had no ratification role—other nations could still not be certain that the United States would deliver on its commitments. Congress could, after all, reject a trade deal. But U.S. negotiating partners *could* be confident that Congress would vote on them, and would not alter them in the process. And in most circumstances, assuming the executive did its political homework, a positive vote could be expected.

The fast-track procedures were incorporated in the Trade Act of 1974, and they have governed, essentially, all major and minor barrier-reducing agreements entered into since that time, up to and including free trade agreements (FTAs) voted on in October 2011. The sequence is as follows: the president seeks and Congress grants authority to engage in trade negotiations, with objectives defined in statute; the USTR and other officials consult with Congress (the trade committees in particular) and private-sector advisory groups during the course of the negotiations; Congress and the advisory groups are notified of the content of an agreement 90 (or 120) days prior to its signing; the groups make independent reports to Congress recommending approval or rejection; the president, after further consultation with Congress, provides draft implementing legislation (introduced without change by congressional leaders); and Congress then acts on this legislation within a limit of ninety legislative days.[6]

The first test came with the Tokyo Round, and the procedures were adapted in practice when leaders of the Senate Committee on Finance pressed USTR Robert Strauss for a role in drafting the president's implementing bill. ("You do want it to pass, don't you?") He agreed, launching what became known as "non-markups"—meetings of congressional committees with executive officials where the legislators discussed and agreed on draft language. These were followed, for the Tokyo Round and typically thereafter, by a "non-conference," where Finance and Ways and Means committee leaders met to reconcile their differences. President Carter submitted the agreed-upon result with few changes, and the legislation passed overwhelmingly (just seven representatives and four senators voted "nay"). The procedures also worked effectively in implementing three subsequent major trade agreements: the Canada–U.S. Free Trade Agreement of 1988, the North American Free Trade Agreement (NAFTA) approved in 1993, and the Uruguay Round/WTO accord ratified in 1994. Essentially, they replicated the legislative process insofar as the statutory language was concerned, though the substance of the bills was, of course, constrained by what the executive branch had negotiated.

The processes favored the committees over other members of congress, and trade "insiders" over those outside the trade policy mainstream. They were condemned by some critics as undemocratic. But from the Tokyo Round through the Uruguay Round, they proved effective. They maintained congressional authority without sacrificing executive negotiating credibility.

A NEW TRADE POLITICS: (1) BUSINESS CHANGES ITS SPOTS

The prime political purpose of the trade policymaking system launched in 1934 was to counter broad business protectionism. American industry had grown strong behind tariff walls, and many of its leaders were committed to maintaining them. By changing the game from unilateral tariff-setting to international trade bargaining, and by shifting the locus of initiative away from the branch most vulnerable to particularist pressures, the system made possible the steady opening up of the American economy.

In the decades after World War II, the need for such institutions and processes seemed to grow. After a brief period of war-generated industrial dominance, U.S. producers began to face fierce international competition—first from Europe, then from a resurgent Japan. Traditionally protectionist sectors like textiles and shoes and steel were joined by newly threatened producers of television sets, machine tools, and even automobiles. Organized labor, in the free-trade camp during the first half-century, moved to the trade-restrictive side. Many Democrats followed, though this was offset by Republicans moving in the free-market direction. And when, in the early and mid-1980s, a suddenly strong dollar generated huge surges in imports and record trade deficits, members of both parties grew increasingly aggressive in demanding forceful responses. Responding to this pressure, Ronald Reagan—committed in principle to free trade—was driven, in the words of his treasury secretary, to "grant more import relief to U.S. industry than any of his predecessors in more than half a century."[7] And his administration, at congressional insistence, grew far more active in pressing foreign governments to lift what U.S. law labeled "unreasonable and unjustifiable" barriers to U.S. trade.

But while Congress insisted on passing broad trade legislation in 1988, its content was moderated after the dollar had declined sharply in value and the trade balance improved with a surge in exports. And when imports surged again in the late 1990s, at rates comparable to the Reagan period, there was no comparable protectionist response. Only the steel industry mobilized for import relief, which it finally received (for twenty-one months) in the first George W. Bush administration. The politically weakened textile industry, by far the most potent force for trade protection from the 1950s through the 1980s, acceded to globalization. Fabric producers now focused on shaping "rules of origin" in bilateral FTAs to assure that clothing shipped here from partner nations used made-in-USA cloth. With such rules in place, the industry actually came out in support of the politically controversial NAFTA agreement.

More generally, U.S. business became globalized. For the U.S. economy as a whole, trade averaged—in 2000—roughly 30 percent of the value of total national goods production, up from about 10 percent in 1970. This meant not only that producers were exporting a larger share of what they made, but also that they were importing many of the inputs into their final products. They now depended on open access to world markets. At mid-century, business protectionism had been the main concern of trade policymakers. By 2000, business was being attacked from the left for its open-market stance.

A NEW TRADE POLITICS: (2) THE RISE OF SOCIAL ISSUES AND PARTISANSHIP

This attack was an element in a broad anti-globalization movement that arose in the 1990s and persisted thereafter. So if business as a whole no longer impeded trade liberalization, other concerns rose to slow its progress. A loose coalition on the left—labor, environmentalists, some nongovernmental organizations (NGOs)—came to argue that trade, and business more generally, imposed serious social costs. Products from third-world nations came from factories that exploited workers, they declared. And this "unfair" competition drove down wages in advanced countries. Moreover, environmental conditions in these plants were often egregious. Not only was this bad for the poor countries themselves, but it also threatened an environmental "race to the bottom" as developed country competitors sought loosening of regulations at home so that they could better compete in the global marketplace.

For some advocates, these concerns were sufficient to justify full-blown opposition to new trade agreements—for their own sake, and (for some in the labor movement) because they provided "cover" for narrower economic interests. Others took a more qualified position—agreements could be beneficial *if* they included measures that addressed these social harms. Bill Clinton gave this stance visibility and credibility in the 1992 election campaign, when he declared he supported NAFTA (negotiated under President George H. W. Bush) but would not send it to Congress for approval unless and until there were appended to it side agreements on labor and the environment.

Clinton's USTR, Mickey Kantor, negotiated such agreements, and the president then sent NAFTA to Congress and won the uphill battle for its ratification. The coalition opposing it—labor, elements of the environmental community, and their allies—was bested in this battle, but they were determined it would not be the last. Through the rest of Clinton's presidency, they resisted new trade initiatives, bringing about failure of his effort to renew fast-track trade negotiating authority in 1997, and contributing to the breakdown of the Seattle ministerial conference of the World Trade Organization (WTO) convened to launch a new round of global trade negotiations. Their resistance also undercut progress on other ambitious undertakings to which Clinton was committed—a Free Trade Area of the Americas (FTAA) and an open trade regime among members of the Asia-Pacific Economic Cooperation (APEC) group.

The administration was able, in 2000, to win congressional approval of permanent normal trade relations with China, an indispensable element of that nation's joining the WTO. But Clinton bequeathed to his successor a polity divided over trade in general and the new social issues in particular. Most Democrats favored, at minimum, strong labor and environmental standards incorporated in the text of any future FTAs. Most Republicans, backed by business, wanted such standards minimized if included at all. This partisan polarization was relatively new to trade policy. But it reflected, and was reinforced by, broader trends in American politics.

In substantive views and voting behavior, the House of Representatives was becoming steadily more divided along partisan lines. One picture may not tell it all, but it shows a lot. Figure 16.1 shows the ideological distribution of liberal and conservative members (measured by voting

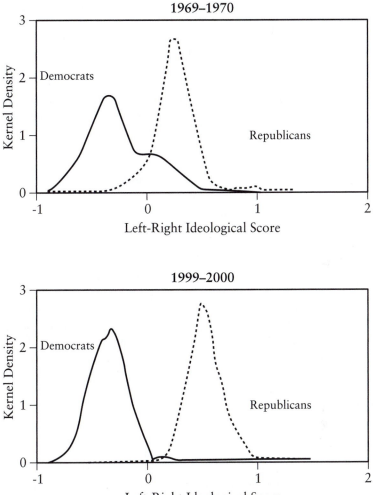

Figure 16.1. Ideological Distribution of the Parties in the U.S. House, 1969–1970 and 1999–2000

record) in 1969–1970, when there was considerable overlap between the two parties, and 1999–2000, when there was virtually none.[8] The causes were several and are addressed by the author in detail elsewhere.[9] But two were prominent.

The first was the sorting out of political party memberships that made them ideologically more cohesive. After the civil rights revolution, southern Democrats became Republicans—and/or their children did. And liberal northeastern Republicans turned into Democrats. As a result, the

Republican Party became, predominantly, the conservative party, and the Democrats, substantially, the liberal party.

The second change was the onset of decennial House redistricting, after the Supreme Court ruled that members must represent constituencies of equal size. This meant redrawing the lines after every census, and state legislatures—under pressure from House members—drew them primarily so as to protect incumbents, and only secondarily (if they controlled both branches of the state government) to increase the number elected from their own party. This produced Representatives safe from challenge by the other party, but vulnerable to challenge within their own party if they strayed too far from the party line.

As substantive polarization deepens, the political party becomes more than a convenient association for politicians seeking election—it becomes a group of like-minded individuals seeking to move public policy in specific, preferred directions. Within Congress, the group is represented by the party leadership and the party caucus, which seeks to shape substantive legislation at the expense of the committees. And the committee majorities are pressed to act in a partisan manner lest they lose power. In the process, members come to communicate mainly with their own kind, and seldom with those on the other side of the aisle. As communication fades, so does trust.

Substantive positions on trade policy do not fit comfortably into this new partisan mold. For decades, congressional Republicans had been growing more pro-trade and congressional Democrats, particularly labor Democrats, more skeptical. But the normal trade liberalization coalition remains a centrist one, as illustrated by the fact that extreme anti-trade sentiment appears almost equally at the fringes of both parties. In 2000 and 2005, for example, the House voted, as required by law, on whether the United States should withdraw from the WTO. Both resolutions were overwhelmingly rejected. The first withdrawal resolution won support from twenty-one Democrats—and thirty-three Republicans! The second was backed by forty-six Democrats and thirty-nine Republicans. General views on trade also do not differ fundamentally between these parties' overall memberships—a poll taken in the heat of the Central America Free Trade Agreement (CAFTA) debate found 51 percent of Democrats in favor—and 50 percent of Republicans![10]

Perhaps for these reasons, it took a while for party polarization to infect trade policy. Through the 1970s and, for the most part, the 1980s, the Ways and Means and Finance committees handled trade on a bipartisan basis. There were occasions when the majority Democrats excluded the minority and/or used trade to advance partisan purposes, but they were the exception. Chairman Dan Rostenkowski maintained the bipartisan tradition at Ways and Means into the early 1990s, resisting House Democratic Caucus pressure to operate in a more partisan manner.

But gradually, growing partisan rancor made trade compromise increasingly difficult to reach in the U.S. House of Representatives. This was reinforced by the fact that labor and environmental issues—unlike trade liberalization—*are* classic issues of liberal versus conservative. When the George W. Bush administration came to power in 2001 determined to pursue an active trade policy agenda, therefore, it and the House Republican leadership faced a choice. As they moved in 2001 for renewal of fast-track, now renamed "Trade Promotion Authority," they could seek compromise on these issues with leading Democrats. Or they could rely instead on their majority control of the chamber, "whipping" an overwhelming majority of their members into line (even though, in recent major votes, one-fourth to one-third of Republicans had voted against trade liberalization).[11]

Pushed by the House leadership, they chose the latter course. Ways and Means Chairman Bill Thomas (R-CA) refused, on more than one occasion, to meet with Democratic counterpart Charles Rangel (D-NY) to determine whether common ground could be found, even though President Bush had encouraged serious compromise talks.[12] The result was that essentially centrist legislation—it did include modest labor and environmental provisions—was adopted in a highly partisan process. With Democrats alienated, Republicans had to pressure their own. Driven by "the Hammer" (a.k.a. Majority Whip Tom DeLay [R-TX]), they extended the December 2001 vote on Trade Promotion Authority for twenty minutes beyond the time that the rules allowed, then had the speaker bang the gavel when one last reluctant Republican was dragged (and bought) into line, and Trade Promotion Authority survived, 215–214. In all, they were able to squeeze the number of "nay" votes from their party down to 23 (out of 217). Out of 210 Democrats, 21 voted in favor. After Senate approval and two more narrowly won House procedural votes, it became law in August 2002. The bill was named, ironically, the Bipartisan Trade Promotion Authority Act.

Bush's first-term trade representative, Robert Zoellick, used the new authority aggressively—not just for the newly launched Doha Round of multilateral trade talks, but also for an unprecedented number of bilateral and regional FTAs. Most were with relatively uncontroversial trading partners, with whom labor and environmental issues were not paramount—deals with Chile, Singapore, Australia, and Morocco won easy bipartisan approval. However, the Central America–Dominican Republic Free Trade Agreement (CAFTA-DR), signed in late 2003, brought back the partisan divisions. The vote was delayed until July 2005. With Democratic support down to fifteen votes, the Republican leadership replicated the 2001 process, holding the ballot open for more than an hour beyond the time decreed by House rules, until it was clear exactly how many GOP votes would be required. CAFTA-DR was approved 217–215, with three additional Republican votes available just in case.

Then, suddenly, the string ran out. Republicans faced defeat in the 2006 midterm election; Tom DeLay was under investigation and forced to resign his post. A new FTA was completed with Peru in December 2005, but Democrats found its labor-environmental provisions wanting, and Republicans no longer could roll it through the House on their own.

2007–2011: DELAY, THEN COMPROMISE

As Democrats prepared to assume power in the House in January 2007, USTR Susan C. Schwab recognized the need for a broader political base. She was completing an FTA with Colombia, and negotiations were well advanced on agreements with Panama and Korea. For these to have a chance in the new political environment, the split over labor and environmental standards needed to be resolved. Ways and Means Democrats were willing to deal, so she negotiated with now-Chairman Rangel what became known as the May 10 agreement. Endorsed by Speaker Nancy Pelosi, it specified provisions that would be added to the Peru and Colombia deals, and negotiated with Panama and Korea. On labor standards, for example, the executive-congressional agreement met the longstanding Democratic demand that trading partners commit themselves to the five core labor standards endorsed in the landmark June 1998 International Labor Organization Declaration on Fundamental Principles and Rights at Work: freedom of association, the right to bargain collectively, elimination of forced labor, effective abolition of child labor, and elimination of employment discrimination. Environmental provisions included pledges to adopt and enforce the obligations under major international environmental agreements and not to lower their own environmental standards.[13]

Business endorsed the agreement. Though it did not accord with the preferences of their members, organizations like the Business Roundtable and the Chamber of Commerce recognized the value of removing what had been, on its face, the primary impediment to bipartisan cooperation on trade over the past decade.

Schwab hoped that the May 10 deal would pave the way for approval of all four FTAs. But Ways and Means Democrats had additional problems with Colombia (on the security of labor leaders) and Korea (on the provisions for autos). Korea was also proving difficult on beef imports—a top priority for Montana Senator Max Baucus, who chaired the Senate Committee on Finance. And Panama developed problems with the United States on other issues. So only the Peru agreement won approval during the Bush years. Moreover, the Schwab-Rangel deal did not generate any momentum for extension of Trade Promotion Authority, which expired at the end of June 2007. Schwab could have used this to strengthen her hand in the Doha negotiations, which would fail to reach a conclusion during her tenure.

Meanwhile, a 2008 episode underscored the shakiness of bipartisan cooperation on trade and the fast-track procedures. President Bush was deeply committed to the Colombia FTA, wishing to reward a stalwart regional ally that was winning its fight against internal insurrection and drug violence. For months, his trade and economic officials sought to strike a deal with Pelosi allowing that FTA to be voted on and approved. Pelosi temporized, not willing to challenge organized labor, which vehemently opposed the pact. With time running out, Bush did what the procedures empowered him to do—he sent to legislation implementing the Colombia FTA to Congress for the requisite up-or-down vote.

Never had a president done this without the cooperation of the House leadership, and Pelosi responded by exploiting fast-track's Achilles heel, its foundation on the rules of each chamber. These were subject to change by majority vote, and Pelosi took the unusual step of having the House vote to remove the time limit as it applied to Colombia. This exposed a fact well known to trade cognoscenti but not to many others—that the seemingly iron-clad promise of expeditious congressional action was not so ironclad after all.

In his campaign, candidate Barack Obama expressed reservations about the Colombia and Korea FTAs as negotiated. In his first fifteen months, President Obama gave priority to domestic legislation—a record economic stimulus bill to counter the Great Recession, and comprehensive health care legislation. It was not until 2010 that he began to move. His January State of the Union address called for improving trade relations with Colombia, Korea, and Panama—though it fell short of mentioning the FTAs themselves. Obama and Korean President Lee Myung-bak met in June and committed themselves to renegotiate sensitive issues, especially the auto provisions. In December, they announced agreement: specifically, changes in how Korea would liberalize car imports and delays in the reduction of tariffs for that nation's vehicles entering the U.S. market. In the spring of 2011, a deal was reached with Colombia on an enhanced program to combat violence against labor leaders. Outstanding issues with Panama were resolved as well.

Since fast-track rules do not limit the time period between completion of an agreement and its submission for legislative action, the Korea and Panama FTAs could be sent to Congress under them—even though the deadline for concluding new agreements under fast-track was June 30, 2007. Colombia had to be considered under normal rules, because of its prior submission in 2008. But with Republicans overwhelmingly support-ive, the way seemed clear for enactment. Yet action was delayed for months over a related issue—the extension of the Trade Adjustment Assistance (TAA) program for workers displaced by imports. Important provisions of this law had expired at the end of 2010, and the White House and con-gressional Democrats wanted them to be extended. Their major leverage with the House, now returned to Republican control, was to hold back on submitting the FTAs until agreement was reached on substance and timing.

Resolution was delayed by lack of trust across partisan lines, but in the end an understanding was struck. After years of delay, the House and Senate conducted a total of seven trade votes on the same day—October 12. The lower chamber approved the three FTAs and the TAA legislation. The Senate, which had already voted the latter, approved the three agreements as well. None of the votes were close.

SECOND-TERM OBAMA: THE TRANS-PACIFIC PARTNERSHIP

As Americans approached the 2012 election, Congress and the Obama administration had finished most of the work the Bush administration began. The large exception was the Doha Round, which marked the end of its tenth year with little prospect of a fruitful conclusion. In the spring of 2011, Schwab put in writing what many had been thinking, labeling the negotiation as "doomed" and urging nations to move beyond it.[14]

By this time, however, the Obama administration was moving ahead on another major initiative—the Trans-Pacific Partnership (TPP) negotiation. Originated in Bush's last year, these talks came to involve twelve nations (Australia, Brunei, Canada, Chile, Japan, Malaysia, Mexico, New Zealand, Peru, Singapore, the United States, and Vietnam). If successful, this promised to be a FTA more comprehensive than any in U.S. history. And the Obama administration also entered, beginning in 2013, into talks with the European Union for a Trans-Atlantic Trade and Investment Partnership (TTIP).

Negotiations on both dragged on. After a seemingly promising launch, the TTIP talks with Europe became hung up on resistance within a number of EU countries, sufficient to push any completion of that accord into a post-Obama administration. TPP fared somewhat better. Originally there was a goal of completing the deal by 2012, then 2013, but the twelve economies were quite different from one another. And the substance was far-reaching and complicated, going way beyond the removal of tariffs which was the basic feature of traditional FTAs. As finally signed by the twelve nations in February 2016, TPP included no fewer than thirty titles, only a minority of which centered on merchandise trade *per se*. Other issues included financial services, telecommunications and electronic commerce, investment, intellectual property, state-owned enterprises, labor and the environment, regulatory coherence, and transparency and anti-corruption.

After years of delay, the Obama administration had proposed—and won—Fast-Track/Trade Promotion Authority for TPP in June 2015. The vote reflected what had become the standard pattern—Republicans substantially in support and Democrats overwhelmingly opposed. The House of Representatives approved Trade Promotion Authority by a ten-vote margin, with just twenty-eight members of the president's party voting in favor. The Senate followed by a more comfortable final vote of 60–38, with thirteen Democrats in favor.

This assured that if and when the president sent a completed TPP to Congress, it would benefit from favorable legislative procedures—limited debate, no amendments. It did not, however, assure legislative approval. Obama faced the same situation with a Republican-controlled House and Senate that Bush had encountered eight years before with Democrats in charge. Bush had forced the matter to get action, only to have Pelosi engineer a change in fast-track rules for the Colombia agreement that he had so wanted, leading to inaction. Obama therefore needed to have the substantive and procedural acquiescence of Republican Senate and House leaders.

He never received it. House and Senate leaders insisted on deferring action until after the November election. And through most of 2016, TPP was being subject to withering political assault. For years, the labor-activist coalition that had fought NAFTA had been mobilizing against what it called "NAFTA on steroids." The Democratic challenger, Vermont Senator Bernie Sanders, was a longtime opponent of FTAs, and he enthusiastically took up the anti-TPP cause. Hillary Clinton felt compelled to play defense, and retreated from the pact she had once labeled (potentially at least) the "gold standard" for international trade agreements. And then came the unexpected rise of Donald Trump, whose sweeping protectionist campaign was beyond anything in American memory since the 1930s if not before. His surprise November victory rendered the issue moot.

Obama had sought TPP not just for the relatively modest economic gains it provided the United States, but also as a centerpiece of his effort to renew U.S. leadership in the Asia-Pacific in response to China's rise. Trump, however, saw it very differently, and three days after his inauguration he signed an order withdrawing the United States from the never ratified pact. As he took this action, he declared it "a great thing for the American worker." And tough early words with Mexico foreshadowed at minimum a difficult NAFTA renegotiation, and at maximum a withdrawal from that agreement as well.

2017FF: A NEW AND UNCERTAIN ERA

Trump has labeled such trade pacts "dumb," with the United States the loser, and prominent among his "America First" policies has been a promise to abandon or renegotiate them to U.S. advantage. The rhetoric of his inaugural address was sweeping and extraordinary. He spoke of "rusted-out factories scattered like tombstones across the landscape of our nation" and of decades of policies that "enriched foreign industry at the expense of American industry." "The wealth of our middle class," he added, "has been ripped from their homes and then redistributed across the entire world."[15]

But "from this day forward," he declared, "a new vision will govern our land." "We must protect our borders from the ravages of other countries making our products, stealing our companies, and destroying our jobs." By contrast, "Protection will lead to great prosperity and strength," he assured his national audience. "We will bring back our jobs. We will bring back our borders. We will bring back our wealth. And we will bring back our dreams."

Taken literally, these words meant a reversal of decades of globalization. They meant breaking up global supply chains on which twenty-first-century U.S. firms and workers depended. How far the Trump administration could move in this direction, how much it would succeed, was anything but clear. A majority of congressional Republicans had long supported open trade policies, including the leaders of both chambers. The United States was bound by multiple trade agreements to keep tariffs low. And, as noted at the outset of this essay, as of late 2016 a majority of Americans still backed trade-expanding agreements and saw globalization as, overall, "a good thing for the United States."

Trump's appeal was strong, though, among those who felt that America was leaving them behind. The message was particularly effective in the "rust belt" states of Ohio, Michigan, Pennsylvania, and Wisconsin. The last three of them had brought Trump the surprise victories that tilted the Electoral College in his favor.

It was, in this analyst's view, a gross exaggeration for Trump to say that trade policies had been pursued with "not even a thought about the millions upon millions of American workers left behind." Calls in fact were prevalent, in the early twenty-first century, for "a new social compact" to ameliorate the concerns and needs of those who were globalization's losers.[16] But while trade had, contrary to Trumpian rhetoric, made the nation richer, overall, by a trillion dollars each year according to one serious analysis,[17] precious little of this increased wealth had gone to those bearing the burden of adjustment. So on this point, America's new president was not entirely off the mark.

Now, early in his administration, the gains from trade are very much at risk. America may be entering, as President Trump proposes, a period of much more restrictive trade policies, with all the disruption of the U.S. economy and of global economic institutions that this would entail. But perhaps reality will constrain Trump administration trade actions, making his commercial bark much louder than its bite. If it does, trade advocates should heed the warning. They should hasten to move with laws to make a "new social compact" a reality. This would mean serious measures aiming to strengthen both American workers and American producers in adapting to globalization. One element would be enactment of truly robust social policies that would offer broad support and recourse for workers that the forces of globalization have driven from their jobs. This would need to be accompanied by a comprehensive set of home-based "policies . . . to make the United States a more attractive location for the production of world-competitive goods and services."[18]

In the polarized political climate of 2016, enactment of such measures was impossible to achieve. In 2017 and thereafter, they might conceivably be attainable.

DISCUSSION QUESTIONS

1. Which branch of government has been dominant in trade policy over the history of the country, and what was the dominant issue that shaped such policy?
2. What precipitated the shift in trade policymaking in the 1930s? What was the significance of the Reciprocal Trade Agreements Act of 1934?
3. How did the President's Special Representative for Trade Negotiations develop, and how did that representative evolve into the present-day USTR?
4. What role does the USTR play in trade policymaking today? Is the USTR an executive office or a congressional office? Explain.
5. What are the functions of the Department of Commerce, USITC, and the Department of Agriculture in trade policymaking?
6. What is meant by the fast-track procedure, or trade promotion authority? How does this procedure work in practice?
7. What are two important changes in trade policy since World War II that have altered the groups that support and challenge the freeing up of international trade by the United States?
8. What factors does Destler point to in explaining the new divisions on trade policy in the U.S. Congress?
9. What was the May 10 agreement and how did it seek to address the congressional stalemate over free-trade agreements negotiated by recent presidents?
10. What have been the changes of U.S. trade policy and institutions under the presidency of Donald Trump?

NOTES

1. "America in the Age of Uncertainty," Chicago Council on Global Affairs, October 2016.

2. Richard E. Neustadt, *Presidential Power: The Politics of Leadership* (New York: Wiley, 1960).

3. James L. Sundquist, *The Decline and Resurgence of Congress* (Washington, DC: Brookings Institution, 1981), 99.

4. E. E. Schattschneider, *Politics, Pressures, and the Tariff* (New York: Prentice-Hall, 1935).

5. For more on these specific episodes, see I. M. Destler, *Making Foreign Economic Policy* (Washington, DC: Brookings Institution, 1980); and I. M. Destler, *American Trade Politics*, 4th ed. (Washington, DC: Institute for International Economics, 2005).

6. For more detail on fast track and how the process functioned through 1996, see I. M. Destler, "Renewing Fast-Track Legislation," Policy Analysis No. 50, Institute for International Economics (September 1997). The procedures were renamed Trade Promotion Authority (TPA) by the George W. Bush administration in 2001.

7. Remarks of Secretary of the Treasury James A. Baker III at the Institute for International Economics, Washington, DC, September 14, 1987.

8. This chart (in Destler, *American Trade Politics*, 283) is reprinted with permission from Sarah A. Binder, *Stalemate: Causes and Consequences of Legislative Gridlock* (Washington, DC: Brookings Institution, 2003), 24–25. Binder's liberal-conservative scores draw upon Nolan M. McCarty et al., *Income Redistribution and the Realignment of American Politics* (Washington, DC: American Enterprise Institute, 1997).

9. Destler, *American Trade Politics*, chap. 11.

10. *Americans on CAFTA and U.S. Trade Policy*, a PIPA/Knowledge Networks study, July 11, 2005. More recent surveys have shown Democrats becoming more positive about trade, and Republicans more skeptical. See, for example, Chicago Council, "America in the Age of Uncertainty."

11. On the Uruguay Round agreements approved in 1994, Republicans split 121–56. On the China/WTO vote, the division was 164–57.

12. I address this matter in detail in "Trade Promotion Authority in 2001: The Bargain That Wasn't," appendix A to Destler, *American Trade Politics*, 331–42.

13. For details, see I. M. Destler, *American Trade Politics in 2007: Building Bipartisan Compromise*, Peterson Institute Policy Brief No. 07-5, May 2007.

14. Susan C. Schwab, "After Doha: Why the Negotiations Are Doomed and What We Should Do about It," *Foreign Affairs* (May/June 2011): 104–17.

15. These and subsequent Trump quotes are from his inaugural address, January 20, 2017.

16. Calls for a "new social compact" were prevalent in the middle of the past decade. For a summary, see Destler, *American Trade Politics*, chapter 2. For a proposal to the Obama administration, see "A New Trade Policy for the United States: A Report to the President-Elect and the 111th Congress from the Trade Policy Study Group," Peterson Institute for International Economics (December 2008). The 2009 stimulus bill included a substantial broadening of trade adjustment assistance, but the sweeping Republican victory in 2010 took the momentum from this achievement and forced its proponents to play defense.

17. See Scott C. Bradford, Paul L. E. Grieco, and Gary Clyde Hufbauer, "The Payoff to America from Global Integration," in C. Fred Bergsten et al., *The United States and the World Economy* (IIE, Washington, DC, January 2005), 65–109.

18. "U.S. Trade and Investment Policy," Independent Task Force Report No. 67, Council on Foreign Relations (September 2011).

III

DECISIONMAKERS AND THEIR POLICYMAKING POSITIONS

Foreign policy choices are often made by a remarkably small number of individuals, the most conspicuous of whom is the president. As Harry S. Truman exclaimed, "I make American foreign policy."

Because of the president's power and preeminence, it is tempting to think of foreign policy as determined exclusively by presidential preferences and to personalize government by identifying a policy with its proponents. "There is properly no history, only biography" is how Ralph Waldo Emerson dramatized the view that individual leaders are the makers and movers of history. This "hero-in-history" model finds expression in the practice of attaching the names of presidents to the policies they promulgate (e.g., the Truman Doctrine, the Kennedy Round, the Bush Doctrine, the Obama Doctrine), as if the men were synonymous with the nation itself and of routinely attributing foreign policy successes and failures to the administrations in which they occur.

The conviction that the individual who holds office makes a difference is one of the major premises underlying the electoral process. Thus, each new administration seeks to distinguish itself from its predecessor and to highlight policy departures as it seeks to convey the impression that it has engineered a new (and better) order. The media's tendency to label presidential actions "new" abets those efforts. Hence, leadership and policy are portrayed as synonymous, and changes in policy and policy direction are often perceived as the results of the predispositions of leaders themselves.

Clearly, leaders' individual attributes exert a potentially powerful influence on American foreign policy, and no account of policy sources would be complete without a discussion of them. Still, many scholars question the accuracy of this popular model. They argue that the hero-in-history, or idiosyncratic, model is misleading and simplistic, that it ascribes too much influence to the individuals responsible for the conduct of American foreign policy and implicitly assumes that this influence is the same for all leaders in all circumstances.

That individuals make a difference is unassailable, but it is more useful to ask (1) under what circumstances the idiosyncratic qualities of leaders exert their greatest impact, (2) what types of institutional structures and management strategies different leaders are likely to follow, and (3) what policy variations are most likely to result from different types of leaders. These questions force us to examine how individual characteristics find expression in foreign policy outcomes and how the policymaking roles that leaders occupy may circumscribe their individual influence.

When we consider the mediating impact of policymakers' roles, we draw attention to the fact that many different people, widely dispersed throughout the government, contribute to the making of American foreign policy. In part II, we examined some of the departments and agencies of government involved in the process. Here, in part III, the concern is with decisionmakers and how the roles created by the government's foreign policy–related organizational structures influence the behavior of the policymakers occupying these roles and, ultimately, American foreign policy itself, even as we acknowledge the powerful influence of individual characteristics. As a rival hypothesis to the hero-in-history image of political leadership, however, "role theory" posits that the positions and the processes rather than the characteristics of the people who decide influence the behavior and choices of those responsible for making and executing the nation's foreign policy. Furthermore, in this view, changes in policy presumably result from changes in role conceptions rather than from changes in the individuals who occupy these roles.

Role theory also leads us to other perspectives on how policymakers make foreign policy choices. Considerable evidence, drawn from foreign policy case studies, points toward the pressures for conformity among those responsible for choosing among competing foreign policy alternatives, pressures that may lead to less than optimal choices. Furthermore, the principal actors in the foreign affairs government often compete with one another as they consider competing policy alternatives, with their respective bargaining positions dictated by organizational preferences rather than national interests. In particular, the "bureaucratic politics" model of decision-making stresses the importance of the roles individuals occupy in large-scale organizations and the struggles that occur among their constituent units. Proponents of the model claim it captures the essence of the highly politicized foreign policy decision-making process more accurately than does the model of rational behavior, which assumes that the government operates as a single, unitary actor. That popular decision-making model maintains that policymakers—notably the president and his principal advisers—devise strategies and implement plans to realize goals "rationally"—that is, in terms of calculations about national interests based on the relative costs and benefits associated with alternative goals and means.

Graham Allison's book *Essence of Decision*, a study of the 1962 Cuban Missile Crisis, is the best-known effort to articulate and apply the bureaucratic politics model as an alternative to the rational actor model. Allison developed two alternative strands of the bureaucratic politics model. One, which he calls the *organizational process* paradigm, reflects the constraints that organizational procedures and routines place on decisionmakers' choices. The other, which he calls *governmental politics*, draws attention to the "pulling and hauling" that occurs among the key bureaucratic participants in the decision process.[1]

How, from the perspective of organizational processes, do large-scale bureaucracies affect policymaking? One way is by devising standard operating procedures for coping with policy problems when they arise. For example, when the George W. Bush administration began talking about options for dealing with weapons of mass destruction in mid-2002, the absence of large forces-in-being in situ constrained its choice of military options. Over the next several months, the administration began deploying large military forces to the Middle East as a prelude to a war with Iraq. Ground forces were moved into Kuwait and surrounding countries; naval forces were dispatched to the Persian Gulf, the Indian Ocean, and the Mediterranean Sea; and reserve forces at home were mobilized to replace and supplement those sent abroad. The deployments' purpose was to maximize the military options available to the administration even as it pursued diplomatic strategies. Still, it is reasonable to assume that the deployments themselves and planning for various military options followed previously rehearsed routines, much as they had more than a decade earlier as a prelude to the Persian Gulf War. The organizational routines of the various units deployed arguably shaped what was possible and what was not (could missiles placed near Islamic mosques be destroyed from the air without also destroying the mosques?), thus constraining the menu of choice available not only to military leaders but also to the president and his civilian advisers.

The Obama administration faced similar kinds of organizational constraints when it was considering the "surge strategy" over Afghanistan in late 2009. The logistics of transferring American military forces to that country rapidly and efficiently were undoubtedly a part of the calculation that went into the decision-making process. Further, when the Obama administration was considering the implementation of a "no-fly zone" over Libya in response to the actions of Muammar Qaddafi's government against its people, the availability of American military personnel for such an operation, with two ongoing wars elsewhere, was undoubtedly one consideration (among others) in the decision-making. Moreover, the Obama administration opted to provide support for that operation, although leaving most of the enforcement of this "no-fly zone" to other NATO nations. In short, organizational processes shape and constrain foreign policy options.

The Trump administration is unlikely to escape such constraints either. Even as President Trump directed the Department of Defense to devise a more aggressive plan for attacking the Islamic State in Iraq and Syria (ISIS), the implementation of such a new strategy will inevitably confront the organizational routines of the military and special operations. Further, when President Trump issued an executive order to halt the admission of persons from seven countries because of past history of terrorist activity, his order was met not only with some confusion over its implementation but also with resistance from judicial decisions over the legality of the actions and criticisms for foreign policy officials.

Governmental politics, the second strand in the bureaucratic politics model as articulated by Allison, draws attention to the way individuals act in organizational settings. Not surprisingly, and as role theory predicts, the many participants in the deliberations that lead to foreign policy choices often define issues and favor policy alternatives that reflect their organizational affiliations. "Where you stand depends on where you sit" is a favorite aphorism reflecting these bureaucratic (role) imperatives. Furthermore, because the players in the game of governmental politics are responsible for protecting the nation's security, they are "obliged to fight for what they are convinced is right." The consequence is that "different groups pulling in different directions produce a result, or better a resultant—a mixture of conflicting preferences and unequal power of various individuals—distinct from what any person or group intended."[2]

Sometimes, however, these bureaucratic differences can lead to policy conflict and stalemates, as witnessed by the Bush administration during the summer of 2002 when options about possible actions toward Iraq were considered. While some within the administration favored quick action to remove Saddam Hussein because of his development and use of weapons of mass destruction, others, including Secretary of State Colin Powell and his deputy, Richard Armitage, contended that that approach had "risks and complexities" that needed more review.[3] Opinion was also reportedly divided within the Department of Defense, with civilian officials favoring military action more than military officers. Furthermore, members of Congress and officials from the earlier George H. W. Bush administration also argued against rapid escalation to military action. Policy development was thus stalled for a time, and the administration pursued resolutions in the UN Security Council and Congress to garner more support for more vigorous action against Saddam Hussein.

The Obama administration experienced the same kind of internal policy dispute over the direction of American policy in Afghanistan in 2009. In the spring of 2009, the American commander in Afghanistan, General Stanley McChrystal, was ordered to conduct a policy review and make a recommendation to the president by the end of the summer. His recommendation called for the addition of American troops and the pursuance of a counterinsurgency strategy, an approach much like the one pursued by the Bush administration in Iraq in 2007. These recommendations set off an extended bureaucratic debate within the national security team. Vice President Biden, for example, opposed the commitment of more troops and favored a counterterrorism, not a counterinsurgency, strategy in Afghanistan, and the president's special representative to Afghanistan and Pakistan, Richard Holbrooke, largely opposed the sending of more American troops. The uniformed military, including General David Petraeus, and Secretary of Defense Robert Gates backed the recommendations in the McChrystal report; Secretary of State Hillary Clinton came to support that position as well. Nonetheless, the bureaucratic debate went on for several months before a presidential decision was announced on December 1, 2009, at West Point.[4]

Although the Trump administration is early in its tenure, there are already signs of bureaucratic divisions over the direction of policy toward Russia. Although President Trump initially indicated that he is receptive to improving relations with Russia (and possibly reducing sanctions against that nation over its Ukraine/Crimea and cyberattacks), some of his principal foreign policy and national security advisers are divided over such a direction. His secretary of defense, James Mattis, is particularly wary of any such accommodation with Russia and expressed so during his confirmation hearing. Earlier, the current chairman of the Joint Chiefs of Staff, General Joseph Dunford, said that he saw Russia as America's principal adversary. President Trump's first national security advisor, General Michael Flynn, however, appears more willing to work with Russia, since he viewed actions against ISIS as crucial and Russia had indicated its opposition to this nonstate actor. Secretary of State Rex Tillerson, while cautious about Russia, has had long-standing involvement with Russia in his role of CEO of EXXON MOBIL and appears unwilling to condemn Russia fully over some of its actions.

More generally, another analyst points to broad divisions about the direction of policy based upon the differing views and supporters of the Trump administration.[5] In this view, some, including President Trump himself, adopt an "America First" approach to policy that will limit and hinder many foreign policy actions. Another set of administration adherents are what are labeled "religious warriors." Their fundamental focus is on Islamic terrorism and particularly ISIS. As such, foreign policy decisions and actions will be largely assessed through that lens. Finally, a third group of support-ers is the "traditionalists," or the Republican foreign policy establishment, who want to foster a foreign policy that maintains a domestic foreign policy consensus and the traditional global role of the United States in leading the international community. How these groups clash (or cooperate) will largely account for future American foreign policy.

The examples are consistent with the logic of the bureaucratic politics model, suggesting that sometimes the explanation for why states make the choices they do lies not in their behavior in terms of one another but because they are constrained by the disputes within their own governments. Furthermore, rather than presupposing the existence of a unitary actor, as the rational model does, the bureaucratic politics model suggests that "it is necessary to identify the games and players, to display the coalitions, bar-gains, and compromises, and to convey some feel for the confusion" in the policymaking process.[6]

In virtually every situation in which the United States has contemplated the use of force in recent years—in the Persian Gulf, Afghanistan, Somalia, Bosnia, Rwanda, Haiti, Kosovo, Iraq, and Syria—policymakers and critics alike have worried about the specter of Vietnam and the "lessons" it taught. In part, this is because the protracted series of decisions that took the United States into Vietnam—and eventually out of it, on unsatisfactory terms after years of fighting and the loss of tens of thousands of lives—is fertile ground for probing how American foreign policy is made and implemented.

Part III of this book begins with an account, informed by role theory and bureaucratic politics, of how the United States became involved in and conducted the prolonged war in Southeast Asia. "How Could Vietnam Happen?" asks James C. Thomson Jr., almost rhetorically. The failure in Vietnam, Thomson contends, was the failure of America's policymak-ing process, not of its leadership. Vietnam shows that some of the most catastrophic of America's foreign policy initiatives have been the result not of evil or stupid people but of misdirected behaviors encouraged by the nature of the policymaking system and the roles and bureaucratic processes embedded in the way the government's foreign policy system is organized. Thomson's argument, however disturbing, provides insight into the milieu of decision-making and identifies many syndromes crucial to understand-ing how the roles created by the decision-making setting influence the kinds of decisions that leaders make and that bureaucracies are asked to implement.

With the Vietnam experience as a backdrop, the next series of policymaking cases examines the impact of role theory, bureaucratic politics, and indi-viduals in accounting for the actions taken more recently. For the individual analyses, the cases point to the impact of the position held by policymakers and to the personal characteristics that they bring to the policy process as explanations. The illustrative cases span several recent administrations—the George H. W. Bush administration's actions over Somalia and Bosnia in the early 1990s, the decision to expand the North Atlantic Treaty Organization (NATO) by the Clinton administration in the mid-1990s, the decision by George W. Bush to initiate the Iraq War in 2003, and the decision-making style of Barack Obama in several decisions, largely during his second term in office. While all the cases highlight the impact (and limitations) of the bureaucratic setting, several of them also highlight the need to consider other factors, including individual mindsets and beliefs, the availability of information, and idiosyncratic characteristics of individual policymakers, in explaining these foreign policy decisions.

Indeed, the mindsets, the perceptions of reality, and the information that policymakers possess also affect the nature of the policy choices they pursue, and these factors are evident in the first case study in part III. In "Sources of Humanitarian Intervention: Beliefs, Information, and Advocacy in U.S. Decisions on Somalia and Bosnia," Jon Western argues that the initial decisions of the administration of George H. W. Bush in these cases were primarily functions of the belief systems among key policymakers and of their ability to use information and advocacy to shape those policy decisions. Yet Western's case study also demonstrates how information and advocacy can change the direction of American policy, as the Bush administration did in late 1992 toward Somalia.

Prior to its 1992 policy shift, Western argues, the Bush administration's policies toward Bosnia and Somalia were a function of the pervasive perception among key officials (the president, his key aides, and especially the Joint Chiefs of Staff) that the events in those two countries did not affect U.S. national interests and American interventions "could only lead to a Vietnam-style quagmire." This perception of the "selective engagers" stood in contrast to the views of the "liberal humanitarians," who sought to intervene to prevent the human tragedies, massive killings, and wholesale starvation then occurring in Bosnia and Somalia. In addition, the perceptions of the key policymakers dominated the policy process because the administration controlled much of the information and more of the policy advocacy machinery. As Western notes, "The U.S. media . . . had little expertise in the Balkans," and "there was no galvanizing force that either linked disparate humanitarian organizations or mobilized the press corps." In short, the selective engagers had a clear edge over the liberal humanitarians in the policy process.

By the summer of 1992, however, perceptions began to change as both the media and liberal humanitarians "gradually developed and dedicated more resources for their own information-collection efforts to challenge the administration's framing of the two conflicts." Most notable were a report by the U.S. ambassador to Kenya about his visit to a refugee camp on the Somali–Kenyan border and a fact-finding visit by two U.S. senators to Somalia. At about the same time, reports surfaced about radical Serb nationalist and paramilitary forces "committing horrific atrocities" and about Serb-run concentration camps in Bosnia. These and other revelations began to challenge seriously the thinking of the selective engagers within the Bush administration, as did the challenge from presidential candidate Bill Clinton, who argued for more robust American actions in Bosnia.

Later that year, the Bush administration began to modify its position. Although President Bush "ordered his team to contest the liberal humanitarian view that U.S. intervention could quickly break the siege of Sarajevo with little cost to American lives," he ordered the Air Force to provide assistance in transporting relief to Somalia and agreed to American funding for Pakistani peacekeepers in that county. Western argues that this shift occurred because of increased political pressure on the administration regarding its policies in Somalia and Bosnia.

The change in policy direction continued even as selective engagers and liberal humanitarians continued their propaganda campaigns. After his victory in early November, Clinton visited Washington for various briefings, contributing to what Western calls the "cumulative pressure" on the selective engagers to change course. Within days, the Joint Chiefs of Staff reversed their opposition to intervention in Somalia. President Bush followed suit a few days later. Western attributes the policy reversal to the "mobilized political opposition" and its ability "to challenge the administration's framing of the crisis."

James Goldgeier, in his "NATO Expansion: The Anatomy of a Decision," supports the argument about the crucial importance of individuals in molding policy and illustrates the limitation on bureaucracies in shaping it. On the basis of extensive interviews with officials knowledgeable or involved in the initial NATO expansion decision during the Clinton administration, Goldgeier demonstrates that bureaucracies—and the individuals in those bureaucracies—can shape debate over an issue and can "pull" and "haul" to promote different positions, but they cannot determine policy. Instead, the issue of whether NATO membership would formally expand or whether the Partnership for Peace option would continue ultimately depended on President Clinton. Not until Clinton made a series of speeches in Brussels, Prague, and Warsaw did bureaucratic differences start to be settled. As Clinton stated, "The question is no longer whether NATO will take on new members but when and how."

The NATO case illustrates the importance of individuals in other ways. For example, Anthony Lake, the national security adviser at the time, and other foreign policy principals were able to move Clinton to make statements that seemingly committed the United States to NATO expansion. They in turn used his remarks as the basis for establishing a working group that set forth an "action plan," thus demonstrating the influence that individuals are sometimes able to exercise in the face of bureaucratic resistance. Particularly interesting is how Richard Holbrooke, assistant secretary of state for European affairs, became the "enforcer" of the NATO expansion decision within the interagency process. Invoking the president's wishes with the argument "either you are on the president's program or you are not," he was able to crystallize the president's key role in the policy choice.

In "President Bush and the Invasion of Iraq," James Pfiffner provides even a more explicit and detailed assessment of the role of an individual in directing American foreign policy: he points to the impact of President Bush on the decision to go to war against Iraq in 2003. Specifically, he argues that the personality and beliefs of President Bush were crucial to this decision as well as his ability to utilize the bureaucratic structures to support his policy direction.

President Bush, Pfiffner contends, rejected "an orderly policy process" in making this decision, displayed personal certainty over the direction of policy, and did not consult "with his top military and civilian officials" prior to making policy decisions. Pfiffner also seeks to show how the president utilized intelligence findings to make the case for the war by linking Saddam Hussein and Al Qaeda, how he overruled his generals, and how he made decisions without consulting his key aides. Moreover, the case carries the analysis through the entire war effort by the Bush administration, including the rise of the insurgency and the adoption of the "surge strategy," and illustrates the important role of the president. Further, the case concludes by discussing the Status of Forces Agreement (SOFA) for the eventual removal of American troops, signed by President Bush, and its possible connection to the role of the ISIS. In all, Pfiffner's case study makes the fundamental argument that individual beliefs and characteristics of policymakers are crucial to foreign policy decisions and actions, but he also contends that, in his judgment, such an approach led to an ill-conceived foreign policy decision.

In "Obama's Decision-Making Style," Fred Kaplan also identifies the role of individual personality characteristics and beliefs in understanding the foreign policy actions of President Barack Obama, much as James Pfiffner did in explaining President George W. Bush's actions in the Iraq War. Kaplan then assesses how these beliefs shaped the foreign policy decisions of President Obama in several recent cases—over American policy toward Libya, Syria, ISIS, and Ukraine. In general, President Obama's beliefs serve as a useful guide to accounting for American policy.

Kaplan begins his analysis with an example of President Obama meeting with military officials early in his presidency and expressing knowledge and flexibility in his foreign policy beliefs and action, but he points out that such a description turned out not to be the way he governed or conveyed his decision-making style, as a number of critics observed. Instead,

Kaplan points to the usual critique of Obama's approach as one in which "he evades hard decisions," "is allergic to military force if it risks American casualties or escalation," and displays "a mismatch between his words and his deeds." Kaplan then proceeds to examine several episodes to weigh the validity of this characterization of Obama's beliefs and decision style.

In the case of the uprising in Libya as part of the "Arab Spring" against long-time dictator Muammar al-Qaddafi, President Obama seemed to follow this decision style in shaping American policy. Although the president was concerned about events unfolding in that country, he stipulated that there would be "no U.S. boots on the ground, no military action at all unless it had a legal basis, and a decent chance of succeeding," and only with "an appropriate division of labor with allies." As a result, the United States provided some initial air strikes and logistical support; the NATO allies were largely responsible for taking action because those countries had more direct interests in Libya than the United States.

The same caution—and even more so—was exercised in attempting to deal with the uprising in Syria against President Bashar al-Assad. Although the president had expressed "uncharacteristic exuberance" in calling for action to stop the killing and his advisors had recommended a more assertive American response, the president ultimately opted for a much more restrained policy in light of the complexity of the situation and the possible responses of other outside forces. This disjuncture between words and deeds was most evident in the Syrian case with the president's announcement of the "red line" over the Syrian government's use of chemical weapons and an American response. Ultimately, the president decided not to take direct action against Syria, as Kaplan catalogues in detail.

In addressing the rise of the jihadist threat of ISIS and dealing with the Russian intervention in Ukraine, President Obama displayed the same kind of caution and selective action in responding to these cases. The responses tended to be "piecemeal" to these crises with the ultimate aim of not getting the United States involved more deeply and to limit American risks. While actions were taken in both instances, the lack of an overall strategy remained an issue. Still, President Obama defended his decision-making and his foreign policy belief in an important commentary that Kaplan captures at the end of his chapter.

Editor's Note: At the end of each chapter entry is a series of discussion questions for use by the students and instructor.

NOTES

1. See Graham T. Allison, *Essence of Decision: Explaining the Cuban Missile Crisis* (Boston: Little, Brown and Company, 1971), and Graham T. Allison and

Philip Zelikow, *Essence of Decision: Explaining the Cuban Missile Crisis*, 2nd ed. (New York: Longman, 1999).

2. Allison, *Essence of Decision*, 145.

3. Todd S. Purdom and Patrick E. Tyler, "Top Republicans Break with Bush on Iraq Strategy," *New York Times*, August 16, 2002.

4. For an extended discussion of the internal debate over Afghanistan policy during the first year of the Obama administration, see Bob Woodward, *Obama's Wars* (New York: Simon & Schuster, 2010). Also see James M. McCormick, "The Obama Presidency: A Foreign Policy of Change?" in Steven E. Schier, ed., *Transforming America: Barack Obama in the White House* (Lanham, MD: Rowman & Littlefield, 2011), 235–66.

5. Thomas Wright, "Trump's Team of Rivals, Riven by Distrust," Brookings, December 15, 2016 at https://www.brookings.edu/blog/order-from-chaos/2016/12/15/trumps-team-of-rivals-riven-by-distrust/, accessed January 5, 2017.

6. Allison, *Essence of Decision*, 146.

17

How Could Vietnam Happen?

An Autopsy

James C. Thomson Jr.

As a case study in the making of foreign policy, the Vietnam War will fascinate historians and social scientists for many decades to come. One question that will certainly be asked: How did men of superior ability, sound training, and high ideals—American policymakers of the 1960s—create such a costly and divisive policy?

As one who watched the decision-making process in Washington from 1961 to 1966 under Presidents Kennedy and Johnson, I can suggest a preliminary answer. I can do so by briefly listing some of the factors that seemed to me to shape our Vietnam policy during my years as an East Asia specialist at the State Department and the White House. I shall deal largely with Washington as I saw or sensed it, and not with Saigon, where I spent but a scant three days, in the entourage of the vice president, or with other decision centers, the capitals of interested parties. Nor will I deal with other important parts of the record: Vietnam's history prior to 1961, for instance, or the overall course of America's relations with Vietnam.

Yet a first and central ingredient in these years of Vietnam decisions does involve history. The ingredient was *the legacy of the 1950s*—by which I mean the so-called loss of China, the Korean War, and the Far East policy of Secretary of State Dulles. This legacy had an institutional by-product for the Kennedy administration: In 1961 the U.S. government's East Asian establishment was undoubtedly the most rigid and doctrinaire of Washington's regional divisions in foreign affairs. This was especially true at the Department of State, where the incoming administration found the Bureau of Far Eastern Affairs the hardest nut to crack. It was a bureau that had been purged of its best China expertise, and of farsighted, dispassionate men, as a result of McCarthyism. Its members were generally committed to one policy line: the close containment and isolation of mainland China, the harassment of "neutralist" nations that sought to avoid alignment with either Washington or Peking, and the maintenance of a network of alliances with anticommunist client states on China's periphery.

Another aspect of the legacy was the special vulnerability and sensitivity of the new Democratic administration on Far East policy issues. The memory of the McCarthy era was still very sharp, and Kennedy's margin of victory was too thin. The 1960 Offshore Islands TV debate between Kennedy and Nixon had shown the president-elect the perils of "fresh thinking." The administration was inherently leery of moving too fast on Asia. As a result, the Far East Bureau (now the Bureau of East Asian and Pacific Affairs—Ed.) was the last one to be overhauled. Not until Averell Harriman was brought in as assistant secretary in December 1961 were significant personnel changes attempted, and it took Harriman several months to make a deep imprint on the bureau because of his necessary preoccupation with the Laos settlement. Once he did so, there was virtually no effort to bring back the purged or exiled East Asia experts.

There were other important by-products of this "legacy of the 1950s."

The new administration inherited and somewhat shared a *general perception of China-on-the-march*—a sense of China's vastness, its numbers, its belligerence; a revived sense, perhaps, of the Golden Horde. This was a perception fed by Chinese intervention in the Korean War (an intervention actually based on appallingly bad communications and mutual miscalculation on the part of Washington and Peking, but the careful unraveling of the tragedy, which scholars have accomplished, had not yet become part of conventional wisdom).

The new administration inherited and briefly accepted *a monolithic conception of the communist bloc*. Despite much earlier predictions and reports by outside analysts, policymakers did not begin to accept the reality and possible finality of the Sino-Soviet split until the first weeks of 1962. The inevitably corrosive impact of competing nationalisms on communism was largely ignored.

The new administration inherited and to some extent shared the *"domino theory" about Asia*. This theory resulted from profound ignorance of Asian history and hence ignorance of the radical differences among Asian nations and societies. It resulted from a blindness to the power and resilience of Asian nationalisms. (It may also have resulted from a subconscious sense that since "all Asians look alike," all Asian nations will act alike.) As a theory, the domino fallacy was not merely inaccurate but also insulting to Asian nations.

Finally, the legacy of the 1950s was apparently compounded by an uneasy sense of a worldwide communist challenge to the new administration after the Bay of Pigs fiasco. A first manifestation was the president's traumatic Vienna meeting with Khrushchev in June 1961; then came the Berlin crisis of the summer. All this created an atmosphere in which President Kennedy undoubtedly felt under special pressure to show his nation's mettle in Vietnam—if the Vietnamese, unlike the people of Laos, were willing to fight.

In general, the legacy of the 1950s shaped such early moves of the new administration as the decisions to maintain a high-visibility Southeast Asia Treaty Organization (SEATO; by sending the secretary of state himself instead of some underling to its first meeting in 1961), to back away from diplomatic recognition of Mongolia in the summer of 1961, and, most important, to expand U.S. military assistance to South Vietnam that winter on the basis of the much more tentative Eisenhower commitment. It should be added that the increased commitment to Vietnam was also fueled by a new breed of military strategists and academic social scientists (some of whom had entered the new administration) who had developed theories of counterguerrilla warfare and were eager to see them put to the test. To some, "counterinsurgency" seemed a new panacea for coping with the world's instability.

So much for the legacy and the history. Any new administration inherits both complicated problems and simplistic views of the world. But surely among the policymakers of the Kennedy and Johnson administrations there were men who would warn of the dangers of an open-ended commitment to the Vietnam quagmire?

This raises a central question at the heart of the policy process: Where were the experts, the doubters, and the dissenters? Were they there at all, and if so, what happened to them?

The answer is complex but instructive.

In the first place, the American government was sorely *lacking in real Vietnam or Indochina expertise.* Originally treated as an adjunct of Embassy Paris, our Saigon embassy and the Vietnam Desk at State were largely staffed from 1954 onward by French-speaking Foreign Service personnel of narrowly European experience. Such diplomats were even more closely restricted than the normal embassy officer—by cast of mind as well as language—to contacts with Vietnam's French-speaking urban elites. For instance, Foreign Service linguists in Portugal are able to speak with the peasantry if they get out of Lisbon and choose to do so; not so the French speakers of Embassy Saigon.

In addition, the *shadow of the "loss of China"* distorted Vietnam reporting. Career officers in the department, and especially those in the field, had not forgotten the fate of their World War II colleagues who wrote in frankness from China and were later pilloried by Senate committees for critical comments on the Chinese nationalists. Candid reporting on the strengths of the Viet Cong and the weaknesses of the Diem government was inhibited by the memory. It was also inhibited by some higher officials, notably Ambassador Nolting in Saigon, who refused to sign off on such cables.

In due course, to be sure, some Vietnam talent was discovered or developed. But a recurrent and increasingly important factor in the decision-making process was the *banishment of real expertise*. Here the underlying cause was the "closed politics" of policymaking as issues become hot: The more sensitive the issue, and the higher it rises in the bureaucracy, the more completely the experts are excluded while the harassed senior generalists take over (that is, the secretaries, undersecretaries, and presidential assistants). The frantic skimming of briefing papers in the back seats of limousines is no substitute for the presence of specialists; furthermore, in times of crisis such papers are deemed "too sensitive" even for review by the specialists. Another underlying cause of this banishment, as Vietnam became more critical, was the replacement of the experts, who were generally and increasingly pessimistic, by men described as "can-do guys": loyal and energetic fixers unsoured by expertise. In early 1965, when I confided my growing policy doubts to an older colleague on the National Security Council (NSC) staff, he assured me that the smartest thing both of us could do was to "steer clear of the whole Vietnam mess"; the gentleman in question had the misfortune to be a "can-do guy," however, and [was subsequently] highly placed in Vietnam, under orders to solve the mess.

Despite the banishment of the experts, internal doubters and dissenters did indeed appear and persist. Yet as I watched the process, such men were effectively neutralized by a subtle dynamic: *the domestication of dissenters*. Such "domestication" arose out of a twofold clubbish need: on the one hand, the dissenter's desire to stay aboard; and on the other hand, the non-dissenter's conscience. Simply stated, dissent, when recognized, was made to feel at home. On the lowest possible scale of importance, I must confess my own considerable sense of dignity and acceptance (both vital) when my senior White House employer would refer to me as his "favorite dove." Far more significant was the case of the former under-secretary of state George Ball. Once Mr. Ball began to express doubts, he was warmly institutionalized: He was encouraged to become the in-house devil's advocate on Vietnam. The upshot was inevitable: The process of escalation allowed for periodic requests to Mr. Ball to speak his piece; Ball felt good, I assume (he had fought for righteousness); the others felt good (they had given a full hearing to the dovish option); and there was minimal unpleasantness. The club remained intact; and it is, of course, possible that matters would have gotten worse faster if Mr. Ball had kept silent, or left before his final departure in the fall of 1966. There was also, of course, the case of the last institutionalized doubter, Bill Moyers. The president is said to have greeted his arrival at meetings with an affectionate "Well, here comes

Mr. Stop-the-Bombing." Here again the dynamics of domesticated dissent sustained the relationship for a while.

A related point—and crucial, I suppose, to government at all times—was *the "effectiveness" trap,* the trap that keeps men from speaking out, as clearly or as often as they might, within the government. And it is the trap that keeps men from resigning in protest and airing their dissent outside the government. The most important asset that a man brings to bureaucratic life is his "effectiveness," a mysterious combination of training, style, and connections. The most ominous complaint that can be whispered of a bureaucrat is "I'm afraid Charlie's beginning to lose his effectiveness." To preserve your effectiveness, you must decide where and when to fight the mainstream of policy; the opportunities range from pillow talk with your wife, to private drinks with your friends, to meetings with the secretary of state or the president. The inclination to remain silent or to acquiesce in the presence of the great men—to live to fight another day, to give on this issue so that you can be "effective" on later issues—is overwhelming. Nor is it the tendency of youth alone; some of our most senior officials, men of wealth and fame, whose place in history is secure, have remained silent lest their connection with power be terminated. As for the disinclination to resign in protest, while not necessarily a Washington or even American specialty, it seems more true of a government in which ministers have no parliamentary back-bench to which to retreat. In the absence of such a refuge, it is easy to rationalize the decision to stay aboard. By doing so, one may be able to prevent a few bad things from happening and perhaps even make a few good things happen. To exit is to lose even those marginal chances for "effectiveness."

Another factor must be noted: As the Vietnam controversy escalated at home, there developed *a preoccupation with Vietnam public relations as opposed to Vietnam policymaking.* And here, ironically, internal doubters and dissenters were heavily employed. For such men, by virtue of their own doubts, were often deemed best able to "massage" the doubting intelligentsia. My senior East Asia colleague at the White House, a brilliant and humane doubter who had dealt with Indochina since 1954, spent three-quarters of his working days on Vietnam public relations: drafting presidential responses to letters from important critics, writing conciliatory language for presidential speeches, and meeting quite interminably with delegations of outraged Quakers, clergymen, academics, and housewives. His regular callers were the late A. J. Muste and Norman Thomas; mine were members of the Women's Strike for Peace. Our orders from above: Keep them off the backs of busy policymakers (who usually happened to be nondoubters). Incidentally, my most discouraging assignment in the realm of public relations was the preparation of a White House pamphlet titled "Why Vietnam," in September 1965; in a gesture toward my conscience, I fought—and lost—a battle to have the title followed by a question mark.

Through a variety of procedures, both institutional and personal, doubt, dissent, and expertise were effectively neutralized in the making of policy. But what can be said of the men "in charge"? It is patently absurd to suggest that they produced such tragedy by intention and calculation. But it is neither absurd nor difficult to discern certain forces at work that caused decent and honorable men to do great harm.

Here I would stress the paramount role of *executive fatigue*. No factor seems to me more crucial and underrated in the making of foreign policy. The physical and emotional toll of executive responsibility in State, the Pentagon, the White House, and other executive agencies is enormous; that toll is, of course, compounded by extended service. Many Vietnam policymakers had been on the job for from four to seven years. Complaints may be few, and physical health may remain unimpaired, though emotional health is far harder to gauge. But what is most seriously eroded in the deadening process of fatigue is freshness of thought, imagination, a sense of possibility, a sense of priorities and perspective—those rare assets of a new administration in its first year or two of office. The tired policymaker becomes a prisoner of his own narrowed view of the world and his own clichéd rhetoric. He becomes irritable and defensive—short on sleep, short on family ties, short on patience. Such men make bad policy and then compound it. They have neither the time nor the temperament for new ideas or preventive diplomacy.

Below the level of the fatigued executives in the making of Vietnam policy was a widespread phenomenon: *the curator mentality* in the Department of State. By this I mean the collective inertia produced by the bureaucrat's view of his job. At State, the average "desk officer" inherits from his predecessor our policy toward Country X; he regards it as his function to keep that policy intact—under glass, untampered with, and dusted—so that he may pass it on in two to four years to his successor. And such curatorial service generally merits promotion within the system. (Maintain the status quo, and you will stay out of trouble.) In some circumstances, the inertia bred by such an outlook can act as a brake against rash innovation. But on many issues, this inertia sustains the momentum of bad policy and unwise commitments—momentum that might otherwise have been resisted within the ranks. Clearly, Vietnam [was] such an issue.

To fatigue and inertia must be added the factor of internal confusion. Even among the "architects" of our Vietnam commitment, there was persistent *confusion as to what type of war we were fighting* and, as a direct consequence, *confusion as to how to end that war*. (The "credibility gap" [was], in part, a reflection of such internal confusion.) Was it, for instance, a civil war, in which case counterinsurgency might suffice? Or was it a war of international aggression? (This might invoke SEATO or UN commitment.) Who was the aggressor—and the "real enemy"? The Viet Cong? Hanoi? Peking? Moscow? International communism? Or maybe "Asian communism"? Differing enemies dictated differing strategies and tactics. And confused throughout, in like fashion, was the question of American objectives; your objectives depended on whom you were fighting and why. I shall not forget my assignment from an assistant secretary of state in March 1964: to draft a speech for Secretary McNamara which would, inter alia, once and for all dispose of the canard that the Vietnam conflict was a civil war. "But in some ways, of course," I mused, "it *is* a civil war." "Don't play word games with me!" snapped the assistant secretary.

Similar confusion beset the concept of "negotiations"—anathema to much of official Washington from 1961 to 1965. Not until April 1965 did "unconditional discussions" become respectable, via a presidential speech; even then the secretary of state stressed privately to newsmen that nothing had changed, since "discussions" were by no means the same as "negotiations." Months later that issue was resolved. But it took even longer to obtain a fragile internal agreement that negotiations might include the Viet Cong as something other than an appendage to Hanoi's delegation. Given such confusion as to the whos and whys of our Vietnam commitment, it is not surprising, as Theodore Draper has written, that policymakers found it so difficult to agree on how to end the war.

Of course, one force—a constant in the vortex of commitment—was that of *wishful thinking*. I partook of it myself at many times. I did so especially during Washington's struggle with Diem in the autumn of 1963 when some of us at State believed that for once, in dealing with a difficult client state, the U.S. government could use the leverage of our economic and military assistance to make good things happen, instead of being led around by the nose by foreign dictators. If we could prove that point, I thought, and move into a new day, with or without Diem, then Vietnam was well worth the effort. Later came the wishful thinking of the air-strike planners in the late autumn of 1964; there were those who actually thought that after six weeks of air strikes, the North Vietnamese would come crawling to us to ask for peace talks. And what, someone asked in one of the meetings of the time, if they don't? The answer was that we would bomb for another four weeks, and that would do the trick. And a few weeks later came one instance of wishful thinking that was symptomatic of good men misled: In January 1965, I encountered one of the very highest figures in the administration at a dinner, drew him aside, and told him of my worries about the air-strike option. He told me that I really shouldn't worry; it was his conviction that before any such plans could be put into effect, a neutralist government would come to power in Saigon that would politely invite us out. And finally, there was the recurrent wishful thinking that sustained many of us through the trying months of 1965–1966 after the air strikes had begun: that surely, somehow, one way or another, we would "be in a conference in six months," and the escalatory spiral would be suspended. The basis of our hope: "It simply can't go on."

As a further influence on policymakers, I would cite the factor of *bureaucratic detachment*. By this I mean what at best might be termed the professional callousness of the surgeon (and indeed, medical lingo—the "surgical strike," for instance—seemed to crop up in the euphemisms of the times). In Washington the semantics of the military muted the reality of war for the civilian policymakers. In quiet, air-conditioned, thick-carpeted rooms, such terms as "systematic pressure," "armed reconnaissance," "targets of opportunity," and even "body count" seemed to breed a sort of games theory detachment. Most memorable to me was a moment in the late 1964 target planning when the question under discussion was how heavy our bombing should be, and how extensive our strafing, at some midpoint in the projected pattern of systematic pressure. An assistant secretary of state resolved the point in the following words: "It seems to me that our orchestration should be mainly violins, but with periodic touches of brass." Perhaps the biggest shock of my return to Cambridge, Massachusetts, was the realization that the young men, the flesh and blood I taught and saw on these university streets, were potentially some of the numbers on the charts of those faraway planners. In a curious sense, Cambridge [was] closer to this war than Washington.

There is an unprovable factor that relates to bureaucratic detachment: the ingredient of *cryptoracism*. I do not mean to imply any conscious contempt for Asian loss of life on the part of Washington officials. But I do mean to imply that bureaucratic detachment may well be compounded by a traditional Western sense that there are so many Asians, after all; that Asians have a fatalism about life and a disregard for its loss; that they are cruel and barbaric to their own people; and that they are very different from us (and all look alike?). And I *do* mean to imply that the upshot of such subliminal views is a subliminal question of whether Asians, and particularly Asian peasants, and most particularly Asian communists, are really people—like you and me. To put the matter another way: Would we have pursued quite such policies—and quite such military tactics—if the Vietnamese were white?

It is impossible to write of Vietnam decision-making without writing about language. Throughout the conflict, words were of paramount importance. I refer here to the impact of *rhetorical escalation* and to the *problem of oversell*. In an important sense, Vietnam became of crucial significance to us *because we said that it was of crucial significance*. (The issue obviously relates to the public relations preoccupation described earlier.)

The key here is domestic politics: the need to sell the American people, press, and Congress on support for an unpopular and costly war in which the objectives themselves [were] in flux. To sell means to persuade, and to persuade means rhetoric. As the difficulties and costs mounted, so did the definition of the stakes. This is not to say that rhetorical escalation is an orderly process; executive prose is the product of many writers, and some concepts—North Vietnamese infiltration, America's "national honor," Red China as the chief enemy—entered the rhetoric only gradually and even sporadically. But there [was] an upward spiral nonetheless. And once you have *said* that the American Experiment itself stands or falls on the Vietnam outcome, you have thereby created a national stake far beyond any earlier stakes.

Crucial throughout the process of Vietnam decision-making was a conviction among many policymakers that Vietnam posed a *fundamental test of America's national will*. Time and again I was told by men reared in the tradition of Henry L. Stimson that all we needed was the will, and we would then prevail. Implicit in such a view, it seemed to me, was a curious assumption that Asians lacked will, or at least that in a contest between Asian and Anglo-Saxon wills, the non-Asians must prevail. A corollary to the persistent belief in will was a *fascination with power* and an awe in the face of the power America possessed as no nation or civilization ever before. Those who doubted our role in Vietnam were said to shrink from the burdens of power, the obligations of power, the uses of power, the responsibility of power. By implication, such men were soft-headed and effete.

Finally, no discussion of the factors and forces at work on Vietnam policymakers can ignore the central fact of *human ego investment*. Men who have participated in a decision develop a stake in that decision. As they participate in further, related decisions, their stake increases. It might have been possible to dissuade a man of strong self-confidence at an early stage of the ladder of decision; but it is infinitely harder at later stages since a change of mind there usually involves implicit or explicit repudiation of a chain of previous decisions.

To put it bluntly, at the heart of the Vietnam calamity was a group of able, dedicated men who were regularly and repeatedly wrong—and whose standing with their contemporaries, and more important, with history, depended, as they saw it, on being proven right. These were not men who could be asked to extricate themselves from error.

The various ingredients I have cited in the making of Vietnam policy created a variety of results, most of them fairly obvious. Here are some that seem to me most central.

Throughout the conflict, there was *persistent and repeated miscalculation* by virtually all the actors, in high echelons and low, whether dove, hawk, or something else. To cite one simple example among many, in late 1964 and early 1965, some peace-seeking planners at State who strongly opposed the projected bombing of the North urged that, instead, American ground forces be sent to South Vietnam; this would, they said, increase our bargaining leverage against the North—our "chips"—and would give us something to negotiate about (the withdrawal of our forces) at an early peace conference. Simultaneously, the air-strike option was urged by many in the military who were dead set against American participation in "another land war in Asia"; they were joined by other civilian peace-seekers who wanted to bomb Hanoi into early negotiations. By late 1965, we had ended up with the worst of all worlds: ineffective and costly air strikes against the North, spiraling ground forces in the South, and no negotiations in sight.

Throughout the conflict as well, there [was] *a steady give-in to pressures for a military solution* and only minimal and sporadic efforts at a diplomatic and political solution. In part this resulted from the confusion (earlier cited) among the civilians—confusion regarding objectives and strategy. And in part this resulted from the self-enlarging nature of military investment. Once air strikes and particularly ground forces were introduced, our investment itself had transformed the original stakes. More air power was needed to protect the ground forces; and then more ground forces to protect the ground forces. And needless to say, the military mind develops its own momentum in the absence of clear guidelines from the civilians. Once asked to save South Vietnam, rather than to "advise" it, the American military could not but press for escalation. In addition, sad to report, assorted military constituencies, once involved in Vietnam, had a series of cases to prove: for instance, the utility not only of air power (the Air Force) but also of supercarrier-based air power (the Navy). Also, Vietnam policy suffered from one ironic by-product of Secretary McNamara's establishment of civilian control at the Pentagon: In the face of such control, interservice rivalry [gave] way to a united front among the military—reflected in the new but recurrent phenomenon of Joint Chiefs of Staff unanimity. In conjunction with traditional congressional allies (mostly Southern senators and representatives) such a united front would pose a formidable problem for any president.

Throughout the conflict, there [were] *missed opportunities, large and small, to disengage ourselves from Vietnam on increasingly unpleasant but still acceptable terms.* Of the many moments from 1961 onward, I shall cite only one, the last and most important opportunity that was lost: In the summer of 1964 the president instructed his chief advisers to prepare for him as wide a range of Vietnam options as possible for postelection consideration and decision. He explicitly asked that all options be laid out. What happened next was, in effect, Lyndon Johnson's slow-motion Bay of Pigs. For the advisers so effectively converged on one single option—juxtaposed against two other, phony options (in effect, blowing up the world, or scuttle-and-run)—that the president was confronted with unanimity for bombing the North from all his trusted counselors. Had he been more confident in foreign affairs, had he been deeply informed on Vietnam and Southeast Asia, and had he raised some hard questions that unanimity had submerged, this president could have used the largest electoral mandate in history to de-escalate in Vietnam, in the clear expectation that at the worst a neutralist government would come to power in Saigon and politely invite us out.

In the course of these years, another result of Vietnam decision-making [was] *the abuse and distortion of history.* Vietnamese, Southeast Asian, and Far Eastern history was rewritten by our policymakers, and their spokesmen, to conform to the alleged necessity of our presence in Vietnam. Highly dubious analogies from our experience elsewhere—the "Munich" sellout and "containment" from Europe; the Malayan insurgency and the Korean War from Asia—[were] imported in order to justify our actions. And later events [were] fitted to the Procrustean bed of Vietnam. Most notably, the change of power in Indonesia in 1965–1966 has been ascribed to our Vietnam presence, and virtually all progress in the Pacific region—the rise of regionalism, new forms of cooperation, and mounting growth rates—has been similarly explained. The Indonesian allegation is undoubtedly false (I tried to prove it, during six months of careful investigation at the White House, and had to confess failure); the regional allegation is patently unprovable in either direction (except, of course, for the clear fact that the economies of both Japan and Korea profited enormously from our Vietnam-related procurement in these countries, but that is a costly and highly dubious form of foreign aid).

There is a final result of Vietnam policy I would cite that holds potential danger for the future of American foreign policy: *the rise of a new breed of American ideologues who saw Vietnam as the ultimate test of their doctrine.* I have in mind those men in Washington who have given a new life to the missionary impulse in American foreign relations, who believe that this nation, in this era, has received a threefold endowment that can transform the world. As they see it, that endowment is composed of, first, our unsurpassed military might; second, our clear technological supremacy; and third, our allegedly invincible benevolence (our "altruism," our affluence, our lack of territorial aspirations). Together, it is argued, this threefold endowment provides us with the opportunity and the obligation to ease the nations of the earth toward modernization and stability: toward a full-fledged *Pax Americana Technocratica*. In reaching toward this goal, Vietnam was viewed as the last and crucial test. Once we succeeded there, the road ahead [was seen to be] clear.

Long before I went into government, I was told a story about Henry L. Stimson that seemed to me pertinent during the years that I watched the Vietnam tragedy unfold—and participated in that tragedy. It seems to me more pertinent than ever.

In his waning years Stimson was asked by an anxious questioner, "Mr. Secretary, how on earth can we ever bring peace to the world?" Stimson is said to have answered, "You begin by bringing to Washington a small handful of able men who believe that the achievement of peace is possible. You work them to the bone until they no longer believe that it is possible. And then you throw them out—and bring in a new bunch who believe that it is possible."

DISCUSSION QUESTIONS

1. What is meant by "the legacy of the 1950s"?
2. What were some of the "by-products" of this legacy?
3. Why were the "experts" unable to fully comprehend what was happening in Vietnam?
4. What does Thomson mean when he discusses the "'effectiveness' trap" and the "curator mentality"?
5. What were some key mistakes that Thomson identifies in American policy toward Vietnam?
6. How much impact did role factors or bureaucratic structures have on policymaking in this case?
7. How would you judge the role of individual factors in affecting policy?
8. What appeared to be the consequences of Vietnam policymaking for American foreign policy, according to Thomson?

18

Sources of Humanitarian Intervention

Beliefs, Information, and Advocacy in U.S. Decisions on Somalia and Bosnia

Jon Western

On November 21, 1992, General Colin Powell's chief deputy on the Joint Chiefs of Staff, Admiral David Jeremiah, stunned a National Security Council Deputies Committee meeting on Somalia by announcing, "If you think U.S. forces are needed, we can do the job."[1] Four days later, President George H. W. Bush decided U.S. forces were needed. On December 9, 1992, 1,300 marines landed in Mogadishu, and within weeks more than 25,000 U.S. soldiers were on the ground in Somalia.

Prior to the November 21 deputies meeting, virtually no one in or out of the administration expected that President Bush or his top political and military advisers would support a major U.S. humanitarian mission to Somalia.[2] For more than a year, the Bush administration, and General Powell and the Joint Chiefs of Staff in particular, had steadfastly opposed calls for humanitarian military interventions in Somalia, Liberia, Bosnia, and elsewhere.[3] None of these conflicts was relevant to U.S. vital interests.[4] They were simply humanitarian tragedies.

With respect to Somalia, senior Bush administration and military officials had argued repeatedly throughout most of 1992 that the deeply rooted inter-clan conflicts that permeated Somalia would make any military intervention extraordinarily risky. The basic position of the Joint Chiefs of Staff and the senior White House staff was that military force would not be able to protect itself or the distribution of humanitarian relief, because the nature of the conflict made it virtually impossible to distinguish friend from enemy or civilian from combatant. In short, the administration argued, roaming armed bandits fueled by ancient hatreds and intermingled with the civilian population was a recipe for disaster.

Yet after nearly a year of extensive opposition to the use of American military force in Somalia, in November 1992 President Bush, with the firm support of all of his key advisers—including General Powell—decided to launch a massive U.S. military intervention in Somalia. Why did the Joint Chiefs of Staff reverse [their] estimates from that of July 1992, that Somalia was a "bottomless pit," to its November proclamation that "we can do the job"? Nothing in that period changed the political, military, or logistical factors on the ground. The crisis had long before reached a critical humanitarian mass. What explains the sudden change of heart within the Bush administration on Somalia?

This chapter details the factors that led to the decision to intervene in Somalia. It reveals the circuitous path by which the Bush administration adamantly opposed intervention for more than a year and then abruptly shifted its position following the election of Bill Clinton in November 1992. It is a case study on the influence of domestic politics, competing elite beliefs, information advantages, and advocacy strategies on military intervention, with the major chasm coming between "selective engagers" in the Bush administration—those who argued that U.S. military intervention should be reserved for those isolated cases when U.S. vital strategic interests were directly threatened, not strictly humanitarian considerations—and "liberal humanitarianists," or those who supported military intervention to provide humanitarian relief to aggrieved populations and to stop or prevent atrocities perpetrated against civilians. Ultimately, the decision to intervene in Somalia became intertwined with the humanitarian tragedy of Bosnia and the presidential election of 1992.

SELECTIVE ENGAGERS AND NO VITAL INTERESTS

In 1990 and 1991 civil wars erupted in Somalia and in Yugoslavia. While neither war captured much U.S. public or elite attention, by the end of 1992 both conflicts had become the focal point of American foreign policy. But in 1990 and 1991, U.S. policy toward Somalia and the former Yugoslavia, respectively, reflected the prevailing views among President Bush and his core advisers—almost all of whom could be classified as selective engagers—that with the end of the Cold War, both the Horn of Africa and the Balkans had dramatically diminished in strategic importance to the United States. For selective engagers, the dissolution of Yugoslavia was of concern to the extent that unleashed ancient ethnic hatreds might create regional instability. The prudent choice in Yugoslavia—despite the profound transitions occurring throughout the rest of Eastern and Central Europe—was to support some form of centralized authority and to press for gradual change. From 1990 until the outbreak of war in Croatia in 1991 and Bosnia in March 1992, the administration devoted its diplomatic energies to strategies to forestall the collapse of the Yugoslav federation. Once violence erupted, the policy shifted from prevention to containment.

In Somalia, U.S. policy was similarly focused. During the Cold War, the United States contributed vast sums to Somali leader Siad Barre in an effort to stabilize the Horn of Africa in the face of the Soviet-backed regime of Mengistu Haile Mariam in Ethiopia. With the erosion of Soviet influence and competition, U.S. contributions to Barre were no longer seen as imperative to U.S. geostrategic interests. Without the financial backing of the United States to prop up Barre's corrupt regime, Somalia quickly disintegrated into interethnic civil conflict. Because the 1991–1992 crisis posed little threat to U.S. political or economic interests and did not constitute a threat to regional or international stability, the Bush administration's position throughout much of 1991 and most of 1992 was that the crisis was an internal Somali problem. The Somali leaders needed to resolve the crisis themselves.

INITIAL INFORMATION AND PROPAGANDA ADVANTAGES

Bosnia

Prior to the war in Bosnia, few Americans or foreign policy elites focused on Bosnia. To the extent that attention was paid to the crisis during the initial months of violence, the widely accepted view was that presented by selective engagers in the Bush administration. The administration criticized the Serb leadership in Belgrade for the violence and worked diplomatically to isolate Slobodan Milosevic's regime, but it nonetheless firmly believed and publicly emphasized the view that the conflict was the inevitable consequence of intractable and primordial hatreds that had been unleashed with the collapse of the tight communist control. On numerous occasions, President Bush and his advisers equated the Bosnian crisis as rooted in ethnic animosities that went back hundreds of years. Based on this analysis of the conflict, the administration argued publicly that the prudent policy was to refrain from involvement in a situation that could only lead to a Vietnam-style quagmire for the United States. Consequently, most Americans came to perceive Bosnia as the tragic but inevitable resurrection of ancient hatreds. The public supported the administration's limited policy to contain the conflict from spreading to areas that were of geostrategic interest to the United States—in particular, Kosovo, Macedonia, Albania, Greece, Turkey, or Bulgaria.

Initially, no one was in a position to challenge critically the administration's paradigmatic framing of the conflict. In the spring of 1992, no clear precedent had been set for post–Cold War humanitarian interventions, and because Yugoslavia had been a relatively advanced economic and political society during the Cold War, very few nongovernmental humanitarian organizations had any presence or experience there. Furthermore, because only a few members of Congress had much interest in or understanding of events in Yugoslavia, most deferred to the administration's resources and expertise on the conflict. As a result, those who might have opposed the administration's analysis—such as a few liberal humanitarianists in Congress who did have some regional interest—lacked a strong organizational and political base on which to mobilize public and political opposition to the Bush administration's policies on Bosnia.

For its part, the U.S. media covering Eastern and Central Europe also had little expertise in the Balkans. Few of the major news organizations had experienced correspondents on the ground. When the war in Croatia broke out in June 1991, journalists scrambled to cover the story. As early as the fall of 1991, American reporters and administration officials began warning that although the violence in Croatia was terrible, conditions in the more ethnically diverse Bosnia would be much worse. Consequently, when violence erupted in Bosnia in March 1992, there was widespread acceptance, at least initially, among journalists that the conflict there was simply a further manifestation of the unchecked nationalist hatreds that had been widely predicted.

In addition, many journalists and editors wanted to ensure "objective" and "balanced" reporting, which meant that stories often identified and reported atrocities as though all sides were equally culpable. All of this produced predictable pressures and influences on the reporting during the first several months of the war in Bosnia, reporting that portrayed the violence as tragic but ultimately endorsed the administration's line that the conflict was caused by age-old ethnic hatreds and was one in which all sides were equally culpable.

Further aiding the Bush administration's policies were the support and informational advantages of Joint Chiefs of Staff chairman General Colin Powell and his senior advisers. Powell and his advisers strongly believed that foreign military intervention in limited conflicts would inevitably degenerate into a Vietnam-type quagmire. The Joint Chiefs stressed the inherent military dilemmas associated with any type of U.S. force deployment in Bosnia. For example, during a discussion in June on whether to use U.S. military aircraft in support of an emergency humanitarian airlift to Sarajevo, senior planners told members of Congress that even such a limited operation would require the presence of more than fifty thousand U.S. ground troops to secure a perimeter of thirty miles around the airport.

Brent Scowcroft, who had been national security adviser during these deliberations, acknowledged that the Joint Chiefs "probably inflated the estimates of what it would take to accomplish some of these limited objectives, but once you have the Joint Chiefs making their estimates, it's pretty hard for armchair strategists to challenge them and say they are wrong."[5]

Consequently, throughout the first four months of the conflict in Bosnia the American public largely accepted the administration's view that the conflict was fueled by ancient hatreds about which the United States could do little. Little information emanated from the scene of the conflict to contradict that judgment, and in the face of a proliferation of "objective" reporting from Bosnia, there was very little discernable tendency within American public opinion toward a more forceful U.S. response to the crisis.

Somalia

Meanwhile, the collapse of nearly all state structures in Somalia and intense fighting between rival factions—led respectively by General Mohamed Farah Aideed and Ali Mahdi Mohamed—in the wake of Siad Barre's flight from Mogadishu in January 1991 left much of the country's civilian population under severe threat of malnutrition and starvation. Amid increasing security concerns, the United Nations withdrew its relief operations in mid-1991, leaving only a few nongovernmental organizations (NGOs) to deal with the escalating humanitarian crisis. By January 1992, the International Committee of the Red Cross was estimating that almost half of the country's six million people faced severe nutritional needs, with many liable to die of starvation without some form of immediate assistance.[6] Three hundred thousand had already died of malnutrition; more than three thousand people were starving to death daily.[7]

As with the former Yugoslavia, selective engagers in the Bush administration did not see any tangible U.S. interests at stake in Somalia. The administration deferred to the United Nations for a response to the crisis. But even here, selective engagers were focused on their own perceptions of U.S. interests and remained wary of supporting new military initiatives through the United Nations. During UN Security Council debates in April 1992, the Bush administration opposed initiatives to create an armed UN security force, fearing that new peacekeeping missions would further bloat an already inefficient UN bureaucracy and inevitably necessitate greater U.S. military involvement.

For liberal humanitarianists, Somalia was significant but only one of many regional conflicts that had humanitarian concerns. Wars in Afghanistan, Angola, Chad, Liberia, Mozambique, southern Sudan, Sri Lanka, the former Yugoslavia, and elsewhere were all producing humanitarian challenges that diverted concentrated liberal attention and resources from Somalia. The few NGOs working in Somalia issued reports beginning in the fall of 1991 citing catastrophic conditions, and efforts were made by UN Secretary-General Boutros Boutros-Ghali to mediate a settlement between the warring factions. But neither the UN mediation efforts nor the ad hoc reports from humanitarian organizations attracted attention. No galvanizing force either linked disparate humanitarian organizations or mobilized the press corps. Consequently, even though the famine intensified dramatically in the fall of 1991 and early 1992, Somalia emerged in the public discourse very slowly in 1992, and there was very little discussion on the crisis within the elite foreign policy community.

By June 1992, nearly 4.5 million were on the brink of starvation in Somalia, and nearly a hundred thousand people were dead in Bosnia, with another million displaced from their homes; still there was no concerted pressure on the selective engagers within the Bush administration to alter their policies on either Somalia or Bosnia. The administration strongly believed that even though both crises were tragic, each was rooted in intractable causes and each ultimately fell outside of U.S. interests. Furthermore, military commanders in the Joint Chiefs who opposed U.S. participation in limited wars remained convinced that military options in both Somalia and Bosnia were wholly untenable.

THE EROSION OF INITIAL INFORMATION ADVANTAGES

The Bush administration's position in Somalia and Bosnia, however, began to come under pressure in the summer of 1992. Throughout the summer, both the media and liberal humanitarianists gradually developed and dedicated more resources for information-collection efforts to challenge the administration's framing of the two conflicts.

In Somalia, in late June, the U.S. ambassador to Kenya, Smith Hempstone Jr., traveled to refugee camps on the Somali-Kenyan border for the first time. He reported his trip in a cable titled "A Day in Hell," which presented a vivid report of the humanitarian suffering. The cable resonated with many liberal humanitarianists in the State Department who believed that the Bush administration needed to do more in Somalia, and it was immediately leaked to the press. Meanwhile, liberal humanitarianists in Congress, led by Senators Nancy Kassebaum (R-KS) and Paul Simon (D-IL), conducted fact-finding missions to Somalia in June and July, and reported horrific conditions. They returned and urged their colleagues to support sending an armed UN security mission to Somalia. As other international aid organizations also began to weigh in heavily on the political debate in Washington, Boutros-Ghali again stressed that a million Somali children were at immediate risk and that more than four million people needed food assistance urgently.

All of this political pressure began to find a response at the White House. In late July, President Bush encouraged his staff to examine additional diplomatic efforts to enhance the UN efforts in Somalia. However, if the president was beginning to feel some political pressure to take action, his concern was limited to finding ways in which the United States could assist the United Nations in dealing with the problem. The United States supported a Security Council resolution passed on July 26 authorizing an emergency airlift to provide relief to southern Somalia, but according to Brent Scowcroft, "there was no discussion of using U.S. force for any purpose at this point."[8]

At the staff level, this constraint led to a bureaucratic deadlock. Some liberal humanitarianists sought to put forward military options for provision of relief, whereas selective engagers remained opposed to the use of force, calling Somalia a "bottomless pit."[9] This opposition frustrated the liberal humanitarianists. James Bishop, who was then acting assistant secretary of state for human rights and humanitarian affairs, recalls,

> I went to one interagency meeting and there was this brigadier general from the Joint Staff. We came up with this option to use helicopter gunships to support relief delivery. This general sat there and said we couldn't use helicopters in such a dusty environment. Hell, we had just fought a massive war in the Persian Gulf desert with lots of helicopters. I was evacuated from Mogadishu in January 1991 in a Marine Corps helicopter that operated just fine. But that was their attitude. They didn't want anything to do with it and they were prepared to lie to keep them out of it. At every meeting, no matter the proposal, the Joint Chiefs opposed it.[10]

By early August, according to Herman Cohen, then the assistant secretary of state for African affairs, "We were [being] told to be forward leaning, but the president paid even less attention to us."[11]

BOSNIA: IMPACT OF CAMP DISCLOSURES

Meanwhile, throughout July and early August, liberal humanitarianists greatly intensified their pressure on the Bush administration to intervene in Bosnia. At the time, the administration's control of the public message on Bosnia began to be challenged as independent reports from Bosnia started to contradict its statements. Instead of suggesting that the conflict was the spontaneous actions of neighbor killing neighbor, journalists reported on the activities of small bands of radical Serb nationalists and paramilitaries accused of committing horrific atrocities in highly organized campaigns.

This view of a highly coordinated and systematic campaign of violence was reinforced in early August by the disclosure of Serb-controlled concentration-style camps in Bosnia. The images were haunting and, for many, conclusive proof that the U.S. administration was deliberately distorting the events in Bosnia, especially given the administration's initial attempts to downplay the reports on the camps.

The pressure on the selective engagers in the wake of the camp disclosures in early August was particularly intense. Between August 2 and August 14, forty-eight news stories on Bosnia, totaling 151 minutes and 30 seconds, were broadcast on the three major network evening news programs.[12] The stories challenged Bush's policies and gave significant attention to the views and criticisms of Bush's political rival, Bill Clinton. Several stories contrasted Clinton's visible outrage at the concentration camps with Bush's tempered reaction.[13] On August 9, *ABC World News Tonight* ran a profile distinguishing Clinton's and Bush's approaches to Bosnia, extensively quoting Clinton on the need for strong, decisive U.S. leadership.

Liberal humanitarianists in Congress also escalated pressure on the president. On August 14, the Senate Foreign Relations Committee released a scathing report on ethnic cleansing, presenting the Serb campaign as a deliberate and highly coordinated, politically driven campaign of violence—not the result of spontaneous, bottom-up hatreds.

Amid this escalation in political pressure surrounding the disclosure of the camps in Bosnia, Bush urgently assembled his national security team on August 8 at his vacation home in Kennebunkport, Maine, to discuss the matter. Although there is no evidence that public opinion had shifted toward greater support for direct U.S. involvement in Bosnia, the 1992 Republican Presidential Convention was only two weeks away, and the mobilized political opposition to Bush's handling of the crisis struck a nervous chord among Bush's political advisers. Bush, who had taken tremendous pride in his foreign policy accomplishments—overseeing the fall of the Berlin Wall, the reunification of Germany, the Persian Gulf War, and the dissolution of the Soviet Union—was now being publicly castigated by highly respected foreign policy commentators. This was a particularly sensitive issue among Bush's senior political advisers—James Baker, Dennis Ross, Margaret Tutwiler, and Robert Zoellick—all of whom had moved from the State Department to the White House on August 1 to take charge of Bush's failing reelection bid.

In particular, selective engagers in Bush's political camp feared that liberal humanitarianists and hard-line interventionists in the bureaucracy were altering the public conception of Bosnia and making the administration look callous in the face of an egregious humanitarian crisis. Several liberal humanitarianists and hard-line commentators and members of Congress suggested that intervention could be done without fear of

U.S. forces becoming embroiled in a Vietnam-style situation. They focused their attention on Serb aggression and on Milosevic as the primary culprit for the violence. Their prescription was that if the United States removed Milosevic or directed a targeted military strike against him and his radical supporters, the violence in Bosnia would quickly dissipate.

Despite the intensity of the political pressure, selective engagers at the White House and within the military remained convinced that Bosnia would be a quagmire. After meeting his advisers on August 8, Bush reiterated his caution: "We are not going to get bogged down in some guerrilla warfare."[14] He also ordered his team to contest the liberal humanitarian view that U.S. intervention could quickly break the siege of Sarajevo at little cost in American lives. Scowcroft recalls his reaction to the domestic criticism unleashed at the time: "I was very suspicious that people who had never supported the use of force for our national interests were now screaming for us to use force in Yugoslavia. . . . I disagreed with the humanitarianists who deliberately down-played the intractability of the conflict, who demonized Milosevic and saw this simply as a war of aggression. Milosevic was a factor, but to that extent there were also national hatreds there, that couldn't be ignored."[15]

Over the next several days, selective engagers in the Bush camp and within the Joint Chiefs intensified their public campaign to sell their beliefs about the potential dangers associated with direct U.S. involvement in the conflict. On August 11, Lieutenant General Barry McCaffrey, a principal deputy to General Powell, publicly discussed the Joint Chiefs' views with *ABC World News Tonight*, saying emphatically that despite the tragedy, "there is no military solution." Earlier that day, senior military planners told a congressional hearing that between 60,000 and 120,000 ground troops would be needed to break the siege of Sarajevo and ensure uninterrupted relief.[16] Other commanders suggested that a field army of at least 400,000 troops would be needed to implement a cease-fire.

SOMALIA: AIRLIFT IS SUPPORTED

In the midst of the public furor over the camp disclosure in Bosnia, President Bush announced an abrupt shift on his Somalia policy and ordered U.S. Air Force C-130s to assist in providing relief to famine victims in Somalia. The president also reversed his opposition to funding the deployment of five hundred Pakistani peacekeepers to Somalia; in fact, he announced that the Pentagon would provide transportation for the five-hundred-man team and its equipment.

Conventional arguments suggest that the media compelled the president to act in Somalia—that vivid images of starving and emaciated children in Somalia provoked a sense of moral outrage within the American populace. However, among the three major U.S. television networks, Somalia was mentioned in only fifteen news stories in all of 1992 prior to Bush's decision to begin the airlift, and nearly half of these "showed only fleeting glimpses of Somalia's plight" as part of other stories.[17]

The evidence suggests that Bush's policy shift on Somalia in fact came in response to both the increasing pressure to do something in Somalia and also in response to the political backlash on Bosnia that occurred on the eve of the Republican Convention. Scowcroft recalls, "[The Bosnian camp issue] probably did have a significant influence on us. We did not want to portray the administration as wholly flint-hearted realpolitik, and an airlift in Somalia was a lot cheaper [than intervention in Bosnia] to demonstrate that we had a heart."[18]

FURTHER MOBILIZATION OF INTERVENTIONISTS

On Bosnia, the selective engagers in the administration continued their public strategy to downplay the magnitude of the violence and to characterize the conflict as one of ancient blood feuds. Acting secretary of state Lawrence Eagleburger proclaimed, "It is difficult to explain, but this war is not rational. There is no rationality at all about ethnic conflict. It is gut; it is hatred; it's not for any common set of values or purposes; it just goes on. And that kind of warfare is most difficult to bring to a halt."[19] Later in a television interview he argued, "I'm not prepared to accept arguments that there must be something between the kind of involvement of Vietnam and doing nothing, that the *New York Times* and the *Washington Post* keep blabbing about, that there must be some form in the middle. That's again, what got us into Vietnam—do a little bit, and it doesn't work. What do you do next?"[20]

By September, liberal humanitarianists began a concerted effort to identify the likely effect of the upcoming winter on the civilian population in Bosnia. As part of the effort, they detailed estimates of civilian casualties that displaced populations would face in the impending winter months. Andrew Natsios, the assistant administrator for food and humanitarian assistance for the Agency for International Development, warned Eagleburger in a letter that "immediate and massive action must be taken now to avert a tragedy by the onset of the winter season."[21] A week later, a secret Central Intelligence Agency analysis estimate that as many as 250,000 Bosnian Muslims might die from starvation and exposure was leaked to the press even before it was briefed to the National Security Council (NSC).[22] NGOs began working with professional staff members of the Senate Intelligence Committee to increase congressional oversight of the intelligence community's collection and analysis of war crimes and atrocities and to report as to whether Serb actions constituted genocide under the 1948 UN Convention on the Prevention and Punishment of the Crime of Genocide.[23]

As liberal humanitarian and hard-line interventionist voices began to permeate Washington's political debate, serious concern emerged among the Joint Chiefs of Staff that the intense political and public debate over intervention was leading toward direct U.S. involvement in Bosnia.[24] In response, General Powell embarked on an unprecedented public campaign to keep U.S. troops out of Bosnia. On September 27, Powell invited Michael Gordon of the *New York Times* to his office for an extensive interview. Gordon describes Powell as at times angry during the interview and says that he "assailed the proponents of limited military intervention to protect the Bosnians." Powell argued that "as soon as they tell me it is limited, it means they do not care whether you achieve a result or not. As soon as they tell me 'surgical,' I head for the bunker." He further complained about the civilians calling for military action in Bosnia:

> These are the same folks who have stuck us into problems before that we have lived to regret. I have some memories of us being put into situations like that which did not turn out quite the way that the people who put us in thought, i.e., Lebanon, if you want a more recent real experience, where a bunch of Marines were put in there as a symbol, as a sign. Except those poor young folks did not know exactly what their mission was. They did not know really what they were doing there. It was very confusing. Two hundred and forty-one of them died as a result.[25]

Two days later, the *New York Times* published a scathing editorial directed at General Powell, "At Least Slow the Slaughter." It strongly criticized Powell and his reluctance to intervene in Bosnia:

> The war in Bosnia is not a fair fight and it is not war. It is slaughter.
>
> When Americans spend more than $280 billion a year for defense, surely they ought to be getting more for their money than no-can-do. It is the prerogative of civilian leaders confronting this historic nightmare to ask the military for a range of options more sophisticated than off or on, stay out completely or go in all the way to total victory.
>
> With that in hand, President Bush could tell General Powell what President Lincoln once told General McClellan: "If you don't want to use the Army, I should like to borrow it for a while."[26]

By all accounts, Powell was livid. In his memoirs, he recalls that he "erupted" in anger. He then dashed off a [furious] rebuttal in which he argued that the conflict is "especially complex" and has "deep ethnic and religious roots that go back a thousand years."[27]

In sum, all of these various pressures put Powell and his advisers on the defensive. The State Department was initiating new policy initiatives that, while stopping short of outright U.S. intervention, were seen by the military command staff as the initial steps to a much greater U.S. involvement. Liberal humanitarianists in Congress were demanding more. In addition, the media was openly questioning Powell's leadership. This was the cumulative pressure on Powell and the Bush administration in early November when Bill Clinton, who had campaigned on an activist policy in Bosnia, won the 1992 presidential election.

Throughout much of September, October, and early November, Somalia again fell off the radar screen. After an initial wave of news broadcasts and printed reports on Somalia following the decision to begin the airlift, the media moved to other international stories. Within the NSC also Somalia quickly disappeared. Those within the NSC who worked on Africa turned their focus toward the negotiations in South Africa leading up to free elections and to the brutal civil wars in Angola and Mozambique—both cases that were deemed more important to overall U.S. geostrategic interests than was Somalia.

This indifference to the situation in Somalia was felt within the bureaucracy and the interagency task force that had been established to monitor the airlift. The U.S. air relief was dropping food into Baidoa, and feeding centers had been established, but those most in need were not able to get to the supplies. On November 6, the Office of Food and Disaster Assistance reported that more than 25 percent of Somali children under the age of five had already died. Despite these conditions, there was very little bureaucratic movement on additional remedies to the crisis.

THE PRESIDENTIAL ELECTION

When on November 8 Bill Clinton won the presidential election, the general belief within the Washington foreign policy elite community was that the new team would shift markedly toward a liberal humanitarian foreign policy agenda.

There was wide speculation that Clinton would take quick action on Bosnia, lifting the arms embargo and possibly using U.S. air power to strike Serb targets. Sensing the power shift, within days of the election liberal humanitarianist staffers at the State Department circulated a new initiative to lift the arms embargo against Bosnia. By November 16, every relevant bureau in the State Department had signed on to the policy proposal. Furthermore, momentum quickly grew for dramatically expanding UN peacekeeping forces in Bosnia and dedicating NATO air assets to support the peacekeepers; the UN Security Council agreed to the measure on November 16.

SOMALIA: PRESSURE BUILDS AGAIN

In early November, dozens of international relief groups and representatives from the UN High Commission on Refugees again urged the international community to step up its efforts to mitigate the famine. InterAction, a coalition of 160 U.S.-based nongovernmental relief organizations, issued public and private appeals to President Bush detailing the extensive problems that relief groups were facing in Somalia without any security from roaming bandits. InterAction requested that the United States increase its support for the UN to provide security for relief operations. Furthermore, the UN secretary-general reiterated his criticism that the Bush administration—with all of its public focus on the Bosnian war in Europe—was ignoring the more acute plight of millions of black Africans in Somalia.

In response to this pressure, a wide range of policy options was discussed at a series of interagency meetings during the first three weeks of November. The question of military intervention was not open for discussion, because of continued and absolute opposition from the military. Instead, the interagency group outlined a series of recommendations short of U.S. military participation and forwarded them to a Deputies Committee meeting of the NSC on November 20.

CLINTON'S FIRST TRIP TO WASHINGTON

On November 19, two weeks after the election, President-Elect Bill Clinton arrived in Washington for separate briefings from President Bush and General Powell. Although both meetings were designed to be thorough discussions of U.S. national security priorities (i.e., U.S. relations with Russia and China, and the future of the NATO alliance, including NATO expansion), in both meetings Clinton pressed Bush and Powell extensively about Bosnia. On this subject, the meeting with Powell was especially tense. Even before the meeting, Powell and his colleagues in the Joint Chiefs had been highly concerned that Clinton might propel the United States into Bosnia on an ambiguous, feel-good mission. According to Powell's account, Clinton started their meeting by asking, "Wasn't there some way, he wanted to know, that we could influence the situation [in Bosnia] through air power, something not too punitive?" Powell lamented later, "There it was again, the ever-popular solution from the skies, with a good humanist twist; let's not hurt anybody." Powell says he didn't want to sound too negative on the first meeting and that he told the president-elect that he would have his staff "give the matter more thought."[28]

CUMULATIVE PRESSURE

By now, liberal humanitarianists had mobilized extensive public and internal political pressure on the administration on both Somalia and Bosnia. At the White House, Scowcroft recalls that the president, coming off of his postelection blues, was personally affected by the reports and by the pressure he was receiving on Somalia from groups like InterAction. Bush began asking his advisers whether anything could be done on Somalia. At the same time, the Joint Chiefs were increasingly anxious that the new president might escalate U.S. military involvement in Bosnia. They were especially embittered—as is strikingly evident in Powell's discussion with Clinton—by liberal humanitarianist claims that intervention in support of humanitarian missions, and in Bosnia in particular, could be done on the cheap.

This cumulative pressure ultimately catapulted a policy reversal by the Joint Chiefs—again, not on Bosnia but on Somalia. The day after Powell's meeting with Clinton, the Deputies Committee met to discuss the situation in Somalia. Three options were put on the table: increasing U.S. financial and material support for the current UN peacekeeping forces in Somalia; coordinating a broader UN effort in which the United States would provide logistical support but no ground troops; and initiating a U.S.-led multinational military intervention to Somalia. According to John Hirsch and former ambassador to Somalia Robert Oakley's account, however, the only consensus at the November 20 meeting was that the third option "was not a serious option."[29] In fact, the option of military intervention was not even raised for discussion.

The next day, however, Admiral Jeremiah returned and, as we have seen, stunned the deputies meeting by announcing that if force was desired in Somalia, the military could do the job. Admiral Jeremiah recalls that by then, the frustration within the Joint Chiefs had reached a critical mass:

> There was a lot of pressure on us to do something. . . . [W]e had [had] weeks of hand wringing and futzing around [by the civilian policymakers] trying to figure out the right thing to do. Nobody wants to send troops . . . [where groups] . . . have been fighting for hundreds of years.
>
> When I said it, I was frustrated because we were taking all of the heat on Somalia and Bosnia. Everyone wanted us to volunteer—to go into Bosnia and to go into Somalia—but nobody was making decisions about what they wanted to do.
>
> During the November 21 deputies meeting, I presented our [the Joint Chiefs of Staff] view that—*if you decide*—this is what it will take to do the job. Were our figures overkill? Probably. But we weren't going to go in with a weak force. We said just give us the resources and let's get on with it already.[30]

Scowcroft recalls that he, too, was startled by the Joint Chiefs' abrupt shift: "I know that the military had long felt that [Somalia would be a quagmire because the combatants would be virtually indistinguishable from the civilians]. I was struck, and I still am, with the alacrity with which Colin Powell changed gears."[31]

THE PRESIDENT'S DECISION

On November 25, after receiving briefings on the famine and the military situation, the president told his advisers that he wanted to deploy U.S. forces to Somalia. The president's decision was directly linked to the cumulative pressures of the public criticism on both Somalia and Bosnia. It was also tied to the fact that the Joint Chiefs were prepared to support the action, and that military commanders now believed they could effectively mitigate the famine. In addition, according to Scowcroft, by this time, Bush had become more sensitive to his presidential legacy, which had become jeopardized by the exhaustive liberal criticism of the administration's apparent callousness to humanitarian crises. Somalia seemed like a good contribution to that legacy.

For their part, the Joint Chiefs' abrupt shift on Somalia also reflected the cumulative pressure and criticism from liberals on them for their reluctance to use force in support of the crisis in Bosnia. Powell's support for intervention in Somalia was explicitly based on the condition that U.S. forces would not be called into a similar effort in Bosnia.

CONCLUSION

The cases of Somalia and Bosnia in 1992 have several idiosyncrasies that make generalizations difficult. But one implication from these cases is that a starting point for future research on why the United States intervenes in some humanitarian crises and not others is to examine competing normative beliefs and the politics of intervention. After Bosnia, Haiti, Kosovo, northern Iraq, Rwanda, Sierra Leone, Somalia, Sudan, and elsewhere, in the past decade American foreign policy elites have expressed differing normative beliefs about when and where the United States should intervene. These competing beliefs appear to rotate around the selective-engager and liberal-humanitarian axis. The cases presented here suggest that these beliefs not only exist but are also significant contributors to our understanding of why the United States intervenes.

This suggests in turn that humanitarian impulses have increasingly become part of the political discourse within American foreign policy and probably cannot be ignored or rejected outright. Indeed, those who seek to establish some universal grand strategy restricting the use of force to only those situations where American vital interests are directly threatened may well find themselves under intense and persistent pressure that will detract attention from other foreign policy initiatives and ultimately could lead to some form of intervention under less than desirable or optimal terms.

In addition to competing beliefs, the intervention decision on Somalia also reveals that advocacy, information, and advocacy resources can also influence American foreign policy outcomes. Initially, President Bush and his advisers faced little opposition to their policies on Somalia and Bosnia. They captured significant information advantages on both Somalia and Bosnia, with little or no liberal humanitarian or media presence on the ground in either; selective engagers effectively portrayed the conflict as one fueled by ancient tribal hatreds about which the United States could do little.

The shifts in the Bush administration's policy on Somalia—first in August 1992 and then again in November 1992—came only in the face of mobilized political opposition. The critical variables behind these policy shifts stemmed from the shift in information and propaganda advantages once competing elites and the media developed and dedicated resources to the conflict areas to challenge the administration's framing of the crisis. Given the vast increases in global telecommunications technologies, future administrations are likely to find it difficult to develop and sustain information advantages.

DISCUSSION QUESTIONS

1. What does Western mean when he classifies people as "selective engagers" and "liberal humanitarianists"?
2. Why did the government initially not want to intervene in either Bosnia or Somalia?
3. Describe the opposition that the liberal humanitarianists faced concerning relief to Somalia.
4. How did the presidential election affect America's intervention decisions?
5. What were some of the major factors that changed the government's position on intervening in Somalia? Why not Bosnia?

NOTES

1. Quoted in John L. Hirsch and Robert B. Oakley, *Somalia and Operation Restore Hope: Reflections on Peacemaking and Peacekeeping* (Washington, DC: U.S. Institute of Peace, 1995), 43.

2. In fact, the option of U.S. military deployment was not even on the agenda for discussion for the November 21 meeting, according to several participants. Author interview with Admiral David Jeremiah, Oakton, Virginia, April 29, 1999; telephone interview with Andrew Natsios, who was then the president's special representative, on Somalia, Boston, Massachusetts, March 29, 1999; interview with Herman Cohen, who was then assistant secretary of state for African affairs, Arlington, Virginia, March 30, 1999; interview with James Woods, who was then deputy assistant secretary of defense for Africa and international security policy, Arlington, Virginia, March 30, 1999; and interview with Walter Kansteiner, who was the staff member responsible for Africa on the National Security Council, Washington, DC, March 29, 1999.

3. Interviews with Kansteiner, Cohen, Natsios, and with James Bishop, who was then acting assistant secretary of state for human rights and humanitarian affairs, Washington, DC, March 29, 1999.

4. U.S. Department of State *Dispatch* Supplement (DSDS), September 1992, 14; interview with Kansteiner.

5. Interview with Brent Scowcroft, Washington, DC, April 29, 1999.

6. Cited in Walter Clarke, *Somalia: Background Information for Operation Restore Hope, 1992–1993* (Carlisle Barracks, PA: U.S. Army War College, December 1992).

7. Mohamed Sahoun, *Somalia: The Missed Opportunities* (Washington, DC: U.S. Institute of Peace, 1994), 16.

8. Interview with Scowcroft.

9. Quoted from Don Oberdorfer, "The Path to Intervention: A Massive Tragedy We Could Do Something About," *Washington Post*, December 6, 1992, A1.

10. Interview with Bishop.

11. Interview with Cohen.

12. Network Evening News Abstracts, Television News Archives, August 2–14, 1992, Vanderbilt University, http://tvnews.vanderbilt.edu/eveningnews.html.

13. See, for example, *ABC World News Tonight*, August 8, 9, and 10, 1992; *NBC Nightly News*, August 7, 8, and 10, 1992; and *CBS Evening News*, August 8 and 9, 1992, all from Network Evening News Abstracts, Television News Archives, Vanderbilt University, http://tvnews.vanderbilt.edu/eveningnews.html.

14. Quoted in Jim Hoagland, "August Guns: How Sarajevo Will Reshape U.S. Strategy," *Washington Post*, August 9, 1992, C1.

15. Interview with Scowcroft.

16. Quoted in Michael Gordon, "Conflict in the Balkans: 60,000 Needed for Bosnia, a U.S. General Estimates," *New York Times*, August 12, 1992, 8.

17. Warren P. Strobel, *Late-Breaking Foreign Policy: The News Media's Influence on Peace Operations* (Washington, DC: U.S. Institute of Peace, 1997), 131–37.

18. Interview with Scowcroft.

19. Quoted in U.S. Department of State *Dispatch* Supplement (DSDS), September 1992, 14.

20. Quoted in U.S. Department of State *Dispatch* Supplement.

21. Quoted in Michael Gordon, "Winter May Kill 100,000 in Bosnia, the CIA Warns," *New York Times*, September 30, 1992, 13.

22. Quoted in Gordon, "Winter May Kill 100,000."

23. Interview with William Hill, director, Office of East European Analysis, Bureau of Intelligence and Research, U.S. Department of State, Washington, DC, March 22, 1999.

24. Interview with Jeremiah.

25. Quoted in Michael Gordon, "Powell Delivers a Resounding No on Using Limited Force in Bosnia," *New York Times*, September 28, 1999, 1.

26. "At Least Slow the Slaughter," *New York Times*, October 4, 1992, 16.

27. Colin Powell, "Why Generals Get Nervous," *New York Times*, October 8, 1992, 35.

28. Colin Powell, *My American Journey: An Autobiography* (New York: Random House, 1995), 562.

29. Hirsch and Oakley, *Somalia and Operation Restore Hope*, 43.

30. Interview with Jeremiah.

31. Interview with Scowcroft.

19

NATO Expansion

The Anatomy of a Decision

James M. Goldgeier ·

In deciding to enlarge the North Atlantic Treaty Organization (NATO), Bill Clinton's administration followed through on one of its most significant foreign policy initiatives and the most important political-military decision for the United States since the collapse of the Soviet Union. The policy involved a difficult trade-off for the administration between wanting to ensure that political and economic reform succeeded in Central and Eastern Europe and not wanting to antagonize Russia, which had received billions of dollars to assist its transition to a democratic, market-oriented Western partner. Skeptics of the NATO expansion policy within the government also worried about its costs, its effect on the cohesiveness of the Atlantic Alliance, and the wisdom of extending security guarantees to new countries. How did President Clinton, often criticized for a lack of attention to foreign policy and for vacillation on important issues, come to make a decision with far-reaching consequences for all of Europe at a time when NATO faced no military threat and in the context of diminishing resources for foreign policy?

This [chapter] analyzes the process the U.S. government followed that led to this major foreign policy initiative. I have based my findings largely on interviews I conducted in 1997 with several dozen current and former U.S. government officials, from desk officers deep inside the State and Defense Departments all the way up to President Clinton's foreign policy advisers. The interviews reveal that the administration decided to expand NATO despite widespread bureaucratic opposition, because a few key people wanted it to happen, the most important being the president and his

---

Some notes have been deleted; others have been renumbered.

national security adviser, Anthony Lake. Other senior officials—particularly those in the State Department—became important supporters and implementers of NATO expansion, but Lake's intervention proved critical early in the process. Keenly interested in pushing NATO's expansion as part of the administration's strategy of enlarging the community of democracies, Lake encouraged the president to make statements supporting expansion and then used those statements to direct the National Security Council (NSC) staff to develop a plan and a timetable for putting these ideas into action. The president, once convinced that this policy was the right thing to do, led the alliance on this mission into the territory of the former Warsaw Pact and sought to make NATO's traditional adversary part of the process through his personal relationship with Russian president Boris Yeltsin.

Rather than being a story of a single decision, this policy initiative came about through a series of decisions and presidential statements made during three key phases of the process in 1993 and 1994. During the summer and fall of 1993, the need to prepare for Clinton's January 1994 summit meetings in Brussels pushed the bureaucracy into action. The product of this bureaucratic activity was the October 1993 proposal to develop the Partnership for Peace (PFP), which would increase military ties between NATO and its former adversaries. In the second phase, which culminated in his January 1994 trip to Europe, Clinton first signaled U.S. seriousness about NATO expansion by saying the question was no longer "whether" but "when." The final phase discussed here encompasses the period from April to October 1994, when key supporters of NATO expansion attempted to turn this presidential rhetoric into reality. At the end of this period, the newly installed assistant secretary of state for European affairs, Richard Holbrooke, bludgeoned the bureaucracy into understanding that expansion was presidential policy, and an idea that had been bandied about for a year and a half finally started to become reality.

PHASE 1: BUREAUCRATIC DEBATE AND ENDORSEMENT OF THE PARTNERSHIP FOR PEACE

In the first few months of his administration, President Clinton had not given much thought to the issue of NATO's future. Then, in late April 1993, at the opening of the Holocaust Museum in Washington, he met one-on-one with a series of Central and Eastern European leaders, including the highly regarded leaders of Poland and the Czech Republic, Lech Walesa and Vaclav Havel. These two, having struggled so long to throw off the Soviet yoke, carried a moral authority matched by few others around the world. Each leader delivered the same message to Clinton: Their top priority was NATO membership. After the meetings, Clinton told Lake how impressed he had been with the vehemence with which these leaders spoke, and Lake says Clinton was inclined to think positively toward expansion from that moment.

At the June 1993 meeting of the North Atlantic Council (NAC) foreign ministers in Athens, Greece, U.S. Secretary of State Warren Christopher said enlarging NATO's membership was "not now on the agenda." But Christopher understood that NATO needed to assess its future, and with White House endorsement, he pushed his fellow foreign ministers to announce that their heads of state would meet six months later, in January 1994.[1] This announcement set in motion a process back in Washington to discuss the contentious issue of expansion. At the White House, Lake wrote in the margins of Christopher's statement, "Why not now?" and his senior director for European affairs, Jenonne Walker, convened an interagency working group (IWG) to prepare for the January 1994 meeting in Brussels and to recommend what the president should do there. The working group involved representatives from the NSC staff, the State Department, and the Pentagon. According to several participants, Walker informed the group at the start that both the president and Lake were interested in pursuing expansion.

On September 21, 1993, nine months into the Clinton administration, Lake gave his first major foreign policy speech, in which he developed ideas on promoting democracy and market economies that Clinton had enunciated during his campaign. Clinton had stressed the theme that democracies do not go to war with one another and thus that U.S. foreign policy strategy should focus on promoting democracy. Lake had helped to develop this approach, which leading campaign officials saw as a foreign policy initiative behind which different wings of the Democratic Party could rally. In the 1993 speech, Lake argued that "the successor to a doctrine of containment must be a strategy of enlargement—enlargement of the world's free community of market democracies." And he added, "At the NATO summit that the president has called for this January, we will seek to update NATO, so that there continues behind the enlargement of market democracies an essential collective security."[2]

Although Lake tried rhetorically to push the process along, the bureaucracy greatly resisted expanding the alliance. Officials at the Pentagon unanimously favored the PFP proposal developing largely through the efforts of General John Shalikashvili and his staff, first from Shalikashvili's perch as Supreme Allied Commander in Europe and then as chairman of the Joint Chiefs of Staff. PFP proponents sought to foster increased ties to all the former Warsaw Pact states as well as to the traditional European neutrals, and to ensure that NATO did not have to differentiate among its former adversaries or "draw new lines" in Europe. Every state that accepted its general principles could join the PFP, and the countries themselves could decide their level of participation. Many officials viewed the partnership as a means of strengthening and making operational the North Atlantic Cooperation Council (NACC), which had been NATO's first formal outreach effort to the East, undertaken in 1991. From the Pentagon's standpoint, it did not make sense to talk about expansion until after NATO had established the type of military-to-military relationships that would enable new countries to integrate effectively into the alliance. Several participants in the IWG say that Pentagon representatives made clear that both Secretary of Defense Les Aspin and General Shalikashvili opposed expansion and, in particular, feared diluting the effectiveness of NATO.

In addition to concern about NATO's future military effectiveness, the bureaucracy also feared that expansion would antagonize Russia and bolster nationalists and Communists there. Many State Department debates at this time focused on this fear, and views on expansion there were more divided than those in the Pentagon. In September, Yeltsin had written a letter to Clinton and other NATO heads of state backtracking on positive remarks he had made in Warsaw on Polish membership in NATO and suggesting that if NATO expanded, Russia should be on the same fast track as the Central Europeans. Then, in early October, Yeltsin's troops fired on his opposition in Parliament, and it appeared to many that the political situation in Russia was deteriorating.

During this period a small group at the State Department—including Lynn Davis, the under secretary for arms control and international security affairs; Thomas Donilon, the chief of staff; and Stephen Flanagan, a member of the Policy Planning Staff—advocated a fast-track approach to expansion. This group argued that in January 1994, NATO should lay out criteria, put forward a clear timetable, and perhaps even offer "associate membership" to a first set of countries. At a series of lunches with Secretary Christopher, organized to present him with the pros and cons of expansion, these individuals pressed him to move the process forward as quickly as possible, saying, as one participant recalled, that NATO should "strike while the iron is hot." Flanagan, Donilon, and Davis worried that without the prospect of membership in a key Western institution, Central and Eastern Europe would lose the momentum for reform. NATO and the European Union (EU) were the premier institutions in Europe, and the EU, absorbed in the internal problems associated with the Maastricht Treaty, would clearly postpone its own expansion. These officials wanted to encourage states such as Poland and Hungary to continue on the path of reform—to adopt civilian control of the military, to build a free polity and economy, and to settle border disputes—by providing the carrot of NATO membership if they succeeded.

This pro-expansion group also drew on compelling arguments from two other government officials. Charles Gati, a specialist on Eastern Europe serving on the Policy Planning Staff, had written a memo in September 1993 arguing that the new democracies were fragile, that the ex-Communists were likely to gain power in Poland, and that if NATO helped Poland succeed in carrying out reforms, it would have a huge impact on the rest of the region. Donilon took this memo straight to Christopher, who found the reasoning impressive. When the ex-Communists did win parliamentary elections in Poland weeks later, Gati's words carried even greater weight.

The other argument came from Dennis Ross, the special Middle East coordinator for the Clinton administration, who had been director of policy planning under Secretary of State James A. Baker III. Given his involvement in the German unification process and the development of the NACC, Ross attended two of the Christopher lunches on NATO. During one, he reminded the group that critics had believed that NATO could not successfully bring in a united Germany in 1990, but it did, and without damaging U.S.-Soviet relations. He suggested that NATO involve Russia in the expansion process rather than confront its former enemy. Ross argued that the previous administration's experience with German unification offered good reason to believe that the current administration could overcome problems with Russia.

Inside the State Department's regional bureaus dealing with Europe and with the New Independent States (NIS), however, bureaucrats expressed tremendous opposition to a fast-track approach and in a number of cases to any idea of expansion. Many who worked on NATO issues feared problems of managing the alliance if Clinton pushed ahead with this contentious issue. Those who worked on Russia issues thought expansion would undermine reform efforts there.

In these State Department debates, the most important proponent of a much more cautious and gradualist approach to expansion was Strobe Talbott, then ambassador-at-large for the NIS. Talbott proved important for two reasons: As a longtime friend, he had direct access to Clinton, and as a former journalist, he could write quickly, clearly, and persuasively. Christopher asked Talbott and Nicholas Burns—the senior director for Russian, Ukrainian, and Eurasian Affairs at the NSC—to comment on the fast-track approach. He and Burns argued to both Christopher and Lake that Russia would not understand a quick expansion, which would impair the U.S.-Russian relationship and, given the domestic turmoil in Russia in late September and early October, might push Russia over the edge.

One Saturday in mid-October, when Talbott was out of town, Lynn Davis forcefully argued to Christopher at a NATO discussion lunch that NACC and the PFP were simply not enough. When Talbott returned that afternoon and learned about the thrust of the meeting, he quickly wrote a paper reiterating the importance of a gradual approach to expansion. The next day, he delivered a memo to Christopher stating, "Laying down criteria could be quite provocative, and badly timed with what is going on in Russia." Instead, he suggested, "Take the one new idea that seems to be universally accepted, PFP, and make that the centerpiece of our NATO position." Talbott argued that the administration should not put forward any criteria on NATO membership that would automatically exclude Russia and Ukraine, and that the administration could never manage the relationship if it did not offer Russia the prospect of joining the alliance at a future date. He firmly believed that Clinton should mention neither dates nor names in Brussels.[3]

By Monday morning, October 18, Christopher had decided to support the gradual rather than fast-track approach, which meant that any agreement among leading officials would place the policy emphasis on the PFP. Among Clinton's top foreign policy advisers, Lake sought to push ahead with expansion, Aspin and Shalikashvili sought to delay consideration of expansion and instead supported the PFP, and Christopher fell somewhere in between, open to gradual expansion but concerned about Russia's reaction. At the White House later that day, Clinton endorsed the consensus of his principal foreign policy advisers that, at the January summit, the alliance should formally present the PFP, and he should announce NATO's intention eventually to expand. This decision reflected the consensus that had emerged from the bargaining within agencies and in the IWG, which had easily agreed on the PFP, but which could not agree on issues such as criteria, a timetable, or "associate membership" status. In the end, the IWG agreed on what its principals in turn could accept: to put forward the PFP and to say something general about NATO's eventual expansion.

The consensus emerged because, as with many decisions, opponents and proponents of expansion had different interpretations of what they had decided, and this ambiguity created support for the decision throughout the bureaucracy. Vociferous opponents of NATO expansion believed the administration's principals had decided to promote the PFP while postponing a decision on enlargement. Those in the middle, who could live with expansion but did not want to do anything concrete in 1994, also saw the October decision as consistent with their preferences. Finally, the decision that Clinton should comment on expansion pleased proponents of near-term enlargement, as they believed such a treatment would help to move the process along on a faster track.

The October 18 meeting would be the last of its kind on NATO expansion for another year. Given the meeting's ambiguous outcome—the foreign policy principals had not given the president a timetable to endorse—confusion reigned concerning the policy's direction. For the moment, the decision to develop the PFP was the Clinton administration's NATO outreach policy.

Yet from the moment the participants went their separate ways, observers could tell they interpreted the decision differently. Secretary of State

Christopher's entourage, on its way to Budapest to brief the Central Europeans (and then on to Moscow to explain the policy to Yeltsin), said the January summit would send the signal that NATO's door would open at some future date (and apparently even State Department officials on Christopher's plane disagreed about how to present the decision). The senior official conducting the airborne press briefing stated, "We believe that the summit should formally open the door to NATO expansion as an evolutionary process."[4] Meanwhile, Secretary of Defense Aspin and his advisers, attending the NATO defense ministers' meeting in Travamünde, Germany, to gain alliance endorsement of the PFP, emphasized that NATO would not enlarge soon. According to one report, Lake called Aspin in a pique saying the secretary of defense had veered from the script.[5]

PHASE 2: THE PRESIDENT SPEAKS

After mid-October, administration officials knew the president would say something about NATO enlargement on his trip to Europe in January. But no one was sure how much he would say and how specific he would be. After all, the bureaucratic wrangling had produced a decision that the president should emphasize the PFP while delivering a vague statement that NATO could eventually take in new members. The first official statement prior to the summit came from Secretary Christopher at the plenary session of the Conference on Security and Cooperation in Europe (CSCE) in Rome on November 30. Noting that the United States was proposing a Partnership for Peace, he also stated, "At the same time, we propose to open the door to an evolutionary expansion of NATO's membership."[6] Two days later, at the NAC ministerial in Brussels, he said, "The Partnership is an important step in its own right. But it can also be a key step toward NATO membership."[7]

Meanwhile, prominent figures from previous administrations pressured Clinton to be more forthcoming on expansion at the summit. Former secretary of state Henry Kissinger complained in an op-ed piece that the PFP "would dilute what is left of the Atlantic Alliance into a vague multilateralism," and he called for movement to bring Poland, Hungary, and the Czech Republic into some form of "qualified membership." Former national security adviser Zbigniew Brzezinski urged NATO members to sign a formal treaty of alliance with Russia and to lay out a more explicit path to full NATO membership for the leading Central European candidates. Former secretary of state James A. Baker III also made the case for a "clear road map" with "clear benchmarks" for the prospective members.[8]

During this time, Brzezinski had been meeting with Lake to share ideas about his two-track approach to expansion, and he also invited Lake to his home to meet a number of Central and Eastern European leaders. Since the debate at the White House focused more on "whether" than concretely "how," these meetings with Brzezinski helped Lake to clarify his own thinking and emphasized to him the importance of keeping the process moving forward. Significantly, Brzezinski argued that Russia would be more likely to develop as a stable, democratic presence in Europe if the West removed all temptations to reassert imperial control and precluded Russia's ability to intimidate its former satellites.

In late December, Lake's staff members, who were in general opposed to moving expansion onto the near-term agenda, presented him with the draft briefing memoranda for the different stops on the president's upcoming trip to Europe. Several of his staffers say he threw a fit on seeing the initial work, because the memos emphasized the PFP. According to Nicholas Burns, Lake wanted a presidential statement in January that would leave no doubt about the policy's direction.

But high-level opposition to any push toward expansion continued to color the agenda. The Pentagon appeared unanimously to share the view that the policy should be sequential; countries would participate in the PFP for a number of years and then the alliance might start addressing the issue of expansion. General Shalikashvili, at a White House press briefing on January 4, emphasized the value of the PFP as a way of ensuring that the alliance create no new divisions in Europe, and he suggested postponing discussions of membership to a future date.

But, he added, in words that Clinton would make much more significant a week later, "It is useful to remember that we are talking so much less today about whether extension of the alliance [should take place], but so much more about how and when." Pentagon officials, however, had a much different view of what "when" meant than did proponents of expansion at the NSC and State, believing the PFP should operate for several years before the alliance began thinking about expansion.

Prior to the summit, even Clinton still seemed unsure of how far he wanted to go. The strong showing of nationalists and Communists in the December 1993 Russian parliamentary elections had sent shockwaves through the administration. On January 4, Clinton said in an exchange with reporters at the White House,

> I'm not against expanding NATO. I just think that if you look at the consensus of the NATO members at this time, there's not a consensus to expand NATO at this time and we don't want to give the impression that we're creating another dividing line in Europe after we've worked for decades to get rid of the one that existed before.[9]

This was hardly the signal the Central Europeans had hoped to receive.

Just prior to his trip, Clinton sent Polish-born General Shalikashvili, Czech-born U.S. ambassador to the UN Madeleine Albright, and Hungarian-born

State Department adviser Charles Gati to Central Europe to explain the administration's policy and to quell criticisms stemming from this region prior to the summit. Albright argued forcefully to the Central European leaders that the PFP would provide the best vehicle for these countries to gain future NATO membership, and she reiterated that it was not a question of whether, but when.

In Brussels, Clinton said that the PFP "sets in motion a process that leads to the enlargement of NATO." According to Donilon, Lake wanted the president to make a more forceful statement in Prague to give a clear impetus to expansion. Sitting around a table in Prague prior to Clinton's remarks, Lake, Donilon, and presidential speechwriter Robert Boorstin wrote the statement that Clinton agreed to deliver. Echoing what Albright had told the Central Europeans, the president said, "While the Partnership is not NATO membership, neither is it a permanent holding room. It changes the entire NATO dialogue so that now the question is no longer whether NATO will take on new members but when and how."[10]

To proponents such as Lake, this statement was a clear victory, and it laid the basis for moving the process along. He wanted the alliance to address the "when" as soon as possible. For expansion skeptics, to whom "when" meant after the PFP had created a new military environment in Europe, the president's words meant nothing specific and reflected, they believed, the outcome of the October 18 decision; they concluded that although the president had stated that expansion was theoretically possible, the administration would not undertake any actual effort to expand the alliance anytime soon. Their failure to recognize the importance of the president's remarks—at least as Lake and other expansion proponents interpreted them—would lead to their surprise later in the year that the process had been moving forward.

Administration critics would later suggest that Clinton supported expansion purely for political purposes, to woo voters of Polish, Czech, and Hungarian descent. Numerous foreign policy officials in the administration, who deny that domestic political considerations came up in their meetings on expansion, hotly dispute this claim. Lake says that although everyone knew the political context of the NATO enlargement debate, he never had "an explicit discussion" with the president about the domestic political implications of expansion. Domestic politics probably played a more complicated role in this policy decision than a simple attempt to court ethnic votes in key Midwestern and northeastern states. First, for several political reasons, Clinton needed to demonstrate U.S. leadership. His administration's policy in Bosnia was failing miserably, and this failure overshadowed every other foreign policy issue at the time. Second, even if ethnic pressures did not drive the decision, Clinton would have alienated these vocal and powerful domestic constituencies had he decided against expanding NATO; Republicans thus would have gained another issue to use in congressional elections later that year. If domestic politics did not drive the decision, it gave it more resonance for the White House, and both parties certainly used the policy for political purposes: Clinton's speeches in places like Cleveland and Detroit in 1995–1996 provide clear evidence of the perceived value of NATO expansion to those communities, and the Republicans included NATO expansion as a plank in their Contract with America during the 1994 congressional campaign.

The bureaucratic decision-making process had not advanced much between October 1993 and the president's trip to Europe in January 1994. But regardless of where the bureaucratic consensus remained, Clinton had opened the door for expansion with his forceful remarks in Brussels and Prague. This is turn gave Lake the impetus he needed, and because of his proximity and access to the president, for the moment he could move the process along without having to gain the backing of the rest of the bureaucracy.

PHASE 3: FROM RHETORIC TO REALITY

For several months after Clinton's pronouncements in January, neither his advisers nor the bureaucracy paid much attention to NATO expansion, largely because of the crises in Bosnia that winter and because of the attention they paid to getting the PFP up and running. In early spring, the NATO expansion process began moving forward again, at Lake's instigation. In April, Lake held a meeting with his deputy, Samuel R. "Sandy" Berger, and one of his staffers, Daniel Fried, a specialist on Central and Eastern Europe, to discuss how to follow up on the president's January remarks and to prepare for the president's trip to Warsaw that July. Lake asked for an action plan on enlargement, and when Fried reminded him of the bureaucracy's continued strong opposition, Lake replied that the president wanted to move forward and Lake therefore needed an action plan to make it happen.

To write the policy paper, Fried brought in two old colleagues: Burns at NSC and Alexander Vershbow, then in the European bureau of the State Department but soon to become the NSC's senior director for European affairs. Despite his NSC portfolio on Russian affairs, Burns was not opposed to NATO expansion, which pleased Fried; Burns likewise appreciated that Fried accepted a gradual approach and understood that the strategy had to include a place for Russia. Unlike the authors of many policy papers that need approval, or clearance, from key actors at each of the relevant agencies, this troika worked alone, thus sidestepping the need for bureaucratic bargaining. Before the president's Warsaw trip, Lake invited Talbott and State Department Policy Planning Director James Steinberg to the White House to discuss the draft paper with Fried and Burns. Talbott sought assurances that the proposed process would be gradual, consistent with the policy he had pushed the previous October.

Many people believe Talbott opposed enlargement during this time, especially because most of the Russia specialists outside government vehemently opposed expanding NATO. Talbott clearly opposed making any immediate moves and emphasized that the process must be gradual and include rather than isolate Russia. But many of Talbott's colleagues say that once he became deputy secretary of state in February 1994 and more regularly considered the broader European landscape and the needs of the Central and Eastern Europeans, he warmed to expansion. Talbott encouraged Christopher to bring Richard Holbrooke back from his post as ambassador to Germany to be assistant secretary of state for European affairs in summer 1994, both to fix the Bosnia policy and to work on NATO expansion. By the following year, Talbott had become one of the most articulate Clinton administration spokespersons in favor of the NATO expansion policy.

By summer, the NSC and State Department positions had converged. Thinking in more gradual terms than Lake had been pushing earlier in the year, the troika's views now coincided with the consensus that had developed in the State Department. The efforts to begin figuring out a way to develop a timetable for both the expansion track and the NATO-Russian track led to a major push in summer and fall 1994 to get an expansion policy on firmer footing.

In Warsaw in July, Clinton spoke more forcefully on the issue than many in the bureaucracy would have preferred, just as he had done in Brussels and Prague earlier in the year. In an exchange with reporters after his meeting with Lech Walesa, he said, "I have always stated my support for the idea that NATO will expand. . . . And now what we have to do is to get the NATO partners together and to discuss what the next steps should be."[11] By emphasizing the need to meet with U.S. allies, the president gave a green light to those who wanted a concrete plan.

Two months later, addressing a conference in Berlin, Vice President Al Gore proved even more outspoken, saying,

> Everyone realizes that a military alliance, when faced with a fundamental change in the threat for which it was founded, either must define a convincing new rationale or become decrepit. Everyone knows that economic and political organizations tailored for a divided continent must now adapt to new circumstances—including acceptance of new members—or be exposed as mere bastions of privilege.[12]

Holbrooke apparently had major input on this speech and one staffer for the JCS said the vice president's remarks gave the military its first inkling that the administration's NATO policy had changed since January. Senior military representatives objected to the draft text of Gore's remarks, but to no avail.

Despite his inclination toward expanding the alliance, Clinton understood concerns about Russia's reaction. After all, Clinton's foreign policy had centered in part on U.S. assistance for the Yeltsin government's reform program, and he did not want to undercut Yeltsin before the 1996 Russian presidential election. In late September, Yeltsin came to Washington, and Clinton had a chance to tell him face to face that NATO was potentially open to all of Europe's new democracies, including Russia, and that it would not expand in a way that threatened Russia's interests. At a White House luncheon, Clinton told Yeltsin that he had discussed NATO expansion with key allied leaders, and he made sure Yeltsin understood that NATO would not announce the new members until after the Russian and U.S. 1996 presidential elections. At the same time, Clinton wanted to ensure that any advances in the process that might take place in the meantime—during the NATO ministerials—would not surprise the Russian president.

With Holbrooke coming back to the State Department and with Vershbow and Fried both now special assistants to the president at the NSC, expansion proponents had gained more power within the bureaucracy than they had during the previous autumn. Lake successfully circumvented bureaucratic opposition to get Clinton to make forceful statements that expansion would occur. His troika had continued to update its action plan throughout the summer and fall, and by October 1994 its strategy paper proposed the timeline that the alliance eventually followed: a series of studies and consultations designed to lead to a membership invitation to the first group and a NATO-Russian accord in 1997. But concerns about the military dimension of expansion still existed in the Pentagon, without whose efforts to address the nuts and bolts of expanding the military alliance the decision could not have moved from theory to practice.

For their next task, proponents had to convince skeptics within the administration that the president was serious. For NATO expansion, the enforcer would be Holbrooke, the newly installed assistant secretary of state, whom Christopher had brought back to the department at the urging of Talbott, Donilon, and Under Secretary for Political Affairs Peter Tarnoff.

Holbrooke held his first interagency meeting on NATO expansion at the State Department in late September, almost immediately after taking office. He wanted to make clear that he would set up and run the mechanism to expand NATO, because the president wanted it to happen. Holbrooke knew that most Pentagon officials preferred concentrating on making the PFP work rather than moving ahead with expansion, and he wanted to make sure everyone understood that he was taking charge. His opportunity came at this meeting when the senior representative from the Joint Chiefs of Staff (JCS), three-star General Wesley Clark, questioned Holbrooke's plans to move forward on the "when" and "how" questions of expansion. To the Pentagon's way of thinking, no one had yet made a decision that would warrant this action. Holbrooke shocked those in attendance by declaring, "That sounds like insubordination to me. Either you are on the president's program or you are not."[13]

According to participants, Deputy Assistant Secretary of Defense Joseph Kruzel, one of the key figures in developing the PFP program, argued that the issue had been debated in October 1993 and the decision at that time, the last formal meeting on the subject at the highest levels, was *not* to enlarge. Other Pentagon officials in attendance argued that only the "principals" could make this decision, and thus another meeting needed to be held at the highest level. Holbrooke responded that those taking this view had not been listening to what the president had been saying. The skeptics simply could not believe that Holbrooke was resting his whole case on remarks Clinton had made in Brussels, Prague, and Warsaw. Former defense secretary William Perry still refers to Holbrooke as having "presumed" at that point that the administration had decided to enlarge NATO, whereas Clinton had made no formal decision to that effect.

After this dramatic outburst, Holbrooke asked Clark to set up a meeting to brief this interagency group on what they would need to do to implement the policy. Through this request, Holbrooke enabled the JCS to voice their concerns but also forced them to begin acting on the issue. At the Pentagon two weeks later, a team with representatives from both the Office of the Secretary of Defense (OSD) and the JCS presented to the interagency group the full range of military requirements each country would need to meet to join NATO. The JCS briefer pointed, for example, to the 1,200 Atlantic Alliance standardization agreements the former Warsaw Pact armed forces would have to address to become compatible with NATO. Holbrooke, now playing "good cop," responded by saying that this briefing was exactly what the group needed, and he invited them to work with him to make the process a smooth one. This briefing would, in fact, serve as the basis both for the briefing to the NAC later in the fall and for the NATO study conducted the following year.

Because Pentagon officials did not believe the administration had ever made a formal decision, Perry called Clinton and asked for a meeting of the foreign policy team to clarify the president's intentions. At the meeting, Perry presented his arguments for holding back and giving the PFP another year before deciding on enlargement. He wanted time to move forward on the NATO-Russian track and to convince Moscow that NATO did not threaten Russia's interests, before the alliance moved ahead on the expansion track. Instead, the president endorsed the two-track plan that Lake and his staff, as well as the State Department, now pushed—the plan that ultimately led to the May 1997 signing of the NATO-Russian Founding Act and the July 1997 NATO summit in Madrid inviting Poland, Hungary, and the Czech Republic to begin talks on accession to full NATO membership.

THE AMBIGUITY OF THE DECISION

Like so many decision-making processes, the NATO expansion process was not at all clear-cut. The best evidence of its ambiguities comes from asking participants a simple question: "When did you believe that the decision to expand NATO had been made?" Their answers demonstrate that what you see depends on where you stand; attitudes toward the decision affected individuals' views of what was happening. Most supporters, including Lake, cite the period between the October 1993 meeting of the principals and Clinton's trip to Europe in January 1994. The answers of opponents, on the other hand, generally range over the second half of 1994, depending on when they finally realized the president was serious. One State Department official who opposed expansion said that when he objected to language circulating in an interagency memo on the issue in August 1994, a colleague told him it was the same language the president had used in Warsaw the previous month. At that point, he says, he understood that the policy had moved from theory to reality. Others, such as Perry, did not start to believe that expansion was on the table until after the Holbrooke interagency meeting in September 1994. In support of this last interpretation, Brzezinski pointed out at the time that until Clinton *answered* the questions "when" and "how," rather than simply *asking* them, the United States had no decisive plan for Europe.[14]

These interpretations vary so widely because the president and his top advisers did not make a formal decision about a timetable or process for expansion until long after Clinton had started saying NATO would enlarge. The when, who, how, and even why came only over time and not always through a formal decision-making process. In January 1994, when the president first said that he expected the alliance to take in new members, no consensus existed among his top advisers on the difficult questions of when and how. Clinton's advisers could as reasonably believe that his remarks amounted to no more than a vague statement that NATO might someday expand as they could believe that the president wanted to begin moving forward *now*. Whereas proponents of expansion took his statements as a signal to begin planning how to put theory into practice, the president did not make an explicit decision in the presence of his top foreign policy advisers until nearly a year later, and some opponents therefore choose to believe that the course was not set until that meeting.

Readers may find it unsatisfying that I have not uncovered either *the* moment of decision or the president's ulterior motive. Truthfully, however, most policies—even those as significant as this one—develop in a more ambiguous fashion. This process was hardly unique to the Clinton administration. White House meetings often result in participants, as well as those they inform, having conflicting understandings of what the administration has decided. Policy entrepreneurs use presidential statements to push forward an issue that remains highly contentious in the bureaucracy. Each step alone seems trivial. But cumulatively, they can result in momentous policies.

As for motive, Walesa and Havel may well have made a huge impression on a president open to emotional appeals. Still, given that Clinton cared so much about the fate of Russian reform, Walesa's appeal to bring Poland and other Central European nations into the West could hardly have been sufficient. Rather, Clinton's motive was probably more complex, and he probably had only a vague idea of when he himself made the formal commitment to expand NATO. For Clinton, the appeal by the Central Europeans to erase the line drawn for them in 1945, the need to demonstrate U.S. leadership at a time when others questioned that leadership, the domestic political consequences of the choice, and his own Wilsonian orientation toward spreading liberalism combined by the second half of 1994—if not earlier—to produce a presidential preference favoring expansion. Once Clinton spoke out in favor of NATO expansion in January 1994, expansion supporters within the administration had what they needed to begin to turn rhetoric into reality.

DISCUSSION QUESTIONS

1. What prompted President Clinton to consider NATO expansion in the first place?
2. Who within the administration was a strong supporter of expansion?
3. What type of policy did the various bureaucracies favor regarding the expansion of NATO?
4. What exactly was President Clinton's position on NATO expansion?
5. Considering the expansion timetable as it developed, whose advice did President Clinton appear to pay most attention to?
6. How did the changing make-up of the State Department affect the debate on expanding NATO?
7. How does the example of the NATO expansion debates illustrate the bureaucratic politics model and the influence of outside factors on presidential decision-making?

NOTES

1. For information on Secretary Christopher's intervention at the June 1993 NAC meeting, see *U.S. Department of State Dispatch* 4, no. 25:3.

2. Anthony Lake, "From Containment to Enlargement," *Vital Speeches of the Day* 60 (October 15, 1993): 13–19.

3. For quotations from the Talbott memo, see Michael Dobbs, "Wider Alliance Would Increase U.S. Commitments," *Washington Post*, July 5, 1995, A1, 16; Michael R. Gordon, "U.S. Opposes Move to Rapidly Expand NATO Membership," *New York Times*, January 2, 1994, A1, 7.

4. The official is quoted in Elaine Sciolino, "U.S. to Offer Plan on a Role in NATO for Ex-Soviet Bloc," *New York Times*, October 21, 1993, A1, 9.

5. Elaine Sciolino, "3 Players Seek a Director for Foreign Policy Story," *New York Times*, November 8, 1993, A1, 12; Stephens Kinzer, "NATO Favors U.S. Plan for Ties with the East, but Timing Is Vague," *New York Times*, October 22, 1993, A1, 8.

6. *U.S. Department of State Dispatch*, December 13, 1993.

7. *U.S. Department of State Dispatch*, December 13, 1993.

8. See Henry Kissinger, "Not This Partnership," *Washington Post*, November 24, 1993, A17; Zbigniew Brzezinski, "A Bigger—and Safer—Europe," *New York Times*, December 1, 1993, A23; and James A. Baker III, "Expanding to the East: A New NATO," *Los Angeles Times*, December 5, 1993, M2.

9. Remarks by the president in a photo-op with the Netherlands prime minister Ruud Lubbers, January 4, 1994, *Public Papers* (1994): 5–6.

10. On the Brussels statement of January 10, 1994, see *U.S. Department of State Dispatch Supplement*, January 1994, 3–4; for the Prague remarks, see Clinton, *Public Papers*, bk. I (1994), 40.

11. For his exchange with reporters in Warsaw after meeting with Walesa on July 6, 1994, see Clinton, *Public Papers* (1994), 1206.

12. *U.S. Department of State Dispatch*, September 12, 1994, 597–98.

13. Quoted in Dobbs, "Wider Alliance." Confirmed by author interviews with numerous officials who attended the meeting.

14. Zbigniew Brzezinski, "A Plan for Europe," *Foreign Affairs* 74 (January/February 1995): 27–28.

20

President Bush and the Invasion of Iraq

Presidential Leadership and Thwarted Goals

James P. Pfiffner

The 2003 Iraq War is a case study in winning the military battle but losing the war. President George W. Bush demonstrated impressive political skills in taking the country to war, despite the reservations of former generals, members of his father's administration, and the doubts of contemporary military leaders. But President Bush's political victory in taking the country to war and the quick military defeat of Saddam's army were undercut by a long postwar insurgency in Iraq, the rise of Iran's influence in the Middle East, and the establishment of ISIS in a broken Iraq. This case study will examine President Bush's campaign for war, his use of intelligence to make his case, and the longer-term consequences of the war.

Many factors determine a decision to go to war, and in the United States, the personality and character of the president as leader of the country and commander in chief of the armed forces are particularly important. To be sure, Congress is constitutionally the institution that must "declare war," but political and governmental dynamics most often favor the president. The president has the advantage of being a single decisionmaker directing the many bureaucracies that gather intelligence and prepare for war. Virtually all intelligence available to Congress originates in executive branch agencies. Publicly, the president can command the attention of the media and strongly shape public perceptions of the national security situation of the United States.

In the case of the Iraq War of 2003, several characteristics of President Bush strongly influenced his war decisions: (1) his disdain for an orderly policy process by making decisions without informing his top national security advisers. For instance, he never held a National Security Council (NSC) meeting to consider the pros and cons of his decision to go to war in Iraq; (2) his self-certainty reinforced by his religious convictions. In 2004, he declared "I'm a war president."[1] He wanted to "rid the world of evil."[2] "This is what I was put on earth for. I'm here for a reason."[3] This moral certitude served him well in convincing the country to go to war with Iraq, but it led him to dismiss advice about the potential consequences of the U.S. war; and (3) his refusal to consult with his top military and civilian officials before making key decisions, for instance, his decisions to appoint Paul Bremer as his viceroy in Iraq and reverse two important NSC decisions.

This chapter will first examine President Bush' public campaign to convince the nation that war with Iraq was necessary. It will then examine his use of intelligence to support his arguments. Finally, it will explore the longer-term consequences of the U.S. war in Iraq.

EARLY PLANNING AND BUILDING SUPPORT FOR WAR

Immediately after the atrocities of 9/11, President Bush deliberated with his war cabinet and decided to go to war in Afghanistan to retaliate against Al Qaeda and to defeat the Taliban, which had harbored Al Qaeda as it plotted its attack on the United States. They also considered attacking Iraq, despite its noninvolvement with the 9/11 attacks. The decision to go to war in Afghanistan was made in full consultation with his advisers, in contrast to the decision to invade Iraq, which was made over the course of more than a year and was characterized by incremental and fragmented decision-making.

But President Bush also decided shortly after 9/11 to begin planning for war with Iraq. In a secret order on September 17, he ordered Secretary of Defense Donald Rumsfeld to begin to plan for war to depose the Iraqi dictator, Saddam Hussein.[4] In December 2001, as the U.S. invasion of Afghanistan was beginning, Bush ordered U.S. General Tommy Franks to work on plans for war with Iraq. Franks was surprised because he thought that the war in Afghanistan was not yet won and that the United States would be stretched thin fighting two wars at once. But the president insisted, and Franks did what he was told, briefing President Bush several times on war plans in the spring of 2002. The United States then began to divert material, personnel, intelligence, and resources from Afghanistan to prepare for a war with Iraq. Despite Bush's declarations that "I have no war plans on my desk,"[5] in March he told National Security Adviser Condoleezza Rice, "We're taking him out."[6]

President Bush began to prepare the American public for war with Iraq in his State of the Union speech in January 2002 when he raised the specter of an "Axis of Evil" comprising Iraq, Iran, and North Korea. He argued that these were rogue nations that sponsored terrorism and had to be stopped. The next major public pronouncement by the president on national security and Iraq came at the June 1, 2002 commencement address he gave at the U.S. Military Academy at West Point. The president said, "The war on terror will not be won on the defensive. We must take the battle to the enemy. . . ."[7] Bush was signaling a shift in U.S. national security policy so that it would not be necessary for a military threat to be imminent, in which case a preemptive war would be justified. The United States would now use preventive war to assure that an enemy would not be able to get to the point where war would be imminent. "If we wait for threats to fully materialize, we will have waited too long."[8] This is the sense in which the Iraq war has been called a "war of choice," rather than of necessity.

Bush had been urging British Prime Minister Tony Blair to join the United States in its war with Iraq, and in July 2002, Richard Dearlove, director of British foreign intelligence (MI6), wrote a memo of a secret meeting he had with his U.S. counterparts. He wrote: "Military action was now seen as inevitable. Bush wanted to remove Saddam, through military action, justified by the conjunction of terrorism and WMD. But the intelligence and facts were being fixed around the policy. . . . There was little discussion in Washington of the aftermath after military action."[9]

Although the wisdom of attacking Iraq was not the subject of any full NSC meeting, Bush did receive warnings about the negative consequences of going to war. In July of 2002, director of policy planning at the State Department, Richard Haass, went to Condoleezza Rice, the president's national security adviser, to express his concern that the president was moving toward war with Iraq and that it would be a mistake. Rice told him that "the president had made up his mind."[10] In August, Secretary of State Colin Powell had dinner with the president to warn him about the dangers of war with Iraq. Powell warned that a war would destroy the Iraqi government. "There will be no government. There will be civil disorder. You break it, you own it. . . . You'll have twenty-five million Iraqis standing around looking at each other."[11]

Public warning also came from Anthony Zinni, retired marine and commander of CENTCOM, who continued to consult with the CIA. Zinni was skeptical of Bush's claims that Saddam was stockpiling weapons of mass destruction (WMD). "In my time at CENTCOM, I watched the intelligence and never—not once—did it say 'He had WMD.'"[12] Even Brent Scowcroft, national security adviser to George H. W. Bush (41) and James A. Baker, Bush 41's secretary of state wrote op-ed article urging caution. Scowcroft wrote an article in the *Wall Street Journal* entitled "Don't Attack Saddam," in which he argued that it would be "very expensive" and that "there is a virtual consensus in the world against an attack on Iraq at this time."[13]

But President Bush was not convinced by their entreaties or Colin Powell's warning. On August 26, 2002, Vice President Cheney told the Veterans of Foreign Wars, "Many of us are convinced that Saddam will acquire nuclear weapons fairly soon. . . . There is no doubt he is amassing [WMD] to use against our friends, against our allies, and against us."[14] In the fall of 2002, the White House began a strong public push for war with Iraq, organizing the White House Iraq Group (WHIG) to prepare the American public for war. Chief of Staff Andrew Card explained the timing of the public push. "From a marketing point of view, you don't introduce new products in August."[15]

The arguments for war were based on Saddam's possession of WMD, referring to chemical, biological, and nuclear weapons. It was not unreasonable to believe that Saddam possessed such weapons. He had been working on them in the 1980s, and he had used chemical weapons on Iraqis who opposed his rule. When UN weapons inspectors went to Iraq after the U.S. victory over Saddam in the Gulf War of 1991, they found stores of chemical and biological weapons and discovered that he was well on the way to building a nuclear bomb. The weapons inspectors then destroyed all of his WMD before leaving Iraq.

Thus, the president and his administration were not unrealistic in asserting that Saddam had reconstituted his WMD. The problem was that there was very little evidence for their claims, which will be examined in the next section.

In a major address on October 7, 2002, President Bush told the nation that Saddam had WMD and was preparing to use them on the United States. Iraq "possesses and produces chemical and biological weapons. . . . The evidence indicates that Iraq is reconstituting its nuclear weapons program. . . . it could have a nuclear weapon in less than a year. . . . we cannot wait for the final proof—the smoking gun—that could come in the form of a mushroom cloud."[16] His speech came a month before the congressional elections of 2002, and the president wanted to put pressure on Congress to adopt a resolution to authorize him to go to war against Iraq. Bush was successful, and within two weeks, Congress passed a joint resolution authorizing the president to go to war in Iraq.[17]

Secretary of State Colin Powell had convinced Bush to seek approval of war with Iraq from the United Nations Security Council. In his address to the Security Council on September 12, Bush urged them to take action. After his address, he framed the issue as a clear obligation of the United Nations to support the United States, "I'm a patient man. . . . But if they cannot bring themselves together to disarm Saddam Hussein, then we will lead a coalition to do just that."[18] If the United Nations did not back the U.S. plan, Bush said it would be "an ineffective debating society" that will be "irrelevant."[19] The Security Council issued the strongly worded

Resolution 1441 on November 8 that ordered Iraq to account for its WMD and allow UN inspectors to ensure they were gone.

As the administration continued to advocate war against Iraq and the military began to deploy troops and assets for the coming war, the UN inspectors went into Iraq. In December, Iraq issued a report on its weapons, but National Security Adviser Rice called the December Iraqi account of its weapons a "12,200 page lie." She argued that the declaration was "intended to cloud and confuse the true picture of Iraq's arsenal. . . . and constitutes a material breach of the United Nations Security Council Resolution 1441. . . ."[20] As the initial reporting date for the UN inspectors (January 27, 2003) approached, the Bush administration became increasingly impatient with the inability of the UN inspection team to locate evidence of Iraq's WMD.

The UN weapons inspectors, headed by Hans Blix, had virtual carte blanch to search Iraq, and they presented four reports to the United Nations, all concluding that no WMD could be found. Their final report was made on March 7 with negative results. These reports were rejected by President Bush who declared "Inspection teams do not need more time or more personnel."[21] On March 17, President Bush insisted that the UN inspectors "should leave Iraq immediately."[22]

The lack of any comprehensive deliberation in the Bush administration about war in Iraq was striking. Paul Pillar noted "the absence of any identifiable process for making the decision to go to war."[23] CIA Director George Tenet agreed: "There was never a serious debate" about options for continuing to contain Iraq.[24]

On March 19, the war began.

THE USE OF INTELLIGENCE

In their efforts to take the country to war with Iraq, President Bush and Vice President Cheney made a number of claims about U.S. intelligence findings. Some of these claims were supported by U.S. intelligence agencies and some were not. The most important claims turned out not to be true. Arguably, they seriously misled the U.S. public in their quest for war. This section will examine the most important claims that convinced Congress and the American people that war with Iraq was necessary. The president claimed that there was a close link between Saddam and Al Qaeda, that Iraq possessed chemical and biological weapons that it intended to use against the United States, and that Saddam had an active nuclear program under way. In addition, intelligence was politicized in the sense that it was used to support the president's preferred policy outcome rather than being used to inform policy choices.

Asserted Link with Al Qaeda

Immediately after the attacks of 9/11, President Bush believed that Saddam Hussein was connected to the attacks; after making this claim repeatedly, a majority of the American public believed it. The problem was that there was virtually no evidence of this link, and the CIA argued that there was no active link. Within twenty-four hours of the attacks, President Bush told Richard Clarke several times to look into "any shred" of evidence that Saddam was behind the attack, despite Clarke's report that the intelligence community had concluded that Al Qaeda perpetrated the atrocities.[25] The administration's argument for going to war in Iraq was based in part on its conclusion that Saddam was allied with Al Qaeda—a conclusion that was explicitly challenged by the intelligence community, especially the CIA and the Bureau of Intelligence and Research of the State Department.

CIA officer Paul Pillar, who was in charge of coordinating the intelligence community's assessment of Iraq from 2000 to 2005, concluded: "the greatest discrepancy between the administration's public statements and the intelligence community's judgments concerned . . . the relationship between Saddam and al Qaeda. The enormous attention devoted to this subject did not reflect any judgment by intelligence officials that there was or was likely to be anything like the 'alliance' the administration said existed."[26]

On October 7, 2002, in his major speech about the need for war, President Bush said, "We've learned that Iraq has trained al-Qaeda members in bomb-making and poisons and deadly gasses."[27] The main source of this claim was the interrogation of Ibn al-Shaykh al-Libi, a Libyan captured in Pakistan, who had been a senior member of Al Qaeda. However, in February of 2002, the Defense Intelligence Agency (DIA) had judged that al-Libi's statements were suspect because he could not provide credible details about the types of weapons involved, the Iraqis he dealt with, or the location of the meetings. In addition, his claims were made under torture.[28]

Chemical and Biological Weapons

Suspicions that Saddam had significant quantities of chemical weapons in 2002 were based on the facts that he had large quantities of chemical munitions in the 1980s and that he had used them internally against the Kurds and in his war with Iran. Saddam's chemical and biological warfare capacity formed much of the basis for the Bush administration's argument that Saddam's WMD were a threat to the United States. President Bush said on September 26, 2002 that "the Iraqi regime possesses biological and chemical weapons. The Iraqi regime is building the facilities necessary to make more biological and chemical weapons."[29]

A report by the DIA from September 2002, however, voiced some skepticism and pointed out that the WMD were destroyed after the 1991 Gulf War. It stated: "There is no reliable information on whether Iraq is producing and stockpiling chemical weapons, or where Iraq has—or will—establish its chemical warfare agent production facilities."[30] After searching Iraq for WMD, Inspector David Kay reported that with respect to chemical weapons, "Iraq's large-scale capability to develop, produce, and fill new CW munitions was reduced—if not entirely destroyed—during Operations Desert Storm and Desert Fox and 13 years of UN sanctions and UN inspections"[31]

The primary, contemporary evidence for the biological weapons and mobile labs claim that Colin Powell asserted in his February 5 UN speech was Curveball, who was an Iraqi defector held by the Germans.[32] Despite doubts about his reliability, the CIA assured Colin Powell before his UN speech that the sources were multiple and credible. Yet senior German officials of the Federal Intelligence Service said that they had warned U.S. intelligence officials in the fall of 2002 that Curveball was unreliable. After hearing the U.S. claims about chemical and biological weapons, the Germans said, "We were shocked. . . . We had always told them it was not proven. . . . It was not hard intelligence."[33]

In May 2003, after the initial military phase of the war, the United States sent nine bioweapons experts, each with ten years of professional experience, to examine two trailers that had been found that were thought to be mobile biological weapons labs. After a careful examination, the technical team reported back to the CIA on May 27, 2003 that the trailers were not designed for bioweapons production but rather for producing hydrogen for weather balloons.[34]

Thus, although the premise that Saddam possessed chemical and biological weapons was plausible, there was no hard evidence for it, and policymakers ignored several warnings that undercut their convictions.

Nuclear Weapons

Although Saddam's supposed participation in 9/11 was a strong political argument for revenge against Iraq, the argument that Saddam was close to obtaining nuclear weapons was the most compelling argument for war. Even those most skeptical about the need for war and its consequences had to be shaken by the possibility of Saddam with nuclear weapons. Therefore, the administration played the nuclear card with significant effects in its public campaign for war.

The suspicion that Saddam was in the process of reconstituting his nuclear capacity was not unreasonable. After the 1991 Gulf War, it was discovered that Saddam had made much more progress toward a nuclear capacity than either the United Nations or the CIA had suspected. That capacity was destroyed by U.S. forces in the war and by UN inspectors after the war. Given Saddam's record, it seemed reasonable that he would again seek nuclear weapons. The problem was that the main evidence upon which the administration relied was dubious: Saddam's attempted purchase of yellow cake (uranium oxide) from Niger and Saddam's attempted purchase of aluminum tubes that the administration claimed were intended to be used as nuclear centrifuges.

In his State of the Union speech on January 28, 2003, President Bush said, "The British government has learned that Saddam Hussein recently sought significant quantities of uranium [necessary for nuclear weapons] from Africa."[35] The claim was also included in the CIA's National Intelligence Estimate (NIE) of early October 2002. The State Department's Bureau of Intelligence and Research, however, wrote in the NIE: "the claims of Iraqi pursuit of natural uranium in Africa are, in INR's assessment, highly dubious."[36] George Tenet had previously warned that the Niger story was probably not true and had to convince the president's advisers to take it out of the president's October 7 speech in Cincinnati.[37]

The problem was that the documents used as evidence were forged and not authentic. The letterhead of one letter was from the military government that had been replaced before the 1999 date on the letter, and the signature on the letter indicated the name of a foreign ministry official who had left his position in 1989. The forgery was made public on March 7, 2003, by Mohamed El Baradei who was director of the International Atomic Energy Agency (IAEA), who reported the findings to the UN Security Council.[38]

In early 2001, a CIA analyst discovered that Iraq tried to buy thousands of highly specialized aluminum tubes. An April 10, 2001, CIA report asserted that the tubes "have little use other than for a uranium enrichment program."[39] The Energy Department, however, said that the tubes were the wrong size for centrifuges and that the openness of the solicitation by Iraq indicated that the tubes were intended for conventional weapons. In June of 2001, a shipment of the tubes was seized in Jordan, and the United States assigned its best nuclear centrifuge engineers to examine the case. The Energy Departments (and British) experts concluded that the tubes were meant for conventional weapons purposes, though the CIA still maintained that they were intended for nuclear centrifuges.[40]

On September 8, 2002, the story of the tubes was leaked to the *New York Times*, but without any of the reservations expressed by the nuclear experts. Cheney and Rice, who expressed certainty that the tubes were intended for nuclear purposes, quickly confirmed the validity of the leak. Rice confirmed that the tubes "are only really suited for nuclear weapons programs."[41] The claim that the aluminum tubes were intended to be nuclear centrifuges was included in the NIE of early October and played an important role in convincing members of Congress to vote for the AUMF in October 2002. But the Energy and State Departments both dissented in the NIE and said the tubes were not likely meant for nuclear purposes.

Politicizing Intelligence

In its pursuit of public support for regime change in Iraq, the Bush administration may also have tried to politicize the intelligence process by putting pressure on intelligence analysts to arrive at the conclusions favored by the administration. During the summer and fall of 2002, Vice President Cheney made multiple visits to CIA headquarters in Langley in order to ask sharp questions about CIA analysis of intelligence relating to Iraq. Senator Rockefeller, ranking minority member of the Senate Select Intelligence Committee, concluded that there was an atmosphere of "intense pressure in which the intelligence community officials were asked to render judgments on matters relating to Iraq when the most senior officials in the Bush administration had already forcefully and repeatedly stated their conclusions publicly."[42]

Confirmation that pressure was applied to the Intelligence Community with respect to the claimed link between Saddam and Al Qaeda came in a special report by a team headed by Richard J. Kerr, former deputy director of central intelligence. With respect to the claimed link between Saddam and Al Qaeda, the report concluded:

> In the case of al-Qa'ida, the constant stream of questions aimed at finding links between Saddam and the terrorist network caused analysts to take what they termed a "purposely aggressive approach" in conducting *exhaustive and repetitive searches* for such links. *Despite the pressure,* however, the Intelligence Community remained firm in its assessment that no operational or collaborative relationship existed.[43] (emphasis added)

Perhaps the most authoritative evidence that policymakers tried to politicize intelligence prior to the Iraq War is the testimony of Paul R. Pillar. Pillar was the national intelligence officer who had responsibility for Middle East intelligence from 2002 to 2005 and directed the coordination of the intelligence community's assessments of Iraq. In an article in *Foreign Affairs,* Pillar charged that (1) "official intelligence analysis was not relied on in making even the most significant national security decisions"; (2) "intelligence was misused publicly to justify decisions already made"; and (3) "the intelligence community's own work was politicized."[44]

David Kay, who had led UN WMD inspectors after the Gulf War in 1991, led the Iraq Survey Group of 1,400 inspectors in 2003 to find the WMD that had been the justification for the U.S. invasion. On January 28, 2004, in testimony before the Senate Armed Services Committee, Kay said, "Let me begin by say-ing that we were almost all wrong about the presence of WMDs in Iraq."[45] A follow-up search led by Charles Duelfer came to the same conclusion.

In summary, President Bush argued that there was a link between Saddam and Al Qaeda, despite CIA evidence and arguments to the contrary. Although there was little contemporary evidence that Iraq possessed chemical weap-ons, President Bush and the allied government believed that it did. Although Saddam had used biological weapons before the 1991 Gulf War, there was little evidence that he still had that capacity. The only evidence for Saddam's possessing nuclear weapons was claims about yellowcake and aluminum tubes, and the administration used those claims with much more confi-dence than the intelligence warranted. Overall, the Bush administration used misleading evidence in an overconfident way to convince Americans that Saddam was a serious threat to the United States, when he was not.

MILITARY VICTORY, OCCUPATION, AND INSURGENCY

The off-the-shelf previous plans for war in Iraq called for many more troops than the United States used in its initial invasion. Previous planning for a U.S. invasion of Iraq had been conducted by General Anthony Zinni, who oversaw the development of plans for a U.S. war with Iraq, which called for 380,000 troops and an occupation of up to ten years.[46] General Tommy Franks had been involved with preparing the troop levels for the plans and told Rumsfeld in December 2001 that 385,000 troops would be necessary for a successful war in Iraq.[47] Colin Powell had also advised Bush that more troops would be necessary.[48] Secretary of Defense Rumsfeld, however, wanted to change the paradigm for war fighting and accomplish more with fewer troops by maximizing mobility, intelligence, and the use of new technology. Rumsfeld thought that a much smaller force would be sufficient for military success.[49]

Bush overruled the generals and the United States ended up invading with 67,700 troops plus allied forces.[50] The number of troops was suf-ficient for the initial military victory, but was woefully inadequate for the following occupation. After attacking Iraqi air defenses with 600 cruise missiles and 1,500 air stories on the first day, U.S. troops moved into Iraq and pushed on to Baghdad, defeating Saddam's military. Though there was resistance, and U.S. forces took casualties, many Iraqi troops abandoned their defensive positions.

Paul Bremer Appointed

President Bush then made the fateful decision to replace Jay Garner, the experienced former general who had been appointed to conduct Phase IV of the war, that is, returning the country to normal functioning after the military victory. With command experience at the end of the Gulf war of 1990–91, Garner was well qualified to do the job. But Bush decided to replace Garner with Paul Bremer, who had State Department experience but who had never been in Iraq. Bush made the decision at lunch with Bremer at the White House and was to meet with his advisers to consider the appointment. He immediately announced his decision, and when his top aides joined them, Bush said, "I don't know whether we need this meeting at all. Jerry and I just had it."[51] Colin Powell recalled "I was stunned," "the plan was for Zal to go back. He was the one guy who knew this place better than anyone." There were "no full deliberations. And you suddenly discover, gee, maybe that wasn't so great, we should have thought about it a little longer."[52]

Bremer was appointed to direct the Coalition Provisional Authority (CPA) and have control of all U.S. policy in Iraq, military and civilian. He considered himself to be responsible only to the president and, in effect, the U.S. viceroy in Iraq. Bremer thought that the Iraqi state was in chaos and that it would take some time before a new political system was able to govern Iraq democratically. Bremer said that Bush had told him in a private meeting on May 6 that "we're going to take our time to get it right."[53] In effect, this changed the U.S. role from liberator to occupier. The decision to extend the U.S. presence in Iraq was made without consultation with Condi Rice, Colin Powell, or Donald Rumsfeld (who objected after the fact).

Coalition Provisional Orders 1 and 2

Bremer then made two decisions that would have seriously negative consequences for the United States: de-Baathification of the government of Iraq and disbanding its army.

An NSC meeting on March 10, 2003 had come to the consensus that the top levels of Saddam's government had to go, but that mid-level managers and technicians had to stay in their positions to run the technical infrastructure of the country. The military understanding of the purge was that it would apply to the top *two* levels of the Baath party, those who were clearly leaders and close to Saddam, which amounted to perhaps 6,000 people. But when Bremer issued Coalition Provisional Authority (CPA) Order Number One, he interpreted the de-Baathification policy to exclude the top *four* levels of the Baath Party as well as the top three levels in each government ministry.[54] This decision effectively eliminated the leadership and top technical capacity for universities, hospitals, transportation, electricity, and communications. Although Bremer said that the order would affect only about 20,000 people, the total amounted to 85,000 to 100,000 people.[55] According to George Tenet, this included "forty thousand schoolteachers, who had joined the Baath Party simply to keep their jobs."[56]

Others in the administration did not believe that there was any consensus or even knowledge of the change in policy. CIA Director George Tenet said, "In fact, we knew nothing about it until de-Baathification was a fait accompli . . . . Clearly, this was a critical policy decision, yet there was no NSC Principals meeting to debate the move."[57] The CIA station chief of Baghdad, when he learned of the decision, warned Bremer that he (Bremer) was about to fire the key technicians who operated the electric, water, and transportation infrastructure of the country. He told Bremer, "By nightfall, you'll have driven 30,000 to 50,000 Baathists underground. And in six months, you'll really regret this."[58]

Bremer put Ahmad Challabi in charge of de-Baathification. Challabi was a Shiite Muslim with close ties to Iran, and took a hard line against former Sunni members of the government by installing Shia Muslims in their places. This began the suppression of Sunnis, many of whom would join the insurrection against the U.S. occupation and eventually join the Islamic State in Iraq and Syria (ISIS).

In a NSC meeting on March 12, 2003, there was a consensus that the U.S. forces would use the Iraqi Army to help provide internal and external security in postwar Iraq.[59] Yet on May 23, CPA head Paul Bremer issued CPA Order Number Two that "dissolved" the Ministry of Defense and the military services. The security forces included 385,000 in the armed forces, 285,000 in the Interior Ministry (police), and 50,000 in presidential security units.[60] Of course those in police and military units who were Saddam's top enforcers (e.g., the Special Republican Guard) had to be barred from working in the new government. But many officers in the army were professional soldiers, and the rank-and-file enlisted soldiers constituted a source of stability and order. The disbanding threw hundreds of thousands out of work and immediately created a large pool of unemployed and armed men who felt humiliated and hostile to the U.S. occupiers. According to one U.S. officer in Baghdad, "When they disbanded the military, and announced we were occupiers—that was it. Every moderate, every person that had leaned toward us, was furious."[61]

How did this crucial reversal come about? In a NSC meeting on May 23, Bremer "informed the president of the plan [de-Baathification] in a video teleconference."[62] President Bush did not formally decide to reverse his decision of March 12, but Bremer interpreted his lack of questions as approval. Importantly, Colin Powell was out of town when the decision was made, and he was not informed about it, much less consulted. "I talked to Rice and said, 'Condi, what happened?' And her reaction was: 'I was surprised too, but it is a decision that has been made and the president is standing behind Jerry's decision. Jerry is the guy on the ground.' And there was no further debate about it."[63] This was Bremer's first time in Iraq, and he had been "on the ground" for only eleven days when he gave the order.

The order had not been cleared through any normal policy process, nor had Bremer consulted the CIA, State Department, or NSC leaders.[64] General McKiernan's (then head of coalition forces in Iraq) said that he was not consulted. "I never saw that order and never concurred." Central Command in Florida was also surprised by the decision.[65] Paul Pillar, national intelligence officer for the Near East and South Asia, said that the intelligence community was not consulted about the decision.[66]

In addition to the dismantling of Iraqi security forces, the decision bred resentment among the Iraqi Army Officer Corps, many of whom had been trained in U.S. professional military training programs. Before the U.S. invasion, U.S. military and intelligence representatives had told senior Iraqi military commanders that if they did not join the resistance to the U.S. invasion, they would be taken care of and would have military roles in the post-Saddam Iraq. When CPA Director Paul Bremer disbanded the Iraqi Army, U.S. military leaders were appalled. But more importantly, the Iraqi officers felt outraged, betrayed, and angry. They then joined the resistance to the U.S. occupation.[67]

Both of these key decisions fueled the coming insurgency by (1) alienating hundreds of thousands of Iraqis who could not support themselves or their families, (2) undermining the normal infrastructure necessary for social and economic activity, (3) ensuring that there was not sufficient security to carry on normal life, and (4) creating insurgents who were angry at the United States, many of whom had weapons and were trained to use them.

Rise of the Insurgency

After the military victory, Donald Rumsfeld and military leaders expected that after the military victory over Saddam the United States would begin drawing down the U.S. troop presence in Iraq and would turn Iraq over to an indigenous government. But when President Bush declared "mission accomplished" on the aircraft on May 1, he declared that "the transition from dictatorship to democracy will take time."[68] In making this declaration, Bush was signaling that the military would not leave Iraq as planned, but would stay to ensure that the new government was a democracy. Bush made this decision without conducting a NSC meeting and without consulting Powell or Rumsfeld.[69] U.S. military and intelligence planners had predicted the rise of an insurgency, but their warnings were ignored by Rumsfeld.[70]

One of the first signs of trouble after the U.S. military victory was the looting of the National Museum by Iraqi looters and the failure of U.S. troops to stop the looting. This signaled that the United States was seemingly not concerned about law and order or preserving the historical heritage of Iraq. Donald Rumsfeld dismissed the looting as "stuff happens."[71]

The broader context of these initial decisions was the bitter enmity that had developed between Sunni and Shiite Muslims in Iraq. Sunnis were a minority in Iraq (about 20 percent of the population), but Saddam and the Baath Party ensured that they controlled the government completely and kept down the Shiites, who composed about 60 percent of the Iraqi population. (Kurds, who were also Sunni but wanted independence from Saddam's government, made up the other major ethnic/religious portion of the population.)[72] With Saddam gone, the Shiites saw an opportunity to rule the country and turn the tables on the Sunnis. After elections that the Sunnis boycotted, Shiites dominated the legislature, and Nouri al-Maliki became the prime minister. The United States was backing the government of Iraq, which was now dominated by Shiites. The United States pressured Maliki and the Shiites to create a government open to Sunnis and not extract revenge for years of oppression, but sectarian hostility was stronger than U.S. admonitions.

With Sunnis regarding U.S. soldiers as an occupying force, they began an insurgency to drive the United States out of Iraq. At first, Rumsfeld denied that there was any insurgency, but in the fall of 2003, after many U.S. casualties, it became clear that a major insurgency, using guerilla tactics, was under way. Over the next two years, U.S. casualties continued to mount, and it became clear that the United States was not "winning," but was under continuous attack by the mostly Sunni insurgents.

Iraq Sunnis resented Maliki and the Shiite-dominated government, which was taking revenge for years of oppression. During this guerilla warfare period, Sunni extremists in northern Iraq and southern Syria declared themselves Al Qaeda in Iraq (AQI), though they were denounced by the original Al Qaeda in Afghanistan. The AQI vicious attacks on the Shiite government and the infamous destruction of the Golden Mosque of Samarra succeeded in provoking the Shiite government to take more repressive measures against Sunnis. AQI calculated that the predictable Shiite repression of Sunnis would drive moderate Sunnis into the arms of AQI as their only protection against Shiite repression.[73]

In 2006, the war dragged on, with the United States continuing to take casualties and the U.S. public opinion turning against the war. President Bush decided to reevaluate U.S. options and calculated that that U.S. efforts could be salvaged by increasing the number of U.S. troops. After replacing Rumsfeld as secretary of defense, he appointed General David Petraeus to replace General Casey in Iraq to implement a counterinsurgency strategy (COIN). This approach stressed providing more security to the Iraqi civilian population and closer interaction of U.S. troops with Iraqis. Petreaus was given additional twenty to thirty thousand troops to implement his strategy in 2007, bringing total U.S. military forces up to more than 165,000 (with 155,000 contractors, 26,800 of them American).[74]

As he was pursuing the counterinsurgency strategy, Petraeus was able to recruit Sunnis to support the United States by paying them well and convincing them that AQI had to be defeated. This was called the "Anbar Awakening." The Sunnis were so enraged by the violence and atrocities of AQI, such as beheadings, that they decided to side with the United States against AQI extremists. In addition, the Shiite religious leader Moqtada al-Sadr decided to stop his Shiite followers in Baghdad from persecuting Sunnis.

These steps led to a sharp decrease in U.S. casualties and Iraqi civilian deaths. This gave President Bush the breathing room to announce a gradual drawdown of U.S. troops in Iraq. In implementing this drawdown, President Bush signed a Status of Forces Agreement (SOFA) with Prime Minister Maliki, in which he agreed that all U.S. forces would leave Iraq by the end of 2011. Maliki refused to agree to a SOFA provision that would ensure that any U.S. soldiers accused of a crime would be tried in a U.S. justice system rather than Iraqi courts. Without such a SOFA, President Bush would not agree to extend the U.S. presence in Iraq. President Obama fulfilled the agreement that Bush had made by withdrawing U.S. troops by the end of 2011. Critics of President Obama, however, criticize him for fulfilling Bush's pledge and not convincing Maliki to allow U.S. troops to stay in Iraq after 2011 in order to thwart the rise of ISIS.[75] But if 165,000 U.S. troops could not stop Maliki from suppression of Sunnis, it is not clear how a much lower level of troops could have succeeded.

Without the presence of U.S. troops, Prime Minister Maliki did not keep his agreement to conduct his government in a way that was open to Sunni citizens; rather, he allowed his government officials to purge Sunnis from the government and vigorously oppress them in other ways.[76] This persecution of Sunnis by the Shiite government of Iraq led to the resurgence of AQI, which, in 2013, declared itself the ISIS. ISIS began to occupy territory in northern Iraq and southern Syria and claimed to establish a new Muslim caliphate. ISIS recruited former Sunni military leaders by presenting itself as the only protector of Sunnis from the depredations of the Shiite government of Iraq.

ISIS began to hold territory and act as a proto-state, rather than merely insurgents. It ruled its territory viciously and undertook terrorist attacks in Europe and the United States. After ISIS committed many atrocities and acts of terrorism, in 2014 President Obama began to send U.S. troops to aid the coalition of forces fighting ISIS; in 2016, there were more than 4,000 U.S. troops aiding the Iraqi government's fight against ISIS.

CONCLUSION

This case study illustrates the importance of the individual personality and character in presidential leadership. If Vice President Al Gore had been elected in 2000, it is highly unlikely that he would have invaded Iraq. Gore was not committed to regime change in Iraq as was President Bush and his neoconservative advisers, particularly Vice President Cheney. Gore did not see the 1991 Gulf War as a failure because U.S. forces did not drive to Baghdad. Gore would probably have ordered military clashes with Saddam's Iraq in enforcing the no-fly zones, but he would most likely have heeded the warnings and advice of top U.S. military and national security leaders that a U.S. invasion of Iraq would lead to a quagmire and disaster, as predicted by President George H. W. Bush and Brent Scowcroft in their book, *A World Transformed*:

> Trying to eliminate Saddam, extending the ground war into an occupation of Iraq, would have violated our guideline about not changing objectives in midstream, engaging in "mission creep," and would have incurred incalculable human and political costs.[77]

Despite the large national security bureaucracies in the executive branch, President Bush was able to overcome their skepticism about invading Iraq by appointing people who shared his world view and ensured that his political appointees imposed their will on the career professionals in their agencies. This is the way the American executive branch is designed to work, for good or for ill.

After more than 4,000 U.S. deaths, 30,000 wounded, and more than 200,000 Iraqi deaths at the end of the Bush administration, the United States withdrew from Iraq.[78] Thus, the U.S. invasion of Iraq resulted in the rise of ISIS, a much greater threat to the United States than Saddam ever was. In addition, the removal of Saddam (a Sunni) and the subsequent takeover of the Iraq government by the majority Shiites eliminated Iraq as a major counterweight to Shiite Iran as a major power in the Middle East.[79] A war that was intended to protect the United States by removing Saddam resulted in the rise of ISIS, which threatened to dominate Iraq and increased the influence of Iran, which President Bush had declared a member of the "Axis of Evil."

Military scholar David Kilcullen, who had been an advisor to Secretary of State Rice and senior counterinsurgency advisor to David Petraeus in Iraq, concluded that the U.S. invasion of Iraq was "the greatest strategic screw-up since Hitler's invasion of Russia."[80] Historian Jean Edward Smith concluded in his biography of President Bush, with a focus on the Iraq War: "Rarely in the history of the United States has the nation been so ill-served as during the presidency of George W. Bush. . . . his decision to invade Iraq is easily the worst foreign policy decision ever made by an American president."[81]

DISCUSSION QUESTIONS

1. How does Pfiffner characterize President Bush's decision style regarding the Iraq War?
2. When did President Bush begin planning for war against Iraq?
3. What was the reaction of various national security personnel when they learned that President Bush was developing war plans?
4. What arguments could be advanced for believing that Saddam Hussein possessed WMD?
5. Does Pfiffner argue that there was a deliberative decision process over initiating the Iraq War?
6. What are some examples that Pfiffner advances to illustrate that intelligence was used to advance the arguments for the Iraq War?
7. What were some problems that developed after the military success in Iraq? How was the reconstruction and the appointment of the provisional authority handled?
8. Why does Pfiffner argue that the Iraq War lead to the rise of ISIS?

NOTES

1. Jean Edward Smith, *Bush* (New York: Simon and Schuster, 2016), 245.
2. Ibid., 227.
3. Ibid., 226.
4. Glenn Kessler, "U.S. Decision on Iraq Has Puzzling Past," *Washington Post* (January 12, 2003), 1, A20.
5. Smith, *Bush*, 306.
6. George Packer, *The Assassins' Gate: American in Iraq* (New York: Farrar, Straus and Giroux, 2005), 45.
7. Weekly Compilation of Presidential Documents, *Administration of George W. Bush, 2002*, "Commencement Address at the United States Military Academy in West Point, New York" (June 1, 2002), 944–48.
8. Smith, *Bush*, 307.
9. "Iraq: Prime Minister's Meeting, 23 July," from Mathew Rycroft (a Downing Street foreign policy aide) to David Manning S 195 /02, "Secret and Strictly Personal—UK Eyes Only," printed in the *Times* online at http://downingstreet-memo.com/memotext.html, May 1, 2005, accessed June 21, 2005. According to James Risen, on July 20, 2002, Dearlove spent the day at CIA headquarters in Langley, VA and spoke alone with George Tenet for ninety minutes. James Risen, *State of War* (New York: Free Press, 2006), 114. Dearlove also met with National Security Adviser Rice, Glen Frankel, "From Memos, Insights Into Ally's Doubts on Iraq War," *Washington Post* (June 28, 2005), 1, A10.

10. Smith, *Bush,* 308.

11. Ibid., 340.

12. Ibid., 313.

13. Ibid., 311.

14. Vice President Cheney, Remarks at the Veterans of Foreign Wars Convention (August 26, 2002).

15. Bob Woodward, *Plan of Attack* (New York: Simon and Schuster, 2004), 172.

16. President Bush Outline Iraq Threat, Remarks in Cincinnati, Ohio, October 7, 2002.

17. Authorization for Use of Military Force against Iraq Resolution of 2002 Public La 107–243, 197th Congress.

18. Smith, *Bush,* 318.

19. Ibid., 319.

20. Condoleezza Rice, "Why We Know Iraq Is Lying," *New York Times* (January 23, 2003), A27.

21. Smith, *Bush,* 349.

22. Ibid., 354.

23. Paul Pillar, "The Right Stuff," *The National Interest,* Vol. 91 (Sept/Oct 2007), 55.

24. Scott Shane and Mark Mazzetti, "Ex-CIA Chief, in Book, Assails Cheney on Iraq," *New York Times* (April 27, 2007).

25. Richard A. Clarke, *Against All Enemies* (New York: Free Press, 2004), 30–33.

26. Paul R. Pillar, "Intelligence, Policy, and the War in Iraq." *Foreign Affairs* 85(2) No. 2 (2006): 15–28.

27. President Bush Outline Iraq Threat, Remarks in Cincinnati, Ohio, October 7, 2002.

28. The unclassified statement of the DIA report (DITSUM#044-02) is contained in the letter from Senators John Rockefeller and Carl Levin to Vice Admiral Lowell Jacoby (October 18, 2005), https://fas.org/irp/news/2005/11/DIAletter.102605.pdf.

29. Dana Priest and Walter Pincus, "Bush Certainty on Iraq Arms Went Beyond Analyst's Views," *Washington Post* (June 7, 2003), 1, 17.

30. Kevin Whitelaw, "We Were All Wrong," *U.S. News & World Report* (February 24, 2004); Bruce B. Auster, Mark Mazzetti, and Edward T. Pound, "Truth and consequences," *U.S. News & World Report* (June 9, 2003), 17.

31. David Kay, "Report on the Activities of the Iraq Survey Group to the House Permanent Select Committee on Intelligence and the House Committee on Appropriations, Subcommittee on Defense and the Senate Select Committee on Intelligence," 6. The page reference is to the unclassified report published on the CNN website, http://cnn.allpolitics (accessed October 10, 2003).

32. Richard J. Kerr, "Intelligence and Analysis on Iraq: Issues for the Intelligence Community." *Studies in Intelligence* 49 (2004), issued in July 2004 and declassified in August 2005. MORI DocID: 1245667, July 29. The Kerr Report said that "different descriptions of the same source" often led "analysts to believe they had more confirmatory information from more sources than was actually the case."

33. David Kay raised the interesting question that "if the BND [German intelligence service] thought he was a fabricator why did not they just throw him to the US instead of trying to protect him as if he was a valuable source?" Personal e-mail to the author, December 13, 2005.

34. Joby Warrick, "Lacking Biolabs, Trailers Carried Case for War," *Washington Post* (April 12, 2006), 1; Joby Warrick, "White House Decries Report on Iraqi Trailers," *Washington Post* (April 13, 2006), 18.

35. See Dana Priest and Kaaren DeYoung, "CIA Questioned Documents Linking Iraq, Uranium Ore," *Washington Post* (March 22, 2003), A30; and Seymour M. Hersh, "Who Lied to Whom?" *New Yorker* (March 31, 2003), 41–43.

36. Central Intelligence Agency. 2002a. "Key Judgments [from the October 2002, NIE]: Iraq's continuing Programs for Weapons of Mass Destruction." Declassified excerpts published on the CIA website, www.odci.gove/nic/pubs/research.

37. Paul Pillar who coordinated the intelligence community's analysis of Iraq said, "U.S. intelligence analysts had questioned the credibility of the report making [the Niger] claim, had kept it out of their own unclassified products, and had advised the White House not to use it publicly. But the administration put the claim into the speech anyway. . . ." (Pillar, 2006: 6).

38. Priest and DeYoung, "CIA Questioned Documents Linking Iraq, Uranium Ore,"A30; and Seymour M. Hersh, "Who Lied to Whom?" *New Yorker* (March 31, 2003), 41–43. It is hard to understand how mere incompetence could have allowed the reference to forged documents get into the president's State of the Union speech. One former intelligence official said, "Someone set someone up." (Hersh, 43).

39. David Barstow, William J. Broad, and Jeff Gerth, "How the White House Embraced Disputed Arms Intelligence, *New York Times*, October 3, 2004. For details and documentation, see James P. Pfiffner, "Did President Bush Mislead the Country in His Arguments for War with Iraq?" *Presidential Studies Quarterly* 34(1) (March 2004), 25–46.

40. Central Intelligence Agency "Key Judgments [from October 2002 NIE] Iraq's Continuing Programs for Weapons of Mass destruction." (2003). Declassified excerpts published on the CIA website, http://www.odci.gov/nic/pubs/research. Retrieved October 10, 2003.

41. Barstow, Broad, and Gerth, "How the White House Embraced Disputed Arms Intelligence."

42. *New York Times*, "Excerpts from Two Senators' Views About Prewar Assessments of Iraq," (July 10, 2004), website.

43. Richard J. Kerr, "Intelligence and Analysis on Iraq: Issues for the Intelligence Community," *Studies in Intelligence* Vol. 49. Issued in July 2004 and declassified in August 2005 (MORI DocID: 1245667, July 29, 2004).

44. Pillar, "Intelligence, Policy, and the War in Iraq."

45. Smith, *Bush*, 378.

46. Michael R. Gordon and Bernard E. Trainor, *Cobra II* (New York: Vintage, 2007), 26.

47. Ibid., 28.

48. Bruce Berkowitz, "The Numbers Racket," *The American Interest* II(1) (2006), 132.

49. David Kilcullen, *Blood Year: The Unraveling of Western Counterterrorism* (New York: Oxford University Press, 2016), 13.

50. Amy Balasco, "Troop Levels in the Afghan and Iraq Wars, FY2001-FY2012," Congressional Research Service (July 2, 2009), 9.

51. Smith, *Bush*, 372.

52. Roger Cohen, "The MacArthur Lunch," *New York Times* (27 August 2007), New York Times website. For an analysis of similar decision-making in the Bush White House, see James P. Pfiffner, "Decision Making in the Bush White House," *Presidential Studies Quarterly* (June 2009), 363–84.

5.3 Smith, *Bush*, 371. For the argument that this was a turning point, see Smith, 356–80.

54. Charles Ferguson, *No End in Sight: Iraq's Descent into Chaos* (New York: Public Affairs, 2008), 155; Rajiv Chandrasekaran, *Imperial Life in the Emerald City* (New York: Vintage, 2006), 78–83; Ricks, *Fiasco*, 159–61.

55. Paul Bremer, *My Year in Iraq* (New York: Simon and Schuster, 2007), 39; Thomas Ricks, *Fiasco* (New York, NY: Penguin Press, 2006), 40, 160; Ricardo S. Sanchez, *Wiser in Battle* (New York: Harper, 2008), 184.

56. George Tenet, *At the Center of the Storm* (New York: HarperCollins, 2007), 427.

57. Ibid., 426.

58. Ricks, *Fiasco*, 159.

59. Michael Gordon, "Fateful Choice on Iraq Army Bypassed Debate," *New York Times* (March 17, 2008), 1. Ricks, *Fiasco*, 160; Gordon and Trainor, *Cobra II*, 492.

60. Ricks, *Fiasco*, 162, 192.

61. Ibid., 164.

62. Bremer, *My Year in Iraq*, 57.

63. Gordon, "Fateful Choice on Iraq Army Bypassed Debate," 1. http://www.nytimes.com/2008/03/17/world/middleeast/17bremer.html?_r=1&pagewanted=print

64. Chandrasekaran, *Imperial Life in the Emerald City*, 86–87.

65. Ricks, *Fiasco*, 163

66. Ferguson, *No End in Sight: Iraq's Descent into Chaos*, 219.

67. Chandrasekaran, *Imperial Life in the Emerald City*, 84–89.

68. Smith, *Bush*, 369.

69. Ibid., 371–72.

70. James Fallows, "Blind into Baghdad," *The Atlantic* (January-February 2004); Kilcullen, *Blood Year*, 19.

71. Smith, *Bush*, 362.

72. Sharon Otterman, "Iraq: The Sunnis," Council on Foreign Relations (December 12, 2003), http://www.cfr.org/iraq/iraq-sunnis/p7678.

73. Kilcullen, *Blood Year*, 31–32.

74. Heidi M. Peters, et al., "Department of Defense Contractor and Troop Levels in Iraq and Afghanistan: 2007–2016," Congressional Research Service, 5.

75. Kilcullen, *Blood Year*, 46–47.

76. Ibid., 46–51, 83–85.

77. George H. W. Bush and Brent Scowcroft, *A World Transformed* (New York: Knopf, 1998), 489.

78. For the number of deaths, see Dan Smith, *The Penguin State of the Middle East Atlas* (New York: Penguin Books, 2016), 111.

79. See the analysis by Kilcullen, *Blood Year*, 25–27.

80. Kilcullen, *Blood Year*, 14–16.

81. Smith, *Bush*, xv, 660.

21

Obama's Decision-Making Style

Fred Kaplan

On January 28, 2009, barely a week into his presidency, Barack Obama met with the U.S. military's top generals and admirals on their own turf, inside "the tank," the Joint Chiefs of Staff's conference room on the second floor of the Pentagon. A senior official recalled the new president as "remarkably confident—composed, relaxed, but also deferential, not trying to act too much the commander in chief." Obama walked around the room, introducing himself to everyone; he thanked them and the entire armed forces for their service and sacrifice; then he sat down for a freewheeling discussion of the world's challenges, region by region, crisis by crisis. He was "the man in full," the official said, fluent on every issue, but more than that—a surprise to the officers, who had been leery of this young, inexperienced Democrat—he displayed a deep streak of realism.

At one point, Obama remarked that he was not the sort of person who drives down a street wishing he could park wherever he likes. If he saw an open spot, even one that required some tricky parallel parking, he would be fine with squeezing into it. Obama's meaning was clear: he had been dealt a bad hand (two unpopular wars, alienated allies, the deepest recession in decades), but he would find a way to deal with the world as it was.

Seven years later, many officers and defense officials, including some who were so impressed with Obama at the start, look back at his presidency as following a different style of governing. They laud the historic accomplishments—the Iran nuclear deal, the opening to Cuba, the Trans-Pacific Partnership, the prevention (so far) of another terrorist attack on American soil—and they acknowledge that he has often tried to make the best of bad choices. But too often, they say, he has avoided taking action, waiting for conditions to get better—circling the block and, in his own metaphor, waiting for a better parking spot to open up.

This is a common critique of Obama's foreign policy: that he evades hard decisions, that he is allergic to military force if it risks American casualties or escalation, and that there is often a mismatch between his words and his deeds. "This is a pattern," one retired four-star general said. "He issues stern warnings, then does nothing. It damages American credibility."

Is the charge true? And to the extent that it has some validity, how much can be laid at Obama's feet, and how much should be attributed to the intractability of the problems he has faced? Would a different sort of president have handled the decade's challenges better, and if so, how?

The following examination of key crises and decisions is based on conversations I have had with dozens of officials across the span of Obama's presidency and with twenty mid- to senior-level officials (past and present, almost all on a background basis) interviewed specifically for this [chapter].

THE LESSON OF LIBYA

In December 2009, Obama journeyed to Oslo to receive the Nobel Peace Prize. The award was premature, to say the least, but he used his acceptance speech to lay down the principles of a foreign policy he hoped to follow—a sophisticated grappling with the tensions between idealism and realism. It was a daring speech for a Peace Prize recipient. "To say that force may sometimes be necessary is not a call to cynicism," he said. "It is a recognition of history, the imperfection of man, and the limits of reason." Nations must "adhere to standards that govern the use of force," and a just, lasting peace must be "based on the inherent rights and dignity of every individual." Still, "America cannot act alone," except on matters of vital national interest, and mere lofty rhetoric about human rights only sustains "a crippling status quo." Engagement with repressive regimes may lack "the satisfying purity of indignation," but "no repressive regime can move down a new path unless it has the choice of an open door."

Benjamin Rhodes, Obama's deputy national security adviser for strategic communications, said, "When people ask me to summarize [Obama's] foreign policy, I tell them to take a close look at that speech." Another former top White House official called it "a template to how he approaches problems," a "framework for how he thinks about U.S. power." Whether he followed the template—how he grappled in action with the tensions he recognized in theory—would be, by his own standard, the measure of his presidency.

The early years of Obama's term were taken up with challenges inherited from the Bush administration, especially the wars in Afghanistan and Iraq.

At the start of 2011, however, a string of new problems emerged, as domestic protests against authoritarian leaders broke out across the Middle East. The Ben Ali regime in Tunisia fell in January, and the Mubarak regime in Egypt followed in early February. By late February, rebels opposed to the Libyan dictator Muammar al-Qaddafi had seized control in cities such as Benghazi, and the dictator's days seemed numbered. But then the tide of war reversed, and Qaddafi's forces moved to crush the uprising.

With tens of thousands of civilian lives at risk, the Obama administration, which had come out in support of the rebels, faced a difficult choice. The members of the Arab League were unanimously imploring the United States to get involved. NATO allies were keen to intervene in support of the armed rebels, and a UN Security Council resolution was in the works. At a National Security Council meeting called to discuss the crisis, Secretary of State Hillary Clinton, U.S. Ambassador to the UN Susan Rice, and some of Obama's National Security Council (NSC) staff argued for action, citing moral imperatives and the prospect of a truly multilateral force. But according to several people present at the meeting, Pentagon officials opposed intervening, pointing out that the United States had no vital interests in Libya and that any serious commitment would get Washington bogged down, possibly for years.

Two options were set before the president: go in all the way as the leader of an alliance, or don't go in at all. Obama's response was to come up with a third way, which emerged as he thought through the problem out loud. Early on, he articulated the principles that would underlie whatever course he chose: no U.S. boots on the ground, no military action at all unless it had a legal basis and a decent chance of succeeding, and, finally, an appropriate division of labor with allies—the U.S. military would provide its unique capabilities (among them precision bombing and intelligence sharing), but U.S. allies, who had a far greater interest in the conflict's outcome, would assume the brunt of protecting Libyan civilians and restoring order after the fighting.

In an interview at the time with *The New Yorker*, an Obama adviser (whose identity remains unknown) dubbed this approach "leading from behind," a term that would come in for much derision. But in context, it made sense, and it fit Obama's outlook on the role and limits of military force, the distinction between interests and vital interests, and the need to align the instruments of power with the intensity of those interests.

The first phase of the resulting operation was ultimately a success. The combination of U.S. air strikes and intelligence, NATO air support, and rebel movements on the ground led to the defeat of Qaddafi's forces and (although this was not an explicit aim of the campaign) the killing of the Libyan leader himself. But the second phase was a failure: a new government was never fully formed, the rebel factions' squabbles degenerated into civil war, and the country's social order (such as it was) collapsed.

The problem was that the NATO allies that had promised to lead the stabilization phase of a post-Qaddafi Libya did not follow through, in part because this phase turned out to be much more violent than they had anticipated. Restoring (or, really, creating) order would have required armed intervention—and possibly serious combat—on the ground, a mission for which European states had little capacity and less appetite.

Obama recognized the failure, acknowledging in his September 2015 speech to the UN General Assembly, "Even as we helped the Libyan people bring an end to the reign of a tyrant, our coalition could have and should have done more to fill a vacuum left behind." And the lesson weighed on him when considering how to handle a similar crisis in Syria.

THE SYRIAN SINKHOLE

As the Arab Spring evolved, demonstrations broke out in Damascus against Syrian President Bashar al-Assad. Assad struck back with extreme force, killing protesters first by the hundreds, then by the thousands. Gradually, a rebel force arose, and the country plunged into civil war. With the United States having already intervened in Libya under similar circumstances, the question naturally arose whether it would intervene in Syria as well.

In an NSC meeting, Obama spelled out the differences between the two conflicts. Libya's fighting had taken place on an open desert, which allowed for clear targeting; Syria was enmeshed in urban warfare, with civilians, rebels, and soldiers intermingled. The Libyan rebels had had a chance at forming a cohesive government; there were no such possibilities in Syria. No other outside power was calling on the United States to intervene this time around. Finally, the conflict was cascading into a proxy war for the regionwide Sunni-Shiite confrontation. Not only did the United States have little at stake in this fight, but it also had little ability to influence its direction or outcome. According to several attendees of the meeting, nobody really disagreed with these points.

And yet the administration had aligned itself with the season's popular uprisings. In May, in a speech of uncharacteristic exuberance, Obama likened the turmoil to previous eras of democratic revolution. He spoke with particular urgency about Syria, proclaiming that Assad "must" stop shooting his own people and allow human rights monitors to enter the country. In August, Obama joined with the leaders of France, Germany, and the United Kingdom in calling on Assad to step down. Syria's ruler was "on the wrong side of history," Obama said, declaring that "the time has come for President Assad to step aside."

Such rhetoric was driven by two factors. First, the aides in Obama's inner circle—few of whom knew anything about Middle Eastern politics—really did think Assad's regime was nearing collapse. Second, given that apparent fact, they felt it was best to put the administration publicly on "the right side of history," especially since allied nations were calling on Obama to show "leadership."

The rhetoric was not entirely empty. Obama did ask his military and intelligence chiefs to come up with plans to speed history along, and in the summer of 2012, CIA Director David Petraeus laid out a scheme to arm a group of "moderate" Syrian rebels. The plan, which Petraeus had formulated with Saudi Prince Bandar bin Sultan and a few other Arab security chiefs, called for shipping small arms, mainly rifles, to a small, select group of the Syrian opposition. Petraeus did not promise the moon; he explicitly said that these rebels could not oust Assad right away and that the goal was to put "pressure" on Assad. If you're saying Assad must go, he was telling the president, here's how the CIA can help. The plan had the backing of Clinton, Secretary of Defense Leon Panetta, and the Joint Chiefs of Staff. But the president rejected it.

Obama was not opposed to taking action; he had asked Petraeus and Panetta for options. But he was opposed to doing something merely for the sake of doing something, and the Petraeus plan seemed to fall into that category. Who were these rebels, he asked? Could the United States really distinguish the good ones from the bad ones? (Petraeus insisted that he could, but Obama was unconvinced.) If these rebels did emerge as a threat to the regime, would Iran, which had invested heavily in Assad, simply stand by, or would it intervene (as Obama thought more likely)?

In NSC meetings, several attendees recall, Petraeus acknowledged that it might take years for the rebels to mount an effective challenge to Assad's rule. Meanwhile, the CIA's plan might throw Assad psychologically and give Washington "skin in the game," a path to influence over the long haul. This was not a winning argument with Obama: he was looking for something that had a chance of succeeding in the near term, and he did not want skin in a game played in the quagmire of a sectarian civil war. While Petraeus was working up the plan, Obama asked the CIA to produce a paper on how often in the past U.S. arms had succeeded in helping rebels oust hostile governments. The answer: not very often. That sealed the case.

Although grounded in logic and history, the rejection of intervention in Syria set off the first waves of discontent over Obama's foreign policy in general—the notion that he did not want to use force, that he was always on the lookout for arguments that rationalized this disinclination, that he talked bold but failed to follow through, which made all his commitments ring hollow.

Later on, as the self-proclaimed Islamic State (also known as ISIS) took control of vast swaths of Iraq and Syria, Obama's critics argued that if only the president had accepted Petraeus' plan, ISIS might not have found a foothold.

But the claim seems far-fetched—even though a few of Obama's close advisers allow, in retrospect, that it might have been worth giving Petraeus' option a chance. In any case, two years later, Obama approved a similar plan. However, when the American-backed rebels started racking up victories on the battlefield and appeared to be closing in on Assad, Obama's prediction of what would happen next came true: the Iranians redoubled their support for Assad, sending Quds Force soldiers to fight the rebels. And Russian President Vladimir Putin, fearing the loss of Moscow's sole outpost outside the former Soviet Union, sent tanks, planes, and missiles to support the Syrian army.

REDLINE, RED FACE

Syria is where Obama's foreign policy met its most brutal challenge, and where his tools for dealing with crises—words, logic, persistent questions, and sequential problem-solving—proved inadequate.

At least five times in the eight-month span between August 2012 and April 2013, Obama or administration officials publicly warned Assad that using chemical weapons against rebels and protesters would cross a "redline." It would mark "a game changer from our perspective," Obama elaborated on one occasion. "There would be enormous consequences," he said on another. It would be "totally unacceptable," and Assad would be "held accountable." Yet despite such utterances, say close aides and officials, the president never ordered up a plan for what to do if Assad crossed the line.

Then, on August 21, 2013, rocket shells containing sarin gas slammed rebel-controlled areas in the Damascus suburbs, killing an estimated 1,500 people. The redline had been crossed. Obama swiftly decided to retaliate. Attack plans were drawn up, most of them designed to destroy not the chemical stockpiles themselves (explosions of which might spread the gas far and wide) but rather the munitions and facilities required to launch them into battle. Assad's regime was not the explicit target in any of these plans, but some White House aides thought, or hoped, that his strength might erode as a side effect.

Obama seemed to be serious about launching the strikes. His aides were instructed to phone legislators and journalists to make sure they had read an unclassified intelligence report that the White House had just released proving that Assad was behind the chemical attacks. A UN resolution backing the use of force in Syria was unlikely; Russia and possibly China would veto it. So Obama rallied Arab and NATO nations to join in the attack, or at least to endorse it. He got no such support, except from France and the United Kingdom—but then British Prime Minister David Cameron requested authorization for an attack from Parliament, which voted it down.

On August 31, the NSC met for more than two hours. Everyone around the table agreed that the United Kingdom's backpedaling, although regrettable, should not affect the president's decision and that he should proceed with the air strikes. Kathryn Ruemmler, the White House counsel, suggested seeking a congressional resolution for the strikes, especially given the lack of support elsewhere, but she also said that Obama had the legal authority to order the strikes on his own. The meeting broke up, with everyone agreeing to proceed with the bombing. Then, Obama took a walk on the White House lawn with Chief of Staff Denis McDonough, returned to the Situation Room, and announced he would put the issue to Congress for a vote. Aides say Ruemmler's suggestion hadn't tilted his thinking; rather, it had reflected his views on the use of force generally.

In any case, everyone in the room was surprised by his reversal. Obama explained that he needed some institutional backing for such a risky move. What if, after the air strikes, Assad launched more chemical attacks? If the United States dropped more bombs, it would risk getting sucked into a civil war, and if it did nothing, that would be worse: the United States would look weaker, and Assad stronger. Some White House aides viewed air strikes as a one-time action, but Pentagon officials had warned that if the president proceeded with the bombing (which they supported), he should be prepared for escalation. Obama suspected they were right. Whatever he did, his actions (or inaction) would trigger criticism and disunity; without a prior vote, his support, slim from the outset, would rapidly erode. In discussions before the meeting, some of his aides had worried that if he bombed Syria on his own and the mission fell apart, he might even face impeachment.

To many senior officials, each separate piece of Obama's argument made sense, but the overall logic did not. Maybe it was a bad idea to proceed with air strikes, but in that case, Obama should not have drawn those redlines: he should not have recited the rationale for air strikes to so many diplomats, journalists, and legislators; he should not have told Secretary of State John Kerry to make a case for the bombings (in a powerful speech just hours before he changed course); and after making this new decision, he certainly should not have gone ahead with a scheduled prime-time television address in which he detailed Assad's perfidy, laid out the national security concerns, claimed he had the legal authority to respond with unilateral air strikes—and then announced that he was sending the matter to Congress.

One NSC official who was relieved that the strikes did not take place nevertheless said, "We paid a price for pulling back. The perception among people in the region was that they couldn't rely on Obama to pull the trigger." A former top White House official said, "When people—serious people—say Obama is indecisive and uncertain, they're talking about this episode with Syria."

The White House lobbied Congress to pass a resolution authorizing the use of force, but the task was clearly futile: most Republicans did not want to do any favors for Obama, and many Democrats were leery of military action. In the end, Russia came to the rescue. At a press conference on September 9, Kerry was asked if Assad could do anything to avoid air strikes. Kerry replied, "Sure, he could turn over every bit of his [chemical] weapons to the international community within the next week, without delay," adding, "but he isn't about to." To everyone's astonishment, Russian Foreign Minister Sergey Lavrov replied that he could make that happen—and he did. Under Russian pressure, Assad surrendered very nearly all of his chemical weapons for destruction.

Obama and his aides declared victory, noting that this diplomatic solution was more effective than military strikes would have been and that the threat of those strikes was what had driven Russia to pressure Assad. The first claim was probably true; the second probably was not. The fact is Congress seemed certain to defeat Obama's motion before Russia stepped in. It is possible that Putin never believed that Obama would feel bound by Congress, that he would find some way to launch the strikes anyway. But more pertinent, Russian leaders have always taken pains to keep weapons of mass destruction—biological, chemical, or nuclear—out of their allies' hands: not so much because they abhor those weapons as because they abhor the loss of control. Moscow had its own interests in stripping the loose cannon Assad of these ghastly weapons, and since the redline crisis had forced Obama to focus on the chemicals and not on Assad's regime, the diplomatic save would serve one of Russia's vital interests—the preservation of Moscow's only foothold in the Middle East.

THE ISIS CRISIS

The redline fiasco was a low point in the administration's foreign policy, but the troubles in Syria were hardly over. Less than a year after the chemical weapons settlement, ISIS—which Obama had recently dismissed as a "JV" version of Al Qaeda—stormed Mosul, the second largest city in Iraq. The U.S.-trained Iraqi soldiers fled at first contact, and the armed jihadists barreled on to Ramadi and Fallujah and, for a while, came perilously close to Baghdad.

The jihadists had started out and were largely based in Syria, but Obama focused his anti-ISIS strategy on Iraq because that's where it might have some effect; the United States, after all, had resources, air bases, and a partnership of sorts with a functioning government in the country—and it had none of those things in Syria, where Obama remained properly wary of diving into a sectarian civil war. Even by September 2014, when Obama realized that Syria couldn't be ignored (it was, after all, the headquarters of ISIS' operations, and he knew very well that the Iraqi-Syrian border was porous to the point of meaningless), he stuck to what his aides called an "Iraq first" strategy. American air strikes, which had long begun against ISIS forces in Iraq, would be extended to Syria, but only over the paths that ISIS used to travel between the two countries. Obama also announced a program to train and equip "moderate" Syrian rebels on bases in Saudi Arabia but noted that they wouldn't be ready to fight ISIS for many months; clearly, Syria was on the back burner, at best.

Days after Obama's announcement, ISIS laid siege to Kobani, a mainly Kurdish town on the Syrian-Turkish border. The town had no strategic significance, but a massacre was in the making. More than that, ISIS was sending thousands of jihadists into the town—forming an easy concentrated target, which neither the Pentagon nor Obama could resist. Obama ordered massive air strikes, which killed an estimated two thousand to three thousand ISIS fighters.

In another unexpected feature of the battle, Kurdish fighters gathered to stave off ISIS, fought very capably, and recaptured the town. Obama had not been opposed to going after ISIS inside Syria; he just had not seen a suitable partner that could carry out the fight on the ground. In the Syrian Kurds, he found one, and U.S. air strikes continued, often in tandem with Kurdish ground assaults. At the same time, the CIA started covertly assisting a group of rebels in southern Syria whose main aim was to overthrow Assad. Again, Obama had opposed Petraeus' plan to arm some rebels not because he was against arming rebels but because he did not see how that particular plan or those particular rebels would succeed. The new plan seemed more plausible, in part because the CIA and the U.S. military had gathered a lot more intelligence and scoped out reliable forces over the previous year. (A separate $500 million Pentagon program to train and equip a small group of northern Syrian rebels to fight ISIS proved publicly disastrous: the rebels turned out to be more interested in fighting Assad's army than ISIS, taking them out of the fight to train in Saudi Arabia only disoriented them, and more militant rebels killed almost all of them on their reentry into Syria.)

Viewed piece by piece, tactical move by tactical move, Obama's operations appeared to be making progress. But foreign fighters kept flooding the region, ISIS was barely budged aside, and although Assad's army seemed imperiled, it was still quite large (at around 125,000 troops) and recovered much of its strength after Russia sent in tanks and jet fighters in September 2015. Russia's move raised the hackles of some of Obama's critics, who saw Putin as trying to revive the Soviet empire. Obama didn't bite, and wisely so. At an NSC meeting, he cautioned against viewing Russia's intervention through a Cold War prism. We are not at war with Russia over Syria, he said, according to officials who were at the meeting. Putin's vital interest in this had much to do with his own domestic politics, and an alarmed American response would play into his game. Finally, Obama doubted that the Russian military campaign would have much impact on the battle.

Nonetheless, Obama was still receptive to attractive options for his own military posture. The Syrian Kurds were racking up more successes (and requiring more protection from Turkey, which was pounding them with air strikes while claiming to be going after ISIS), and so Obama approved plans to send the Kurds more ammunition—and to deploy U.S. Special Forces to join them in raids on ISIS strongholds, secret missions that resulted in six fatalities before Obama announced the actions publicly.

Obama has a keen legal mind, which serves him and the country well when he pokes holes in specious arguments for risky policies. But it also enables him to rationalize his own porous positions: for instance, that conducting joint raids falls in the category of "advise and assist," not "boots on the ground." He can also make firm assurances that he will not push these ground forces any further, ignoring that he has laid the groundwork and set the logic for his successor in the White House to escalate the fight, if he or she is so inclined. (Not to draw precise parallels, but in a similar vein, President John F. Kennedy firmly resisted pressure from the Joint Chiefs of Staff to deploy "combat troops" to Vietnam yet expanded the scope and numbers of "advisers" there, leaving President Lyndon Johnson to believe he was following in his predecessor's footsteps when he poured five hundred thousand U.S. troops into the fight.)

THE SEARCH FOR ORDER

What has been missing in Obama's Syria policy, in all its phases, is a coherent strategy. His two aims—defeating ISIS and pressuring Assad to step down—are in some ways contradictory. Assad's continued reign has been a magnet for foreign Sunni fighters to join ISIS. But in the short run, Assad's army, if properly directed, could be the most potent anti-ISIS force—second perhaps only to Iran, which has been sending members of its elite Quds Force to protect Assad's regime. Obama has been constrained from forming an overt alliance with Assad or Iran, in part because he has needed Sunni allies—Egypt, Turkey, and the Gulf states—to delegitimize and defeat the Sunni radicals of ISIS; if he bonded with Shiite Iran or its client Assad, those countries might drop out of the coalition.

Therein lies the heart of the problem not only with Obama's strategy against ISIS but with any U.S. president's stab at such a strategy. If all the countries that feared and loathed ISIS—which is to say, almost all the countries in the region—joined forces, ISIS would crumble in short order. But each of those countries has more fear and loathing for at least one of its potential allies (Turkey for the Kurds and Saudi Arabia for Iran, for example). Forming an effective coalition has therefore been all but impossible—a fact that ISIS commanders have shrewdly exploited.

As many of Obama's critics contend, a coherent regional strategy—not just a series of piecemeal responses to crises—is needed to solve this problem. But what is this regional strategy? Who should lead it? What incentives might lure the potential coalition's players to subordinate their individual interests to the larger goal? (In October [2015], Obama dropped his reluctance and invited Iran and Russia to join talks in Vienna to discuss a political solution to the Syrian crisis and a joint fight against ISIS. The prospects seemed dim, until—on the very eve of the conference—ISIS agents mounted coordinated terrorist attacks in Paris. Although the odds remain long, a plausible path to a settlement opened up. Obama seems to have recognized, along with others, that transcending the sectarian divide rather than accommodating it—and forming alliances with rivals against larger, common threats—is the only way toward a peaceful transition.)

These complexities are symptomatic of a larger phenomenon that accounts for the surge of violence throughout the Middle East: the breakdown of the colonial order imposed at the end of World War I. This order, with its artificial borders designed to split or suppress tribal identities, would have collapsed after World War II (along with the British and French colonies) but for the deep freeze imposed by the Cold War. When the Soviet Union imploded, the Cold War too dissolved, along with the international security system that it had created and sustained for nearly half a century. With the subsequent diffusion of global power and fragmentation of power blocs, the collapse of the Middle East's borders and authorities resumed—a process accelerated by President George W. Bush's 2003 invasion of Iraq, which disrupted the balance of power among nations, sects, and tribes that had kept an uneasy peace between Shiites and Sunnis, not only within Iraq but across the region, as the disruption's ripples spread.

Some of Obama's critics claim that if he had found a way to keep ten thousand American troops in Iraq instead of going through with a complete withdrawal in 2011, the renewal of sectarian violence and the rise of ISIS to fill the subsequent power vacuum would never have happened. But this is extremely unlikely, given that in an earlier era it took close to 170,000 U.S. combat troops using extraordinary measures to stem a similar tide, and even then they were able to do so only temporarily. In any case, Obama had no choice in the matter. The status-of-forces agreement (SOFA) that Bush signed in 2008 demanded, "All the United States Forces shall withdraw from all Iraqi territory no later than December 31, 2011." Obama was, in fact, amenable to keeping five thousand troops in Iraq for the long haul and sent emissaries to Baghdad to see if an extension could be negotiated, but revisions to the SOFA, including a U.S. demand that American troops enjoy immunity from Iraqi law, required parliamentary approval, and no factions in the Iraqi parliament, except perhaps the Kurds, would vote for the Americans to stay. (Obama has been able to send military forces back to Iraq only because the SOFA expired after three years.)

LIMITED INTERESTS, LIMITED RISKS

As the ISIS imbroglio widened, yet another crisis erupted, this time in Ukraine. After Putin bribed Ukrainian President Viktor Yanukovych with an aid package to stop him from signing an association agreement with the European Union, popular protests broke out in Kiev. When Yanukovych cracked down, the protests widened, and he was ultimately forced to flee. Putin responded by sending Russian forces to seize the Crimean Peninsula and support a secessionist rebellion in eastern Ukraine.

In NSC meetings held to decide how to respond to Russia's move, Obama quickly approved a script of denunciation, reinforcements of U.S. military exercises in and around eastern Europe's NATO allies (especially the Baltic states), and a string of economic sanctions.

Some Pentagon officials wanted to go further and supply the Ukrainian army with "lethal defensive weapons," especially tow antitank missiles. According to NSC officials, Vice President Joe Biden strongly endorsed this position, saying that the United States had a moral obligation to help the Ukrainians defend themselves, as well as a strategic interest in making Putin pay for his land grab and in deterring him from going further. (No one in any NSC meeting, however, advocated sending Ukraine offensive weapons or deploying U.S. troops to the country.)

In the end, Obama approved the provision of nonlethal military assistance, such as night-vision and radar equipment, and training for Ukraine's National Guard. Beyond that, he was opposed. The United States had interests in Ukraine, but not vital interests. There were reasons two previous presidents had considered, then decided against, inviting Kiev's leaders to join NATO. First, polls had suggested that less than half of Ukrainians wanted membership. Second, Russia's interests in Ukraine, unlike the United States', were vital: Russia and Ukraine shared a border and a long history of trade, cultural exchange, and even common statehood. No Russian leader would stand by as Ukraine drifted too far from Moscow's orbit.

Obama likes to look ahead two or three steps. (His critics have seen this as a technique for avoiding the use of force; others see it as a method of rational decision-making.) Moscow could and would match or surpass any lethal weapons that the West supplied to Kiev. Then what? If Washington sent still more arms, it would risk getting sucked into an arms race, and the violence would intensify. If the United States did not respond in kind, the

West would have lost the contest; Obama would look weaker, and Russia stronger, than if he had not sent any arms in the first place.

This was Obama's first principle in all discussions about the crisis: he was not going to risk a war with Russia for the sake of Ukraine. At one meeting, he said, "If I wanted to invade Canada or Mexico, no one could do much about it." The same was true of Putin and Ukraine.

Still, Obama put a high value on enforcing international norms, one of which was the inviolability of borders. He felt it necessary to make Russia pay for its violation; the question was how. Military escalation, in this context, was a game Russia would win, but escalation of sanctions was one the United States could win, if Obama could keep European states on board. This was a challenge, for many European countries were more reliant on Russian energy supplies than the United States was and therefore more vulnerable to economic reprisals from Russia. They were also dead set against risking war over Ukraine. If Obama went up the military ladder, he knew they would drop out of the sanctions regime.

At least through the fall of 2015, Obama's policy worked. Despite Putin's efforts to split the transatlantic alliance, its members have held tight on the sanctions, and the cease-fire negotiated in Minsk in February [2015] has held, too. Putin's likely goal in Ukraine was to weaken the country's central government and keep it from moving closer to the West. At that, he has succeeded. If Obama and the western European nations had wanted to strike back on that front, tens of billions of dollars in economic aid would have meant a lot more than a few hundred antitank missiles. But beyond a relatively paltry International Monetary Fund grant, no one seemed to want to go down that road.

PATIENCE AND PRAGMATISM

So how does Obama's record stack up? The president has been besieged by foreign policy crises, constrained by diminished American power, and pressured by opponents at home and allies abroad to take action and show leadership, even when dealing with intractable problems. He has learned on the job, with his instincts for caution reinforced by the ill-fated Libyan intervention. And he has, at times, talked more boldly than he has acted, creating a needless gap between words and deeds.

And yet for the most part, he has stayed true to the template of his Nobel address, keeping sight of the big picture as others have gotten lost in the shrubs. His caution about embarking on unnecessary military adventures and desire to avoid escalatory military spirals seem wise. Obama also proved remarkably patient with drawn-out diplomatic negotiations, even those unlikely to bear fruit. Some of these, such as the

Israeli-Palestinian peace talks, have predictably gone nowhere, but others, such as the opening to Cuba and the nuclear deal with Iran, have been strikingly successful.

On April 5, 2015, the president delivered a spirited speech at American University defending the nuclear deal that he and five other world powers had negotiated with Iran. Several times, he quoted Kennedy's famous American University speech in 1963 calling for an end to the Cold War mindset and a new strategy based on a "practical" and "attainable peace," one based "not on a sudden revolution in human nature but on a gradual evolution in human institutions—on a series of concrete actions and effective agreements."

Later that day, Obama held an on-the-record roundtable discussion with ten columnists in the White House. When my turn came to ask a question, I noted that Kennedy had delivered his speech after several crises in which he realized that his advisers were often wrong and that he should place more trust in his own instincts. What lessons, I asked Obama, had he learned in his crises? What decisions might he have made differently, had he known then what he knows now? He answered:

> I would say that I have been consistent in my broad view of how American power should be deployed and the view that we underestimate our power when we restrict it to just our military power . . . There's no doubt that, after six and a half years, I am that much more confident in the assessments I make and can probably see around the corners faster than I did when I first came into office. The map isn't always the territory, and you have to kind of walk through it to get a feel for it.
>
> In terms of decisions I make, I do think that I have a better sense of how military action can result in unintended consequences. And I am confirmed in my belief that much of the time, we are making judgments based on percentages, and . . . there are always going to be some complications.
>
> And so maybe at the same time as I'm more confident today, I'm also more humble. And that's part of the reason why, when I see a situation like this one [the possibility of a nuclear deal with Iran], where we can achieve an objective with a unified world behind us and we preserve our hedge against its not working out, I think it would be foolish—even tragic—for us to pass up on that opportunity.

DISCUSSION QUESTIONS

1. How does Kaplan characterize the foreign policy decision style of President Obama?
2. According to Kaplan's discussion, how does Obama think about the use of American power?

3. What were some of the restrictions that President Obama placed on the American response to the Libyan crisis? Did those restrictions fit with the Obama decision style?

4. How would you summarize the response by President Obama to the Syrian crisis, and how was the Syrian response different than the response to the Libyan crisis?

5. What was the "redline" regarding Syria, and was President Obama's response consistent with his decision style?

6. Do the U.S. actions with regard to ISIS comport with President Obama's foreign policy style?

7. How do the U.S. actions over Russia's involvement in Ukraine reflect the foreign policy views of the president regarding American interest and power?

8. At the end of the chapter, how does President Obama assess his own approach to dealing with foreign policy?

Index

About the Editor and Contributors

EDITOR

James M. McCormick is professor in the department of political science at Iowa State University. He has also held positions at the University of New Mexico, Ohio University, the University of Toledo, and Texas A&M University. He received his PhD from Michigan State University and served as an American Political Science Association Congressional Fellow in 1986–1987. McCormick is the author of *American Foreign Policy and Process* and editor of *A Reader in American Foreign Policy*. He has published numerous articles and chapters on foreign policy and international politics in such journals as *World Politics, American Political Science Review, American Journal of Political Science, International Studies Quarterly, Journal of Politics,* and *Legislative Studies Quarterly*. He was a recipient of the Iowa State University Foundation Award for Outstanding Research at Mid-Career in 1990, a Fulbright Senior Award to New Zealand in 1993, the Fulbright-SyCip Distinguished Lecturer Award to the Philippines in 2003, the 2010 Iowa State University International Service Award, and the 2011 Quincy Wright Distinguished Scholar Award by the International Studies Association—Midwest. In fall 2017, he was the recipient of the Fulbright Canada Research Chair in U.S.-Canada Relations at Carleton University.

CONTRIBUTORS

Adam J. Berinsky is a professor of political science at the Massachusetts Institute of Technology.

Joshua W. Busby is an associate professor of public affairs at the LBJ School of Public Affairs, University of Texas.

Ivo H. Daalder is the president of the Chicago Council on Global Affairs and former American ambassador to NATO. Along with I. M. Destler, he coauthored *In the Shadow of the Oval Office: Profiles of the National Security Advisers and the Presidents They Served—from JFK to George W. Bush.*

I. M. (Mac) Destler is the Saul I. Stern Professor at the School of Public Policy, University of Maryland. Along with Ivo H. Daalder, he coauthored *In the Shadow of the Oval Office: Profiles of the National Security Advisers and the Presidents They Served—from JFK to George W. Bush.*

Colin Dueck is a professor in the School of Policy, Government, and International Affairs at George Mason University.

Robert M. Entman is the J.B. and M.C. Shapiro Professor of Media and Public Affairs in the School of Media and Public Affairs at the George Washington University.

Peter D. Feaver is a professor of political science, director of the Triangle Institute for Security Studies, and director of the Program in American Grand Strategy at Duke University.

Louis Fisher is a scholar in residence with the Constitution Project. He worked from 1970 to 2010 as senior specialist in separation of powers for the Congressional Research Service at the Library of Congress and as a specialist in constitutional law with the Law Library.

Michèle A. Flournoy is cofounder and chief executive officer of the Center for a New American Security (CNAS) and former undersecretary of defense for policy in the Obama administration.

Christopher Gelpi is chair of Peace Studies and Conflict Resolution at the Mershon Center for International Security and professor of political science at the Ohio State University.

James M. Goldgeier is dean of the School of International Service at American University.

Robert Jervis is the Adlai E. Stevenson Professor of International Politics at Columbia University.

Craig Kafura is a research associate at Chicago Council on Global Affairs.

Fred Kaplan is national security columnist for *Slate.*

James M. Lindsay is senior vice president, director of studies, and the Maurice R. Greenberg Chair at the Council on Foreign Relations.

John Mearsheimer is the R. Wendell Harrison Distinguished Service Professor of Political Science at the University of Chicago.

Jonathan Monten is a lecturer in political science in the School of Public Policy at University College London.

Henry R. Nau is a professor of political science and international affairs in the Elliott School of International Affairs at the George Washington University.

Michael Nelson is the Fulmer Professor of Political Science at Rhodes College, a senior fellow at the University of Virginia's Miller Center of Public Affairs, and senior contributing editor and book editor of the *Cook Political Report.*

James P. Pfiffner is a university professor in the Schar School of Policy and Government at George Mason University.

Dina Smeltz is a senior fellow, public opinion, and foreign policy at Chicago Council on Global Affairs.

Tony Smith is the Cornelia M. Jackson Professor Emeritus at Tufts University.

Jordan Tama is an associate professor in the School of International Service at American University.

The late **James C. Thomson Jr.** was a professor emeritus of journalism, history, and international relations at Boston University.

Stephen Walt is the Robert and Renee Belfer Professor of International Affairs at the Kennedy School of Government at Harvard University.

Jon Western is vice president for academic affairs and dean of faculty and Carol Hoffmann Collins '63 Professor of International Relations and Five College Professor of International Relations at Mount Holyoke College.